Active Credit Portfolio Management – Bringing the Capital Market Perspective into Bank Lending

European University Studies
Europäische Hochschulschriften
Publications Universitaires Européennes

Series V
Economics and Management

Reihe V Série V
Volks- und Betriebswirtschaft
Sciences économiques, gestion d'entreprise

Vol./Bd. 3276

PETER LANG
Frankfurt am Main · Berlin · Bern · Bruxelles · New York · Oxford · Wien

Jochen Dürr

Active Credit Portfolio Management – Bringing the Capital Market Perspective into Bank Lending

A Practitioners' View

PETER LANG
Internationaler Verlag der Wissenschaften

Bibliographic Information published by the Deutsche Nationalbibliothek
The Deutsche Nationalbibliothek lists this publication in the Deutsche Nationalbibliografie; detailed bibliographic data is available in the internet at <http://www.d-nb.de>.

Zugl.: Rostock, Univ., Diss., 2007

28
ISSN 0531-7339
ISBN 978-3-631-56935-1

www.peterlang.de

Preface

Profound and sustainable changes in the credit market environment have motivated banks to improve their lending business through actively managing loan exposures instead of holding the assets on their books until maturity of the contracts. Based on an empirical study among the largest and most significant Western European financial institutions, this dissertation provides a detailed exploration of the business models that are available to implement this innovative approach to conduct lending business. Moreover, the thesis particularly addresses the question regarding the optimal business model that should be established depending on specific determining factors.

Writing a dissertation is not an individual achievement but the result of support from and discussions with a number of individuals.

In the first instance, I would like to express my particular gratitude to Professor Dr. Wilfried Siebe for supervising the dissertation and for taking the time to hold numerous fruitful discussions. I also wish to thank very much my co-supervisor Professor Dr. Guido Eilenberger for the time and effort he devoted to my thesis.

I am particularly indebted to Dr. Patrick Beitel and Dr. Uwe Stegemann for various invaluable discussions which sharpened my understanding of the topic, challenged my findings and, hence, contributed strongly to the quality of this thesis.

I am also much obliged to my friend lic. oec. Jörg Kinberger who thoroughly corrected a first version of the manuscript as well as to Ginni Light who was a great support for the linguistic finetuning of the document.

Finally, I would like to thank my parents for their ongoing care and support throughout my entire life. To them I dedicate this dissertation with gratitude.

Dr. Jochen Dürr

Table of contents

Table of figures

Table of abbreviations

ABB	Asset Backed Bond
ABS	Asset Backed Security
ACPM	Active Credit Portfolio Management
ALCO	Asset-Liability-Committee
BAFin	Bundesanstalt für Finanzdienstleistungsaufsicht
BBA	The British Bankers' Association
BP	Basis Point
BU	Business Unit
CAGR	Compound Annual Growth Rate
CAPM	Capital Asset Pricing Model
CBO	Collateralized Bond Obligation
CDO	Collateralized Debt Obligation
CDS	Credit Default Swap
CEO	Chief Executive Officer
CFO	Chief Financial Officer
CLO	Collateralized Loan Obligation
CMBS	Commercial Mortgage Backed Security
CML	Capital Market Line
CMO	Collateralized Mortgage Obligation
COO	Chief Operating Officer
CPM	Credit Portfolio Management
CRO	Chief Risk Officer
CVaR	Conditional Value at Risk
DAX™	Deutscher Aktienindex
EAD	Exposure at Default
EC	Economic Capital
EDS	Equity Default Swap
E.g.	Exempli gratia (*lat.* for example)
EL	Expected Loss
Et seq.	And the following page

Et seqq.	And the following pages
EU	European Union
EUR	Euro
Euribor	Euro Interbank Offered Rate
EVA™	Economic Value Added
FASB	Financial Accounting Standards Board
FDIC	Federal Deposit Insurance System
FinDAG	Finanzdienstleistungsaufsichtsgesetz
GDP	Gross Domestic Product
HypBG	Hypothekenbankgesetz
i.e.	Id est (*lat.* that is)
IACPM	International Association of Credit Portfolio Managers
IAS	International Accounting Standards Board
IRB	Internal Ratings-Based
ISDA	International Swaps and Derivatives Association, Inc.
KfW	Kreditanstalt für Wiederaufbau
KWG	Gesetz über das Kreditwesen (Kreditwesengesetz)
LGD	Loss Given Default
Libor	London Inter Bank Offered Rate
LLP	Loan loss provisions
LPM	Lower Partial Moments
MaK	Mindestanforderungen an das Kreditgeschäft der Kreditinstitute
M&A	Mergers and Acquisitions
MBS	Mortgage Backed Security
MDAX™	Midcap Index of the Deutsche Börse AG
MPL	Maximum Probable Loss
MSP	Minimum Shortfall Portfolio
MSPCML	Mean-Shortfall Probability Capital Market Line
MSPEF	Mean-Shortfall Probability Efficient Frontier
MVCML	Mean-Variance Capital Market Line
MVEF	Mean-Variance Efficient Frontier

MVP	Minimum-Variance Portfolio
n/a	Not applicable
NPV	Net Present Value
OCC	Office of the Controller of the Currency
OGAW	Organisation für Gemeinsame Anlagen in Wertpapieren
OTC	Over the Counter
p.	page
PD	Probability of Default
P&L	Profit and Loss
QBI	US Quarterly Bankruptcy Index
RAROC	Risk-Adjusted Return on Capital
REIMC	Real Estate Mortgage Investment Conduit
RMA	Risk Management Association
RMBS	Residential Mortgage Backed Security
ROA	Return on Assets
ROE	Return on Equity
ROI	Return on Investment
RORAC	Return on Risk-Adjusted Capital
RWA	Risk-Weighted Asset
SEC	Securities and Exchange Commission
SME	Small and Medium-Sized Enterprises
SML	Security Market Line
SPCML	Shortfall Probability Capital Market Line
TRS	Total Return Swap
UK	United Kingdom
UL	Unexpected Loss
US	United States
USD	United States Dollar
VaR	Value at Risk
vs.	versus

Table of symbols

Latin symbols

A	Symbol for absolute risk aversion
c	Share of wealth W
D	Debt capital
E	Equity capital
E(.)	Expected value
F	Symbol for fees related to a loan
I_{CML}	Inflection point of capital market line
I_{EF}	Inflection point of efficient frontier
k	Coefficient for scenario
L	Symbol for loan amount
M	Symbol for market portfolio
$N(\mu;\sigma)$	Normal distribution having mean μ and standard deviation σ as characteristic elements
n	Symbol indicating number
P	Symbol for asset portfolio
r	Interest rate
r_f	Risk-free interest rate
r*	Target return/target interest rate
p	Symbol for probability
RORAC*	RORAC hurdle rate
S	Payment stream of a secondary market transaction
t	Point of time
U	Utility value
U(.)	Utility function
V(.)	Function indicating value in dependence of a variable
W	Symbol for wealth
X	Symbol for asset portfolio
x	Symbol for individual asset
Y	Symbol for asset portfolio

y	Symbol for individual asset

Greek symbols

α	Risk aversion of a utility preference function
β	Beta of pricing models
γ	Confidence level
Δ	Linear change of a variable
$\Phi(.)$	Risk preference function
κ	Coefficient for shortfall probability
μ	Expected return, mean
ρ	Correlation coefficient
σ	Standard deviation
σ^2	Variance

Mathematical symbols

~	Coefficient indicating a stochastic variable
=	Equals
<	Smaller than
>	Larger than
$\in$	Element of
'	Coefficient for first order derivation
''	Coefficient for second order derivation
'''	Coefficient for third order derivation
∞	Coefficient indicating eternity
Σ	Sum of
$\forall$	All values
i !	i-factorial
$[0;1]$	Interval between 0 and 1 (including 0 and 1)

Part I: Introduction, current status of research, motivation, goals, and structure of dissertation

1 Introduction

1.1 Recent developments in the global capital market

The global capital market has been growing tremendously of late. At the end of 2004, the total value of the world's financial stock was as high as USD 136 trillion, up from USD 12 trillion in 1980 and USD 53 trillion in 1993. This growth has been accompanied by an increased deepening of the financial sector, measured as the ratio between financial stock and GDP: the global financial stock augmented from roughly the size of the world's GDP in 1980 to more than three times the size (334%) of the global GDP in 2004 (see Figure 1).

The global financial stock can be divided into asset classes that are intermediated by banks on the one hand, and by securities markets on the other hand. The first asset class comprises illiquid bank deposits, representing the capital, which the banking system channels from savers to borrowers. In a simplified view, deposits provide the funding for bank loans. Therefore, deposits can be used to measure the extent of bank lending activities. The stock of these non-tradable debt instruments represents the degree of bank intermediation in an economy.[1] In contrast, the second asset class represents tradable debt and equity securities. It is the capital markets that directly match investors in and borrowers of these assets, hence, dis-intermediating the banking channel.[2]

Debt assets have the greatest share in the global financial stock and their growth has been the main driver for its rapid expansion. In particular, it has been the strong rise in tradable private and government debt securities – at the expense of the share of illiquid bank deposits – which has fostered this tremendous growth: the share of bank deposits in the global financial stock has sharply decreased from 45% in 1980 to 29% in 2004, while the share of private and government debt securities has increased significantly from 32% to 42% in the same time period (see again Figure 1).[3]

---

1 See chapter 1.4.3 for a more detailed description of bank deposits

2 See McKinsey & Company (2005), p. 25 et seqq. In order to avoid double-counting, portfolios of these asset classes set up by mutual and pension funds or insurance companies, for example, are excluded from the analysis. Inter-bank loans are not included in this approach, either

3 However, there are significant regional differences regarding (I) asset composition, (II) growth rates, and (III) level of deepening of the financial sector (see McKinsey & Company (2006), p. 5):

(I) While the US financial system is clearly market-dominated with bank deposits having a share of merely 19% in its total financial stock, countries such as China, India and Eastern European countries have a clear banking system dominance as their financial stock mainly consists of bank deposits (63%, 43% and 44%, respectively). The Eurozone is about at global average concerning asset composition, having 28% of bank deposits in its financial stock.

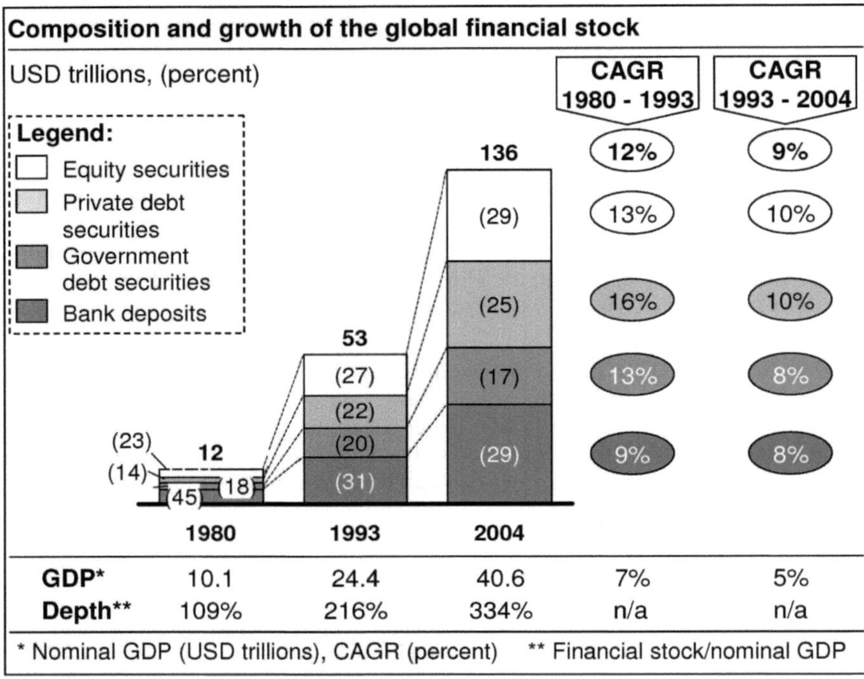

Figure 1: Composition and growth of the global financial stock[4]

The recent deepening of the financial sector can be regarded as a beneficial development because it better enables an inter-temporal transfer of savings, setting the basis for an efficient allocation of the available savings pool to new investment opportunities. This is in particular because deeper financial systems have a greater

(II) Though still constituting only a small fraction of the total financial stock of countries such as China and India, debt securities have grown particularly strongly from a low basis in these nations.

(III) Countries such as Japan, the US, the UK and the Eurozone have reached the highest levels of financial deepening (420%, 309%, 354% and 346%, respectively). By contrast, China, India and especially Eastern European countries have significantly lower levels of financial depth (311%, 175%, and 105%, respectively).

A similar analysis to McKinsey & Company (2006) showing the dwindling market share of bank loans for the benefit of bonds and other funding instruments in the US large corporate banking market can be found in Celent Communications (2002), in particular p. 11 Figure 4

[4] Source: Own illustration based on McKinsey & Company (2006), p. 4

variety of financial intermediaries and can provide users of capital with a more extensive scope of instruments. There is a positive correlation between the depth of a country's financial system and its national income.[5]

However, the flip side of the coin is that improved financial deepening may also be caused by price bubbles and excessive debt leverage. Market corrections and financial crises because of these developments may have serious consequences for an economy, such as increasing bankruptcies of corporations and private individuals as well as dropping aggregate demand. In particular, while the ability to take on debt is advantageous for an economy since it allows inter-temporal income transfer and the funding of investment projects, excessive debt leverage can promote systemic instability.[6]

1.2 Implications for bank lending business – the ACPM approach

The profound developments in the global capital market outlined above have had a strong influence on banking business. Especially, they have challenged the institutions' way of performing conventional lending business, i.e., issuing loans that, in a simplified view, are financed by customer deposits. These traditional activities, despite a lately dwindling significance, still constitute the core business for most banks.[7]

Institutions that are engaged in conventional lending business have recently felt a strong pressure to rethink and improve their business model. As a consequence, the idea of implementing a portfolio view on loan exposures and actively managing the loan portfolio, mainly by means of transactions on secondary credit markets, has emerged. The goal of this newly developed active credit portfolio management

---

5 See McKinsey & Company (2006), p. 8, illustrating the positive correlation between financial stock as percent of GDP and GDP per capita for 29 countries from different regions of the world. See also Barton, Newell et al. (2003) for a similar illustration. Furthermore, Nourzad (2002) shows a positive correlation between financial system development and economic growth

6 It seems as though the indubitable trend towards financial deepening has been accompanied by a strong increase in financial crises:

During the past ten years, there has been a strong increase in crises in the financial sector. While in the 1980s the World Bank registered 45 systemic crises world-wide, this number increased to 63 in the 1990s, see Caprio and Klingebiel (1999) (a crisis is defined as systemic if most of or all the capital in a banking system is eroded, see Caprio and Klingebiel (1999) p. 2).

One driver for this worldwide rise has been the significantly growing number of financial crises in emerging market economies, both in Latin America and Asia as well as in transitional socialist countries of the former Eastern Bloc. Especially in Argentina and Mexico, excessive government debt crowding out private lending and inhibiting economic growth is regarded as a key driver for these crises; see Barton, Newell et al. (2003), p. 30 et seqq.

7 For an illustration of the German banking market see, e.g., Figure 4 displaying loans and deposits as a share of total German banking assets

(ACPM) approach is to achieve a risk-return optimal portfolio composition instead of pursuing the conventional transaction-oriented approach whereby bank loans are statically held until maturity or default.[8]

[8] See Smithson (2003) for an introductory publication concerning the ACPM approach

2 Current status of research on ACPM

A number of introductory articles outlining the principles of the ACPM approach have been published.[9] Particularly, suggestions for business models according to which institutions can actively manage their loan portfolios have been made.[10] Furthermore, ideas regarding the practical implementation of ACPM business models have been developed.[11]

Besides theoretical research, some empirical studies on ACPM have recently been conducted.[12]

---

9 Further to Smithson (2003), publications in the area of ACPM have been made by Hayt and Smithson (2001a), Hayt and Smithson (2001b), Hammes and Shapiro (2001), Altman, Caouette et al. (1998), Kuritzkes (1998) and Wilson (1997)

10 Guill and Hennessey (1997), p. 21 describe that banks have developed different options regarding organizational structures and management principles of units to actively manage loan portfolios, e.g., regarding ownership of credit assets.

More concrete suggestions for ACPM business models have been made by Hammes and Shapiro (2001), p. 108 et seqq. who have developed three generic business models according to which credit portfolios can be actively managed. These models will be described in greater detail in chapter 2.3.2 of part II

11 Due to the complexity of this topic, the practical implementation of an ACPM business model is regarded as a multi-step approach taking several years to complete. Each implementation step is seen to be associated with substantial changes in organizational structure, performance measurement principles and management processes within a banking organization. As a major implementation hurdle for such a new business model, political challenges within the organization need to be overcome. See Asarnov (1996) suggesting a four-step approach to implement an ACPM business model

12 The most relevant, albeit only partially publicly available empirical study in the field of ACPM is a biannual survey performed by Rutter Associates LLC. The first version of the survey was conducted in 2000 (see Smithson (2000)). Since 2002, it has been sponsored by the IACPM, the ISDA and the RMA

The 2002 version of the survey included 71 institutions receiving a 58% response rate and covered five major topics, see Smithson, Brannan et al. (2002): characteristics of credit portfolios (e.g., composition by type of obligor), portfolio management (e.g., management styles of credit portfolios, tools used to manage the portfolio), formal portfolio management (i.e., measurement tools and credit portfolio models used), modeling of individual transactions (e.g., number of rating grades and responsibility for assigning and reviewing ratings), and evaluation of credit assets (e.g., marking the assets to market or model)

The latest version of the biannual survey was performed in 2004 among 83 financial institutions. It received a 53% response rate. The survey included 54 questions, covering six different topics. The content primarily focused on capital modelling at both individual transaction and portfolio level: the participants were asked twenty questions on modelling of individual credit transactions and nine on modelling of the participant's credit portfolio. Eight questions covered CPM topics and seven questions focused on performance measurement. Furthermore, the survey included four questions on the organization and objectives of the institution's CPM unit and three questions on characteristics of their credit portfolio. Excerpts from the survey, including around one fourth to one third of the empirically collected information, have been published for non-participants, see Rutter Associates LLC (2004)

However, research in the field of ACPM has by and large been limited to the aforementioned publications.

Although having developed different generic ACPM business models, the existing theoretical publications on this topic have not described in greater detail which characteristics these models should have. In particular, the business models have not been portrayed more specifically concerning typical objectives pursued as well as regards their functional competencies. Besides this, it has not yet been examined which factors trigger the establishment of a particular model.

This leaves a range of open questions regarding how ACPM units should actually conduct their businesses, in particular vis-à-vis other units within the banking organization, and which instruments they should ideally use to achieve their goals. Moreover, although the aspiration to improve bank lending has been a main motivation for developing the ACPM approach, there has not yet been a methodical examination whether the active management of loan exposures promises to improve lending business by creating additional value for an institution over the conventional lending approach. Correspondingly, the value-maximizing ACPM business model has not yet been deducted. Furthermore, it is unclear which is the optimal business model according to which loan portfolios should be actively managed, depending on a range of determining factors.

The empirical information available on ACPM is limited to the abovementioned studies. These surveys have primarily covered selected specific themes by mainly focusing on technical issues such as capital modeling, for example. They have not, for example, put an emphasis on the different ACPM business models currently implemented by financial institutions as well as specifics of these models such as objectives and functional competencies. Likewise, the empirical research on the financial instruments used by ACPM units has not been differentiated according to different business models and for which purpose these instruments are mainly applied. Also, the value-creation potential of the ACPM approach in general and the different business models, in particular, has not been empirically surveyed yet. This leaves a range of open questions concerning how financial institutions perform ACPM in practice and to which extent the theoretical concepts have actually been implemented.

3 Motivation, goals, and structure of dissertation

It seems as though recent market developments have caused an exigent need for banks to restructure their lending business model. The ACPM approach may be a concept to address these challenges, hence aiding to the improvement of bank lending business. However, as shown above, detailed research in the field of ACPM has been rather limited so far. Bearing in mind the relevance of this topic, it appears necessary to address and bridge the aforementioned existing research gaps concerning ACPM.

This dissertation aims at making a contribution to close the deficiencies in knowledge related to ACPM. The core of the thesis will be an illustration of the results of an empirical study on ACPM, which has been conducted among financial institutions that have been supposed to be leading in this field.

The dissertation is structured in four parts. Following the opening part I, parts II and III constitute the body of the dissertation before part IV concludes the paper.

3.1 Part II

The main objective of part II is to provide a profound fundament for the empirical study whose results will be presented in part III. Accordingly, part II will describe in detail the development and principles of the ACPM approach and give an up-to-date overview of the secondary credit market instruments currently available to actively manage credit portfolios. Furthermore, the theoretical background of the ACPM approach will be outlined and it will be examined whether it creates economic value from a theoretical point of view.

A range of recurrent terms and concepts related to financial markets and banking business will be mentioned in the course of this dissertation. Therefore, chapter one of part II will provide relevant definitions, introduce banks as financial intermediaries, and provide an overview of the different banking systems and types of banks that can currently be differentiated. Furthermore, as the thesis places an emphasis on credit business, an overview of related activities and concepts typically applied by the types of banks that are in the focus of this dissertation will be given.

The introductory remarks above have already indicated that banks' lending business activities have been crucially influenced and challenged by profound developments in the global capital market. These observations will be further elaborated in the more specific context of credit markets in chapter two. Commencing with a description of the conventional approach to lending business, major recent trends and developments in credit markets that have stimulated the development of the ACPM approach will be displayed. Further to the brief description above, the ACPM approach will subsequently be described in greater detail by outlining its central idea and introducing the different generic ACPM business models developed by literature according to which it can potentially be implemented in an institution. Furthermore, an illustration of the internal and external factors that can be deducted as determinants for the design of ACPM units will be given.

It will be shown that a central feature of the ACPM approach is the execution of transactions on secondary credit markets. For this purpose, a variety of secondary credit market instruments has been developed in recent years. There has been a high rate of innovation for these instruments and related markets have experienced soaring growth of late. Hence, it seemed appropriate to provide an up-to-date overview of the options a credit portfolio manager has to actively manage loan exposures on secondary credit markets. Accordingly, chapter three will give a comprehensive outline of the secondary credit market instruments currently available to optimally structure a credit portfolio according to the principles of the ACPM approach. Additionally, related market developments will be portrayed and a comparison of the different instruments will be performed, aiming at facilitating a credit portfolio manager's decision to choose the appropriate instrument for a particular purpose.

Part II of the dissertation will conclude with chapter four. This chapter will introduce the theoretical background of the ACPM approach. In particular, this illustration shall serve as basis for the subsequent examination whether, and if so, under which conditions the active management of a loan portfolio by means of secondary credit market transactions can generate additional value over the conventional approach towards bank lending from a theoretical point of view.

3.2 Part III

It has been shown above that the field of ACPM is still relatively unexplored with publicly available information by and large being limited to the aforementioned sources. At the same time, leading financial institutions seem to have already moved towards actively managing credit assets.[13] Therefore, it seemed necessary to provide transparency regarding what is currently regarded as state-of-the-art in terms of ACPM in practice. Consequently, an empirical study on ACPM was conducted among 22 Western European financial institutions in the first half of 2005, which have been supposed to have established a "best-practice" ACPM approach. Conducting this empirical study has particularly been motivated by the aspiration to confront the theoretical findings of part II with empirical results as well as to provide advice and decision support for practitioners in financial institutions who are currently evaluating establishing an ACPM business model.

The description of the empirical study and its key results will be illustrated in the five chapters of part III.

---

13 For example, HypoVereinsbank has recently implemented such an ACPM business model for its largest corporate lending customers, see Flämig (2005)

Chapter one of part III will outline the goals underlying the empirical study: the main objective of the effort has been to obtain empirical evidence on the ACPM business models identified in part II and to get a profound understanding of the approaches to CPM currently taken by the leading institutions included in the study. Furthermore, based on the empirical sample of the supposedly "best-practice" players in terms of ACPM, the deduction of the optimal ACPM business model an institution should implement provided it faces certain constellations of determining factors is aspired to.

Following a characterization of the data sample in chapter two, chapter three will outline the methodology applied to gather the empirical information. After having described the form of data collection chosen, it will give an overview of the structure and content of the interrogation tool applied in the empirical study and portray how the information has been analyzed.

Chapter four will describe the results of the empirical study in greater detail. In particular, it will depict the CPM business models found in the empirical sample and compare them to the generic models previously introduced in part II. Subsequently, an in-depth description of the business models identified will be provided, focusing on their objectives, related degrees of implementation and implementation barriers as well as their functional competencies. Among others, this analysis will cover the secondary credit market instruments that are characteristic for the different business models. Moreover, the value creation potential of the different CPM business models found in practice will be illustrated and the value-maximizing model will be identified. Chapter four will conclude with a summary of the empirical findings on the CPM business models by also providing a comparison to previously conducted empirical research.

The goal of chapter five will be to deduct the optimal ACPM business model an institution should implement depending on certain specifications of the internal and external determinants for ACPM business models described in part II. This deduction will be made by comparing the conditions faced by the "best-practice" ACPM players covered in the empirical sample with the business models they have implemented to manage their loan portfolios. Especially, it will be argued whether and if so in which situations the value-maximizing business model identified in chapter four can be regarded as the optimal approach according to which credit portfolios should be actively managed.

3.3 Part IV

Part IV will conclude the dissertation by giving a summary of the key findings and results illustrated in parts II and III. Moreover, it will provide a critical evaluation of the approach taken to examine the subject, outline remaining open issues, and illustrate further research requirements in the field of ACPM and related topics.

Part II: The ACPM approach – development, instruments, theoretical background, and value creation potential

1 Credit business of wholesale banks

1.1 Market definitions

A financial market (capital market) is a specialized market on which financial contracts are traded.[14] Financial market theory differentiates between the primary and secondary financial market: on the primary financial market, financial contracts between borrower(s) and lender(s) are concluded (originated), i.e. come into existence. The secondary financial market is the place where existing financial contracts are exchanged between market participants.[15] A loan is a special type of financial contract.[16] It comes into existence on the primary loan market. Existing loans are traded on the secondary loan market (secondary credit market).[17] Participants in this market are primarily banks, but also corporations and private individuals.[18]

Banking theory describes the secondary loan market as a secondary financial market for "activities of buying, selling, dealing, brokering and trading interests in and derived from commercial loans and other credit facilities."[19] According to this definition, the creation of new assets through bundling and (re-)structuring of existing loans within a loan portfolio (securitization) and the selling of these new instruments to another party is considered a primary rather than a secondary loan market transaction.

Banking practice, however, increasingly uses the term "secondary loan market" in a broader sense by including all available financial market instruments that can be used to manage loan portfolios. According to this interpretation, the secondary loan market comprises instruments and activities such as loan sales and syndication, credit derivatives, and securitization transactions.[20] Hence, the securitization transaction

14 A market is defined as a formal or informal institution on which buyers and sellers meet tc trade goods. Financial contracts are contracts which represent claims for current or future payments, see Hartmann-Wendels, Pfingsten et al. (2004), p. 2. The terms "financial market" and "capital market" are used as synonyms in this dissertation

15 See Hartmann-Wendels, Pfingsten et al. (2004), p. 6

16 See chapter 1.4.1 for a classification of loans

17 The terms "loan" and "credit" are used as synonyms in this dissertation

18 Chapter 3 describes, among others, typical parties involved in secondary market transactions. See also Poppensieker (2002), p. 100 figure 16 showing the dominant market share of banks in the secondary loan market

19 See Rhoades (2000), p. 407

20 See, e.g., Kuritzkes (1998). For a comprehensive overview of secondary market instruments see chapter 3

mentioned above is considered a secondary loan market transaction. This dissertation will apply the broader practice definition for secondary loan markets.[21]

1.2 Banks as financial intermediaries

1.2.1 Definition of banks and their role according to banking theory

Banks operate as intermediaries between supply of and demand for capital on financial markets.[22] According to a narrow definition, banks are financial institutions borrowing funds from investors and investing these funds by lending them to capital seekers. A broader definition includes such financial intermediaries which facilitate trading between investors and capital seekers by effectively serving as pass-through vehicles for financial funds. Such institutions include, e.g., brokers as well as mutual and pension funds.[23]

In view of the recent trends and developments in the global capital market illustrated in the opening chapter, particularly in the light of the dwindling significance of "traditional" bank products, it could be argued that the banking business and hence the institutions themselves become redundant as they get more and more disintermediated by capital markets. Therefore, after having briefly described the role of these institutions according to banking theory, it shall be examined whether banks still have an economic right to exist as financial intermediaries.

Freixas and Rochet (1997) describe an Arrow-Debreu model of resource allocation under the assumption of complete capital markets.[24] In market equilibrium, there is a Pareto efficient resource allocation, implying that welfare cannot be improved through the existence of financial intermediaries.[25] Freixas and Rochet (1997) show that under these assumptions banks have an equilibrium profit of zero. Their existence has no influence on other players in this market. Hence, banks are redundant institutions in complete capital markets.[26]

---

[21] There have been attempts in banking theory to develop more extensive definitions for secondary loan markets which are closer to the practice definition. However, they still fail to reach the scope of the market definition according to banking practice as they neglect the significance of the secondary loan market especially for refinancing transactions and regulatory arbitrage; see Poppensieker (2002), p. 86 et seq.

[22] A legal definition for banks can be found, e.g., in §1 Abs. 1 KWG.

[23] See Hartmann-Wendels, Pfingsten et al. (2004), p. 3. In general, a financial intermediary can be defined as an organization that raises money from investors and provides financing for individuals, corporations, or other organizations, see Brealey, Myers et al. (2004), p. 31

[24] A definition of complete capital markets will be provided in chapter 4.2.1.1

[25] Generally speaking, a condition is Pareto efficient if no agent's expected utility can be increased without decreasing another's; see, e.g., Pratt (2000), p. 1547

[26] This is also a reason why many capital market models (e.g., the Capital Asset Pricing Model (CAPM)) do not include banks; see Freixas and Rochet (1997), p. 8 et seqq.

Finance theory, however, assumes incomplete capital markets in reality and differentiates between three main types of market incompletions: limited market access, market frictions and information asymmetries.[27]

Generally, market frictions occur in the form of transaction costs that reduce the returns on assets of a corporation as opposed to the yield such a corporation generates through its investments.[28] According to finance theory, such transaction costs particularly include taxes and default costs.[29]

Neoclassical models prove that due to the existence of transaction costs, market participants have an incentive to enter into fewer contracts with one another than necessary to guarantee an optimal level of diversification. A financial intermediary between borrowers and lenders can create value by reducing the total amount of contracts necessary in the market.[30] However, critique of these models has been raised on the grounds that there has been a tendency towards more complete financial markets in recent years which has caused a decline in transaction costs.[31]

As the transaction cost theory has been met with criticism, the second type of market incompletions has been the center of attention in recent years: the existence of information asymmetries between borrowers and lenders, which only allows second-best solutions for financial contracts between these parties.[32]

---

27 See Hellwig (1994)

28 See Freixas and Rochet (1997), p. 18

29 For an overview see, e.g., Brealey, Myers et al. (2004), p. 403 et seqq. and p. 407 et seqq.

30 See Hartmann-Wendels, Pfingsten et al. (2004), pp. 109-110

31 An overview of transaction cost theory and its critique can be found in Breuer (1993), p. 79 et seqq., Hellwig (1994), p. 42 et seqq. and Santomero (1984), p. 577 et seqq.

32 Information asymmetries can occur in the form of hidden information leading to adverse selection issues and in the form of hidden action resulting in conflicts of interest between contract parties in the sense of moral hazard. Hartmann-Wendels, Pfingsten et al. (2004) give an overview of problems related to information asymmetries on p. 97, Abb. B1.4

Adverse selection refers to quality uncertainty in a contractual relationship as well as to issues regarding the design of optimal contracts in view of this uncertainty. An example can be the issuance of a loan given that the borrower has better information about the particular risks of the project he wants to finance than the lender has (hidden information). The difficulties arising from adverse selection issues as well as possible solutions for optimal contract design were first raised by Akerlof (1970) using the market for used cars as an example

Moral hazard refers to the problem that a market participant uses an information advantage that cannot be observed by his counterpart to achieve an outcome that has negative implications for the latter. Moral hazard issues play a major role in principal-agent relationships, in which the principal cannot observe the agent's activity (hidden action), and where the agent only accomplishes a task in the best interest of the principal if he is given sufficient incentives to do so. See Hartmann-Wendels, Pfingsten et al. (2004), p. 100 et seqq. as well as Bamberg and Spremann (1989)

These information asymmetries can trigger two types of costs: On the one hand, there are costs to reduce the asymmetries, e.g., through the establishment of better supervision mechanisms. When reducing this first type of costs, one can typically benefit from positive economies of scale. On the other hand, a second type of costs induced by information asymmetries are contract costs arising from the need for specifically designed contracts which include incentives for the parties to disclose true information to each other.

Instead of each market participant entering into financial contracts with a counterparty and individually facing the costs related to gathering information about the counterparty as well as supervising it, an intermediary can collect the respective individual information from market participants and hand it on to their counterparties at reduced costs.

The existence of an intermediary, however, induces a double-sided information asymmetry: one party (e.g., an entrepreneur receiving a bank loan) needs to be supervised by the intermediary through an appropriately designed contract; the other party (e.g., investor(s) providing funds for the loan) has an interest to close a contract with the intermediary which ensures he receives correct and true information from the intermediary.[33]

Leland and Pyle (1977) are the first ones to show that, despite this double-sided information asymmetry, the existence of a financial intermediary can reduce the total cost in a market, thus increasing welfare. Diamond (1984) enhances this idea and argues that investors should ideally delegate the monitoring effort to financial intermediaries ("delegated monitoring") who can diversify their investments among several projects and consequently achieve cost savings.[34] Diamond's financial intermediary acts as an asset transformer as it provides a risk-free claim for depositors while lending funds to risky entrepreneurs.[35]

The delegated monitoring theory is based on the assumption of imperfect loan markets derived from the hypothesis that financial contracts (bank loans) – and with them their credit risks – are illiquid.

Indeed, the nature of a bank loan makes it difficult to assume its tradability: relationships between borrowers and lenders are characterized by asymmetric information due to the borrower's private information which the lender does not know about. Therefore, a lender has to acquire information about the borrower before granting a loan and also needs to monitor the borrower during the maturity of the contract. Insofar, the lender himself becomes an insider regarding private information of the borrower. As a consequence, if the lender wants to sell a loan to another party,

[33] See Hartmann-Wendels, Pfingsten et al. (2004), pp.115 – 116

[34] See Diamond (1984) and Hartmann-Wendels, Pfingsten et al. (2004) pp.112 – 131

[35] See Bhattacharya and Thakor (1992), p. 13

the same information asymmetry, which used to exist between borrower and lender, now exists between the lender and the potential acquirer of the loan. This potential buyer has to assume that he is being offered a bad risk without actually knowing it. He also has to analyze and, after the transaction, frequently monitor the borrower's creditworthiness as there is no incentive for the original lender to do so any more.

In order for an original lender to continue his credit monitoring services after having sold a loan, a corresponding loan sale contract must be structured in an incentive-compatible way. For example, the originating bank (i.e., the seller of the loan) can either be contractually obliged to provide an implicit guarantee for the loan or be required to retain a portion of the loan itself.[36]

1.2.2 Legitimization for banks despite recent market developments

The potential issues related to a sale of bank loans show that one can rightfully have doubts regarding their tradability.[37]

Nevertheless, it can be observed that bank loans and their related credit risks have been traded for many years on secondary loan markets through various instruments: according to Greenbaum and Thakor (1994), loan sales already existed before 1880.[38] Furthermore, in recent years there has been a tremendous growth not only in bank loans but also in other financial instruments allowing a trading of credit risks: for example, while around 1980 the annual volume of loans sold in the US was approximately USD 20 billion,[39] this volume had risen strongly to USD 145 billion by 2003. In Europe, this volume grew from USD 5 billion in 1997 to USD 45 billion in 2003.[40] Moreover, there has been an exponential increase in the traded volumes and liquidity of securitized loans and credit derivatives allowing the trading of the underlying credit risks without having to physically transfer the assets.[41]

These developments show that bank loans and their related credit risks have become increasingly tradable in the past years. Advancements in credit analytics and technological improvements such as online platforms providing loan information services through the Internet[42] have significantly contributed to a reduction of

---

36 See Gorton and Pennacchi (1995)

37 See Hartmann-Wendels, Pfingsten et al. (2004), pp. 259 – 260

38 See Greenbaum and Thakor (1994), p. 387

39 Most loan sales transactions at that time were initiated between banks if an originating institution exceeded its legal lending limit for an individual borrower. See Gorton and Pennacchi (1995), p. 391

40 See Figure 16 as well as chapter 3.1 for a detailed description of loan sales

41 See chapter 3.3 for details on securitization and chapter 3.2 on credit derivatives

42 See Footnote 268 for examples of such platforms

information costs and asymmetries and have led to an increase in loan market liquidity.[43]

This increased loan market liquidity can be regarded a trend towards complete capital markets which might make the right to exist for banks as intermediaries in these markets questionable. Furthermore, as already outlined in the opening chapter, tradable debt securities have increasingly replaced bank-intermediated instruments. In particular, such a development can be observed in the market for large corporate loans.[44] The declining importance of bank lending in this market for the benefit of raising funds in the public debt securities markets seems to underline a dwindling significance of banks as financial intermediaries.[45]

However, as will be shown later in this dissertation, despite the above-mentioned observed tendency towards more complete loan markets, incompletions on capital markets still prevail. It will be illustrated in chapter 3 that, regardless of extensive innovations and the tremendous growth of secondary credit market instruments fostering an improved tradability of credit risks, not all loan market segments by far have sufficiently benefited from this development yet. Furthermore, chapter 4.4 will describe the aforementioned existing capital market incompletions limited market access, market frictions and information asymmetries in greater detail.

Moreover, despite a measurable disintermediation of banks in recent years, there has not been a decline in the need and demand for financial intermediation. Rather, a growing importance of specialized financial intermediary services could be observed, e.g., in the private customer segment: in past years, direct investments in financial instruments have increasingly reduced. Private individuals have significantly decreased their share of direct asset holdings. Instead, they have increasingly invested in securities in an indirect way through specialized intermediaries. Such intermediaries offer brokerage services, for example. Others such as mutual and pension funds or insurances collect funds from investors and invest them in better diversified or specifically tailored portfolios. As a consequence of the increased demand for these services, the asset holdings of these intermediaries have strongly increased during past years.[46] The need for specialized intermediation services is fostered by the growing

---

43 See Allen and Santomero (1998), p. 1465 as well as chapter 2.2.3 which gives an overview on recent advancements in credit analytics by describing the development of credit portfolio models

44 See also chapter 2.2.4 further behind

45 See chapter 2.2.4 for a more detailed description of these disintermediation trends

46 Allen and Santomero (1998), pp. 1468 and 1470 show this development using the share of equity ownership by private individuals in the US as an example: the share of private equity ownership has fallen from approx. 85% in the beginning of the 1960s to approx. 50% in 1995. At the same time, the accumulated share of equity ownership by insurance companies, mutual and closed-end funds as well as pension funds has increased from approx. 15% in the 1960s to approx. 40% in 1995, with the share of insurance companies staying flat during this time period

complexity and sophistication of financial instruments such as derivatives. While such mediators are often specialized non-banks, bank financial intermediaries increasingly offer such specialized services as well by refocusing their product and service offerings.[47]

Two main developments have contributed to the recently increased importance of such specialized financial intermediaries: firstly, market participants have seen an increasing need to better manage their risks. As, by nature of their business – the origination and trading of financial assets – financial intermediaries manage and trade risks, they enable market participants with limited own market access to transfer their risks to the capital market.[48] Secondly, an increasing complexity of financial instruments results in mounting costs of direct market participation for individuals. An example is the time which investors need to understand these instruments as well as to review and shift their asset portfolios. Due to their ability to perform risk management on a larger scale than individuals, financial intermediaries can create relatively simple instruments that can easily be understood and that have predictable cash-flows. Acquiring these instruments instead of directly participating in financial markets reduces the participation costs for individuals.[49]

This brief overview shows that banks have a legitimate right to exist as financial intermediaries on capital markets: although "traditional" bank products have recently lost market share in the global financial stock, they still represent the most important asset class with a correspondingly high importance of bank intermediation services. Besides this, not all capital market segments by far have experienced a strong development towards higher degrees of completion. Finally, in view of an increasing significance and typically higher complexity of capital market instruments for private individuals, there has been a growing demand for specialized financial intermediary services in this field.

1.3 Banking systems and systematization of banks

After having introduced banks and given a legitimization for their existence, this chapter aims to display the different types of banks that have been developed. Firstly, a differentiation of banks according to their field of activity will be made. As the US and Germany have developed banking types with characteristic activities which can also

[47] According to Flesch and Gerdsmeier (1998), changes in the competitive environment will result in the creation of three specialized types of banks: distribution banks, production banks and portfolio banks. While these types can be integrated within the legal structure of a universal bank, they will operate independently of their overarching legal structure, focusing on their individual strengths and being able to purchase services from third-party providers if necessary. Hence, they can work as specialized intermediaries, offering their services in competition with specialized non-bank intermediaries

[48] See Allen and Santomero (1998), pp. 1474 – 1480

[49] Allen and Santomero (1998), pp. 1481 – 1482

be found in other countries, this illustration will be made using the example of the US and the German banking system. [50] Besides this, other criteria according to which banks can be systematized will be described.

1.3.1 The US banking system

Due to the Glass-Steagal Act of 1933, which was enacted after the economic crisis between 1929 and 1933, the US banking system has traditionally been a separate banking system. Banks had to classify themselves either as commercial banks, i.e., engaging in the business of taking deposits and granting loans, or investment banks, i.e., engaging in the underwriting and dealing of securities. However, the institutions managed to bypass this strict regulation through, for example, the foundation of subsidiaries that were active in a field their parent company was not allowed to operate in. Eventually, by passing the Financial Services Modernization Act in 1999 – also known as the Gramm-Leach Bliley Act – the Glass-Steagal legislation was abolished.[51] However, despite facilitating the cooperation between different banking types, the new legislation does not annul the basic principles of the separate banking system.[52]

As Figure 2 shows, the structure of the US banking system is still determined by the Glass-Steagal legislation. There are four main types of banks in the US:[53] (I) commercial banks are the dominant type of institutions, holding about 50% of total banking assets in the US market, (II) thrift institutions whose main activity is to receive savings and term deposits and issue real estate and consumer loans, (III) investment banks and securities brokers and dealers offering capital market-related services, and (IV) other non- or near-banks including, e.g., mutual and pension funds.

[50] An overview of banking systems in other countries can be found in Kaufman (1992) or Allen and Gale (2000)

[51] See Hartmann-Wendels, Pfingsten et al. (2004), pp. 66 – 67

[52] See Hartmann-Wendels, Pfingsten et al. (2004), pp. 69 – 72 for a detailed description of the new legislation

[53] See Hartmann-Wendels, Pfingsten et al. (2004), pp. 62-66

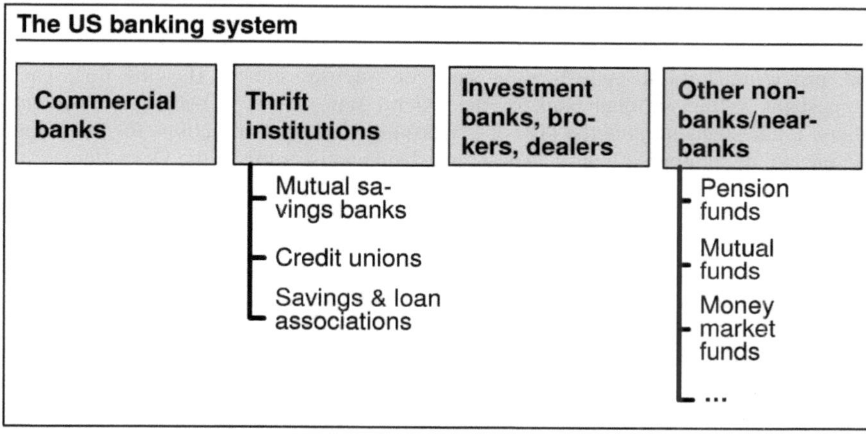

Figure 2: The US banking system[54]

1.3.2 The German banking system

The German banking system is known as a universal banking system.[55] German banking law basically allows financial institutions to perform all kinds of banking transactions. Therefore, there have been no legal requirements to force banks to specialize, although some have chosen to do so in recent years.[56] Three main types of universal banks can be distinguished (see Figure 3):[57]

Credit banks are private banks and can be split into four groups: (I) large private banks having both a nationwide focus and operating on international capital markets[58], (II) regional private banks whose activity is limited to a certain geographic region, (III) other credit banks, and (IV) subsidiaries of foreign banks.

Savings banks are regionally focused banks under public law. They are owned by municipalities or German federal states. Savings banks have the mission to ensure that private individuals, SMEs, and municipalities have access to loans, investment

[54] Source: Own illustration based on Hartmann-Wendels, Pfingsten et al. (2004), p. 63

[55] Universal banks are banks performing both commercial and Investment Banking activities, see Börner (2000), p. 181

[56] See Hartmann-Wendels, Pfingsten et al. (2004) p. 25

[57] See Hartmann-Wendels, Pfingsten et al. (2004), p. 28 et seqq. An overview of German banking types can also be found in Bundesbank (2004), p. 108 et seqq.

[58] These are the biggest four banks in terms of total assets: Deutsche Bank, HypoVereinsbank, Commerzbank and Dresdner Bank. Dresdner Bank was acquired by Allianz in 2001. HypoVereinsbank was acquired by Unicredit in 2005

opportunities and payment services.[59] State banks ("Landesbanken") support savings banks through, e.g., offering services, which exceed the savings banks' capacities,[60] and providing liquidity equalization between savings banks. Besides this, each Landesbank is the regional bank of the federal state which it belongs to. Among others, Landesbanken have the task of performing banking transactions for their state and providing communal loans.[61] The Landesbanken also support the Deka Bank with their services. The Deka Bank is the central institution of the savings banking organization. Besides doing business with public institutions, Landesbanken typically focus on banking activities with large and medium-sized corporations.[62]

Cooperative banks were originally advocacy organizations with the goal of supporting the business activities of their members through their banking business. Since 1974, they can also engage in business activities with non-members. They have a similar regional focus and a comparable business structure to savings banks. Their main business activity is to grant loans which they mostly refinance through savings deposits. The DZ and WGZ-Bank serve as central bank institutions heading this banking type.[63]

It has been shown that savings and cooperative banks operate significantly less competitively than credit banks. Regional demarcation for cooperative and savings banks might be the main reason for this observation.[64]

Besides universal banks, there are banks subject to public law such as the KfW which administrates investment programs of the federal government. Also, there are a variety of specialized banks in Germany, many of them having been acquired by universal banks or founded as subsidiaries of universal banks.[65] In this context, the emergence and increasing importance of so-called direct banks is worth mentioning. Based on the idea that private customers are increasingly aware of fees related to their daily banking business, these institutions – often founded as subsidiaries of established banks – offer

59 See Geiger (1992), p. 25 as well as chapters 2 and 6 for a more detailed overview on the German savings bank organization

60 For example, Landesbanken typically organize the underwriting of syndicated loans through their "Girozentralen"

61 Until July 2005, the Landesbanken were backed by the federal states' "owners' statutory obligation" ("Gewährträgerhaftung") and "maintenance obligation" ("Anstaltslast"). As of July 2005 these obligations have been abolished; see Hartmann-Wendels, Pfingsten et al. (2004), pp. 31 – 34 for details

62 See Geiger (1992), p. 89. For an overview of "Landesbanken" including their business focus, see Geiger (1992), chapter 3 and Sinn (2003)

63 For a more detailed overview of the cooperative banking system see Institut für Genossenschaftswesen an der Humbold Universität zu Berlin (1993) and Laudi (2003)

64 See Hempell (2002)

65 See Hartmann-Wendels, Pfingsten et al. (2004) pp. 35 – 40

a reduced product scope such as brokerage services, payment transactions, and granting of private loans. Their main distribution channel is the Internet.[66]

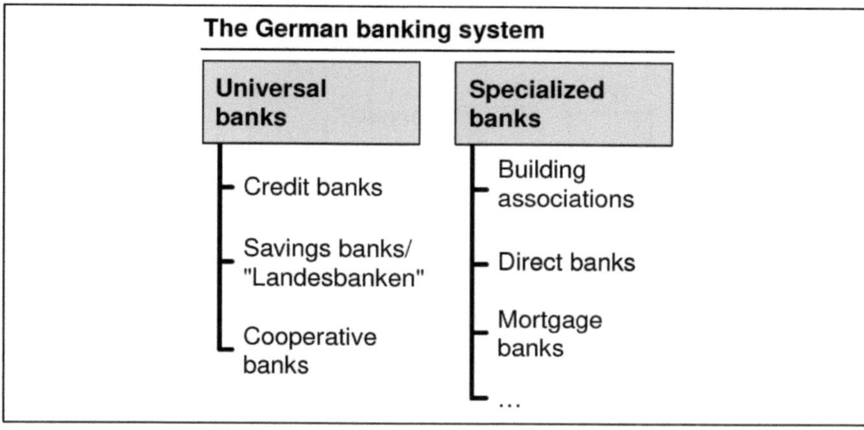

Figure 3: The German banking system[67]

In terms of balance sheet volume, commercial banking is the core activity of German banks. Despite a declining share of lending and deposit volumes in relation to total banking assets, commercial banking activities still account for more than two thirds of total German banking assets (see Figure 4).

[66] See Nöth (2004) for a detailed description of the direct banking concept

[67] Source: Own illustration based on Hartmann-Wendels, Pfingsten et al. (2004), p. 27

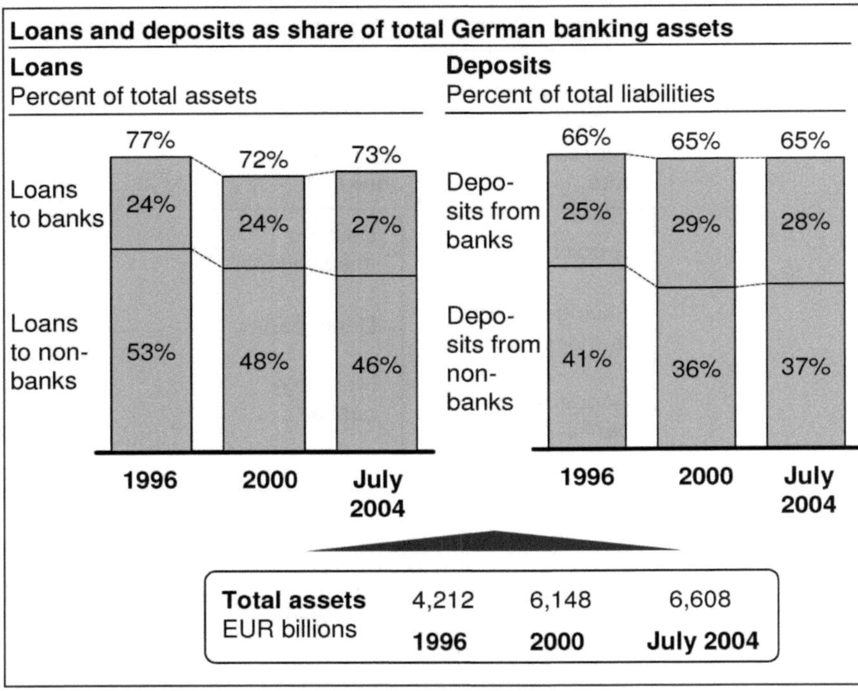

Figure 4: Loans and deposits as share of total German banking assets[68]

1.3.3 Retail vs. wholesale banks

Further to differentiating banks according to their major activity, these institutions can be systematized according to several other criteria. As Figure 5 illustrates, different types of banks can be distinguished according to criteria such as geographic focus, size, ownership and clientele. The subtypes may overlap.[69]

68 Source: Bundesbank (2004), p. 6 and p. 8

69 See Börner (2000), pp. 181-183, referring to Hahn (1981)

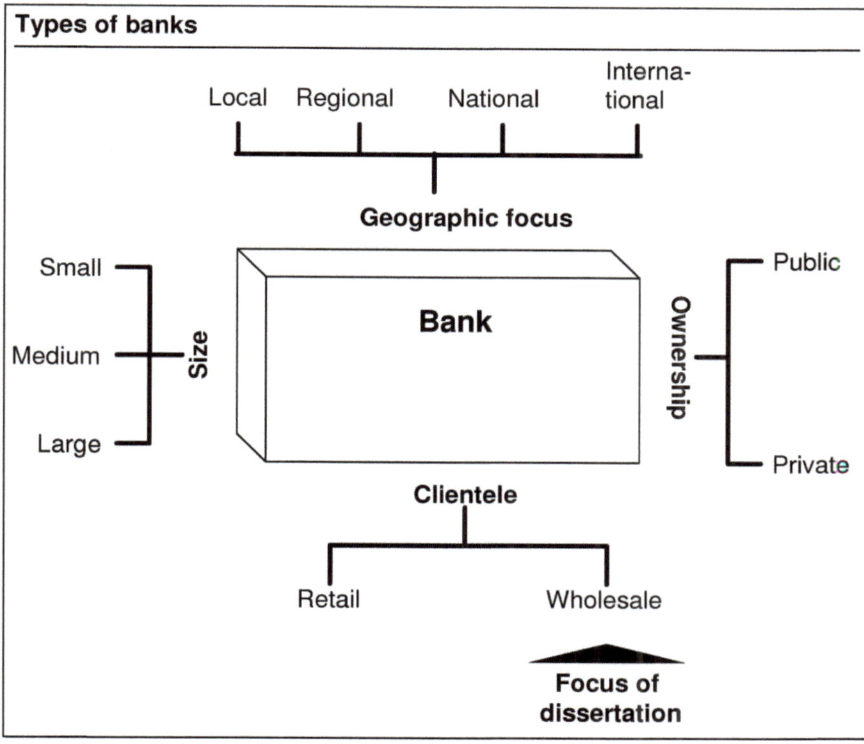

Figure 5: Types of banks[70]

Regarding clientele, one can differentiate between retail and wholesale banks. Retail banks, on the one hand, deal with private and small corporate customers.[71] Wholesale banks, on the other hand, serve individual large and medium-sized corporate and institutional customers.[72] Following this distinction, the focus of this dissertation will

---

70 Own illustration based on Börner (2000), p. 182

71 Wicki (1996), S. 34 defines retail banking as a relatively broad business for private clients, self-employed individuals, and small corporations. Retail banking provides standardized products and services which require little explanations

72 See Büschgen (1998), p. 238 and p. 624 for a definition of wholesale banks.

There is no consistent definition for large, medium, and small corporations. Key criteria to divide corporations in these classes are their number of employees and annual turnover.

Accordingly, the European Commission (2003) defines medium-sized corporations as companies having

primarily be on wholesale credit business with non-private customers.[73] The reason for this focus is that the ACPM concept has primarily been triggered by developments in the wholesale loan market. Furthermore, as will be seen in part III of the dissertation, banks have started the implementation of an ACPM unit for their most liquid large corporate loans so that it is currently mostly wholesale credit portfolios that are actively managed according to the principles of this new lending approach.[74]

Chapter 1.4 gives an overview of the typical characteristics of wholesale credit business.

1.4 Overview of wholesale credit business

This chapter describes characteristic credit arranging (origination) activities of wholesale banks and illustrates typical risks these institutions face when holding such loan portfolios as well as associated performance measurement concepts. Furthermore, related refinancing and workout activities are depicted.[75]

---

less than 250 employees and a turnover of at most EUR 50 million p.a. Small corporations employ less than 50 people and have a turnover of not more than EUR 10 million p.a; see European Commission (2003), Appendix, Title 1, Article 2.

The Institut für Mittelstandsforschung (2005) sticks to the categories of the EU Directive but defines them differently: large corporations employ 500 and more employees, generating revenues of EUR 50 million p.a. or more. Medium-sized enterprises generate between EUR 1 and 50 million in revenues p.a., employing between 10 and 499 people. Companies below these thresholds are defined as small. It is also noted that, if necessary, qualitative characteristics are to be included to classify a corporation.

Banks typically do not follow this segmentation, having higher revenue thresholds for their segments. For example, the definition of large corporations at Commerzbank includes enterprises with annual revenues between EUR 250 million and EUR 5 billion. Companies with higher revenues are assembled in a separate category, namely a multinational segment. The medium-sized segment includes corporations with annual revenues between EUR 2.5 and up to 250 million. The small corporations segment includes corporations with revenues below EUR 2.5 million. Institutional customers (i.e. primarily financial institutions) typically form a separate customer segment; see Teller (2004), p. 7

73 Credit business is the typical business activity between banks and corporate customers, see Schierenbeck (2001), p. 188 and p. 189. While multinational corporations, however, often have access to cheaper funding than bank loans (e.g., through the commercial paper market), smaller corporations typically do not have these options and are more dependent on banks loans regarding funding needs. Commercial papers are short-term unsecured notes typically issued by large, creditworthy corporations with a maximum maturity of 270 days. For a description of the Commercial Paper market and its typical issuers and investors see, e.g., Hahn (1993) and Brealey, Myers et al. (2004), p. 524

74 See again Flämig (2005) describing that the HypoVereinsbank concluded the implementation of its new ACPM business unit for its 400 largest corporate debtors at the beginning of 2005

75 It is important to note that all these banking activities can also be part of retail banking operations. Yet, following the focus of the dissertation, the subsequently introduced concepts and activities will be described from a wholesale banking perspective

1.4.1 Origination, credit approval and monitoring

A loan is typically arranged (originated) through personal negotiation and a contract between a borrower and a lender. This is a key difference compared to the acquisition of securities, such as bonds on the capital market, for example.[76] In return for granting the loan, the originating institution receives payment of interest from the borrower.

Different types of loans can be distinguished. A wholesale loan portfolio typically consists of commercial and industry loans, loans to financial institutions, and commercial real estate loans. Furthermore, loans to brokers and dealers for the purpose of carrying securities as well as agricultural loans are also classified as wholesale loans. Wholesale loans can be secured or unsecured.[77]

Performing credit analysis is the basis for lending and pricing decisions during the origination process. Banks are legally required to undertake a credit analysis.[78] It is usually performed in a standardized way: the credit analyst judges the prospective borrower's creditworthiness based on information provided in the loan application form. The methodology used for a credit analysis is usually the same for retail and wholesale customers: banks typically use standardized scoring systems to develop a credit rating which implicitly describes the prospective borrower's probability of default (PD) and hence determines the borrower's risk category. In contrast to retail customers, however, more detailed financial data is available for wholesale customers. The evaluation of wholesale customers is typically performed by calculating a set of ratios based on their financial reports.[79] Predefined thresholds in the rating scale determine whether a prospective borrower will be granted the requested loan or not. Furthermore, a credit rating can serve as a basis for a model-based risk-adjusted pricing of loans.[80] Additionally, "soft" factors stemming from private information due

---

[76] See Roussakis (1997), p. 285

[77] See e.g., Roussakis (1997), pp. 290-310. For a detailed description of loan types see Büschgen (1998), p. 327 et seqq., Eichwald and Pehle (2000) and Grill and Perczynski (2003)

[78] In Germany, the requirement to perform a credit analysis is regulated in KWG (1998). § 18 KWG (1998) requires banks to demand disclosure of a borrower's economic circumstances if they lend more than EUR 250.000 to this customer

[79] See Crouhy, Galai et al. (2001) for a description of typical ratios calculated in the course of such an analysis

[80] See Büschgen and Börner (2003), p. 281. Altman (1993) p. 186 developed a "Z-Score" model which takes all relevant financial ratios of a corporation into account and develops the "Z-Score" as a weighted sum of the ratios. Should the score be significantly far under a certain threshold, the loan application is immediately rejected; in other cases, dependent on the score level, the application is either scrutinized more thoroughly or approved without closer analysis. Altman and Saunders (1997) provide an overview of the development of credit scoring procedures during the past 20 years

While in 1999, rating scales were still quite unsophisticated (the rating systems of German banks did not comprise more than 10 rating classes, see Kirmße (2001), p. 115 figure 6), they have become more sophisticated in the meantime: Deutsche Bank, e.g., uses a 26-step rating scale, which is calibrated with a

to a long-relationship with the prospective borrower as well as market aspects, such as an evaluation of the economic conditions in which the client operates and the analyst's intuitive judgment of the applicant contribute to a lending decision.[81]

Regarding lending decisions, banks are legally required to establish a clear functional separation between customer BUs and loan approval units: while customer BUs are responsible for initiating the loan origination process by setting up client relationships, performing credit analyses of prospective loan customers, and later on maintaining close customer contact to service and monitor the lending assets, loan approval units provide an independent "second" vote whether to grant a loan or not.[82]

Banks have the obligation to regularly analyze and monitor the financial situation of their borrowers during the entire maturity of the loan contract.[83] In practice, the results of such a credit analysis are noted down in a credit report. Credit reports are regularly updated and are relevant for both initial and follow-up lending decisions. Should a credit analyst realize a significant deterioration of the borrower's creditworthiness in the course of the lending period, he is required to create a new credit report which is equivalent to making a new lending decision.[84]

Monitoring of debtors gains particular importance in the case of deteriorating solvency of credit users. A short description of typical banking activities related to the treatment of problem loan engagements is provided at the end of this chapter.

1.4.2 Credit portfolio risk and performance measurement

A credit portfolio is the sum of all open loan positions. A financial institution's target is to maximize the portfolio income, which is fraught with different types of risks. The auxiliary constraints that need to be fulfilled to achieve this target are to refinance the loans granted through taking on debt and equity as well as to act in compliance with regulation.[85]

After a qualitative description of typical credit portfolio risks, it will be illustrated how these risks can be measured. Then, the concept of economic capital (EC) will be described and strategies how to minimize unexpected credit risks will be presented.

PD based on statistical analyses of historical losses within their loan portfolio, see Deutsche Bank (2003), p. 141

81 See Graddy and Spencer (1990), pp. 460 and 461

82 In Germany, organizational separation between origination and credit approval has been regulated by the BaFin in its minimum requirements for credit business (MaK guidelines), see BaFin (2003) chapter 4.1. It is to be implemented by all institutions classified as a bank according to § 1 Abs. 1 KWG (1998), see BaFin (2003), chapter 2. See also Hannemann, Hanenberg et al. (2003) for a comment on the MaK guidelines

83 See BaFin (1995)

84 See, e.g., Deutsche Bank (2003), p. 142 for a description of the credit analysis process within Deutsche Bank

85 See Poppensieker (2002), p. 8

Afterwards, an overview of common performance measurement concepts applied to credit assets and their portfolios will be given.

1.4.2.1 Credit portfolio risks

Banks face three key types of risks within their credit portfolios, which they aim to minimize in the context of their CPM activities: credit risks, interest rate risks, and prepayment risks (see Figure 6).[86]

Credit risks are related to an unexpected deterioration of borrowers' financial solvency resulting in a possible shortfall to pay interest and the principal of a loan. Two different sub-types of credit risks can be distinguished:

Default risks, on the one hand, describe the risks of debtors failing to meet the agreed-upon payment obligations.[87] On a single loan basis, the extent of the default risks depends on the credit exposure at default and the recovery rate of the loan. The existence of collateral increases the recovery rate. Should the realization of collateral be fraught with risks, however, this would result in additional collateral risks. Default risks between different borrowers are typically imperfectly correlated.[88] Therefore, the default risk of an entire credit portfolio is usually lower than the sum of the individual default risks of the loans within the portfolio. A growing number of loans within a credit portfolio lowers the relative share (concentration) of an individual loan in the total risk of the portfolio – the concentration risk in the portfolio is thus reduced.[89]

Spread risks, on the other hand, are market-related risks. While default risks exclusively refer to the borrowers' probability of insolvency, spread risks cover a worsening of the market value of loans due to a different market perspective on the solvency of the debtors. A deteriorating estimate for a certain borrower's solvency – which is usually reflected through a migration of the borrower into a lower rating class – increases the credit spread, i.e., the spread between the risk-free market interest rate and the individual interest rate the debtor has to pay. This is equivalent to a lower market value of the loan.[90]

---

86 A comprehensive overview on other types of risks that banks typically face can be found in Allen (2003), chapters 5 – 12. Main risk types covered include market risks, options and forward risks, model risks as well as credit risks. Schierenbeck (2003) describes five main types of banking risks: credit risks, interest rate risks, currency risks, share price risks, and operational risks

87 See Hartmann-Wendels, Pfingsten et al. (2004), p. 505 and Schierenbeck (2003), p. 154

88 See footnote 114 for a definition of correlation

89 See Poppensieker (2002), p. 11 and p. 12

90 Spread risks are primarily related to bond markets. Schierenbeck (2003), p. 154, however, defines spread risks as a form of credit risks for loan portfolios.

Spread risks can be regarded as indicators for future anticipated default risks as they refer to changes in the value of a loan before maturity. When a loan matures, its spread risk is identical to its default risk.[91]

While spread risks relate to a changing credit spread following a different perspective on borrowers' solvency, interest rate risks are related to a changing market value of loans as a consequence of changes in the risk-free market interest rate. On a single loan basis, the extent of these market value changes is determined by the duration of the asset and the volatility of the market interest rate.[92] The interest rate risk of a credit portfolio can be aggregated from the interest rate risks of the individual loans analogical to default risks, provided correlations between interest rates are taken into account.[93]

Finally, prepayment risks are reinvestment risks for lenders resulting from borrowers' options to render extraordinary repayments of a loan. A borrower will exercise this option if market interest rates have fallen to such an extent that it is cheaper for him to repay the loan and close a new contract at a lower rate despite the costs he faces as a consequence of such a debt conversion. The lender faces the problem that he can only reinvest the returned funds at a lower rate.[94]

---

91 See Poppensieker (2002), p. 14. See also Anson, Chen et al. (2004), chapter 2 who split credit spread risks in two components: (I) Credit spread risks (i.e. changes in credit spreads due to fundamental factors) (II) Downgrade risks (i.e. changes in actual and/or anticipated rating changes affecting credit spreads)

92 The term duration originally refers to bonds. It is a measure of how long, on average, the holder of a bond has to wait before receiving cash payments; see Hull (2006), p. 89. Duration can also be defined as a measurement for the interest rate sensitivity of a financial instrument or of a portfolio of instruments; see Marrison (2002), p. 391. As duration represents the average maturity of cash flows, it is always positive. Therefore, the interest rate sensitivity of a loan is negative. Accordingly, the value of a loan increases with falling and decreases with rising interest rates; see Hull (2006), p. 90

93 See Poppensieker (2002), p. 16

94 See again Poppensieker (2002), p. 16. Apart from changing interest rates, prepayments of loans can also be triggered by other factors such as changing income of borrowers and the general economic environment, see Poppensieker (2002), p. 31

Overview of key credit portfolio risks

	Credit risks		Interest rate risks	Prepayment risks
	Default risks	**Spread risks**		
Risk type	Counter-party-related	Market-/counter-party-related	Market-related	Market-/counterparty-related
Description	Default of debtor	Change in market perspective on debtor's solvency	Movement of market interest rate	Movement of market interest rate/rationale of debtor

Focus of dissertation (Default risks, Spread risks)

Figure 6: Overview of key credit portfolio risks[95]

Further to the above-mentioned risk types, banks that operate in international credit business typically face country-specific risks not directly related to a specific borrower. Country risks can be regarded as an additional risk component in a credit portfolio in addition to the credit portfolio risks which are directly associated with a debtor. This is due to the fact that cross-border capital transactions can be influenced or even prohibited by mandatory regulations of a state. Thus, even under the absence of risks related to a borrower, country risks can be relevant and may need to be taken into account in the process of lending and CPM decisions.[96]

While the instruments used by CPM to perform transactions on the secondary loan market (described in detail in chapter three) are primarily used with the intention of managing the credit risks of a portfolio, some of them also allow the management of interest rate risks.[97] However, particularly in view of the comparably sophisticated and large interest derivatives market,[98] the management of interest rate risks by means of

[95] Source: Own illustration

[96] See Benthien (1993), pp. 306 and 307, Schierenbeck (2003), p. 154

[97] These are in particular instruments transferring liquidity as well as Total Return Swaps (TRS)

[98] It will be shown in chapter 3.2.4 that the worldwide outstanding volume in credit derivatives only constitutes around 2% of the global derivatives market, whereas interest rate derivatives account for almost 75% of the outstanding derivatives volume worldwide

secondary credit market instruments does not seem to be appropriate. It can rather be assumed that the interest rate risks of a credit portfolio can be managed independently of credit risks through comparably simple instruments such as Interest Rate Swaps. Therefore, the management of interest rate risks will not be examined more closely in this dissertation.

As prepayment risks are primarily influenced by interest rate changes, they can be regarded as derivative interest rate risks. Consequently, they can also be managed independently of credit risks through interest rate instruments as part of the overall interest rate risk within a credit portfolio.[99] Besides this, European banks in particular demand high fees in case of early repayments of loans so that at least in Europe prepayment risks within credit portfolios are generally rather low.[100]

Therefore, the focus of this dissertation will lie on the credit risk component of credit portfolios.[101]

After this qualitative overview of types of risks banks face within their credit portfolios, the next section describes how the credit risks within such portfolios can be quantified and measured.

1.4.2.2 Measurement of credit risks

1.4.2.2.1 Probability distribution and expected loss

The value of an asset can be regarded as a random variable as it can take on an infinite number of possible outcomes. The probability distribution of these outcomes and hence the stochastic asset return can be described through a probability density function.[102] Returns of exchange and interest rate instruments or equity securities are often assumed to follow a normal distribution, implying that the asset prices can be

99 However, the prepayment risks which are not induced by changing interest rate risks (see Footnote 94) can only be managed through secondary credit market instruments. According to empirical examinations for the US market, the prepayment risk is primarily influenced by interest rate changes as opposed to other economic factors; see Poppensieker (2002), p. 17. Consequently, this component will not be considered further

100 See Poppensieker (2002), p. 95. In the case of Mortgage Backed Securities (MBS) – see chapter 3.3.3 for a detailed description of these products – an innovation to mitigate prepayment risks is prepayment penalty mortgages; see Bhattacharaya (2001) for a detailed description of this product type

101 Poppensieker (2002) p. 93 et seqq. leads a similar argumentation

102 A probability density function is an equation giving a value for the probability density as a function of the possible value of the random variable: it has the advantage that the complete probability distribution can be approximated without the necessity to gather huge amounts of data; see Marrison (2002), p. 37. See Marrison (2002), p. 27 et seqq. for a sample case on how to construct a probability density function from historical data

described by a log-normal distribution. This assumption is mostly regarded as a sufficiently accurate picture of reality.[103]

Credit assets have significantly different characteristics, however. The probability distribution function of their values is asymmetric and typically characterized by "fat tails".[104] The shape of a typical probability distribution for credit asset values is illustrated in Figure 7.

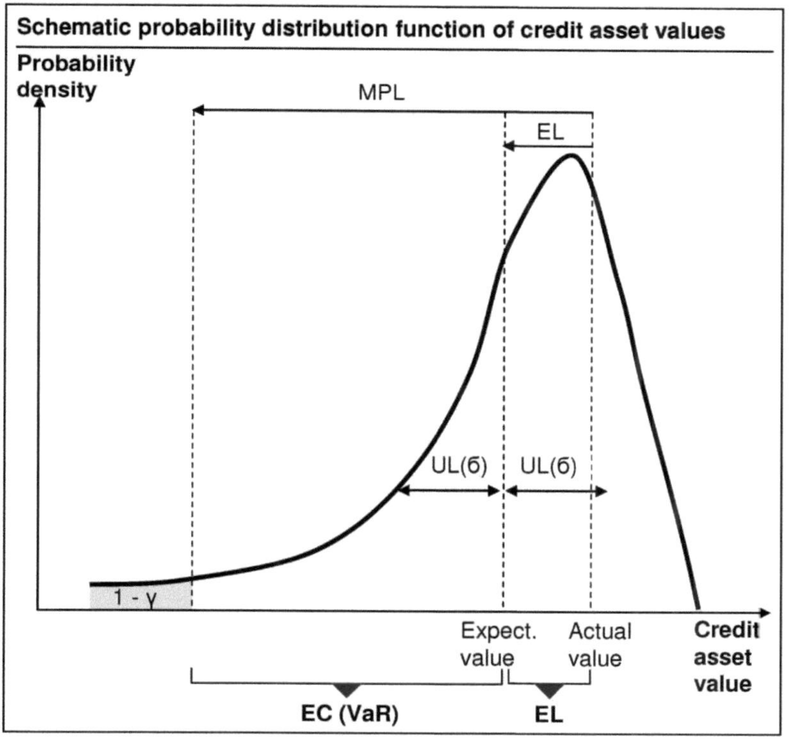

Figure 7: Schematic probability distribution function of credit asset values[105]

[103] See Marrison (2002), p. 37 et seqq. See, e.g., Smithson (2003) p. 36 Panel A for an illustration how the historical distribution of daily price changes of IBM stocks deviates from the normal distribution

[104] Asymmetry of a probability distribution is typically measured by its skewness; "fatness" of a distribution, i.e., the likelihood of suffering extreme losses, is measured by its kurtosis; see Marrison (2002), p. 32 et seq.

[105] Source: Own illustration based on Hartmann-Wendels, Pfingsten et al. (2004), p. 506 and Marrison (2002), chapter 2

As a consequence of this asymmetry, credit asset returns cannot be described by a normal distribution. Instead, value changes of credit assets are often approximated by the Beta distribution function.[106]

As shown in Figure 7, the expected value (mean) of (a) credit asset(s) can be lower than the actual value.[107] The difference between these two values is referred to as expected loss (EL). The EL of a single credit facility can be calculated as

$$EL = EAD * LGD * PD$$

with EAD (Exposure at Default) being the expected credit exposure at the time of default, LGD (Loss Given Default) being the loss in the event of default and PD (Probability of Default)[108] being the probability that default occurs.[109] The EL of a credit portfolio is the sum of the expected losses for the individual loans within the portfolio.[110] It is to cover for the EL of a credit exposure that standard risk costs are calculated and included in its profitability computation.

While the EL describes the average loss from an engagement, it is through risk measures that the risks inherent in a credit asset or portfolio beyond the EL are determined. It can generally be distinguished between symmetric and shortfall risk measures.[111]

1.4.2.2.2 Symmetric risk measures

Most common symmetric risk measures are the standard deviation (δ) and the variance.[112] The standard deviation of the probability distribution is typically defined as unexpected loss (UL).[113]

---

[106] See Marrison (2002), p. 41 for a description of the Beta distribution as well as for an illustrative comparison of the Beta distribution with actual credit loss data

[107] Generally, the expected value or mean value of a random variable is the sum of all possible results, each result being weighted with its probability of occurring. This can be applied for a discrete as well as a continuous number of results; see Marrison (2002), p. 31

[108] The PD is also known as default rate or expected default frequency. It strongly depends on the characteristics of the counterparty/customer (see Marrison (2002), p. 231). For ways to determine values for the PD see Marrison (2002), p. 269 – 281

[109] In this context, one cannot assume that the EAD and the LGD take on given values. In fact, they can be stochastic variables like the PD. In this case, they need to be interpreted as expected values. Furthermore, these expected values need to be stochastically independent because, only in this case, the expected value of a product of stochastic variables is equivalent to the product of the expected values of these stochastic variables, i.e., $E(X*Y) = E(X)*E(Y)$; see Hartmann-Wendels, Pfingsten et al. (2004), p. 505

[110] See Marrison (2002), p. 296 et seq.

[111] See Hartmann-Wendels, Pfingsten et al. (2004), p. 334

[112] The standard deviation measures the degree to which the random results vary from the mean, indicating how

It is important to note that the UL of a credit portfolio (UL_P) can be reduced through portfolio diversification or risk transfer. In the case of two loans within a portfolio, it can be calculated as follows:

$$UL_P = \sqrt{UL_1^2 + 2\rho_{1,2}UL_1UL_2 + UL_2^2}$$

with ρ being the loss correlation between loan 1 and loan 2 of the portfolio.[114] It is appropriate to use the UL as a risk measure whenever sufficiently symmetric distribution functions can be assumed.

1.4.2.2.3 Shortfall risk measures

As shown in Figure 7, credit asset values are characterized by an asymmetric distribution function having "fat tails". This is because there is a greater likelihood of incurring large loan losses than under a symmetric distribution. Therefore, through using symmetric risk measures, the "fat tail" of the probability distribution would be underestimated resulting in a possible loss of information.[115] From an investor's point of view, symmetric risk measures have been criticized on the grounds that they do not correspond to the way investors perceive risks: symmetric risk measures, such as the standard deviation, ascribe the same importance to both positive and negative deviations from the mean. However, investors typically do not have a symmetric attitude towards return variability as they merely regard negative deviations as economic risks.[116] Another argument against symmetric risk measures and in particular

different the actual results can be from the expected result. The square of the standard deviation is the variance; see Marrison (2002), p. 31 et seq.

Classical portfolio theory is based on these risk measures, see chapter 4.1

113 See Marrison (2002), p. 254

Concerning credit risks, it is necessary to consider the EL and UL due to a borrower's default as well as EL and UL due to a change in a borrower's spread risk (i.e. as a consequence of a rating downgrade). It can be shown that downgrades have significant impact on the EL of a borrower but are relatively insignificant to its UL. The UL is mainly determined by extreme losses which primarily derive from defaults. See Marrison (2002), p. 258 et seqq. for a description on how to determine losses due to both defaults and downgrades

114 The correlation is a measure of the tendency for two variables to move together. It is calculated by dividing the covariance (σ_{12}^2) between the variables (i.e. the expected average value of the product of the deviation of the variables, a measure of how much the two variables tend to move together) by the individual variances (σ_1, σ_2) of each of the variables, hence $\rho_{12} = \frac{\sigma_{12}^2}{\sigma_1\sigma_2}$. ρ is a standardized measure taking on values of $[-1;1]$; see Marrison (2002), p. 296 et seq.

115 See Swalm (1966), p. 123 et seqq.

116 See Mao (1970), p. 349 et seqq. and Smith (1971), p. 72 et seq.

against standard deviation is that they necessitate very restrictive assumptions for individuals' utility functions and return distributions so that standard deviation can be applied to the so-called Bernoulli principle.[117]

In order to remedy the deficiencies accompanied by symmetric risk measures, shortfall risk measures have been developed. These risk measures have attracted early attention in financial literature.[118]

From the perspective of shortfall risk measures, risk is defined as "deviations below some exogenously prespecified target rate of return".[119] Hence, they only focus on the "unfavorable" part of a probability distribution.[120] Following this characteristic, shortfall risk measures are typically subsumed under the term Lower Partial Moments (LPM).[121]

One can differentiate between different orders of LPM.[122] Commonly used LPM are zero-, first-, and second-order LPM: zero-order LPM are defined as shortfall probability, first-order LPM as shortfall-mean and second-order LPM as shortfall variance.[123] Shortfall probability will be dealt with in greater detail at a later stage of this dissertation. It is defined as the probability that the return of an asset portfolio is below its target rate of return.[124] If there is no defined specific target rate of return, typically used return targets are the risk-free rate or real or nominal maintenance of capital.[125] It is a common view that the parameter shortfall probability of an asset portfolio can be interpreted more easily than standard deviation.[126]

---

117 See Bawa (1978), p. 255 et seq. Chapter 4.1.1 illustrates the Bernoulli principle and restrictions for utility distribution functions so that standard deviation can be applied as a risk measure

118 See Roy (1952) and Markowitz (1959) for first research on this topic. See also Leibowitz and Henriksson (1989) and Leibowitz and Kogelman (1991)

119 See Harlow and Rao (1989), p. 285. The authors define shortfall risk as downside risk

120 See Hartmann-Wendels, Pfingsten et al. (2004), p. 334. Consequently, shortfall risk measures correspond to a widespread definition of risk, namely the danger that the actual value of an event is lower than its expected value; see Mülhaupt (1980), p. 188

121 Bawa (1975) has developed a formal analysis of LPM of asset distributions for different utility functions

122 See Albrecht (2001), p. 1 for a definition of LPM of order $k \geq 0$ as well as Fishburn (1977), p. 116

123 See Albrecht (2001), p. 2

124 See Rudolf (1994), p. 1 and Footnote 1. The focus on shortfall probability also follows Roy (1952) who defines the probability of falling below a predefined target rate of return as risk. Accordingly, chapter 4.1.3 will deal with portfolios that are efficient in a mean-shortfall probability context

125 See Albrecht (2001), p. 3

126 See, e.g., Zenger (1992)

1.4.2.2.4 VaR as shortfall risk measure used by practitioners

LPM have strongly contributed to an enrichment of portfolio theory in past years. Among practitioners and regulators, however, Value at Risk (VaR) has become the most popular shortfall risk measure of late. The VaR concept was developed in the early 1990s by leading financial institutions as a measure of market risk.[127] Yet, it can be applied for credit risks as well: depending on a predefined confidence level $\gamma \in [0;1]$, the credit VaR measure indicates, which loss compared to a reference asset value (e.g., the mean of the probability distribution) is exceeded only with a probability of $1-\gamma$ in a certain time horizon. In other words, for the time period considered, with a probability of at least γ the loss compared to the expected credit value at the end of the time period is not higher than the VaR.[128]

The VaR can be calculated for any time horizon at any level, be it single-name exposure, portfolio or bank level.[129] For credit risks, the time horizon chosen is usually longer than for market risks.[130] While it is possible that the actual loss on a credit exposure can be higher than the VaR, the confidence level γ is typically chosen so that the default probability is as high as the default probability related to the aspired external credit rating of an institution.[131]

There are three common methods to calculate the VaR: the parametric or variance-covariance approach assuming a normal probability distribution, the historical simulation approach taking market data for usually the past 250 days and calculating the percentage change for each risk factor on each day, and finally the Monte Carlo simulation approach estimating the VaR by randomly creating scenarios for future exposure values.[132]

---

127 JP Morgan produced the first practicable VaR platform for market risk. See, e.g., Rolfes (1998), p. 20 et seqq. for a description on how to use the VaR concept for market risks as part of managing a risk portfolio. Hull (2006), p. 435 notes that VaR is widely used by corporate treasurers, dealers, fund managers, and financial institutions

128 See Hartmann-Wendels, Pfingsten et al. (2004), p. 336

129 See Marrison (2002), p. 98

130 See Hull (2006), p. 499 et seq.

131 See Hartmann-Wendels, Pfingsten et al. (2004), p. 506. Figure 69 gives an overview of long-term credit rating classes and related cumulative default probabilities, using an example of corporate default probabilities measured by Standard & Poor's

132 A more detailed description and comparison of the approaches can be found in Marrison (2002), chapter 6 and Hartmann-Wendels, Pfingsten et al. (2004), p. 339 et seqq. Marrison (2002) chapter 7 provides an overview on how to overcome the limitations related to the VaR approach, such as the assumption that variances and correlations between risk factors are stable, the issue that extreme losses beyond the 99% confidence level are typically not sufficiently described by VaR and the fact that VaR does not account for the fact that exposures may be illiquid

While being popular among practitioners, the use of VaR as a risk measure has been frequently criticized in the academic world. The key point of criticism is its lack of sub-additivity for non-normally distributed asset returns. This means that the diversification of a portfolio is not always adequately represented by the VaR so that it is possible that a diversified portfolio with several credit assets might have a different VaR than the sum of the individual assets' VaR.[133] Hence, VaR risk measurement might cause concentration risks to remain undetected and might not properly reflect diversification effects within a credit portfolio.[134] It is also argued that the VaR approach also does not support a reasonable risk allocation among agents.[135] Finally, certain characteristics of the VaR function such as non-convexity and the existence of multiple local minima make a VaR optimization difficult under discrete return distributions.[136]

In view of the deficiencies of the VaR concept, the Conditional VaR (CVaR) has been introduced. As for the VaR calculation, it is necessary to determine a confidence level and a time horizon to determine the CVaR. While a portfolio's VaR determines the maximum loss that can be expected at the chosen confidence level during the respective investment period, it does not describe the magnitude of the losses outside this confidence level. The CVaR addresses this issue by describing the loss that can be anticipated given that the loss is equal to or larger than the VaR. In other words, the CVaR measures the tail risks of the portfolio distribution function and gives an answer to the question of "how bad is a bad event".[137] As the CVaR is always greater than or at least equal to the VaR, it is a more conservative risk measure than the VaR.[138] The CVaR is sub-additive and fulfills the requirements for a coherent risk measure set up by Artzner, Delbaen et al. (1999).[139] The CVaR is also a tractable measure, i.e., it can be used to solve linear optimization problems.[140]

---

[133] See Artzner, Delbaen et al. (1999), p. 216 showing that VaR is not a "coherent" risk measure as it fails the "sub-additivity" property for non-normal distributions. Jorion (2001), p. 147 et seqq. shows that VaR is additive if it is applied to normal or other elliptic distributions; see also Zagst (2002), p. 253

[134] See Albanese (1997)

[135] See Artzner, Delbaen et al. (1999), p. 218 and also Marrison (2002), chapter 7 describing the limitations of the VaR concept and developing suggestions on how to overcome the weaknesses

[136] See Jobst and Zenios (2001), p. 9

[137] For continuous distributions of asset values, the CVaR is also known as Mean Excess Loss or Tail-VaR. For general distributions, including discrete ones, CVaR is defined as weighted average of losses strictly exceeding VaR; see Rockafellar and Uryasev (2000)

[138] See Jobst and Zenios (2001), p. 9 and Krokhmal, Palmquist et al. (2001), p. 6 et seqq.

[139] See, again, Rockafellar and Uryasev (2000) showing the sub-additivity. Artzner, Delbaen et al. (1999), p. 218 et seqq. and p. 223 et seqq. as well as Zagst (2002), p. 254 et seqq. list coherency criteria: a risk measure is coherent if it is translation-invariant, convex, positively homogenous, and monotonic with respect to

1.4.2.3 Determination of EC

On a bank-wide level, the EC is the cushion an institution needs to have in order to be protected against default.[141] This concept is typically broken down to the individual asset level.

For market risks of trading operations, the EC required is typically determined based on a daily VaR computation.[142] For credit risks, the EC necessary to protect against losses is determined with help of the asset values' probability distribution (see Figure 7):[143] As the EL is typically included in profitability calculations for credit assets,[144] it is for the "uncovered" shortfall component of the probability distribution that EC needs to be held in order to be protected against credit defaults. When assuming a maximum probable loss (MPL) compared to the actual asset value at a confidence level γ such that there is only a small probability $1-\gamma$ that credit losses could be worse than the MPL (see Figure 7), the required EC can be approximated as

$$EC \approx MPL - EL$$ [145]

As illustrated schematically in Figure 7, determining the EC based on the UL of the probability distribution is not sufficient to exclude insolvency with a sufficiently high probability. Therefore, it is rather a downside risk measure, such as the credit VaR that should be chosen as a risk measure to determine the EC required. However, a problem of the VaR calculation is that the entire probability distribution of the asset values needs to be known. As it is generally much easier to determine the UL of an exposure,[146] a common procedure is to allocate EC according to an estimated multiple of the UL so that the default probability is in a satisfactorily low range.[147]

---

stochastic dominance of order 1. Coherency of the CVaR was first proved by Pflug (2000). Zagst (2002), p. 257 et seqq. also proves that VaR is not a coherent risk measure

140 See Di Clemente and Romano (2003), p. 2

141 EC needs to be demarcated from regulatory capital, see chapter 2.2.2 for a description of regulatory capital and related regulatory requirements.

142 See Marrison (2002), p. 18 et seq.

143 Strictly speaking, this definition does not include the spread risk component of credit risk. However, as the spread risk of a loan can be regarded as an anticipated default risk and is identical to its default risk at maturity of the contract, this deficiency can be ignored

144 This is, for example, the case if performance is measured with RAROC, see chapter 1.4.2.5

145 See Marrison (2002), p. 17 et seq.

146 It can be shown that the only parameters which need to be known to calculate the UL are the PD and the variance of the LGD. Assuming the LGD is constant, the PD is sufficient to determine the UL; see Hartmann-Wendels, Pfingsten et al. (2004), p. 507

147 See Hartmann-Wendels, Pfingsten et al. (2004), p. 508

1.4.2.4 Strategies to minimize unexpected credit risks

As already mentioned above, the UL of a credit portfolio can be reduced through portfolio diversification or risk transfer. These activities can be integrated into a systematization of strategies to minimize unexpected credit risks. According to such a systematization, one can differentiate between strategies limiting the causes and others limiting the impact of credit risks (see Figure 8).

Strategies to minimize unexpected credit risks

	Limitation of cause		Limitation of impact		
Strategy	**Avoidance**	**Reduction**	**Diversification**	**Transfer**	**Provision**
Description	• Waive or severely restrict lending business	• Conduct efficient credit analysis • Ensure thorough loan monitoring	• Spread loan volume over many borrowers • Avoid exposure to highly correlated borrowers	• Transfer credit risks between parties	• Ensure sufficient capital to cover credit risks
			Major field of activity of ACPM units		

Figure 8: Strategies to minimize unexpected credit risks[148]

There are two types of strategies aiming at limiting the causes of unexpected credit risks: risk avoidance and risk reduction. Risk avoidance means either waving credit business entirely or at best doing credit business only with extremely high collateral requirements. Risk reduction strategies try to ensure that the borrowers' creditworthiness is properly judged if collateral cannot fully insure the lender against credit losses. In order to successfully achieve a reduction of credit risks, it is essential

[148] Source: Own illustration based on Schierenbeck (2003), p. 194 et seqq.

to have an efficient credit analysis process established. These strategies are typically within the responsibility of origination and not of CPM.

Risk diversification, risk transfer/acceptance, and risk provision are strategies limiting the impact of unexpected credit risks. It will be shown that these strategies are a major field of activity for ACPM units. Risk diversification aims at reshuffling the credit portfolio so that unsystematic portfolio risks are mostly eliminated.[149] This can be achieved, e.g., by distributing the lender's loan volume among as many individual borrowers as possible, as well as by avoiding concentrating the loan volume on certain segments whose creditworthiness is highly correlated.[150] The impact of unexpected risks can also be limited by transferring risks within a credit portfolio back to the borrower or to third parties or by acquiring specific risk components from other parties or on secondary loan markets.[151] Through risk provisions the remaining unexpected risks are covered.

1.4.2.5 Performance measurement

This section introduces concepts that can be used to determine the performance of credit assets and related portfolios, putting an emphasis on risk-adjusted performance measurement.

Commonly used ratios to evaluate single transactions as well as an entire credit portfolio are return on investment (ROI) measures. They put the surplus created by a business activity in relation to the underlying assets (return on assets = ROA) or equity (return on equity = ROE[152]). However, as these ratios do not reflect the risks related to a transaction, they provide an incentive to take on high risk transactions, thereby yielding higher surpluses but ignoring the increased riskiness.

To overcome this deficiency, risk-adjusted performance measures have been developed. Generally speaking, these ratios relate a surplus term to a risk term. The most prominent risk-adjusted performance measures are the return on risk-adjusted

[149] Analogous to capital market theory, credit risk can be split into a systematic and an unsystematic component. Unexpected credit risk (UL) is the unsystematic component and can be reduced/eliminated through diversification of the loan portfolio. A fully diversified loan portfolio would only bear the systematic risk component, which is the credit risk of a so-called market portfolio containing all credit assets of a market, country, region, etc; see Schierenbeck (2003), p. 156 as well as chapter 4.2.1.2

[150] Strictly speaking, risk diversification can both limit cause and impact of unexpected credit risk: on the one hand, the probability and level of possible loan losses can be positively influenced through risk diversification (limitation of causes). On the other hand, the negative impact of loan losses can be alleviated through risk diversification; see Schierenbeck (2003), p. 156

[151] As indicated in Figure 8, it will be shown later in chapter 2.3.2 that risk diversification and risk transfer are among the key activities of an ACPM unit

[152] The equity underlying this ratio is either book capital (i.e., the net value of a single asset, a portfolio or the entire institution as measured by accounting standards) or regulatory capital (i.e., the minimum amount of capital that must be held according to regulatory requirements); see Marrison (2002), p. 21

capital (RORAC) and the risk-adjusted return on capital (RAROC), developed by Bankers Trust (1995). For a loan transaction, RORAC can be defined as

$$RORAC = \frac{A_0 r_L + F - D_0 r_D - OC}{EC}$$

with the following parameter definitions:[153]

L_0 is the initial loan amount, r_L the interest income on the loan (loan price), F any fees related to the loan, D_0 the amount of debt (taken on to give out the loan), r_D the interest to be paid on the debt, OC the operating cost and EC the EC.

The numerator of the RORAC equation contains the net income of the loan engagement. It does not subtract the loan's EL, thus assuming that it is covered by the net income, which the exposure generates.

RAROC, by contrast, is a more conservative ratio as it additionally includes risk adjustment of the net income by deducting the EL. Hence, the RAROC equation for a loan is as follows:[154]

$$RAROC = \frac{A_0 r_L + F - D_0 r_D - OC - EL}{EC}$$

Including the EC in the denominator of the equations for RORAC and RAROC follows the idea that the net income of a loan engagement needs to generate a sufficiently high return on the scarce underlying risk capital. As described above, the most commonly used risk measure to determine the EC in the denominator of the equation is the VaR.

Risk-adjusted performance measures allow the decision for loan engagements according to risk-return aspects. However, such a procedure does not guarantee yet that the value of the capital invested will be maximized. In order to ensure that an intended engagement is value-creating, its minimum return ("hurdle rate") must be higher than the capital costs of the risk capital invested. These capital costs can usually be derived from the market returns for risks.[155] Combining the risk-adjusted

153 See Hartmann-Wendels, Pfingsten et al. (2004), p. 349 in combination with Marrison (2002), p. 21 et seq.

154 See again Marrison (2002), p. 21 et seq. Furthermore, Chorafas (2000), chapter 14 and chapter 1 gives a detailed description of the RAROC measure

The illustration of RAROC depicted here is strictly speaking RAROC for a transaction that happens over a single time period, e.g., a year. If a loan is granted over multiple years, the RAROC calculation becomes more difficult. See Marrison (2002), p. 334 et seqq. for a more subtle definition of RAROC, taking these difficulties into consideration

155 The Capital Asset Pricing Model (CAPM), which will be introduced in chapter 4.1.3, is a widespread tool used to determine these market returns

performance measure from a loan engagement (e.g., RAROC) with a required hurdle rate $RORAC^{*}$ on the risk capital leads to the so-called Economic Value Added (EVA^{TM}):

$$EVA = RAROC - \frac{EC * RORAC^{*}}{EC}$$

A positive EVA^{TM} indicates that earnings from a loan engagement exceed all its costs, hence, the contract is creating value for the institution.[156]

A key advantage when using risk-adjusted performance measures is the ability to integrate the risk component into lending decisions. However, the above-mentioned shortcomings of the VaR concept need to be taken into consideration when interpreting RORAC ratios. The application of more sophisticated risk measures such as the CVaR can improve the explanatory power of the risk-adjusted ratios described above, especially in the context of credit assets.[157]

As mentioned at the beginning of chapter 1.4.2, an auxiliary constraint for CPM to achieve the goal of optimally structuring its portfolio from a risk-return point of view is the refinancing of the lending activities. This will be topic of the next section.

1.4.3 Refinancing

Refinancing refers to raising capital that banks need to perform their lending business. Banks face two options to refinance their activities: on the one hand, they can raise debt capital by accepting deposits from individuals or take on public debt on capital markets. On the other hand, they can raise equity capital from their owners. In recent years, so-called "hybrid securities" which combine elements of equity and debt have become increasingly popular.[158]

Taking on deposits represents the traditional form of bank refinancing, constituting around two thirds of banks' balance sheets in Germany (see again Figure 4). They can be characterized as non-tradable debt instruments with short-term maturity.[159] Another characteristic of deposits is their sequential service constraint, i.e., when withdrawing a deposit, the depositor's ability to withdraw his funds is mainly dependent on the

---

[156] See, e.g., Schierenbeck and Paul (2000), p. 210. See e.g., Ehrbar (1998) for a description of the EVA^{TM} concept. The EVA^{TM} performance measurement method fits to the shareholder value concept developed by Rappaport (1997)

[157] See also Hartmann-Wendels, Pfingsten et al. (2004), p. 356 et seq. for a brief overview on the limitations of RORAC measurement, as well as an evaluation of the approach

[158] See, e.g., Schierenbeck (2003), p. 25 et seq.

[159] See Hartmann-Wendels, Pfingsten et al. (2004), pp. 207 – 208. Regarding different types of deposits and their maturity see Hartmann-Wendels, Pfingsten et al. (2004), p. 201 et seqq. An overview on different types of deposits can also be found in Büschgen and Börner (2003), p. 152 et seqq. and Greenbaum and Thakor (1994), p. 450 et seqq.

behavior of other depositors.[160] It is the sequential service constraint of deposits that makes banks vulnerable to sudden withdrawals of their deposits, so-called "bank runs".[161]

Refinancing options for banks are determined by assumptions regarding capital market liquidity:

Under the hypothesis of illiquid markets for banking capital, a bank can refinance itself exclusively through acceptance of customer deposits. Besides guaranteeing the profitability of its business, the crucial task for a bank under this assumption is to ensure its ability to meet its financial obligations through optimally structuring the volume and duration of its assets and liabilities.[162] The management of this so-called structural liquidity is the key task for banks under the hypothesis of capital market illiquidity.[163]

Given the "modern" hypothesis of liquid banking capital markets, a bank can raise funds on the capital market in addition to funding through deposit taking. Even if certain banking asset classes are illiquid, there is no need to have special provisions in order to maintain liquidity, provided that funding activities are not inhibited by information asymmetries between banks and their investors.[164] In this case, maintenance of liquidity is no longer an issue. A bank does not need to actively manage its structural liquidity any longer – the lending activities can be managed and refinanced independently from the availability of deposits.

It seems as though banking theory, which does not put a particular emphasis on liquidity risks for banks any longer,[165] regards issues concerning management of

160 See Greenbaum and Thakor (1994), p. 452 et seq.

161 Diamond and Dybvig (1983) develop a fundamental model showing that a deposit contract can lead to two equilibriums: in the positive equilibrium, all deposits are paid back to the depositors. The negative equilibrium, however, results from a panic reaction ("bank run") of depositors who suddenly excessively withdraw their funds and can cause a breakdown of the banking system. An overview on theoretical models related to bank runs and the concept of deposit insurance can, for example, be found in Freixas and Rochet (1997), chapter 7

162 According to § 11 KWG (1998) banks are required to invest their funds in such a way that they are always able to meet their financial obligations. This requirement is elaborated further in the liquidity guidelines of the BaFin (so-called "Grundsatz II" from 1 July 2000). See Schierenbeck (2003), p. 120 et seqq. for an overview of the BaFin liquidity guidelines

163 Regarding structural liquidity, see Büschgen (1998), pp. 565 – 567 and Süchting and Paul (1998), pp. 593 – 595. The structural liquidity is typically managed within the Asset Liability Management (ALM) unit of a financial institution; see Marrison (2002), p. 175

164 Hartmann-Wendels, Pfingsten et al. (2004), p. 425 use the example of the illiquid asset of human capital to prove that there are no issues related to liquidity management even if assets are illiquid provided a bank operates in a complete capital market

165 In his overview on bank risk controlling (chapter C of chapter two), Schierenbeck (2003) does not address

structural liquidity and related risks as less and less relevant for banks. The increasing significance of tradable debt instruments in recent years (see part I) and a growing, albeit still not optimal, liquidity of secondary credit markets (see chapter 1.2 for the development of secondary loan markets as well as chapter three describing the emergence of various secondary credit market instruments and related markets in greater detail) seems to support this view as these developments allow banks to raise funds on capital markets in addition to taking on deposits. Assuming that management of structural liquidity is not an issue for banks, the form of bank refinancing is merely relevant for institutions' capital costs.[166]

After a description of refinancing activities, this overview of wholesale credit business will be concluded with a brief description of loan restructuring and workout business.

1.4.4 Loan restructuring and workout[167]

It has been shown in chapter 1.4.1 that a lending institution is required to regularly analyze and monitor its borrowers' financial situation during the entire maturity of a loan contract in order to recognize changes in the borrowers' solvency as well as to detect behavioral changes of the borrowers. However, a close personal contact with debtors is most of the time not only more insightful in view of the changing risk profiles of customers than analyses of financial statements but can also provide more up-to-date information for the lending institution.

Before closing a loan contract, a bank can demand preventive measures from prospective borrowers such as collateral or the agreement to special contract clauses. These measures can help preventing debtors from undertaking risky projects that could endanger their ability to repay a loan.[168] After having closed the contract, should the bank identify a significant deterioration in the credit quality of a debtor during its monitoring activities, a credit workout process is initiated. At the beginning of this process, the troubled debtor is monitored with a higher frequency than debtors with healthy contracts. The bank evaluates whether it seems useful to restructure the loan or whether it should recall the loan completely and unwind the collateral and other assets of the troubled borrower. Hereby, a perspective on the overall exposure to the distressed lender is taken into consideration.[169]

liquidity risks any longer

166 See Poppensieker (2002), p. 9

167 Workout is an agreement between a company and its creditors establishing the steps the company must take to avoid bankruptcy, i.e. to avoid the company's reorganization or liquidation following a default on its debts; see Brealey, Myers et al. (2004), p. 574 as well as Hartmann-Wendels, Pfingsten et al. (2004), pp. 590 – 596

168 According to Figure 8, such measures can be classified as risk avoidance strategies

169 See Berg (1994) for an overview of activities a bank can undertake in view of ailing loans

Restructuring a loan includes negotiations between borrower and lender to undertake actions that help to cure an ailing engagement. Examples of restructuring activities are conversion of debt to equity, the abandonment of interest payments or even the cancellation (partly) of a loan. Often, it is specialized workout groups or accountants who deal with these problematic engagements.[170]

If restructuring activities have failed or do not seem promising, e.g., due to over-indebtedness of a borrower, the lending institution typically recalls the loan and aims at commercializing the lender's collateral or other assets. This can happen through an extrajudicial agreement, with the help of judicial execution or in the course of a bankruptcy proceeding.

The above-mentioned activities and instruments used for monitoring, restructuring and workout of loan contracts can be subsumed under activities of passive credit risk management. A common feature of these strategies is that they focus on minimizing a bank's credit risks after having concluded a lending agreement.[171] They do not aim at transferring risk positions.[172] The remainder of this dissertation will focus on methods and strategies aiming at actively managing a credit portfolio through, e.g., transferring credits or related risks to other players. Methods of passive credit risk management will not be considered any further in this dissertation.

1.5 Summary

This chapter has given an introduction to the dissertation and has targeted the containment and the focus of the topic.

Common definitions related to financial (capital) markets have been provided, defining the primary financial market as a market on which financial contracts come into existence. Consequently, the primary loan market has been defined as a market on which loans are originated. The primary loan market has been demarcated from the secondary loan market, which, according to banking practice, has been defined as a market on which all available financial instruments that can be used to manage loan portfolios are traded.

Afterwards, banks have been introduced as financial intermediaries between the supply of and demand for capital on financial markets. While they are redundant in complete capital markets, it is due to market incompletions such as limited market access, market frictions and information asymmetries that the existence of banks can improve welfare in a financial market. Following a tendency towards more complete financial markets in recent years – induced by a growing liquidity of loan markets – one could argue that banks are increasingly becoming redundant institutions.

---

[170] Lauer (2004) provides a detailed description of loan restructuring activities

[171] See, again, Figure 8 for a classification

[172] See Hartmann-Wendels, Pfingsten et al. (2004), p. 590

However, the tendency toward market completion along with increased secondary credit market liquidity has been focused on certain market segments only. Besides this, traditional bank lending activities as a counterpart for bank deposits still constitute the major share in the global financial stock. There has also been an increasing demand for specialized financial intermediation services in recent years: in view of limited direct market access for individuals and due to a growing complexity of financial instruments, specialized financial intermediaries have increasingly been gaining in importance on capital markets. Consequently, despite profound changes in capital market, banks still have a legitimate right to exist as financial intermediaries on these markets.

After the introduction of banks as intermediaries in financial markets and a justification of their legitimacy, an overview of the banking systems in the US and in Europe has been given in order to show the different types of institutions that have emerged. The US banking system is still coined by the recently abolished Glass-Steagal legislation: commercial and investment banking activities are typically performed by separate institutions. Besides these two main types of banks, there are thrift institutions and non-or near-banks such as mutual and pension funds. The German banking system, by contrast, is a universal banking system, with financial institutions being allowed to perform all kinds of banking businesses under one roof. Three main groups of banks can be distinguished: besides private banks, there are publicly owned and primarily regionally focused savings banks, supported by state banks (Landesbanken), as well as cooperative banks, which have a similar regional focus to savings banks and are headed by the DZ and WGZ-Bank as their central bank institutions. Further to distinguishing banks according to their field of activity, they can be systematized according to other criteria, in particular according to their target clientele. Retail banks, focusing on private and commercial mass market customers, can be differentiated from wholesale banks targeting their business activities mainly at individual large and medium-sized corporate and institutional customers. The primary focus of this dissertation has been narrowed down to the credit business of wholesale banks.

Accordingly, an overview of the different activities related to wholesale banking credit business has been given:

Loan origination initiates a lending relationship. The key task in the course of the origination process is a credit analysis, which is not only based on "hard" factors, such as financial data of the prospective borrower, but also on "soft" factors related to an intuitive judgment of the credit analyst about the loan applicant. Banks are legally required to keep on performing a regular analysis of their borrowers' financial situation throughout the entire maturity of a loan contract.

Following the origination process, the credit portfolio, which is fraught with different types of risks, is managed in order to maximize the income from credit assets.

Thereby, the interest and prepayment risk component of a credit portfolio can be managed independently of its credit risk component. How to manage the latter component will be in the focus of the dissertation.

Credit risks can be defined as an unexpected deterioration of borrowers' financial solvency. Two subtypes of credit risks can be distinguished: default risks describe risks that debtors fail to meet agreed-upon payment obligations. Spread risks refer to risks that a loan may lose value in view of a different market perspective on the debtors' solvency.

In order to be able to measure the credit risks inherent in a credit portfolio, it is essential to know the probability distribution function of the credit assets' values. Such a function is typically asymmetric and characterized by "fat tails", reflecting the higher possibility of extreme outcomes (i.e., large losses of the outstanding loan volume) than under a symmetric probability distribution. The difference between the actual and expected value of a credit asset is defined as EL. The EL describes the average loss from a loan engagement.

The risks inherent in a credit asset or an entire credit portfolio above the EL can be determined through risk measures. Symmetric risk measures ascribe the same importance to both positive and negative deviations of the actual return from the mean of the distribution. Most common representatives of this type are standard deviation and variance. In particular due to the asymmetric risk distribution of credit assets, however, shortfall risk measures seem to be more appropriate to describe the risks inherent in this asset class. Shortfall risk measures focus on the lower part of a probability distribution, describing risk as deviations below a predefined rate of return. Typically, they are referred to as LPM. Shortfall probability, which is defined as zero-order LPM, will be dealt with in greater detail in this dissertation.

The VaR is a very common shortfall risk measure used by practitioners. It describes which loss compared to the mean of the probability distribution is exceeded only with a significantly low probability within a certain time horizon. While the EL is an additive risk measure, this is neither the case for the UL nor for the VaR as correlations between single positions need to be taken into account to be able to determine the aggregated value of these risk measures. The deficiencies of the VaR approach have been addressed through developing the CVaR, being a sub-additive risk measure, which quantifies the tail risks of a distribution function.

The EL is typically included in the profitability calculation for a newly originated loan. Any shortfall risk beyond the EL, however, is not considered in asset pricing and consequently needs to be covered with EC in order to guarantee the solvency of the lender following a possible adverse movement in the asset value.

The performance of a credit asset or an entire credit portfolio can be measured through ratios such as the ROI or the ROE. Yet, these ratios do not reflect the risks related to credit assets. In order to integrate this risk component, risk-adjusted performance measures have been developed. RORAC and RAROC are the most prominent ones. They can also be applied to determine the EVA™ of an engagement, indicating whether this engagement creates economic value or not.

Banks can refinance their lending activities through raising equity capital from their owners. Alternatively, they can access debt capital on the capital markets or accept deposits from individual investors. Deposits are non-tradable short-term debt instruments, characterized by a sequential service constraint. The increasing liquidity of banking capital markets allows the institutions to alternatively refinance themselves on the capital markets, thus making it increasingly redundant to be concerned about an active management of the structural liquidity.

If, in the course of its regular monitoring activities, a bank recognizes a significantly worsening credit quality of a debtor, it usually initiates a credit workout process. Such a procedure typically comprises multiple steps with different escalation levels, ranging from an increased, more frequent monitoring of the troubled debtor to restructuring or ultimately recalling the loan, should other activities have failed or not seem promising. In general, these are activities of passive risk management as opposed to the ACPM approach that will be introduced in the next chapter.

Starting with a description of the hitherto predominant approach towards wholesale lending, the next chapter will describe the key forces of change in credit markets that have been challenging this concept and that have been putting pressure on the institutions to rethink the way to conduct their lending credit business. The establishment of the ACPM approach has been the key innovation in this context. The main ideas behind this new approach towards lending business and the ACPM business models through which it can be implemented according to existing literature on this topic will be outlined. Furthermore, determinants for the design of ACPM units will be introduced.

2 Development, principles, and implementation of the ACPM approach

2.1 The conventional wholesale lending approach – "originate and hold"

Wholesale banks have conventionally followed an "originate and hold" approach towards lending business: under this approach, credit assets are originated, monitored, managed and serviced by an integrated customer BU – i.e., by the individual customer relationship managers. This customer BU owns and holds the assets until maturity (or default) and is responsible for origination, management and, often, problem loan management/workout of these assets. Independently of the BU, there is typically another unit (or a credit committee) which is responsible for credit approval ("second vote") decisions, as well as for collection and analysis of portfolio information. This conventional "hold to maturity" approach is characterized by a one-way flow of credit assets from borrowers onto the banks' balance sheets – consequently, banks virtually fully absorb credit risks and passively accept upcoming loan losses.[173] There is typically no connection between the customer BU and secondary loan market units. Therefore, the composition of the credit portfolio is solely changed via the loan origination side of an institution. Figure 9 gives a schematic illustration of the "originate and hold" lending approach.

2.2 Forces of change in credit markets

During the past years, there have been important changes and developments in the banking environment and particularly in credit markets. Many of these changes and developments have presented opportunities for banks to improve their business practices and provided them with tools and instruments to do so. At the same time, however, they have also challenged the institutions to adjust the way they conduct their lending business to remain competitive in a changing environment.

This chapter gives an overview of the key forces of change in credit markets during past years. Afterwards, the impact of these changes on how wholesale banks organize and manage their lending business will be described.[174]

2.2.1 Increasing secondary credit market liquidity

In recent years, banks have been able to operate in increasingly liquid secondary loan markets. Increasing volumes in secondary loan sales and the emergence and growing liquidity of a variety of secondary credit market instruments enabling the exchange of credit risks has provided the institutions with the prerequisites to reshuffle and diversify their loan portfolios through, e.g., transferring their credit risks to other

[173] See, e.g., Flämig (2005)

[174] For a summary of the key forces of change in credit markets, see Hammes and Shapiro (2001), p. 98 et seq. and Kuritzkes (1998), p. 1 et seq.

players. However, these developments are still in an early phase. For example, chapter three will show that sufficiently liquid credit trading activity is still mainly focused on large corporate credit names.

Conventional wholesale lending approach

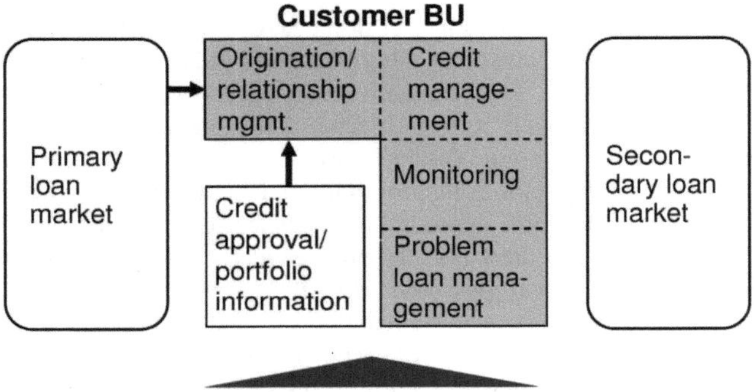

- Credit assets owned by a customer BU, which is responsible for origination, monitoring, management, and servicing of loans
- Independent credit approval unit with second vote authority regarding lending decisions; collection and analysis of portfolio information
- Typically "one-way" asset flow
- No connection between customer BU and secondary loan market

Figure 9: Conventional wholesale lending approach[175]

2.2.2 Opportunities to perform regulatory capital arbitrage

It was shown in chapter 1.4.2.3 that EC is used as a cushion for unexpected credit risks in order for the lending institution to be protected against default of a debtor. The EC is determined according to economic concepts such as the VaR. Independently of holding the economically reasonable capital, however, banks need to conform to regulatory requirements with regard to their capital provisions.

2.2.2.1 Current regulation "Basle I"

The current regulation for provisions of default risks trace back to the guidelines of the Basle Committee of Banking Supervision as of 1988 ("Basle I"), which were introduced with the goal of achieving an international harmonization of capital

[175] Source: Own illustration based on Kuritzkes (1998), p. 2

requirements.[176] The agreement has been implemented through national laws. In Germany, financial institutions are regulated by the "Gesetz über das Kreditwesen (Kreditwesengesetz)" (KWG (1998)), which has been amended by several ordinances. Further to the regulation of liquidity risks mentioned above,[177] §§ 10, 12 and 13 KWG in combination with the so-called "Grundsatz I" regulation of the BaFin regulate the limitation of credit risks in relation to available equity.[178]

According to the currently valid regulatory requirements, the individual creditworthiness of a borrower is not taken into consideration when determining the necessary equity provision. It is differentiated rather between debtor categories such as public debtors, banks, mortgage exposures and corporations/private individuals, with all borrowers of the same category requiring the same equity provision. The required equity is determined by means of the loan volume which is multiplied with an arbitrarily defined risk weighting, depending on the respective debtor category: loans to sovereigns from OECD countries have a 0% risk weight, exposures to banks from OECD countries have a 20% risk weight, real estate loans have a 50% risk weight, and loans to corporations and private individuals have a 100% risk weight. The regulatory required equity to be held needs to be at least 8% of these risk-weighted assets (RWAs).[179]

---

176 See BIS (1988)

177 See Footnote 162

178 In this context, it is important to note that the regulatory definition for equity significantly differs from the EC definition. § 10 articles 2-7 KWG (1998) determine the equity capital components that are considered by regulation. Grundsatz I concretizes according to which criteria the BaFin evaluates the appropriateness of an institution's equity provision.

See, e.g., Hartmann-Wendels, Pfingsten et al. (2004) p. 403 et seqq. for a detailed overview of the regulatory definition for equity according to § 10 KWG

In Bundesbank (2002a), p. 42 et seqq., an overview of the different components included in regulatory equity is given.

Regulatory equity consists of three components: (I) Tier-1 capital (core capital) including the balance sheet equity (mainly consisting of the basic capital, retained earnings and hidden reserves). (II) Supplementary capital first class including provident funds and tax provisions as hidden reserves as well as capital stemming from profit participation rights. (III) Supplementary capital second class comprising long-term subordinate liabilities. Due to its lower qualification, supplementary capital is considered as regulatory equity only to a lower extent than core capital: total supplementary capital may not exceed 100% of the core capital, supplementary capital second class may be at most 50% of the core capital

179 See BIS (1988), p. 8 et seqq. and, e.g., Hartmann-Wendels, Pfingsten et al. (2000), p. 366 et seqq. for a summary of the regulatory requirements. In addition to the above-mentioned risk weights, single loan exposures may not bind more than 25% of the liable equity. Furthermore, the amount of all large exposures (loans whose volume binds more than 10% of the liable equity) is not allowed to exceed eight times the liable equity (see § 13 KWG (1998))

2.2.2.2 Regulatory arbitrage

These relatively gross classifications of risk weights may result in an identical capital requirement for loan positions of different creditworthiness within the same category and, therefore, do not adequately reflect the true economic risks behind individual engagements. Consequently, there is an opportunity for banks to exploit the differences between the true economic risks embedded in their credit portfolios and the notions and measurements of risks that are incorporated in regulatory standards. Such a procedure is known as regulatory capital arbitrage.

Regulatory capital arbitrage can be performed, e.g., by selling off high-quality assets that have comparably low credit risks but are usually subject to the same regulatory capital requirements as riskier assets within the same category. A very popular form of regulatory capital arbitrage is performed through bundling and selling off the highest quality assets by means of securitization,[180] thus reducing the economic risks on the books to a far lesser extent than regulatory required capital.[181] Following this sale, the freed-up regulatory capital can be returned to shareholders or employed in other, more profitable business.[182]

The "originate and hold" lending approach, however, is inefficient from a regulatory capital point of view as it does not allow to perform such arbitrage transactions, which enable the most profitable regulatory capital allocation.[183]

2.2.2.3 Changes following proposal for new capital adequacy rules "Basle II"

In view of the deficiencies of the currently valid requirements, the Basle Committee of Banking Supervision has developed new proposals for capital adequacy rules ("Basle II").[184] As far as credit risks are concerned, the requirement to underlay the risk-

---

180 See chapter 3.3 for a comprehensive description of securitization transactions

181 In an empirical analysis of mortgage loans originated between 1995 and 1997, Ambrose, LaCour-Little et al. (2003) find empirical evidence that securitization transactions are driven by regulatory arbitrage

182 Besides selling off high quality assets, there are other ways to perform regulatory arbitrage which include, e.g., the conversion of credit exposures into contractual agreements that, although providing some loss protection for investors, are not recognized as financial guarantees and do not fall under regulatory capital requirements; see Jones (2000), p. 40 et seqq. for more details on common regulatory capital arbitrage in practice

183 See Kuritzkes (1998)

184 The fact that regulators have become increasingly concerned with the risks of regulatory capital arbitrage, in particular, fearing a deterioration of banks' average credit quality and an erosion of regulatory capital standards has also contributed to a revision of the regulation; see Jones (2000), p. 49 et seq.

After several amendments, the revised version of these requirements is aimed at being implemented by year-end 2007; see BIS (2004c), p.1.

The guidelines include three pillars: the first pillar deals with the calculation of minimum capital requirements, focusing on credit risks, market price risks and, as a new category, operational risks. The second pillar regulates the supervisory review process, and the third pillar deals with issues regarding market

weighted assets with 8% equity remains the same under the new guidelines. However, the key innovation of the new regulation is that the risk weights are to be linked to the assets' actual credit risks. To determine these risk weights, banks can decide whether to implement a so-called standardized approach or one of two types of internal ratings-based (IRB) approaches.

When calculating risk weights under the standardized approach, the debtors' creditworthiness is determined with the help of external ratings from credit rating agencies.[185] Under the IRB approaches, the creditworthiness is determined by means of internal bank ratings.[186] As an incentive for banks to implement advanced risk measurement procedures, the required equity provision is lower the more sophisticated the approach applied is.

Following the implementation of "Basle II", a better alignment between regulatory risk measures and true economic risks of credit assets will be achieved, thus reducing the incentive to undertake regulatory capital arbitrage transactions. Yet, due to the fact that the new guidelines still include a categorization of assets, some amount of regulatory capital arbitrage is still expected following the implementation of "Basle II".[187]

However, to be able to exploit the opportunities for regulatory arbitrage and to optimally allocate regulatory capital, banks need a more flexible approach towards management of credit risks.

2.2.3 Advancements in credit risk analytics[188]

Advancements in credit risk analytics have enabled banks to measure credit portfolio risks in a more refined way than before and to compute the required EC for an individual asset or a credit portfolio. This allows credit assets to be priced from a risk-

discipline of institutions such as disclosure requirements; see BIS (2004c), p. 6 for an overview of the topics covered by the new regulation. The new guidelines also include a separate chapter on regulatory capital requirements for securitizations, aiming at curbing regulatory arbitrage by means of these transactions, see chapter 3.4.4.3

185 See BIS (2004c), p. 15 et seqq. For example, loans to corporations which have a long-term external credit rating between AAA and AA- require a risk weight of 20%, between A+ and A- a risk weight of 50% , between BBB+ and BB- a risk weight of 100% and below BB- a risk weight of 150%. Unrated corporations require a risk weight of 100%; see BIS (2004c), p. 19 as well as the left-hand column of Figure 31 for an illustration. Figure 69 gives an overview on long-term Standard & Poor's credit rating classes and related default probabilities

186 See BIS (2004c), p. 48 et seqq. A basic and an advanced IRB approach are differentiated, with the difference being that the advanced approach can only be applied if the institutions dispose of particularly qualified procedures to measure credit risks

187 See, e.g., Poppensieker (2002), p. 28 et seq.

188 See Marrison (2002), chapter 20 and 21 for a detailed description of the different credit portfolio modelling approaches mentioned in this chapter

adjusted point of view and enables the creation of an optimally structured loan portfolio.

In recent years, five different approaches to measure credit risks of a portfolio and to compute EC have been developed. These approaches were implemented in a number of first-generation credit portfolio models in the mid- and late 1990s.

All these models have in common that they estimate the probability distribution for the asset value of a credit portfolio by determining the portfolio's EL and UL. Based on this estimation, they also determine the amount of EC a bank needs to hold for its credit portfolio in order to be able to compensate losses to maintain its envisaged credit rating. Main differences between these models are the approaches they use to estimate the loss distribution and to determine default correlations between individual credit assets.

Different software solutions have been developed to implement the theoretical concepts. Figure 10 gives an overview of the assumptions behind the first generation of credit portfolio models and their common software implementations. They will briefly be described in the following. Afterwards, a brief illustration of second-generation models will be given.

First-generation credit portfolio models

Model	Key assumptions	Software implementation
Covariance model (Markowitz model)	• Historical losses or asset correlations determine default correlations • Portfolio losses can be approximated by Beta distribution function	• n/a
Actuarial model	• Loan portfolios can be divided into independent groups of loans • Losses within these loan groups are uncorrelated	• CreditRisk^{+TM}, Portfolio Risk^{+TM} (Credit Suisse Financial Products)
Merton model	• Companies' asset values determine loan defaults • Asset values are correlated • Loss distribution function can be determined through simulation	• PortfolioManager™ (Moody's KMV) • CreditMetrics™ (Risk Metrics)
Macroeconomic default model	• Default rates are functions of macro-variables (e.g., GDP growth) • Loss distribution function can be determined through simulation	• CreditPortfolioView™ (McKinsey & Company)
Macroeconomic cash flow model	• Changes in macro-variables drive changes in cash flows which can trigger defaults • Loss distribution function can be determined through simulation	• n/a

Figure 10: First-generation credit portfolio models[189]

2.2.3.1 The covariance credit portfolio model (Markowitz model)

According to the covariance credit portfolio model (often referred to as the Markowitz model), credit risks can be modeled in a four-step approach:

[189] Source: Own illustration based on Marrison (2002), chapters 20 and 21 and Banks (2004), chapter 12

In a first step, a formula for calculating the EL and UL of the credit portfolio is determined using the respective parameters of the individual loans within the portfolio.[190]

As the calculation of the portfolio UL requires the knowledge of correlations between the individual ULs (see the formula in chapter 1.4.2.2), the second step estimates these correlations. A relatively simple and quick way to do so is through considering historical losses (ULs) in the bank's credit portfolio.[191] However, this method only provides one correlation for the whole portfolio and does not allow the differentiation between loans that have different correlations. Besides this, historical loss data of a credit portfolio, if taken from publicly available information, for example, is often biased due to "window-dressing" efforts of bank managers who want to improve their earnings picture. Therefore, a more reliable approach is to calculate loss correlations between individual borrowers (e.g., based on correlations between their net asset values or equity prices) and to use these correlations to determine the probability that loans granted to these individual companies will default at the same time (joint default probability).

The results of these first two steps allow the credit portfolio's EL and UL to be calculated. In a third step, these results are used to determine the portfolio's EC. This requires the estimation of the probability distribution of the assets included in the portfolio. The covariance model assumes a Beta distribution.[192] Based on this distribution function, the EC required to cover potential portfolio losses is determined.

Finally, in a fourth step, EC is allocated to the individual loans within the credit portfolio. It is assumed that each individual loan contributes to the entire UL of the portfolio in such a way that the UL of each individual loan adds up to the total UL of the portfolio. Following the individual EC allocation, the risk-adjusted profitability for each loan and a price for the loan, serving as a basis for a model-based loan price, can be determined.

The main drawback of the covariance model is that the Beta distribution is not necessarily the best approximation for the probability distribution of credit assets. Other models try to overcome this issue by using alternative approaches to estimate a credit portfolio's probability distribution.

190 See chapter 1.4.2.2 above for a description of how to calculate the portfolio EL and UL from the respective values for individual assets

191 See Marrison (2002), p. 297 et seqq. for the detailed calculation method

192 See chapter 1.4.2.2 above for a description of the Beta distribution

2.2.3.2 The actuarial credit portfolio model

Instead of assuming a Beta distribution as an approximation for credit asset values, the actuarial credit portfolio model determines the probability distribution function using statistics of historical losses. It is also calculated according to a four-step approach:

In a first step, the PD for each asset in the loan portfolio is determined. Then, different and independent groups of loans according to sector and size are generated. It is assumed that, for a given "state of the world", losses within one group of loans are independent of each other – accordingly, the default correlation within all different loan groups is zero for this "state of the world". Based on this assumption, the loss distribution for one particular group of loans (including the mean PD of this group) in that particular "state of the world" is approximated as a Poisson distribution.[193] Afterwards, the "state of the world" is alternated, which changes the average PD of the loan group; e.g., if a recession is simulated, the PD will increase.[194] The goal is to determine a mean PD and a standard deviation for each loan group for all different "states of the world". Finally, in the fourth step, the results from all independent groups of loans at all "stages of the world" are aggregated and a cumulative PD function for the potential losses is calculated. Based on this distribution function, the required EC for the portfolio can be determined.

The actuarial credit portfolio model has been implemented by Credit Suisse Financial Products with their CreditRisk$^{+\text{ TM}}$ software. In early 2002, a follow-on model was introduced (PortfolioRisk$^{+\text{ TM}}$), including enhancements such as a methodology which allows adding up non-normal distributions without the need for a simulation.[195]

2.2.3.3 The Merton model

In contrast to the models described so far, the Merton model does not assume a certain statistical probability distribution function for asset values but rather generates the distribution through simulation. Based on the idea that a company's PD is determined by changes in the value of its assets, the simulation generates random values for the assets of each company included in the loan portfolio. If the value generated by the simulation is below a certain pre-defined threshold, the model simulates a default. In this case, the model registers the LGD. The loss of the entire portfolio is calculated by summing up the losses of all companies in the portfolio. This simulation process is

---

[193] Assuming that borrowers default independently but with an identical PD, the distribution for credit losses can be described by a binominal distribution. For low PDs, the binominal distribution can be approximated by a Poisson distribution, which has the advantage that the assumption of identical PDs can be given up. See Schierenbeck (2003) p. 162 – 167 as well as Bleymüller, Gehlert et al. (2004), p. 52 et seqq. for the binominal and p. 55 et seq. for the Poisson distribution

[194] The PD (mean of the Poisson distribution) can be approximated by a Gamma distribution, see Schierenbeck (2003), p. 170 and Bleymüller, Gehlert et al. (2004), p. 62 for a description of the Gamma distribution

[195] See Credit Suisse (1997), Schierenbeck (2003), pp. 160 – 173 and Banks (2004), p. 377 et seq.

repeated with different sets of random asset values until there are enough results to create the loss distribution.

The Merton model foresees the determination of correlations between asset values of different companies based on the correlations between equity values. However, this approach can be very time-consuming. Especially, if there is a large amount of companies in the portfolio, the respective correlation matrix can become extensive. Therefore, an alternative to calculating correlations between individual equity values is frequently used: the asset value for each individual company is modeled according to its sensitivity towards changes of one or several equity indices. This is based on the assumption that the value of each company is correlated to these indices.

Further to modeling PDs through simulations, the Merton model can be extended and, for example, the LGD or EAD can be modeled as random variables as well. It is also possible to simulate rating changes, assuming that, e.g., a downgrade will reduce the value of a loan, even though there has not been a default yet.

Several software implementations of the Merton model have been developed. For example, Moody's KMV developed their PortfolioManager™ software based on the Merton approach.[196] J.P. Morgan implemented the Merton approach in their CreditMetrics™ software.[197]

2.2.3.4 The macroeconomic default model

The macroeconomic default model is similar to the actuarial model regarding the assumption that for a certain "state of the world" all loan defaults are independent. Only if the "state of the world" changes, does the PD of the borrowers change.

A basic version of the macroeconomic default model can be described as follows: in a first step, a "cycle-neutral" PD for each company within the loan portfolio is calculated.[198] Then, a model is created that links economic conditions (e.g., GDP growth) to the overall PD for all loans – the PD of all loans is determined as a function of macro-variables. Afterwards, different economic scenarios (e.g., different GDP growth scenarios) are simulated.

The results of these three steps are combined in a simulation procedure: macroeconomic scenarios are randomly created and the overall PD is calculated in each scenario. Based on the overall PD, the PD for the individual companies in each scenario is determined.[199]

---

[196] See Kealhoffer (1995)

[197] See Gupton, Finger et al. (1997) and Schierenbeck (2003), pp. 174 – 180

[198] The "cycle-neutral" PD is defined as the average PD for this company across all phases of the business cycle, i.e., from boom to recession

[199] The PD for each company under different scenarios is calculated according to the following formula:

Once the individual PD for each company in a certain macroeconomic scenario has been calculated, it is randomly decided whether this PD means the company is in default or not. In the case of default, the LGD is calculated. This default/non-default decision is made for all companies in each scenario and, based on an aggregation of individual LGDs, the total loss for the loan portfolio is determined under the respective macroeconomic scenario. Repeating this process for thousands of macroeconomic scenarios provides a loss distribution function for the loan portfolio.

Several enhancements can be added to this basic macroeconomic model, e.g., other variables such as inflation can be included. McKinsey & Company developed such a macroeconomic default model and implemented it in their CreditPortfolioView™ software.[200]

2.2.3.5 The macroeconomic cash flow model

The PD of a company can be calculated through developing a cash flow model that is linked to a macroeconomic simulation. Based on a random macroeconomic scenario, the model determines a company's cash flow as well as related profits and losses. Under certain scenarios, the cash flows will not be sufficient to service the company's debt, resulting in a state of default. The simulation of many scenarios provides a loss distribution. The company's PD is calculated by dividing the number of defaults by the total number of scenario runs.

Such a cash flow approach can also be used to calculate the loss distribution for a portfolio of loans or also for individual projects. If applied for loan portfolios, a cash flow model has to be set up for each loan in the portfolio and each model needs to be run through the same macroeconomic scenario. Thus, the distribution for the value of each loan under a given macroeconomic scenario is calculated. Summing up the individual distributions of all loans provides a distribution of the portfolio value in the respective scenario. As in the macroeconomic model described above, the whole process can (and should) be repeated for different macroeconomic scenarios.[201]

$$PD_{Company,k} = \frac{PD_{Overall,k}}{PD_{Overall}} * \overline{PD_{Company,k}}$$

$PD_{Company,k}$ is the PD for the individual company in scenario k, $PD_{Overall,k}$ is the overall PD in scenario k, and $\overline{PD}_{Company,k}$ is the cycle-neutral PD for the individual company; see Marrison (2002), p. 326

200 See McKinsey & Company (2000a) and McKinsey & Company (2000b); see also Schierenbeck (2003), pp. 180 – 191 and Wilson (1997)

201 See Marrison (2002), pp. 279 – 281 as well as Marrison (2001b) describing the application of this approach in project finance

2.2.3.6 Second-generation credit portfolio models[202]

Towards the end of the 1990s, the development of more sophisticated second-generation credit portfolio models was initiated. The motivation was to overcome limitations of the first-generation models, which derive from their often simplified assumptions or as a consequence of technical restrictions.

For example, first-generation models merely focused on a fixed (deterministic) computation of credit exposures. Second-generation models address this issue. They are based on simulation techniques, which consider market and credit exposures as random variables, focusing in a first step on the output of market-driven stochastic credit portfolio exposures and, in a second step, including credit losses and capital by applying default and transition probabilities, correlations, etc.

Iscoe, Kreinin et al. (1999) developed one of the early second-generation models. Their approach was later adopted by Algorithmics Inc. in their "Mark-to-Future" model. The model uses a multi-step simulation process, which jointly considers market and credit risks across time as well as over different scenarios. The model output allows the appropriate capital to be provided for the credit portfolio to be determined.

The model developed by Jobst and Zenios (2000) integrates different sources of risks. Key features are the calculation of correlations among different credit and market risk factors and the application of a simulation to take into consideration the probability of extreme events as well as portfolio values at the end of a specific time frame. An important feature of this model is its ability to price credit derivatives.

Driven by advancements in computing power, improved analytics techniques, better data access and more transparent credit markets, even more sophisticated and accurate credit portfolio models are expected to be developed in the next few years.

2.2.3.7 Credit portfolio models used in practice

As shown in Figure 11, most banks currently use internally developed credit portfolio models and software implementations of the Merton model, mostly Moody's KMV PortfolioManager™ software, to measure their credit portfolio risks and to compute the required EC. Only few banks use CreditRisk^{+} as an implementation of the actuarial model. Macroeconomic credit portfolio models seem to play an insignificant role in practice.

---

[202] See Banks (2004), p. 318 et seqq.

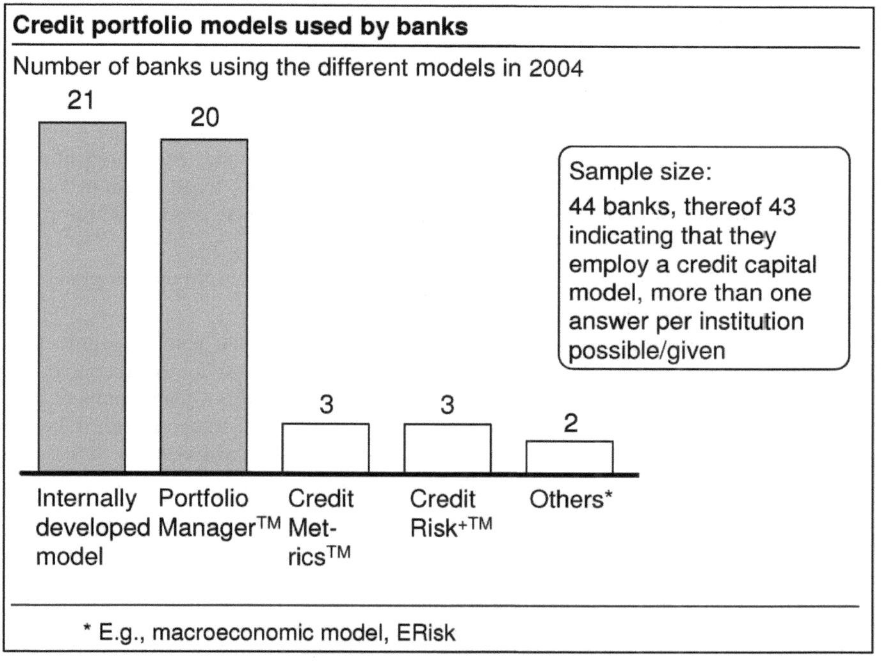

Figure 11: Credit portfolio models used by banks[203]

* * * * *

Through applying the credit portfolio models described above, banks have the possibility to measure credit risks on a portfolio level and to determine the probability of changes in the value of a credit portfolio. The models help to compute the amount of EC required to cover credit portfolio risks. They also allow banks to determine the marginal risk contribution of a newly acquired credit asset to the entire portfolio, thus facilitating the decision whether to accept the asset or not. Thus, the emergence and growing sophistication of credit portfolio models has had a considerable impact on banks' ability to manage their credit portfolios.

[203] Source: Own illustration based on Rutter Associates LLC (2004), p. 5

2.2.4 Declining profitability of banking business

2.2.4.1 Falling new lending margins

An important catalyst for structural changes in wholesale lending has been the significant squeeze of lending margins in recent years. For example, average margins earned by banks on new lending business to corporations in the Euro area almost halved from ~220 BP[204] in 1997 to ~115 BP in 2000.[205] This trend continued until 2004.[206] A similar development can be observed in the US since 1998.[207] Three main reasons for this margin squeeze can be identified:

Firstly, the significant decline in market interest rates in recent years has generally lowered bank lending margins.[208]

Secondly, there has been mounting competition in the corporate lending segment.[209] This competitive pressure has mostly been caused by a growing overcapacity of lenders. In particular, wholesale banks have had to face the entry of new players into their markets. Eager to take on risks, they have been fierce competitors for credit assets. For example, there has been a growing demand for credit risks by non-bank financial institutions such as pension and hedge funds, insurance/reinsurance companies as well as by corporate treasury departments.[210]

Thirdly, banking institutions are confronted with growing disintermediation because large corporate borrowers increasingly replace bank loans with tradable debt instruments such as bonds to finance their investments.[211] This decreasing demand for "traditional" credit assets issued by banks has not only contributed to the squeeze of lending margins but has also been a major driver for declining RWAs at many institutions and subsequently growing Tier-1 ratios in recent years, putting pressure on the institutions to profitably redeploy the excess regulatory capital. Figure 12

[204] A BP is a hundredth of one per cent. See Rhoades (2000), p. 471

[205] Comparison of third quarter data in 1997 and 2000, see ECB (2000), p. 11 chart 3. The margin calculation is based on a separate investigation of lending and deposit margins following the Monti-Klein model of banking competition, which assumes monopolistic banks with some pricing power in the deposit and loan market. See Freixas and Rochet (1997) chapter 3.2 – 3.10 for a description of the model applied

[206] See ECB (2004), p. 12 et seq., in particular p. 12 Table 5. It needs to be noted, however, that there are significant differences in the economic conditions of European credit markets, see Figure 64 behind

[207] See Hayt and Smithson (2001b), p. 45 Figure 1

[208] See again ECB (2004), p. 12

[209] See ECB (2000), p. 14 et seqq. While there are other factors than increased competition that have an impact on bank lending and deposit taking activities, it is shown that increased competition is the major influencing factor for declining new business lending margins

[210] See Hammes and Shapiro (2001), p. 98 et seq.

[211] See again Figure 1 showing the declining share of bank deposits, regarded as a complement to outstanding loans, in the global financial stock for the benefit of tradable debt instruments

illustrates the changes in RWAs and Tier-1 capital ratios of a range of major European institutions in past years.

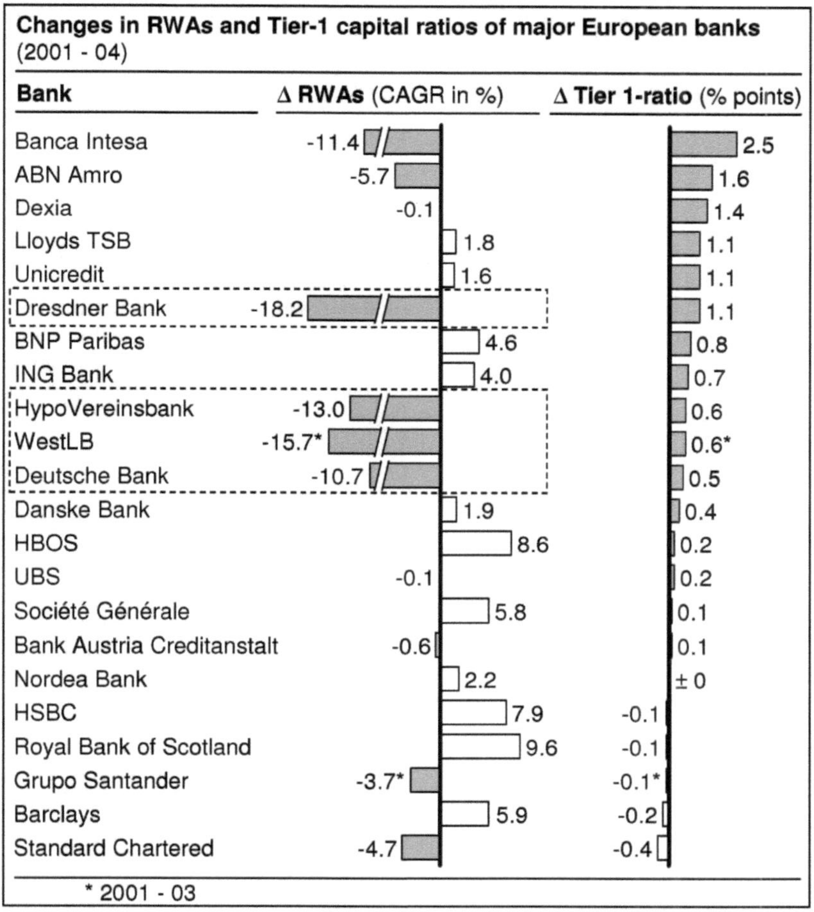

Figure 12: Changes in RWAs and Tier-1 capital ratios of major European banks[212]

212 Source: Own illustration based on Bankscope database. The analysis reveals that it is in particular German institutions, which have faced the strongest RWA decline

As a consequence of the lending margin squeeze faced, wholesale banks can often only generate returns on their corporate loan exposures that are below certain profitability hurdles, forcing them to cross-subsidize their lending business and to perform cross-selling of other products to a credit customer in order to ensure the overall profitability of the customer relationship. In particular, the institutions need to rethink their approach towards lending business in order to tackle these profitability issues.[213]

2.2.4.2 Growing loan losses

Besides facing declining new business margins, a lot of wholesale banks – in particular many German institutions – have had to deal with strongly growing loan losses in recent years. These loan losses caused a sharp upsurge in risk provisions (see Figure 13 showing operating profit and loan loss provisions of German "Landesbanken"[214]). A key reason for these losses has been the fact that the institutions carried large single-name concentration risks on their books. In the course of the economic downturn after 2000, many of these debtors defaulted, causing major losses for the lending institutions.[215] The hitherto predominant "originate and hold" lending approach supported the generation of concentration risks because its characteristic one-way asset flow provides significantly limits the possibilities to diversify a credit portfolio.

[213] See again Flämig (2005)

[214] As mentioned in chapter 1.3.2, Landesbanken focus on business with medium-sized and large corporations and can, therefore, regarded as typical wholesale banks

[215] The existence of high single-name concentration risks is typical for wholesale banks due to their strong lending relationships with only few large corporations; see Hammes and Shapiro (2001), p. 100. Examples of failing single-name debtors of German wholesale banks are the Kirch Group whose bankruptcy resulted in enormous losses for Bayerische Landesbank (the bank had lent around EUR 2 billion to the Kirch group) or the insolvency of Boxclever to which WestLB had a large loan exposure requiring a risk provision of almost EUR 700 million; see N.N (2003a) and N.N (2003b)

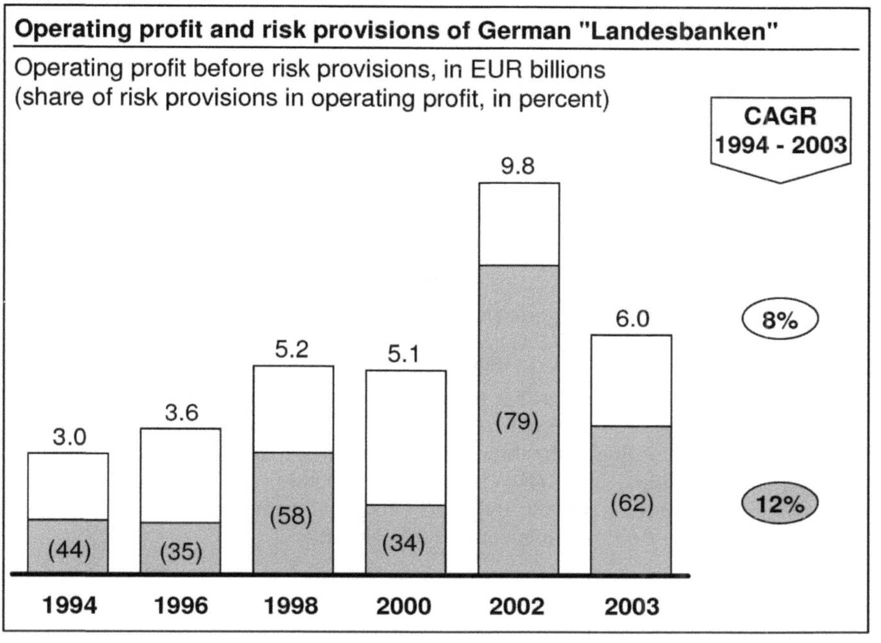

Figure 13: Operating profit and risk provisions of German "Landesbanken"[216]

2.3 The ACPM approach – "originate and trade"

In order to benefit from the opportunities and to master the challenges that have accompanied the changes in credit markets described above, banks need to overcome the deficiencies of the conventional lending business model. A more flexible approach towards lending and managing of credit assets, capitalizing on the benefits which come along with financial innovations, is required. In this context, the ACPM approach has emerged.[217]

[216] Source: Own illustration based on banking statistics in Bundesbank (1994), Bundesbank (1996), Bundesbank (1998), Bundesbank (2000), Bundesbank (2002b), Bundesbank (2003a)

[217] See Kuritzkes (1998)

2.3.1 Central idea

The ACPM approach applies the principles of classical portfolio theory to the management of credit assets: Central idea is to create a credit portfolio, which is efficient from a risk-return point of view.[218]

The optimal portfolio composition can be achieved and kept throughout different economic conditions and stages of the credit cycle by influencing the acquisition of new credit assets on the primary credit market as well as by performing secondary market transactions to acquire or dispose of credit risks through secondary credit market instruments.[219]

2.3.2 Implementation of approach through ACPM business models

2.3.2.1 Generic ACPM business models

There are different options regarding the implementation of the ACPM approach and organizational design of ACPM units. In existing literature on this topic, ACPM units are characterized according to the three design criteria (I) mandate for credit functions, (II) asset ownership, and (III) reporting structure within the institution. Correspondingly, three generic business models with different degrees of responsibility for the ACPM unit have been developed:[220]

One of these business models is referred to as "advisor". Advisor ACPM units have the mandate to perform credit risk measurement functions as well as to give recommendations to customer BUs (i.e., to loan origination/relationship managers) on how to possibly rebalance the credit portfolio composition. The final decision for such activities, however, remains with the asset-owning BUs or senior management. Advisors are seen to be located within the risk unit or customer BU of their institution.

"Active portfolio managers" have the mandate to take over ownership for credit risks from origination. Accordingly, they dispose of the functional authority to sell off these risks on secondary markets in case the risk-return relationship of the portfolio is not within a pre-defined range any longer. These units operate as cost centers and are situated in a central location within the banking organization, effectively between risk unit and customer BUs.

The third generic type of ACPM business models is defined as "proprietary investors". Also taking over credit assets from customer BUs and centrally located within the banking organization, they have P&L responsibility for the credit portfolio owned. Proprietary investors are entitled to independently take positions based on their views

---

218 See Hayt and Smithson (2001), p. 34 et seq. The principles of classical portfolio theory will be described in detail in Chapter **Error! Reference source not found.**

219 Secondary credit market instruments will be introduced in depth in chapter 3

220 See Hammes and Shapiro (2001), p. 107 and in particular p. 108 Figure 8

regarding the future development of credit markets. Based on Kuritzkes (1998), the principles of this ACPM business model will be described in greater detail in the following section.[221]

2.3.2.2 Proprietary investor business model

The proprietary investor ACPM business model foresees the establishment of an empowered ACPM unit taking over the credit assets from loan originating customer BUs and owning the entire credit portfolio of the bank. It acts like an independent manager of the bank's credit assets on the financial markets, having the objective to optimally structure the portfolio from a risk-return point of view. In doing so, the ACPM unit requires the loan portfolio to earn a risk-adjusted return on the underlying EC above a predefined hurdle rate – otherwise the bound-up capital should be released and reinvested into more profitable assets.

The loan origination/relationship management function within the customer BU focuses on granting loans to primary market customers. A separate credit rating/valuation unit has the task of rating and valuing assets independently of opinions from origination or ACPM.[222] An independent risk management unit formally reviews the riskiness of positions and the credit portfolio.[223]

Yet, the ACPM unit only "buys" those credit assets from origination – at a settlement price determined by ACPM[224] – which add value to the existing portfolio, i.e. it only acquires the assets that contribute to achieving the risk-return optimal portfolio composition.[225] The loans that ACPM does not take over must be distributed outside the organization, of course under the precondition that they earn a competitive yield. The close interaction between ACPM and the origination/relationship management function also has the goal of increasing the relationship managers' underwriting discipline as to loan acceptance or rejection decisions as well as regarding pricing and structuring of loans, aiming at increasing profitability from primary market credit business, particularly in highly competitive lending environments.

221 This fully empowered ACPM unit is also described as the "purest form" of ACPM, see Asarnov (1996), p. 19. Asarnov (1996), p. 21 also describes an alternative business model to the proprietary investor in case implementing this model raises too many internal difficulties. This alternative business model is essentially an active portfolio manager described above

222 This organizational split is in line with MaK guidelines, see Footnote 78

223 See Hammes and Shapiro (2001), p. 108 Figure 8

224 See Asarnov (1996), p. 20 briefly outlining the settlement pricing procedure

225 See Hayt and Smithson (2001a), p. 68. The evaluation whether to acquire an asset or not is typically performed with help of the credit portfolio models described in chapter 2.2.3. For example, these models enable the determination of the appropriate amount of EC to be held for a newly acquired asset; see Hayt and Smithson (2001), p. 36

The ACPM unit is seen to be located at a central, independent place within the organization between loan origination, secondary market and risk units. As opposed to the "originate and hold" lending approach, there is an exchange of credit assets between ACPM, origination and the secondary market units. Insofar, the gap that existed between the origination and secondary market side of a banking institution under the conventional lending approach is filled.

In order to execute secondary market transactions, ACPM closely interacts with loan sales, loan syndication, credit derivatives, and securitization desks.

The ACPM approach also foresees the creation of a separate unit responsible for problem loan management and workout of ailing credit assets. This service function can potentially be outsourced to third-party providers.

The proprietary investor is not in direct contact with the bank's primary market credit customers. This follows the idea that its decisions to reshuffle and optimize the credit portfolio composition are not to be influenced by subjective judgments, e.g., due to long-standing customer relationships.[226]

Figure 14 illustrates the suggested schematic set-up of the proprietary investor ACPM business model within a banking organization.

Flesch and Gerdsmeier (1998) see three different sub-banks arising that are completely independent of each other. One of them is a specialized portfolio bank, taking over market and default risks from the production and distribution units and subsequently managing them in its portfolio. Such a portfolio bank can be regarded as a legally independent proprietary investor ACPM unit.[227]

---

[226] See Asarnov (1996), p. 19 et seq.

[227] Flesch and Gerdsmeier (1998) see this development as a continuation of similar development processes taking place in other sectors such as the airline and communication industry

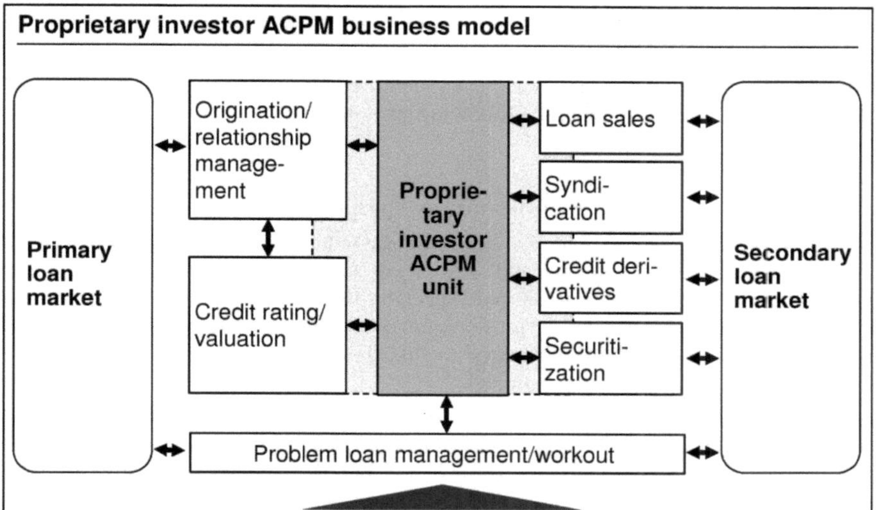

- Centrally located ACPM unit
- Ownership of credit assets, responsibility for profitability of credit portfolio, empowerment to set price hurdles for newly originated assets and to structure and execute secondary market credit transactions
- Close interaction with origination and secondary market trading units
- Objective credit risk rating/asset valuation independently performed in credit rating/valuation unit
- Separate problem loan management/workout unit

Figure 14: Proprietary investor ACPM business model[228]

2.3.3 Determinants for design of ACPM units

Chapter 2.2 has described that the emergence of the ACPM approach has been triggered by a range of profound changes in credit markets. Obviously, while these developments have been a crucial catalyst for the revised approach towards lending business, the extent to which they have been established in the surroundings of a financial institution determines the design of its newly set-up ACPM unit. Further to

[228] Source: Own illustration based on Kuritzkes (1998), p. 2

these external parameters, there are several internal determinants influencing the design of these units.[229]

Internal and external factors that have been identified as determinants for the design of ACPM units will be outlined in the following section.

2.3.3.1 Internal determinants

2.3.3.1.1 Economic performance of institution

It has been shown before that the extent of secondary credit market liquidity is a critical enabler for the set-up and design of an ACPM unit. As a result, the composition of a bank's loan book and especially the decision on which asset classes are to be covered by an ACPM unit determines to which extent ACPM can actually reap the benefits of liquid secondary credit markets and especially which is its correspondingly optimal business model.[230]

Shrinking profitability of credit activities and the subsequent pressure to restructure an institution's lending business model has not only been driven by external conditions like increased competitive pressure, for instance, but also by bank-internal issues such as growing loan losses of institutions. The losses were often induced by a lending policy focusing on few large single name customers whose defaults have been particularly grave.[231] As a consequence of these issues, the institutions have not only been forced to adapt their overall business strategy but especially to alter the objectives of their lending business model.[232] Consequently, the individual economic performance of an institution, mostly driven by the creditworthiness of the credit assets in its loan book, can be regarded a determinant for the objectives and, hence, for the design of its ACPM unit.[233]

---

229 See, for example, Kuritzkes (1998), p. 3 stating that there is no single right answer for the optimal design of an ACPM business model. Rather, each institution needs to determine its optimal approach based on a set of given parameters

230 This finding will be confirmed in chapter 4.3.2 of part III showing that the secondary credit market conditions crucially determine to which extent the objectives of a particular CPM unit can be realized

231 See again chapter 2.2.4.2 and especially Footnote 215

232 See, for example, Busse (2003) on the reorganization of Bayerische Landesbank from an internationally represented institution towards a regional player. Among others, exploding risk provisions in consequence of the default of Kirch group as a major borrower have driven the refocusing of this institution. The reorganization has particularly impacted the bank's approach towards lending business: it has been envisaged to reduce the high dependence on pure lending business by increasingly focusing on selling non-credit products to the largest borrowers. From this, a significant increase of customer profitability has been aspired to

233 See also Hayt and Smithson (2001a), p. 69 on goals and organizational structures of banks' credit portfolio activities

2.3.3.1.2 Initiator for setting up ACPM unit

It has been shown in chapter 2.3.2 that a key question to be answered when setting up an ACPM unit is its optimal location within the banking organization to ensure successful performance of its activities. For example, literature on ACPM sees the proprietary investor ACPM business model to be ideally located at an independent central location within the institution between origination, credit rating/valuation, and secondary market units.[234] The open questions on the reporting structure of an ACPM unit reveal that there has not been a unique and ideal way defined as to how to position such a unit within a financial institution's organizational structure. Therefore, the initiator for setting up such a unit has a crucial influence on its eventual location within the organization. The unit's organizational location, in turn, determines the possible ACPM business model that can be pursued.[235]

2.3.3.1.3 Governance principles of institution

The governance principles of an institution critically determine the design of its ACPM unit.

It is argued that setting up a proprietary investor ACPM unit not only implies a shift of power from originators to portfolio managers. A key requirement seen for successfully setting up such a unit is the redefinition of a bank's lending business strategy from a typical commercial banking-type customer relationship focus towards a more product-/capital market orientation.[236] Consequently, the institution's business strategy can be regarded an essential determinant for setting up an ACPM business model. Furthermore, the institution's governance principles determine if, to which extent and in which time frame such a possibly necessary redefinition can be undertaken and to which extent a targeted ACPM business model that requires a different business strategy can be implemented.[237]

---

234 See again Figure 14

235 See also again Kuritzkes (1998), p. 3 on questions regarding organizational design of an ACPM unit.

Another factor determining the specifications of an ACPM business model with regard to its organizational location is regulatory requirements, e.g., the MaK guidelines, see again Footnotes 78 and 222. According to these guidelines, for example, an asset-owning proprietary investor would not be entitled to be located in an institution's risk unit

236 See Asarnov (1996), p. 19 et seq.

237 This can also be concluded, for example, from the fact that restructuring an organization implies an "inevitable resistance to change", see Asarnov (1996), p. 16. Such a resistance to organizational changes may also be induced by movements of power and responsibility for credit business from origination to ACPM, see Asarnov (1996), p. 18. Therefore, the flexibility and willingness of an organization to adapt to required changes following the establishment of an ACPM business model determines to which extent a different approach towards lending business can be established in an institution. As implementing an asset-transferring proprietary investor business model implies most organizational changes for an institution, see

A major challenge seen in the transition towards an ACPM approach is the issue how to achieve the changes in responsibilities implied by this new business model without demotivating existing staff, in particular the employees located in origination and credit risk units. The issue becomes particularly relevant if a proprietary investor business model is to be implemented.[238] Hence, a profound change in an institution's lending approach, such as the move from the conventional lending business model towards an asset-transferring ACPM model, can only be successfully implemented if there are clearly defined incentives for the different units involved that provide a motivation for employees to act in accordance with the objectives of the newly set up ACPM unit. This makes the existence of such an incentive structure a key determinant for implementing an ACPM unit.

2.3.3.2 External determinants

Increasing liquidity of secondary credit markets has been identified as a major driver and enabler for the development from the conventional bank lending to the ACPM approach. This is due to the fact that the thereby induced tradability of credit assets allows banks to reshuffle their loan portfolios by transferring related risks.

Consequently, successfully setting up an ACPM unit requires both the existence and sufficient liquidity of such a secondary credit market. The fact that especially liquid secondary credit markets are a crucial precondition for establishing an ACPM approach that particularly emphasizes on reshuffling credit risks on these markets also implies that the extent of secondary market liquidity is a central determinant for how an ACPM unit can be set up. Therefore, when thinking about not only whether but especially how to design an ACPM unit, an institution needs to take into consideration the given conditions of the secondary credit market its ACPM unit is supposed to operate in.[239]

While evolving secondary credit market liquidity is seen as an essential enabler for developing the ACPM approach, it has been shown before that a major pressure on banks to restructure their lending business model stems from dwindling profit margins in their primary credit markets. Among others, this is triggered by increasing competition in the corporate lending segment, growing disintermediation of banks and sluggish demand for credit assets. Further more, growing loan losses have put a strong pressure on the profitability of lending business. On the one hand, these market

again Asarnov (1996), p. 21. A precondition for successfully setting up such a model is a sufficiently flexible organization supportive of such transformations

238 See Kuritzkes (1998) p. 3

239 This can, for example, be concluded from Kuritzkes (1998), p. 3 who shows that the initial steps for ACPM are mostly taken in the most liquid large corporate credit market. Furthermore, Asarnov (1996), p. 20 states that limited loan market liquidity is a central external constraint to overcome in the goal of developing an ACPM unit that aims at performing secondary market transactions

developments require the institutions to change their approach towards lending business. On the other hand, they provide the opportunity for the banks to secure a "first-mover advantage" over competitors if they are among the first ones to establish a new lending business model.[240]

The fact that banks adjust their lending approach following changing market conditions implies that the credit market environment they operate in is a determinant for the objectives pursued with their lending activities and hence the set-up of their lending business model and corresponding units responsible to manage loan portfolios. It is especially in highly competitive market environments which are coined by low profitability that the institutions face the pressure to not only change their lending business model but are also strongly incentivized to rapidly implement this new approach if they want to benefit from a competitive advantage over rivals.[241]

The determinants for design criteria of ACPM units are listed on the left-hand side of Figure 36 in part III of this dissertation.

* * * * *

The generic ACPM business models introduced above will be empirically tested through a study that has been held among 22 leading European banks. Subsequently, the ACPM business models found in the empirical sample will be described in greater detail. This enables seeing where banks currently stand in terms of ACPM as well as updating and refining the design criteria described in literature.

Founded on the existing literature on ACPM, a set of factors determining the design of ACPM units has been identified above. With the help of the empirical study, it will be examined which of these determining factors has led participants to the choice for a particular ACPM business model and for certain design criteria of their ACPM unit. The goal of this analysis is to illustrate the relationship between determining factors and design criteria for ACPM units. This aims at supporting the decision-making process regarding which ACPM business model an institution should ideally introduce when facing a set of given internal and external determinants.

* * * * *

The close interaction between ACPM units and loan origination BU is essential with regard to ACPM exerting influence on the acquisition and pricing of new as well as regarding renewals of existing business.[242] However, merely exerting influence on

---

240 See, e.g., Hammes and Shapiro (2001), p. 98

241 See also again Flämig (2005) stating that through implementing an asset-transferring ACPM unit for its largest 400 corporate customers, HypoVereinsbank managed to assume a leading position in the German banking market, with only Deutsche Bank being similarly innovative. The major driver for the establishment of this unit was the bank's intention to enhance its cross-selling activities in order to increase income from its corporate lending business which is currently not sufficiently profitable in the German banking market

242 The establishment of effective feedback loops between ACPM and origination is seen as a major enabler to

primary market transactions is not regarded as sufficient to achieve an optimal portfolio composition. This is mainly because the final decision for primary market transactions and the timing of such activities is not within the influence of ACPM but remains under the control of loan origination. Besides this, there are other reasons why the active management of a credit portfolio by means of primary market transactions is typically perceived as being limited.[243] Therefore, it is of vital importance that ACPM units are able to perform transactions on secondary loan markets, having the goal of diversifying and transferring credit risks to other parties as well as reinvesting freed-up capital into more profitable credit assets.

In recent years, a variety of instruments has been developed that can be used by an ACPM unit to acquire and distribute credit risks on secondary loan markets. In view of the high rate of product innovation as well as the rapid development and growth of markets for secondary credit instruments, it seems necessary to give a detailed overview of the latest developments by comprehensively describing these instruments as well as by outlining the past and, where available, expected growth of their respective markets. Furthermore, an evaluation and comparison of the instruments will be provided with the objective of giving an orientation for credit portfolio managers which of the instruments should best be applied to reshuffle their portfolio composition. The profound illustration of the secondary market instruments will also serve as a basis for part III of this dissertation in which the instruments applied by the CPM units included in the empirical study will be described.

2.4 Summary

This chapter has outlined the key changes in credit markets during past years that have propelled the development of the ACPM approach among wholesale banks. A description of this newly developed approach and the generic business models found in literature on this topic has been provided.

---

achieve an optimal risk-return profile of the credit portfolio. This is mainly for three reasons: firstly, ACPM has deep insights into trends for credit markets and is, thus, able to early detect early on tendencies of worsening credit quality in certain segments. Secondly, through its proximity to and knowledge of secondary credit markets, allowing a judgement which credit risks can be placed on these markets, ACPM is in the position to enable origination BUs to underwrite transactions even if they do not fit to the risk-return structure of the portfolio or exceed certain pre-defined counterparty limits. Thirdly, having knowledge about defaults across industries, ACPM can help to minimize credit losses by supporting origination to select the right criteria and analyses when underwriting loan transactions; see Hammes and Shapiro (2001), p. 107

243 There are three more reasons for the potentially limited ability to use primary market transactions with the goal of actively managing credit portfolios: (I) A specific distribution strategy or specific market conditions typically limit the primary market business of banks to certain market segments, resulting in concentration of credit exposures to certain regions or industries, (II) Customers' demand for high-volume loans often results in single name concentration risk and (III) Banks very often face problems when trying to implement their overall credit policy because loan sales units are typically decentralized within banking organizations; see Poppensieker (2002), p. 93 et seq.

First of all, the conventional wholesale lending approach has been introduced. Under this approach, the management style for credit assets can best be described as "originate and hold": the assets are typically originated, monitored, managed and serviced by a customer BU holding them until maturity or default. The customer BU is supported by a credit approval unit which typically provides a second vote on lending decisions.

Profound changes and developments in credit markets have challenged this "originate and hold" approach:

The fact that banks have increasingly been able to operate in growingly liquid secondary loan markets has provided them with the prerequisite to diversify their credit risks through trading them on these markets.

One motivation to perform such secondary credit market transactions is regulatory capital arbitrage. It is triggered by the fact that the currently valid regulatory capital requirements (Basle I) do not adequately reflect the "true" economic risks of credit assets held. While the "Basle II" requirements will better align the economic risks embedded in credit assets with the regulatory capital to be provided for these loans, there will still be an opportunity to optimize regulatory capital consumption of an institution. However, banks can only exploit this opportunity provided they have a flexible enough approach towards the management of credit risks.

Significant advances in credit risk analytics – particularly the development of sophisticated credit portfolio management models – have equipped banks with the necessary tools to measure and quantify the risks inherent in their credit portfolios and the EC required. Hence, the institutions meanwhile dispose of the necessary prerequisites to accurately evaluate the credit assets they intend to acquire or sell on the loan markets. The basic ideas and theoretical concepts underlying the different first- and second-generation credit portfolio models have been outlined in section 2.2.3 of this chapter, and an illustration of their usage in practice has been given.

Wholesale lending business has become increasingly competitive in past years, and conventional bank loans have increasingly been disintermediated by tradable debt instruments. Consequently, banks have faced strongly falling profitability margins in their new lending business. Furthermore, many banks – especially German ones – have had to digest significantly rising loan defaults. The losses were, among other things, triggered by large single-name concentration risks that the institutions carried on their books, mainly as a consequence of the static approach towards managing their credit assets.

These changes and developments in credit markets bring along opportunities but also pose challenges for wholesale banks. Clearly, they require a more flexible approach towards lending and managing of credit assets. In this context, the ACPM approach has been developed.

The central idea of this approach is the creation of a risk-return efficient credit portfolio. The optimal portfolio composition can be achieved and kept throughout different economic conditions and stages of the credit cycle. Based on the design choices mandate for credit functions, asset ownership and reporting structure, three generic ACPM business models (advisor, active portfolio manager and proprietary investor) have been developed by literature on ACPM.

Core to the proprietary investor business model is the establishment of a central ACPM unit owning the bank's credit assets and having the power to act as an independent proprietary investor on the financial markets with the goal of optimizing the risk-return structure of its credit portfolio. The unit closely co-operates both with primary and secondary market units, regarding acquisition and sale of credit assets. It determines the settlement price for which it is willing to take over the assets from origination that fit into its portfolio structure and business strategy.

Based on existing literature on ACPM, several factors determining the design of ACPM units could be identified. They have been distinguished in external and internal determinants.

External determinants for the design of ACPM units are the existence and liquidity of secondary credit markets as well as the competitive situation and profitability of the market in which the institutions operate. A bank-internal factor impacting the set-up of an ACPM unit is the institution's economic performance, influencing the objectives to be pursued with an ACPM unit and hence the chosen ACPM business model chosen. Furthermore, the organizational location of the ACPM unit, crucially driven by its initiating executive, is an internal determinant for the envisaged business model. Besides this, the governance principles of an institution, in particular its business strategy and the structure of its incentive systems, determine to which extent a certain ACPM business model can be successfully set up.

While a close cooperation between ACPM and origination BUs is essential concerning acceptance and renewal of loan contracts, limitations related to the management of credit portfolios through the primary market side make it essential that an ACPM unit is able to buy and sell credit risks on secondary loan markets. In order to do so, a variety of secondary credit market instruments can be used. It will be the goal of the next chapter to give a comprehensive overview of these instruments and their underlying markets. Chapter 3.1 will focus on loan sales and loan syndication, chapter 3.2 will introduce credit derivatives, and chapter 3.3 will describe asset securitization. Chapter 3.4 will then summarize the findings by providing an evaluation and comparison of the different instruments introduced before, aiming at facilitating a decision-making process regarding which instruments to best use under which conditions.

3 Secondary credit market instruments to actively manage loan portfolios

3.1 Loan sales and loan syndication

3.1.1 Definition and motivation for loan sales and loan syndication

3.1.1.1 Loan sales

While conventional bank lending usually implies that the originating institution holds loans until maturity or default, it is through loan sales that a bank can diverge from this procedure by transferring loans partly or entirely from its own portfolio to that of another institution. Hence, all credit risks related to this asset are transferred to the acquiring institution.[244] Insofar, the loan sales market represents a secondary loan market according to the definition of banking theory.[245]

An increasing amount of literature and empirical studies have tried to investigate banks' motivations for loan sales activities.[246] Three hypotheses have been developed to try to test and demonstrate their motivations for selling and buying loans:

The comparative advantage hypothesis, going back to Pennacchi (1988), states that banks engage in loan sales activities because they have a comparative advantage over competitors in either originating or refinancing loans: banks with a comparative advantage in originating and with a comparative disadvantage in refinancing loans engage in selling of loans. Banks purchasing loans typically have opposite characteristics. Gorton and Pennacchi (1995) developed their work on this hypothesis assuming that banks engage in loan sales because loan sales is a cheaper form of refinancing than deposit taking.

According to the diversification hypothesis, banks use loan sales to diversify their credit portfolios. The hypothesis states that it is limited opportunities to diversify their origination business (e.g., due to limitations in their geographical scope) which trigger loan sales activities of banks. Consequently, the institutions act as purchasers and vendors on the secondary loan market to diversify a loan portfolio of a given size.[247]

A third hypothesis asserts that there are reputation barriers limiting the access to secondary banking markets. Institutions with a reputation for strong credit quality are more prone to act as buyers or sellers on secondary loan markets.

---

244 See Gorton and Haubrich (1990), p. 85

245 See again chapter 1.1 for definitions

246 See, for example, Demsetz (2000), pp. 200 – 203 for a detailed overview of literature regarding loan sales

247 The diversification hypothesis can be regarded as a special version of the comparative advantage hypothesis as a bank can use its proximity to local lending markets to have a comparative advantage over its competitors; see Carlstrom and Samolyk (1995)

There has been a set of empirical studies confirming evidence for the above-mentioned hypotheses.[248]

Before engaging in a loan sales transaction, it may be necessary for the selling institution to get the consent of the respective borrower. This might endanger a long-standing client relationship. In order to circumvent this issue, a loan sale is typically arranged through a participation contract between the original lender and a participation buyer, giving the participation buyer a claim on the loan's cash flows without making him owner of the loan contract.[249] There is usually no relationship between the buyer of the participation and the borrower. The original lender remains the only direct lender to the borrower.[250]

3.1.1.2 Loan syndication

A syndicated loan is originated by one or more banks, afterwards split into several tranches, and finally distributed among member banks belonging to a syndicate of lenders.[251] Each member bank of such a syndicate acts as a direct lender to the borrower, hence having a direct relationship with the borrower and acquiring credit risks according to its share in the total arrangement.

Banks can have several motives for taking part in a syndicate of lenders: an individual lender might want to shed a credit risk exposure, which would be too large for its book. The goal of performing a syndication transaction might also be initiated because the institution wants to avoid that a single loan exposure, which it would like to grant to an individual borrower, exceeding mandatory regulatory requirements.[252] A loan syndication can also be driven by a bank's motivation to diversify its loan portfolio, e.g., in the context of an adjusted portfolio management strategy requiring the reduction of a certain credit exposure.[253] Finally, a reason might be the attempt to seek

---

248 For example, Berger and Udell (1993), Demsetz (1994) and Haubrich and Thomson (1996) find evidence for the comparable advantage hypothesis. Pavel and Phillis (1987) find a positive relationship between loan sales activity and concentration of a credit portfolio, giving an indication for the diversification hypothesis. Demsetz (2000) finds confirmation for both the comparative advantage and the diversification hypothesis and sees evidence for reputational barriers to participation in secondary market transactions

249 For an overview on legal constructions to transfer a loan to a third party under UK, German, French, and US law see, e.g., Rhoades (2000), pp. 409 – 427

250 See Dennis and Mullineaux (2000), p. 6 and BIS (2003b), p. 32

251 In a legal sense, the syndicate of lenders is an association of banks for the purpose of granting a loan together. See Büschgen (1998), p. 338

252 For example, according to § 13 Abs. 1 KWG a loan is classified as large single loan (Grosskredit) if the entire loan volume to a single borrower exceeds 10% of the liable equity of a bank. Granting of large single loans is restricted; e.g., the sum of all loans to one borrower cannot exceed 25% of the bank's liable equity (see § 13a KWG). In this context, syndication can help to avoid large single exposures to one borrower

253 See Dennis and Mullineaux (2000), p. 6 et seq.

access to certain geographic regions or certain types of transactions a lender does not have the necessary origination capabilities for.[254]

Institutions participating in a syndicated transaction commit themselves to common terms and conditions of the credit facility but do mostly not contribute to the loan exposure with equal amounts. Each member bank of the syndicate has the obligation to evaluate and monitor the borrower as though it was lending the committed loan amount on a bilateral basis.[255]

3.1.2 Types of syndicated loans and structure of typical transactions

A syndicated loan usually has a medium-term maturity between three and ten years. Among the variety of syndicated loan types developed in recent years, it is the term loan and the revolving credit facility, which are by far the most frequently used, contracts (see Figure 17 and Figure 18).

A term loan entitles the borrower to draw down an agreed-upon loan amount either in one single amount or in tranches during a defined period. The loan can be repaid either in a single amount at maturity of the contract (bullet loan) or based upon a defined repayment schedule (amortizing term loan). Characteristics of a term loan are that the borrower may not redraw the repaid amounts again, even if they are paid back earlier than agreed in the loan contract. This restriction is the key difference between the term loan and the revolving credit facility.

In contrast to a term loan, a revolving credit facility offers the borrower the right to drawdown, repay and redraw the entire agreed-upon loan amount or part of it at his discretion during the entire maturity of the facility. Variations of the revolving credit facility are the standby facility (here, it is agreed that the borrower will keep the facility only as a standby, i.e. as an undrawn reserve) and the standby letter of credit (under this construction banks augment the existing credit of a borrower, thus granting the borrower access to additional sources of funds).[256]

A typical loan syndication transaction is structured in three phases (see Figure 15): the pre-mandate phase, the post-mandate phase and the post-signing phase. In each of these phases there are typical tasks and milestones for the parties involved which will be briefly touched on in the following section.[257]

---

[254] See Rhoades (2000), p. 15

[255] See Rhoades (2000), p. 14

[256] An overview of the syndicated loan types mentioned above and other instruments which often include derivative instruments can be found in Rhoades (2000), p. 16 et seqq.

[257] See Rhoades (2000), chapter 3 for a detailed description of these phases

Key tasks and milestones during a loan syndication transaction

	Pre-mandate	Post-mandate	Post-signing
Borrower	• Contact bank(s) regarding financing need • Initiate bidding process	• Sell transaction during road shows	• Receive/draw loan amount according to type of loan
Arranger(s)	• Design loan structure • Determine loan price, hand in offering memorandum	• Prepare information memorandum • Identify and approach potential participants and negotiate pricing • Prepare syndication book and other legal documents • Allocate loan amount among participants	• Provide services for borrower and participants to facilitate information flow
Participants	• –	• Perform credit analysis • Communicate acceptance/decline to arranger, commit loan amount	• Perform loan monitoring/servicing tasks
Key milestones at end of phase	• Submission of bid by arranger(s) • Award of mandate(s) by borrower	• Closure and signing of syndication	• Repayment of loan

Figure 15: Key tasks and milestones during a loan syndication transaction[258]

During the pre-mandate phase, the borrower contacts potential lenders, expresses his intention to raise funds, discusses details of his required transaction, and seeks bids from the institutions. Sometimes, a bank might be aware of a borrower's need to raise funds (e.g., through a relationship officer). The urgency of the prospective borrower's financing need determines the timing of the pre-mandate phase. Should, for example,

[258] Source: Own illustration based on Rhoades (2000), chapter 3

an M&A transaction be the reason for a need to raise funds, it might be necessary to assemble a syndicate within a few days only. Under "normal" circumstances, however, a prospective borrower will typically discuss a transaction with a group of interested banks for some weeks before assigning a mandate.

After having been asked to submit bids, the potential future lenders structure and price the required transaction. This necessitates close cooperation between the syndication, credit approval and relationship management units of the bidding banks. It is important for potential lenders to find a balance between their objectives to win the syndication mandate and be able to arrange a successful and profitable syndication and the offer conforming to their credit standards.

Finally, the institutions hand in an offering memorandum containing the suggested structure and conditions of the lending arrangement as well as their underwriting commitment.[259] The borrower, in turn, usually selects one bank among the applicants and assigns it with the mandate to act as arranger of the transaction.

In the subsequent post-mandate phase the loan origination and syndication takes place. Keeping the agreed-upon timing is particularly crucial during this phase as the parties involved commit themselves to raising funds on the credit market during this phase. The consequence of a failure during this period can imply financial penalties but also reputation losses for the parties involved.

The selected arranger – sometimes supported by one or several co-arranger(s) – raises the required loan amount by assembling the syndicate of lenders. The arranger has the task of coordinating all negotiations, payments and administrative tasks between the parties involved and tries to align the objectives of the participating lenders in the syndicate with his own ones and those of the borrower.[260] The arranger's higher efforts compared to participating lenders are reflected in his higher share in the fee distribution.[261]

During the post-mandate phase, the arranger prepares and completes the information memorandum. This document provides information about the borrower to potentially participating lenders in the transaction. The arranging institution also has the task of running and eventually closing the syndication book. The syndication book is a

---

259 From an individual bank's point of view several bidding constellations are possible. The preferred bidding constellation is a sole bid in which the winning bank has the sole authority regarding forming an underwriting group/sub-group as well as regarding fee distribution, etc. The formation of a multi-bank bidding group is less satisfactory from the individual bank's point of view because in this case issues such as management of the bidding process or fee distribution need to be agreed upon by several parties; see Rhoades (2000), p. 174 et seq.

260 See Rhoades (2000), p. 13

261 For details on pricing and fee structures of syndicated loan arrangements, see Rhoades (2000), p. 160 et seqq., Armstrong (2003), p. 6 chart 2 and Miller (1998)

standardized document incorporating details of the institutions the arranger ("book-runner") invites to participate in the transaction – including their committed loan amount if they participate in the transaction.[262] During so-called "road shows" – bank meetings organized by the arranger – the borrower has the opportunity to present himself and his desired transaction to interested banks. The arranger finally allocates the committed and underwritten loan amount among the participating institutions according to their desired participation while at the same time ensuring that the aggregate amount provided by the individual banks matches the amount required by the borrower. A typical target for the arranger is to keep a participation of around 10% in the entire loan volume on its own book. All relevant parties complete the syndication with the signing of the documents.

During the post-signing phase, the arranger services the borrower and the participating banks by, e.g., facilitating the information flow between the parties. The arranger usually performs this task during the entire maturity of the loan.[263]

After the syndication of the loan has been completed, each member of the loan syndicate can transfer its commitment partly or entirely to a third party through a loan sale arrangement on the secondary loan market. This is the connection between loan sales and syndication transactions.[264]

Banking practice distinguishes between the primary and secondary syndication market. All activities before signing the syndication documents are regarded as primary syndication market activities. Therefore, each bank joining as a participating lender in the syndication during the primary market phase of a transaction will appear as an originating party in the documentation. This does not correspond to the theoretical market interpretation, however, because according to this definition, the participating lenders perform a secondary market transaction – they acquire a part of a loan which has already been underwritten, i.e., originated by the arranger. The term secondary syndication market in this context refers to the sale of syndicated loan tranches on the secondary loan sales market after the syndication has been signed.[265]

262 See Rhoades (2000), p. 192 for contents of a typical information memorandum and Exhibit 3.2 for an example of a syndication book

263 As mentioned above, each member of the syndicate acts as a direct lender to the borrower according to its individual participation and is, thus, required to perform its own credit analysis and monitoring tasks with regard to the credit risk it acquires in the course of the transaction. A consequence of this requirement is that the arranger is legally protected against distribution of misinformation among the participating banks except for cases of gross negligence or unlawful misconduct; see Rhoades (2000), p. 224

264 See Rhoades (2000), p. 407

265 See Rhoades (2000), p. 15. Poppensieker (2002) provides a graphical illustration of the syndication activities and phases on p. 36, Figure 1. The distinction between primary and secondary syndication market needs to be applied with care, however, in the case of acquisition finance transactions. Characteristics of these transactions are that the arranger needs to sign the documentation as soon as the transaction is underwritten,

3.1.3 Market development

Due to the strong integration of the secondary loan sales with the syndication market, both markets have developed quite similarly in the past years. Common feature for both markets has been strong volume growth – albeit at different absolute volumes.[266]

3.1.3.1 Loan sales

Secondary market loan sales transactions appeared in the US at the end of the 1980s as banks became increasingly worried about their concentrations of highly leveraged loans on their books following a period of intense financing of leveraged buy-out transactions. Therefore, some commercial and investment banks established loan sales desks allowing lenders to balance and diversify their positions.[267]

Towards the end of the 1990s and continuing in the new millennium, secondary loan sales volumes (both in syndicated and "traditional" corporate loans) strongly increased in the US as well as in Europe. This growth is expected to continue (see Figure 16). The upsurge of information platforms[268] contributed to the increasing growth and liquidity of secondary loan sales markets. In Europe, the secondary loan sales market was established much later than in the US – before 1997 there was no significant market volume observable. Since 1997, the European market has experienced growth with a CAGR of around 45 %, albeit at comparably low absolute numbers. Today's trading volume is still less than a third of the volume in the US.

although it is the intention to run a general – primary – syndication at a later stage

[266] Compare the outstanding volumes in Figure 16 with the ones in Figure 17 and Figure 18

[267] See Barnish, Miller et al. (1997)

[268] Examples of such platforms are the Loan Pricing Corporation (http://www.loanpricing.com) providing its customers with loan information services through the Internet. LoanX, Inc. (http://www.loanx.com) provides a platform and market-related data to institutional portfolio managers and other dealers trading syndicated bank loans; and Debt Exchange (http://www.debtx.com) supports financial institutions to generate a better return on their loan portfolios by providing advisory services and supporting the creation of a more active secondary loan market through its Internet platform

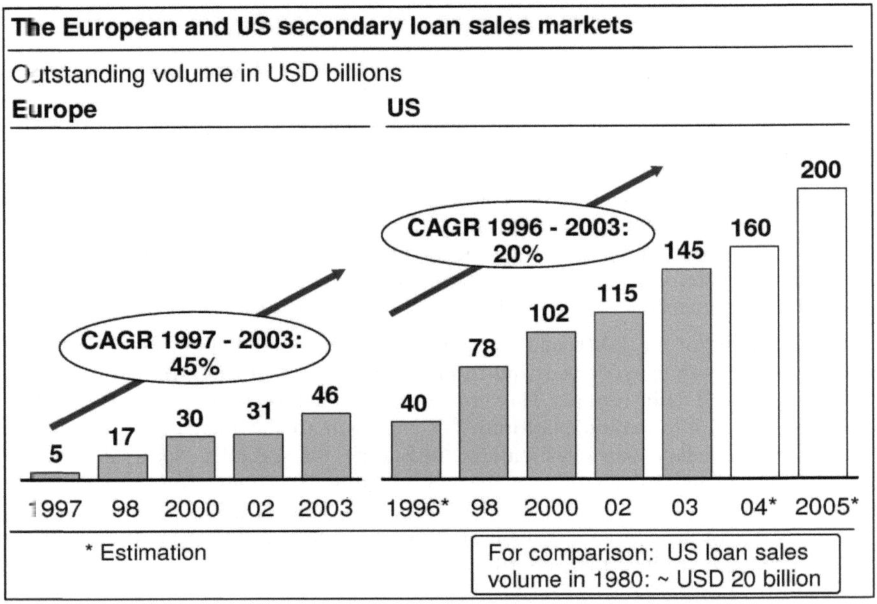

Figure 16: The European and US secondary loan sales markets[269]

Despite the recent strongly increasing trading activity, however, the secondary loan sales market is still a comparably unregulated and decentralized market.[270] There is little information about market shares of banks in the secondary loan sales market, but it seems as if the leading commercial banks dominated this comparably private market segment.[271] It is also important to note that it is virtually only large corporate loans that can benefit from the recent increasing tradability. For most of the loans in the small- and mid-cap segments there is practically no secondary market yet.[272] Innovations such as the "Deutsche Kreditbörse", an electronic trading platform for loans to medium-sized enterprises which was initiated in October 2004, try to address this issue.[273]

[269] Source: Own illustration based on BIS (2003b), p. 10, Gadanecz (2004), p. 85 and N.N (2002)

[270] See Celent Communications (2002), p. 16

[271] Leading secondary loan sales firms in the US are JP Morgan Chase, Credit Suisse First Boston, Goldman Sachs, Citigroup/Salomon Smith Barney, Bear Stearns, Bank of America, Wachovia Securities, UBS Warburg, Merrill Lynch and Morgan Stanley; see Celent Communications (2002), p. 16, Table 2

[272] See Bavaria (2002)

[273] See Franke (2005) and http://www.dekrebo.de

3.1.3.2 Loan syndication

The loan syndication market has its origin in the 1960s because the emergence of the Eurodollar and the launch of the cross-border inter-banking market gave banks the opportunity to assemble lenders from different regions into loan syndicates.[274] After strong growth in the 1980s due to the requirement to finance leveraged buy-out transactions,[275] the need to finance the M&A boom in the 1990s triggered another growth phase for syndicated lending in Europe as well as in the US.[276] Between 1994 and 2004, the new business volume in the European syndicated loan market grew at a CAGR of around 19%. Starting at higher absolute volumes, the US market grew at around 6% annually in the same time period (see Figure 17 and Figure 18). It was also in the mid 1990s when, beginning in the US, institutional investors started to consider syndicated loans as an alternative asset class, trading them on the secondary loan sales markets comparable to trading bonds and shares.[277] Syndicated lending volumes shrank significantly after their peak in 2000. This was mainly attributable to the declining M&A activity in the beginning of the 21st century. However, after having hit a low in 2003, there was a strong upswing in the market in 2004, with new business volume growing by more than 25% compared to 2003 in Europe as well as in the US.

The most recent volume growth is driven by a shift in demand from bilateral to syndicated loans and, particularly in Europe, by an increasing demand for syndicated loans by medium-sized companies. The upsurge of an integrated European syndicated loan market has propelled this growth and, particularly in Germany, syndicated loan volumes have been driven by a recent growing number of leveraged buy-out transactions, which are mostly initiated by corporations that sell off their non-core business to financial investors such as private equity funds. Many corporations also use syndicated loans to secure their liquidity, thus often benefiting from a positive evaluation by rating agencies as they can prove long-term credit lines.[278]

---

274 See Rhoades (2000), p. 2. Syndication was mainly seen as a means to share very large loans through an informal "loan club" of banks

275 See Loan Pricing Corporation (2001)

276 See Poppensieker (2002), p. 37

277 See Armstrong (2003), p. 12 and p. 26

278 See N.N. (2004b)

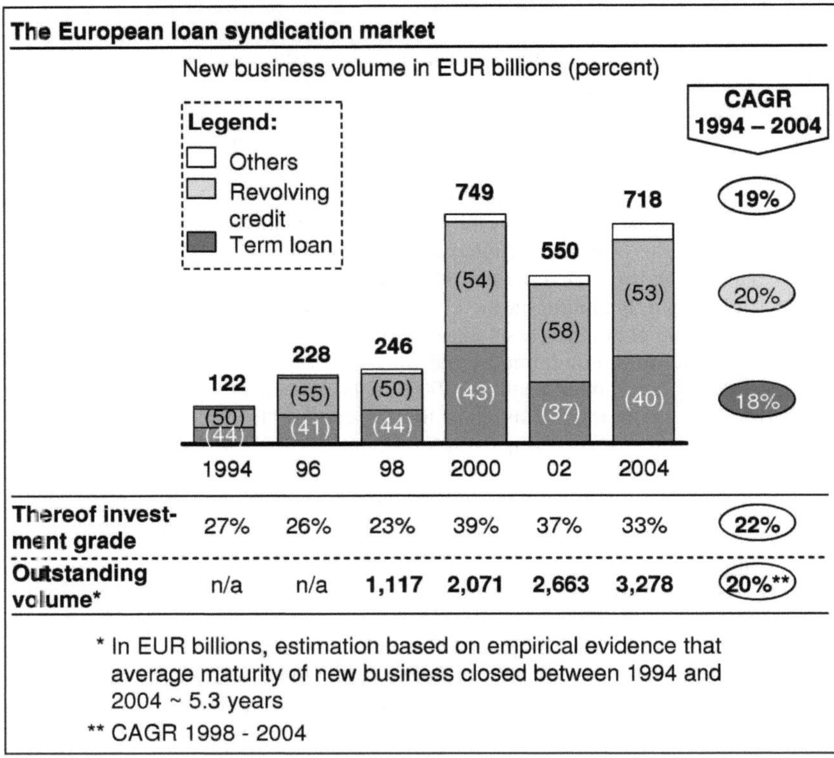

Figure 17: The European loan syndication market[279]

Starting from low absolute volumes in 1994, the European syndicated loan market grew at a CAGR of around 20% until 2004 (new and outstanding volume). Starting at significantly higher absolute volumes in 1994, the US market grew more slowly in the same time period. Revolving credit facilities are the dominating type of syndicated lending instruments in the US market, constituting around 70% of the entire new business volume. In Europe, this product type only has a market share of around 50%, followed by term loans (approximately 40% share of new business volume as opposed to less than 30% in the US). Other product types only play a subordinate role in both markets. The share of investment grade syndicated loans is slightly higher in the US than in Europe (around 40% vs. around one third share in new business volume,

[279] Source: Own illustration based on Dealogic Loanware

respectively). Key difference between the two markets is the maturity of loans: in the US, the average maturity of new business closed between 1994 and 2004 is significantly lower (around 3.6 years) than in Europe (around 5.3 years).[280]

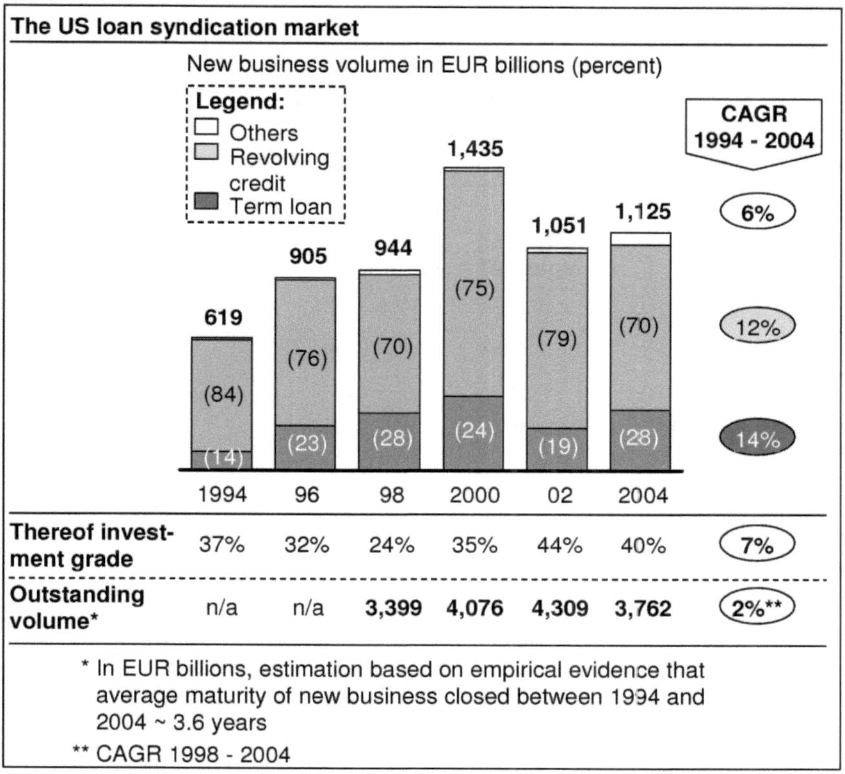

Figure 18: The US loan syndication market[281]

The banks' increased risk aversion and reduced willingness to lend to higher-risk companies has attracted non-bank lenders such as mutual, pension, and hedge funds as

[280] See Figure 70 in Appendix A showing the average maturity of syndicated loans in both markets. Also note that large syndicated loans in Europe often include a tranche with a maturity of only 364 days because there is no need to hold regulatory equity for credit lines with maturity < 1 year; see N.N. (2004b)

In the Moody's rating system, e.g., securities with a credit rating of Baa or above are considered to be investment grade, see Hull (2006), p. 481

[281] Source: Own illustration based on Dealogic Loanware

well as insurance companies to enter the syndicated loan markets.[282] However, despite these new market entrants, the syndicated loan market is still dominated by a few large commercial banks. Especially in the US there is a high concentration of banks in this market: while in both markets more than 50% of the entire market volume is concentrated on the top-ten banks, the largest three arrangers in the US issue around 40% of the entire new business volume, compared to around 23% issued by the top-three arrangers in Europe. See Figure 19 and Figure 20 for league tables of the EU and US loan syndication markets.

League table European loan syndication market 2004

Arranger	Deal volume*	Percent of total volume	Top 3 (percent)	Number of deals	Top 3 (deals)
1 Barclays	54	7.8		252	
2 Citigroup	53	7.7	22.7	194	693
3 BNP Paribas	50	7.2		247	
4 Royal Bank of Scotland	41	6.0		263	
5 Deutsche Bank	40	5.8		131	
6 ABN Amro	36	5.2		159	
7 HSBC	32	4.6		181	
8 JP Morgan	32	4.6		90	
9 Calyon	29	4.2		120	
10 DrKW**	20	2.8		91	
Total	**387**	**54.0**		**1,728*** **	

* In EUR billions

** Dresdner Kleinwort Wasserstein

*** 42% of all deals in 2004

Figure 19: League table European loan syndication market 2004[283]

[282] See Celent Communications (2002), p. 12 and Figure 5 on p. 13 for the US loan syndication market

[283] Source: Own illustration based on Dealogic Loanware

League table US loan syndication market 2004

Arranger	Deal volume*	Percent of total volume		Number of deals	
1 JP Morgan	158	16.9		825	
2 Bank of America	131	14.0	40.6	840	2,067
3 Citigroup	91	9.7		402	
4 Deutsche Bank	40	2.8		198	
5 Wachovia	41	4.4		382	
6 CSFB	29	3.1		149	
7 BNP Paribas	22	2.4		166	
8 Barclays	18	2.0		99	
9 Sun Trust Bank	16	1.7		184	
10 UBS	14	1.5		101	
Total	**560**	**58.5**		**3,346****	

* In EUR billions
** 47% of all deals in 2004

Figure 20: League table US loan syndication market 2004[284]

3.2 Credit derivatives

3.2.1 Definition and classification

A derivative can be defined as an instrument whose value depends on (is derived from) the value of another underlying variable.[285] The maturity of the derivative does not necessarily have to match the maturity of the underlying instrument. Derivatives can be used to transfer risks between the two parties closing the derivative contract. They can be traded on exchanges or over the counter (OTC) – in the latter case the terms of a contract can be negotiated at the discretion of the contract parties and do not need to comply with the rules of an exchange.[286]

[284] Source: Own illustration based on Dealogic Loanware

[285] See Hull (2006), p. 1

[286] See Hull (2006), p. 2 et seq.

There are derivatives such as forward and futures contracts[287] as well as swaps[288] having a symmetric payment structure in relation to their underlying. Other derivatives, such as options, are characterized by an asymmetric payment structure, as a payoff to their holders only takes place if the underlying exceeds or undershoots a predefined exercise or strike price.[289]

In accordance with the general definition for derivatives, credit derivatives are bilateral financial contracts enabling the transfer of the credit exposure of an underlying asset or of an asset portfolio between two counterparties isolated from the other types of risks associated with the underlying asset(s). Hence, by means of credit derivatives a credit portfolio manager can acquire or sell credit risk exposure independently of other risk types.[290]

There are several ways to classify and differentiate credit derivatives. Like derivatives in general, they can be differentiated according to the symmetry of their payment structure. It can also be distinguished between funded and unfunded credit derivatives: the buyer of a funded derivative is obliged to make an upfront payment to the issuer when purchasing the contract. When entering unfunded derivatives contracts, except for regular premiums paid by the protection buyer to the protection seller, payments are made upon termination of the contract only.[291]

In order to analyze the risk transfer impact of credit derivatives, it is useful to split these instruments according to the type of credit risks which can be transferred as well as according to the type of underlying on which the derivative is based. Also, these instruments can be differentiated according to the way they transfer risks among market participants.[292] Accordingly, Figure 21 gives an overview of credit derivative instruments along the following categories:

---

287 A forward is a customized off-exchange (OTC) contract allowing the parties to buy or sell an underlying asset at a predetermined forward price. A future also allows parties to buy or sell an underlying asset at a pre-determined forward price. In contrast to a forward, however, it is a standardized contract traded on exchanges; see Banks (2004), p. 4

288 A swap is a customized off-exchange (OTC) contract enabling parties to exchange periodic cash flows based on an underlying reference; see Banks (2004), p. 5

289 An option grants its buyer the right, but not the obligation, to buy or sell an underlying asset at a predetermined strike price. It can be traded in standardized form on an exchange or customized as an off-exchange (OTC) contract; see again Banks (2004), p. 5

290 See Anson, Chen et al. (2004), p. 1 as well as BBA (2003/2004), p. 10. It will be shown later in this chapter that some instruments also allow the transfer of interest rate risk

291 Examples of funded credit derivatives are Credit-Linked Notes (CLNs). Typical unfunded credit derivatives are Credit Default Swaps (CDS); see Anson, Chen et al. (2004), p. 2. These instruments will be introduced in detail in the next chapters

292 See Poppensieker (2002), p. 40 et seq.

Concerning types of credit risks they transfer, it can be differentiated between derivatives transferring default risks (Credit Default Instruments) and derivatives transferring spread risks (Replication Instruments).[293]

Furthermore, these instruments can be distinguished according to their underlying credit assets: they can be based on single-name credit exposures (e.g., on loans or bonds), on baskets/portfolios of credit assets or on credit indices.

Finally, they can be segmented according to the way they transfer risks among the contract parties: straight derivatives transfer risks directly among the parties involved. Repackaged and tranched derivatives are characterized by an indirect risk transfer:[294] there is a Special Purpose Vehicle (SPV) between risk shedder and investor(s). Through entering into derivatives contracts with the risk shedder, this SPV takes on the risk shedder's (credit) risks. It then repackages these risks into multiple tranches of securities, each of which have a different creditworthiness.[295] The common definition for derivatives also includes repackaged and tranched instruments such as synthetic Collateralized Debt Obligations (synthetic CDOs) and synthetic Mortgage-Backed Securities (synthetic MBS).[296] Repackaged and tranched derivatives as well as a description of the procedure leading to their issuance – securitizations – will be discussed in greater detail in chapter 3.3, which also covers cash-based securitizations.[297]

To complete the product spectrum, Figure 21 also includes Asset Swaps which are straight cash-based products used to transfer credit risks. Strictly speaking, they are hybrid instruments but are often included in the definition for credit derivatives.[298]

[293] This differentiation is also applied by Das (2000), p. 8 Figure 1.2

In this context, it needs to be noted that derivative instruments transferring spread risks also transfer interest rate risk related to one (several) underlying credit asset(s). See, again, the description of risk types above in chapter 1.4.2.1

[294] An exception are the single-name tranched instruments introduced in chapter 3.2.3.1. They directly transfer credit risk

[295] It will be shown in chapter 3.3.2.2.2 that there are also single-tranche securitizations

[296] See BBA (2003/2004), p. 10

[297] As they are typically structured with the help of several other credit products and instruments, repackaged and tranched derivatives are also referred to as "structured derivatives". Accordingly, repackaged and tranched cash products are described as "structured cash products"

[298] See BBA (2003/2004), p. 10

In practice, Asset Swaps are often used to extract default probabilities from bond prices, see Hull (2006), p. 486

Overview of derivative and cash-based instruments

Instrument type	Underlying	Types of credit risks: Default risks[1]	Types of credit risks: Spread risks[2]
Straight cash-based	Single-name	• Asset Swap	
Straight derivative	Single-name	• CDS/Default Option • Equity Default Swap • Credit Default Linked Note	• Spread Forward/Option • Single-name TRS • Total Return CLN • Credit Spread Linked Note
	Basket/ portfolio	• CDS/Default Option • First-to Default CLN	• Basket TRS
	Index	• Default Index Forward/Future/Option	• Spread Index Forward/Option • Index TRS • Total Return Credit Linked Index Note
Repackaged and tranched derivative	Single-name	• Geared Default Swap/ Option	
	Basket/ portfolio	• Synthetic bond • Synthetic securitization	
Repackaged and tranched cash-based[4]	Basket/ portfolio	• Cash-based securitization	

1 Credit default products
2 Replication products
3 Also referred to as "structured derivative"
4 Also referred to as "structured cash product"

Figure 21: Overview of derivative and cash-based instruments[299]

[299] Own illustration based on Poppensieker (2002), p. 41 Figure 3, BBA (2003/2004) and Anson, Chen et al. (2004)

3.2.2 Straight derivatives

3.2.2.1 Single-name credit default instruments

Single-name credit default instruments are bilateral contracts providing protection against the default of a single reference asset.

3.2.2.1.1 Single-name Credit Default Swaps (CDS)

Single-name CDS are the most common single-name credit default instruments. They are the basis for most of the more complex repackaged and tranched credit derivatives instruments. Also, they are the main product of the "traded component" of the credit derivatives market.[300] Following the conclusion of such a contract, the protection buyer pays a periodic fixed fee or a one-off payment to a protection seller.[301] In return, if a credit event happens, the swap contract is terminated and the protection seller makes a payment to the protection buyer to reimburse him for the losses on his credit asset. CDS are typical unfunded instruments as there is no upfront payment between the two parties when closing the contract. Figure 22 illustrates the payment structure of a CDS.[302]

Crucial elements which need to be specified when closing a CDS contract are the definition of a credit event of the reference asset and the type of settlement. These specifications are usually the main causes for disputes between counterparties.[303]

The agreement on what constitutes a credit event triggering a default payment is the most important chapter of the legal documentation for a CDS contract. The International Swaps and Derivatives Association (ISDA) has listed events that can cause the credit quality of a reference entity to deteriorate or cause its value to decline. These events include bankruptcy, credit event upon merger, cross acceleration/cross default (cross default being the event of default with respect to another outstanding obligation of the reference entity), downgrade, failure to pay, repudiation (i.e. the reference entity refuses to pay on any of its obligations), and restructuring of the underlying asset.[304] It is up to the contract parties which of these events they want to include in their agreement.

---

300 These instruments constituted more than 50% of the outstanding volume in the credit derivatives market in 2003; see BBA (2003/2004), p. 21.

301 Strictly speaking, one has to differentiate between the CDS and the Credit Default Option: under a CDS, periodical fee payments were agreed. If the entire fee is paid up front, the product is a Credit Default Option. However, in practice it is referred to both variations are referred to as CDS; see Tavakoli (2001), p. 73

302 See Poppensieker (2002), p. 43 and Choudhry (2004a), p. 16 et seq.

303 See BBA (2003/2004), p. 26

304 See ISDA (2003)

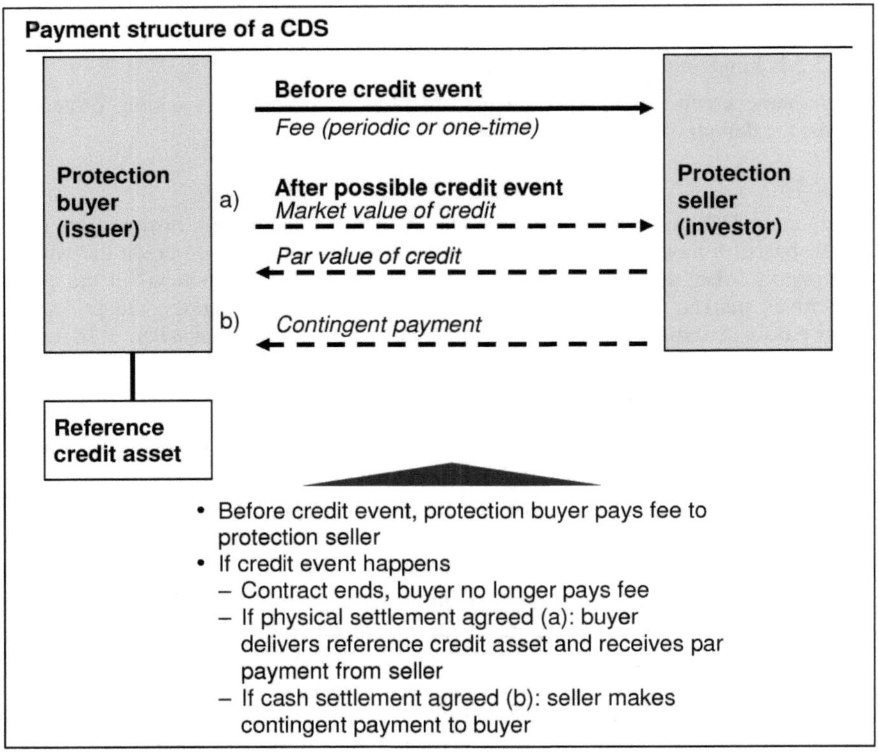

Figure 22: Payment structure of a CDS[305]

Regarding type of settlement, following the termination of a CDS contract, physical settlement is the most frequently used type. It implies that the protection buyer can deliver the defaulted asset in exchange for the asset's par value from the protection seller.[306] Cash settlement implies payment of an agreed-upon cash amount by the protection seller following a credit event. This may be the nominal value of the swap contract or the difference between the par value of the reference obligation and its market value at the time of the credit event.[307]

305 Source: Own illustration based on Choudhry (2004a), p. 16

306 See BBA (2003/2004), p. 25. Among all institutions asked in a survey, 86% responded that they use physical settlement as the most common payout structures. Among leading institutions, it was even 93% settling their contracts in this way

307 See Anson, Chen et al. (2004), p. 63

The latest developments in unfunded default instruments are Equity Default Swaps (EDS). They have the same payment structure as CDS with the difference being that the reference asset is not a credit but an equity asset. Instead of the occurrence of a credit event, the triggering event is the moment when the reference equity hits a specified barrier. Settlement always takes place in cash. In the case of settlement, the protection seller reimburses its counterparty for the loss on its underlying by paying the difference between the equity value at closure of the contract and the recovery value of the asset. The recovery value is typically set at a fixed level when entering the swap.[308]

3.2.2.1.2 Single-name Credit Default Linked Notes (CLNs)

While CDS are unfunded instruments, CLNs are funded credit derivatives: the buyer of a CLN (credit protection seller), makes an upfront payment to the issuer of the note (credit protection buyer) when purchasing the product.[309]

Traditional types of CLNs are Credit Linked Structured Notes. They are structured instruments combining a fixed income security with a credit derivative, linking either the coupon or principal payment of the security to their credit risk component.[310] These instruments allow an investor to replicate an exposure to the credit risks inherent in bonds or loans without having to directly invest in the securities.[311] The major types of Credit Linked Structured Notes include Credit Default Linked Notes, Credit Spread Linked Notes, and Total Return CLNs.

Single-name Credit Default Linked Notes are mainly used to reduce the issuer's default exposure related to an underlying credit asset. They are created by combining a credit asset with a CDS. The investor in the note is the provider of default protection for the underlying asset to the issuer. If no credit event happens in the course of the maturity of the note, the issuer pays back the par value of the note. Should a credit event occur the par value will be reduced by the losses on the reference asset(s) to which the note is linked.[312] Figure 23 illustrates the payment structure of a single-name Credit Default Linked Note.

308 See Choudhry (2004a), p. 18 et seq.

309 As notes, these instruments are tradable on-balance sheet securities as opposed to CDS, e.g., which are typical off-balance sheet instruments, i.e., not appearing on a bank's balance sheet; see Hartmann-Wendels, Pfingsten et al. (2004), p. 312

310 The derivative component can be a CDS, a Total Return Swap (TRS) or a Spread Forward or Option. Issuers of these instruments usually have a high creditworthiness (AAA or AA); see Das (2000), p. 69 and Anson, Chen et al. (2004), p. 119

311 See Das (2000), p. 69

312 See Das (2000), p. 73

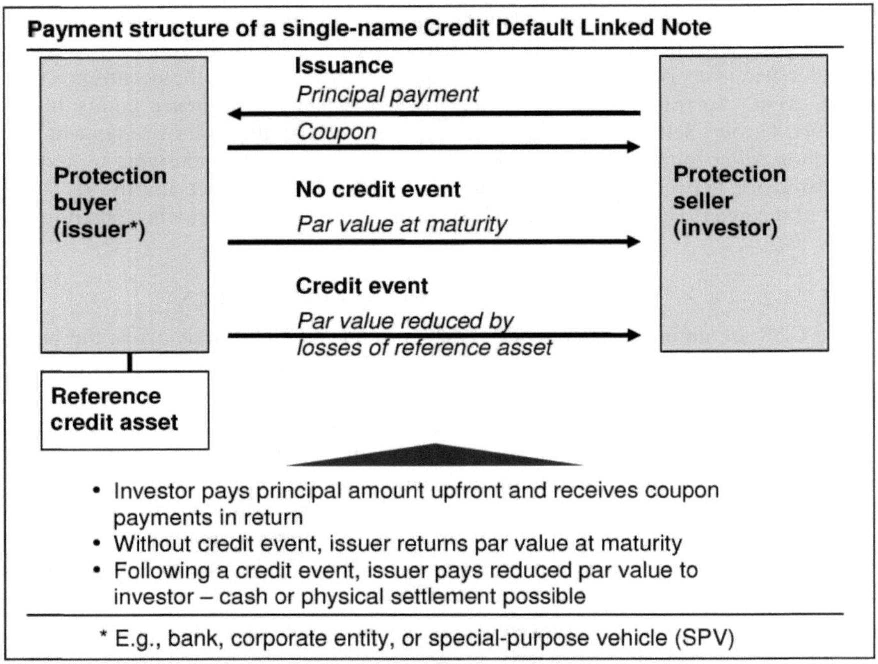

Figure 23: Payment structure of a single-name Credit Default Linked Note[313]

As with CDS, settlement may take place in cash or through physical delivery. If cash settlement has been agreed, the protection seller receives his investment minus the losses which the protection buyer incurred on the underlying asset(s) at the time of the credit event. Under physical settlement, the protection buyer delivers the reference asset at maturity.[314]

3.2.2.2 Single-name spread (replication) instruments

Credit derivatives can also transfer the risks stemming from unexpected changes in the market value of an underlying credit asset. These market value changes stem from a changing credit spread of the underlying.[315]

313 Source: Own illustration based on Choudhry (2004a), p. 47 et seq.

314 See Das (2000), pp. 84 – 87. For variations of the Credit Default Linked Note see Das (2000), chapter 2.7.2

315 The credit spread of an asset is the difference between the yield of an asset and the yield of a risk-free security (e.g., a Government Bond) or between the asset's yield and a risk-free yield (e.g., Euribor); see Banks (2004), p. 504. Euribor is a trimmed average of interest rates quoted for term deposits in the Euro area

3.2.2.2.1 Single-name Spread Forwards and Options

It can be differentiated between spread instruments with a symmetric payment structure (Spread Forwards) and instruments with an asymmetric payment structure (Spread Options).[316] While there is no need to define default criteria for spread instruments, the existence of a sufficiently liquid market price for the respective underlying asset is necessary in order to be able to determine spread changes. Settlement can be in cash or through physical delivery of the reference asset against payment of either the nominal or the original market value.[317]

3.2.2.2.2 Single-name Total Return Swaps (TRS)

Another type of spread instruments are Total Return Swaps (TRS). By means of a single-name TRS, the owner of a credit asset transfers all cash flows from the asset as well as a potential capital appreciation to the receiver of the total return. In turn, the owner will earn the agreed-upon floating rate plus or minus a spread and will be reimbursed should there be a depreciation of the asset under the initial value.[318] Figure 24 outlines the payment structure of a TRS.

interbank market. Strictly speaking, as the underlying instruments for Euribor are unsecured interbank deposits, Euribor is not totally risk-free but reflects a certain degree of credit risk. As most of the banks in contributing to the Euribor setting have a AA long-term credit rating, however, this credit risk is regarded as negligible and Euribor is taken as a proxy for the risk-free interest rate; see BIS (2003a), p. 50 and p. 53.

As mentioned above in Footnote 91, the credit spread is determined by a changing market view on the assets' creditworthiness (spread risk) as well as by a changing market interest rate (interest rate risk)

316 See Das (2000), p. 18

317 See Poppensieker (2002), p. 45 et seq. and Choudhry (2004a), p. 28 et seq.

318 See Anson, Chen et al. (2004), p. 99 as well as Francis, Frost et al. (1999)

While the TRS is a typically an instrument protecting against spread risk of an underlying asset, it can also cover default risk: in the event of default, the total return swap payment will reflect the impact of default through the fall in price of the underlying asset (effectively, this is the expected recovery level of the asset). Therefore, the asset holder will also be indemnified against any loss resulting from default, through receiving the difference between the price when closing the transaction and the price following default; see Das (2000), p. 16

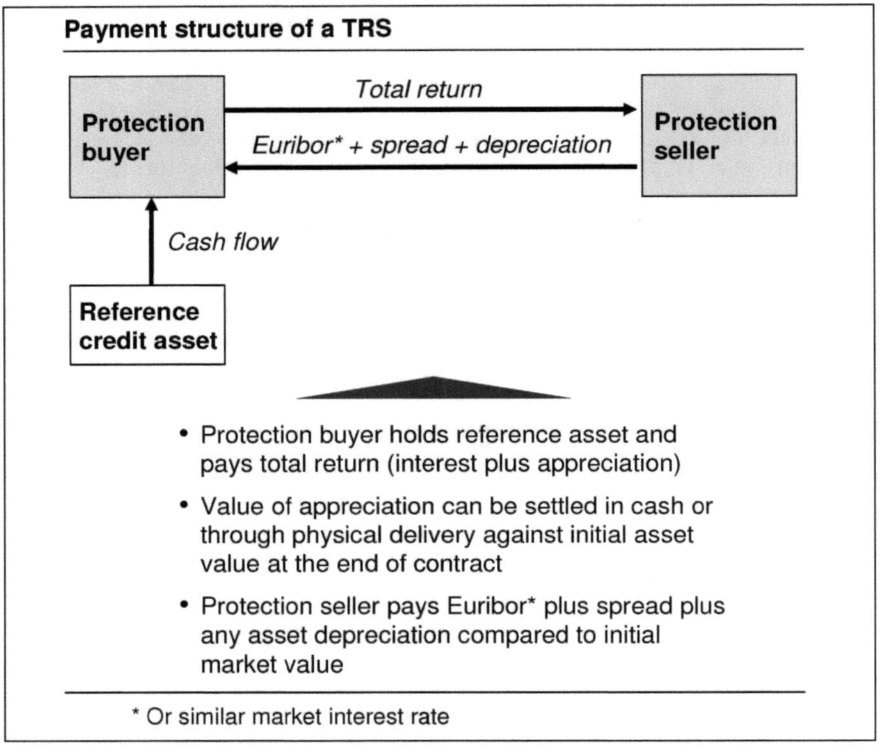

Figure 24: Payment structure of a TRS[319]

Precondition for the determination of the underlying asset's appreciation or depreciation is a sufficiently liquid market price of the asset. In cases where the market price of an asset is not or only inaccurately available, it is common to balance out losses or gains on asset holdings at the moment they arise.[320]

As the actual credit asset remains on the owner's balance sheet, the owner must continue to pay for its funding as well as for the opportunity cost of capital invested in the asset. In turn, the receiver of the total return acquires the entire credit and interest

[319] Source: Own illustration based on Anson, Chen et al. (2004), p. 100 Exhibit 5.1 and Choudhry (2004a), p. 22 Figure 2-4

[320] See Poppensieker (2002), p. 47

rate risks from the underlying but does not need to buy and finance the asset – hence owning a synthetic bond.[321]

In their basic structure, TRS are unfunded instruments.[322] The total return of (an) underlying asset(s) can also be transferred using the above-mentioned (funded) Total Return CLNs.

3.2.2.2.3 Single-name Total Return CLNs and Credit Spread Linked Notes

Analogous to single-name Credit Default Linked Notes, single-name Total Return CLNs transfer the total return of an underlying asset to the investor in these structured notes.[323] Accordingly, single-name Credit Spread Linked Notes allow the transfer of the spread risk component of an underlying asset.[324]

3.2.2.3 Basket default instruments

Basket instruments refer to several underlying credit assets. Like single-name instruments, they can transfer default and spread risks.[325]

3.2.2.3.1 Basket CDS

Basket CDS are CDS referring to several underlying credit assets. Typically, three to five reference entities are included in such an instrument, although a basket CDS may also refer to twenty or more underlyings.

It is common that basket CDS do not provide protection on all assets in the basket but covers the default risks of a selection of names only. Accordingly, one can distinguish between First-(Second-) to-Default baskets, providing credit protection on the first (second) default in the basket only, first *n*th-to-Default baskets protecting the first *n* defaults and last *p*th to Default baskets covering the default risks of the last *p* defaults in the basket. Subordinate and Senior Basket Default Swaps are other variations of default baskets: Subordinate Basket Default Swaps fix a maximum payout for each

---

321 See Choudhry (2004a), p. 21

322 The receiver of the total return may also fully fund a TRS by investing a cash equivalent in an asset yielding a return related to the risk-free market interest rate (e.g., Euribor) so that the floating rate payments to the asset owner are covered; see Das (2000), p. 11

323 See Das (2000), p. 73 et seq.

324 See Poppensieker (2002), p. 52 and Das (2000), p. 80 et seq.

As opposed to default instruments, spread instruments also transfer interest rate risk besides transferring credit risk. Under certain conditions this can lead to offsetting effects: if, e.g., an asset manager uses a TRS to receive credit protection for a reference asset, he is exposed to both credit and interest rate risk. If the credit spread declines following an improvement of the asset's creditworthiness (which results in an increasing price of the credit asset), this gain can be offset by a rising market interest rate (which usually induces a declining price of credit assets); see Anson, Chen et al. (2004), p. 101

325 See Poppensieker (2002), p. 48

defaulted reference entity. Besides this, they determine a maximum aggregate payout. When, as a consequence of several defaults, the maximum aggregate payout is reached, the contracts are terminated and settlement is performed between the parties. Senior Basked Default Swaps also determine a maximum payout for each reference entity but payouts are only triggered after a certain threshold is reached.[326]

The default baskets mentioned above transfer credit default risks of only one or several credit assets within a basket or portfolio of instruments, leaving the protection buyer with a residual default risk. It is through Pro-Rata Default Baskets that the entire default risk of a basket of credit assets can be transferred. For this purpose, these credit derivatives pool several single-name CDS or credit default options, referring to the credit assets of a particular portfolio. The main advantage over a risk transfer by means of a number of separate single-name derivatives is the lower administration cost of these instruments.[327]

3.2.2.3.2 First-to Default CLNs

A characteristic funded basket credit derivative is the First-to-Default CLN, transferring the default risks of an underlying credit basket or portfolio. When issuing a First-to-Default CLN, a market participant can acquire credit protection for one reference asset within a basket of credit securities whichever is the first one to default. If any of the assets in this basket defaults, this will trigger the early maturity of the CLN. In this case, either physical or cash settlement takes place between the contract parties.[328]

From an investor's point of view, the risk exposure at default of First-to-Default CLNs is the same as that of a "standard" CLN because the recovery value of a defaulted credit asset does not change whether the asset is in a portfolio or not. Before default, however, the risk exposure of a First-to-Default CLN is theoretically lower because the diversification in the basket can reduce the default probability. Thus, through using First-to-Default CLNs linked to a diversified credit portfolio, investors can select a credit mix in a basket with a widely diversified exposure. The return on First-to-Default CLNs is a multiple of the average spread of the basket.[329]

---

326 See Das (2000), p. 39, Choudhry (2004a), p. 18 and Anson, Chen et al. (2004), p. 51

327 See Tavakoli (2001), p. 186 et seq.

328 If physical settlement has been agreed, the defaulted asset is delivered to the holder of the note. Cash settlement implies that the CLN issuer pays a cash amount to the investor, calculated as a principle amount of the asset times the asset's recovery value. Physical settlement is typically preferred because the calculation of the recovery value may be rather difficult; see Anson, Chen et al. (2004), p. 128 et seq.

329 See Anson, Chen et al. (2004), p. 130 Exhibit 6.14

3.2.2.4 Basket spread (replication) instruments

It is through basket TRS that the spread risks of a group of assets can be transferred to another party. The basket TRS function is analogous to the single-name Total Return Swap (TRS) mentioned above, with the difference being that they refer to the total return of a basket or portfolio of credit instruments instead of a single credit asset.[330]

3.2.2.5 Credit index derivatives

In general, credit index derivatives are instruments that have credit-risk related market indices as their underlying reference value. They can be used as hedging tools for a credit portfolio if the credit risk of the portfolio has a significantly high correlation with their underlying market indices. In this case, a risk minimizing hedging strategy aims at acquiring one unit of index credit derivatives per unit of acquired credit volume.[331] As with single-name and basket credit derivatives, one can distinguish between credit default index and credit spread index instruments.

3.2.2.5.1 Credit default index instruments

The payment structure of default index credit derivatives depends on a default rate or insolvency index. One can distinguish between instruments with a symmetric payment structure (e.g., forwards, futures) and instruments with an asymmetric payment structure (e.g., options).

However, since it is unrealistic that a credit portfolio is perfectly correlated with an index, the protection buyer faces a basis risk when entering a bankruptcy index derivative contract to protect his portfolio.[332] Also, as it is required to ensure a significantly high correlation between the credit portfolio and the index, the risk

---

330 See Anson, Chen et al. (2004), p. 99

331 For example, through purchasing a future on the bankruptcy index a protection seller can insure its portfolio against default rate changes (rising as well as declining default rates); through purchasing a call, the portfolio can be insured against rising default rates, see Poppensieker (2002), p. 50

There was a future on the US Quarterly Bankruptcy Index (QBI), traded at the Chicago Mercantile Exchange between 1998 and 2003. The QBI contained quarterly insolvency figures from the US. The idea of this derivative was that in a well diversified credit portfolio the default rates should be strongly correlated with changes in the bankruptcy index. However, these instruments have never been traded. Therefore, the Chicago Mercantile Exchange Board of Directors decided to de-list all contracts in the QBI; see Chicago Mercantile Exchange (2003)

332 The basis arises because the spot price of an asset to be hedged is not the same as the futures price of the contract used to hedge the asset. It is defined as the spot price of the hedged asset minus the futures price of the contract used.

Consequently, basis risk is defined as the risk to a hedger arising from uncertainty about the basis at a future time, see also Hull (2006), p. 742. Basis risk can lead to an improvement or worsening of the hedger's position, depending on whether the hedger holds a short or a long position in the hedge; see Hull (2006), p. 53 et seqq.

management of these instruments is more difficult compared to managing a credit derivative directly referring to a loan. Besides this, currently valid regulation still does not consider the risk minimization effect of credit index derivatives in its capital requirements for banks.[333]

3.2.2.5.2 Credit spread index instruments

Analogous to single-name spread instruments, spread instruments referring to a credit index can transfer the risks stemming from unexpected market value changes of a credit portfolio, provided the portfolio has a sufficiently high correlation to the credit market index underlying the derivative. The assets included in such an index serve as a reference portfolio. The payment structures of spread index instruments are determined by changes in the credit spread of the underlying index. One can distinguish between spread index forwards and spread index options. As with default index derivatives, a protection buyer has to take into consideration the basis risk between the index and his portfolio.[334]

Index TRS are TRS referring to the return of a credit market index, thus enabling a portfolio manager to create diversified credit exposure. Relevant indices can refer to a certain credit sector (e.g., the mortgage sector) or to certain loan classes.[335]

There are also CLNs transferring the credit risks of an index: typical instruments of this type are Total Return Credit Linked Index Notes.[336]

3.2.3 Repackaged and tranched derivatives

3.2.3.1 Single-name instruments

Single-name CDS (and respectively Credit Default Options) can be structured so that the credit risks are split into a senior and subordinate tranche. One of these tranches is hedged against default through the contract. Such instruments are called Geared Default Swaps/Options. As opposed to "plain" CDS, the protection buyer only acquires protection for a part of its credit risk.[337]

---

[333] See Hartmann-Wendels, Pfingsten et al. (2004), p. 602. These issues might have been key reasons for the lack of success of the QBI future mentioned above in Footnote 331

[334] In the case of spread index instruments the basis risk does not only evolve from an imperfect correlation between the protection buyer's portfolio and the index portfolio but also due to the fact that the credit spread of an index also includes subjective risk preferences of market participants; see Poppensieker (2002), p. 50

[335] For example, referring to the Citicorp/IFR European Impaired Loan Index tracking a basked of impaired loan assets. The credit sectors mentioned are usually referred to as a "spread sectors" compared to the risk-free Treasury sector, with the spread being a reward for investing in these sectors as opposed to a risk-free investment; see Das (2000), p. 15 et seq.

[336] See Das (2000), p. 76

[337] If credit protection is only granted up to a certain maximum level, the product is a default swap/option with

3.2.3.2 Basket instruments

The traditional types of CLNs introduced above (Credit Linked Structured Notes) can be extended by including an SPV that uses credit derivative contracts to take on the credit risks of an underlying basket or portfolio and repackages these risks by creating multiple tranches of securities/notes with different credit ratings. These securities – essentially, they are synthetic bonds – are sold to investors afterwards.[338]

As the issued securities typically include a first loss (or equity) tranche, these repackaged structures essentially represent an enhancement of the First-to Default CLNs introduced above – with the key difference being that now risks are transferred indirectly through an SPV.

The procedure entailing the repackaging of portfolio credit risks – both through transferring the risks by means of credit derivatives and through physically transferring the underlying assets – is called securitization. Hence, the repackaged CLNs described here can be interpreted as securitization instruments. Essentially, they resemble so-called synthetic CDOs.[339] Synthetic CDOs and other securitization instruments will be described in detail in chapter 3.3.

3.2.4 Market development

Credit derivatives were introduced by commercial banks in 1994 as tools to protect against losses on their corporate loan books.[340] In the following years, the global credit derivatives market experienced a tremendous growth, which is expected to continue strongly. Ten years after its introduction, the market size (outstanding volume) is expected to be as large as USD 5 trillion in 2004 with further growth of over 60% to be expected until 2006 (see Figure 25 for an illustration).[341] London could establish itself as the global trading center for credit derivatives, with around 45% of the global volume being traded there in 2004. The US (New York) is the second-largest market with around 40% of the global volume, followed by Asia/Australia (~8% market share). The rest of Europe holds most of the remaining market share. Market participants expect a continuation of these rankings throughout 2006, although growth

first-loss coverage. In the opposite case, if protection is only guaranteed above a certain minimum limit, the product is a default option with a minimum fixed amount; see Poppensieker (2002), p. 44

338 See Das (2000), p. 120 for a detailed description of synthetic bonds

339 See Anson, Chen et al. (2004), p. 132. More precisely, the repackaged CLNs described here resemble fully-funded synthetic CDOs, see chapter 3.3.2.2

340 See Choudhry (2004a), p. 59

341 In this context, the market size is measured by the outstanding nominal volume (notional amount outstanding) of credit derivative contracts. This is the gross nominal or notional value of all deals concluded and not yet settled at the reporting date. For contracts with variable nominal or notional volume, the volume at the time of reporting is used as a basis. See BIS (2004d), p. 4 for definitions

in Asia/Australia might accelerate at the expenses of the London and New York markets.[342]

Following the need of commercial banks to hedge their large syndicated loan exposures in the US in the early 1990s, it was the major financial crises in the mid of the 1990s, in particular 1997 in Asia and 1998 in Russia, which triggered the banks' need for better credit protection. Financial institutions increasingly aimed at hedging their country risk exposures in the wake of these crises, thus furthering the explosive growth of these instruments. The increased demand for credit protection following defaults of well-known investment grade debtors in the beginning of the 21st century was the key driver for the continuing augmentation of the credit derivatives market. Another factor fostering the credit derivatives growth in recent years has been declining bond yields. In view of the declining yields of direct investments in these credit assets, investors growingly turned towards higher yielding investments in derivatives, often accepting higher risks. Credit Derivatives frequently pay higher returns to investors than investments in the underlying assets (e.g., bonds).[343] Finally, the tendency towards actively managing credit portfolios has been a key driver for the demand for credit derivatives in recent years.[344]

342 See BBA (2003/2004), p.12 et seq. Regarding booked transactions, London is even more important and could recently significantly expand its market share, having a 66% market share globally before New York (14%), rest of Europe (14%) and Asia/Australia (6%)

343 CDS typically yield higher returns than direct investments in the underlying credit assets. Investments in CDO tranches typically also generate higher yields than equivalently rated cash assets; see, e.g., Schüler (2003)

344 See BIS (2004b), p. 14, Schüler (2003), BBA (2003/2004), Hayt and Smithson (2000a), p. 60 and Anson, Chen et al. (2004), p. 5 – 16. See also chapter 4.4.4.3 of part III for a description of typical secondary market instruments used by EU institutions in order to actively manage their credit exposures

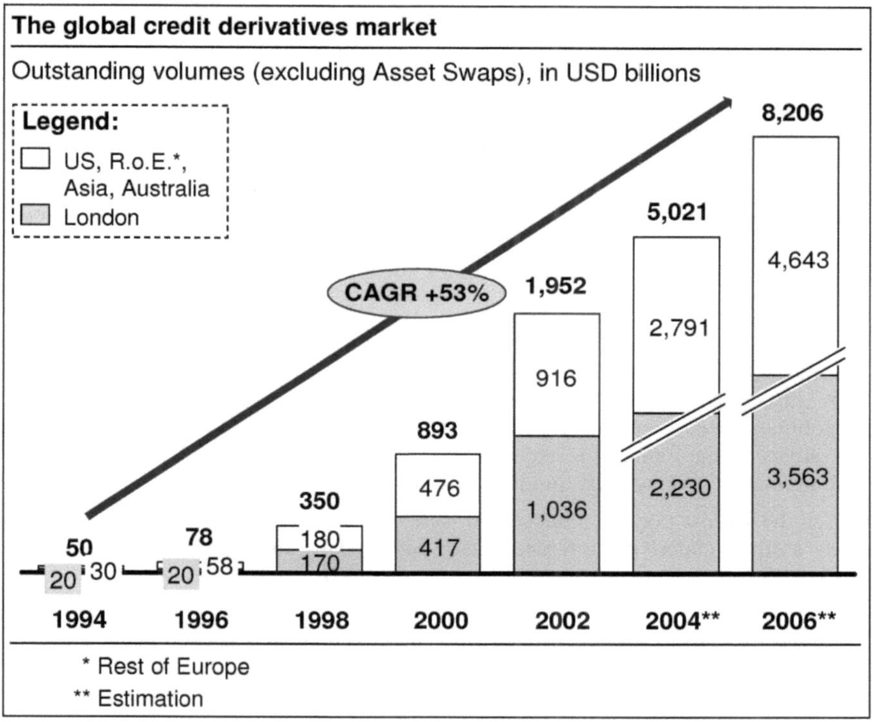

Figure 25: The global credit derivatives market[345]

Since the emergence of credit derivatives, the single-name CDS has been the most popular product, accounting for around 50% market share. In recent years, however, there has been a clear trend towards more complex instruments, in particular synthetic CDO structures but also – albeit less common – complex CDS baskets such as First-to Default and *n*th to Default CDS. Synthetic CDOs are the second-largest group of credit derivatives holding around 20% market share. In the future, the market share of plain vanilla single-name CDS is expected to drop, especially due to the increasing significance of credit index instruments.

Although only introduced recently, credit index instruments already capture more than 10% market share and are expected to gain significant importance with an estimated

345 Source: Own illustration based on BBA (2003/2004) and BBA (1996)

market share of around 17% in 2006.[346] Credit index families such as the iTraxx[347] instruments, for example, consist of market indices segmented by geography, creditworthiness, sectors and maturity. The indices aim at including the large and liquid credit names of their particular segment and allow the trading of credit risks OTC through funded and unfunded instruments. Currently, exchange-traded credit index instruments are being developed. Market participants believe that the credit indices will attract new players into the market, allowing them to perform business under greater transparency and market liquidity. Despite still lacking proper standardization and documentation of credit index derivatives, it is expected that OTC as well as exchange-traded credit index instruments will be important future developments.[348]

Asset swaps will be the product type to lose further significance in the market.[349]

The importance of credit derivatives as instruments for ACPM is rising. According to BBA (2003/2004), until now leading financial institutions have ranked "active portfolio/asset management" at position five on the list of top applications for credit derivatives. In the future, it is expected to move up towards position three, right after "trading/market making" and "product structuring".[350]

By far the largest portion (almost two thirds) of derivatives traded have corporate assets as their underlying reference asset, followed by financial assets (around one fifth), and emerging market sovereign assets (about 8%).[351]

Although banks will continue to be the main market participants – on the buy side as well as on the sell side of credit protection – their market share is continually shrinking on both sides. It is mainly due to mutual, pension and hedge funds that they will further lose market share. In 2006, hedge funds are expected to be the second largest group of protection buyers, with a market share of around 17%. On the sell side of credit risk protection, insurance companies have recently become growingly significant. The fact that a large part of protection buyers and sellers are non-banks

346 See BBA (2003/2004), p. 6 and BIS (2004b), p. 14

347 The iTraxx group (www.itraxx.com) is the result of a merger between two major index families which took place in mid 2004: The TRAC-X and the iBoxx group

348 See BBA (2003/2004), p. 36 and BIS (2004b), p. 54 et seqq.

349 As mentioned above, many institutions include Asset Swaps in their definition of credit derivatives. However, they will continue to lose share in the credit derivatives market: coming from a global market share of 12% at the end of 1999, their market share has continually dropped in recent years and will fall to around 3% in 2006; see BBA (2003/2004), p. 21

350 See BBA (2003/2004), p. 29

351 See BBA (2003/2004), p. 23

emphasizes the fact that many bank-originated loans or related risks are meanwhile held by these non-bank institutions.[352]

Despite its tremendous growth, however, the credit derivatives market is still tiny compared to the entire OTC derivatives market. The total global notional amount of outstanding OTC contracts was as high as USD 197 trillion at the end of 2003, with around USD 142 trillion stemming from interest rate derivatives. Credit derivatives only had a share of around 1.8% in the total global volume (around USD 3.5 trillion outstanding volume).[353]

The amount of reference credit entities on whose debt credit derivatives are traded with sufficient liquidity – most instruments being CDS – exceeds the amount of debt being traded on the cash credit market. This is mainly due to the reason that credit derivatives are bilateral contracts which can be closed independently of the agreement or knowledge of the reference asset's owner.

However, liquid trading of credit derivatives in the CDS market is still highly concentrated in top investment-grade credit names. Globally, it is estimated that there are CDS prices quoted for around 1,200 reference entities. However, there are several layers of liquidity of the traded contracts.[354] Within this group, there are around 50 German reference entities on which CDS prices are quoted and contracts are traded with sufficient liquidity.[355] Although dealers are increasingly putting an effort in creating a continuous price curve for CDS contracts with maturities between < 1 and 10 years, the liquid market is strongly concentrated on medium-term contracts.[356] To date, there has only been modest trading activity and price quotation in markets for non-investment grade and small- and mid cap credit names, although there are efforts under way which can have the potential to increase the liquidity in these segments.[357]

---

[352] See BBA (2003/2004), p. 17 et seq.

[353] See BIS (2004d), p. 1 and BBA (2003/2004), p. 5

[354] See BIS (2004b), p. 14. According to an unpublished estimate by McKinsey & Company, the top 300 names within the group of reference entities on which CDS are traded account for approximately 84% of trading activity. Most of this trading activity is even further concentrated in the top 100 names

[355] See Schüler (2003)

[356] Credit derivatives with very short (< 1 year) and very long (> 5 years) maturities are relatively rare; whereas maturities between 1 and 5 years account for 75% of all trades; see BBA (2003/2004), p. 24

[357] Since the beginning of 2005, HypoVereinsbank continuously quotes 5-year CDS prices on all German corporations included in the DAX, thus creating a liquid credit market in the entire DAX. segment. This allows market participants, among other things, to perform credit index trading in the DAX. It is aimed to expand the approach to medium-sized corporations that are, e.g., listed in the MDAX segment. The pricing for names without liquid bonds that usually provide reference spreads for the CDS prices is based on an internal shadow rating process combined with a Merton pricing approach; see Johannsen (2005)

3.3 Securitization

3.3.1 Definition and classification

In a general sense, securitizations are transactions through which heterogeneous, often illiquid individual assets or claims on these assets are aggregated and tranches of homogeneous tradable securities, secured by these assets, are issued.[358]. The main motivation for these transactions is, on the one hand, to refinance credit exposures as an alternative to acquiring funding through traditional bank debt and, on the other hand, to transfer the risks of the underlying assets.[359] Furthermore, balance sheet and capital management (in particular the reduction of regulatory capital committed to support loan portfolios) are key driving forces for these structures.[360] In principle, all kinds of assets can be used as a basis for a securitization transaction.[361]

The key element of a securitization is typically a so-called SPV. This is a legal entity founded with the exclusive purpose of acquiring the underlying physical assets or claims on the assets and to issue homogeneous tranches of securities with different creditworthiness that are secured by this asset pool.[362] The SPV is usually owned or controlled by the originator but is supposed to have an independent management. This independence, together with its exclusive business purpose, ensures that the SPV will not be liable for claims other than from its securities holders.[363]

The original asset owner (originator/creditor of the assets) has two alternatives regarding how to transfer the asset risks to the SPV:

In the traditional form of a securitization transaction (cash-based securitization), the assets are sold to the SPV. In this case, they disappear from the originator's balance sheet. In case of the originator's bankruptcy, creditors are not able to draw on the assets any more – the structure is "bankruptcy remote". After having sold the assets, the originator can either provide a liability to the SPV for payment defaults stemming from the assets or exclude such a responsibility, thus transferring the default risks to the investors. In the first case, this is a so-called recourse or fully-guaranteed

358 Rating agencies typically provide a credit rating for the different tradable tranches; see, for example, Gehring (1997), p. 27

359 See Hartmann-Wendels, Pfingsten et al. (2004), p. 262 and Ambrose, LaCour-Little et al. (2003), p. 1

360 See Das (2000), p. 128

361 The type of securitization introduced here is often referred to as asset securitization; see Poppensieker (2002), p. 59

362 See Hill (1996), p. 1067. The legal form of the SPV can be a corporation, a partnership or, as it is most frequently the case, a trust. See Gehring (1997), p. 18 et seqq. for the legal structure of SPVs under US law and Gehring (1997), § 11 for the relevant acts under German law. For a discussion on whether an SPV constitutes a financial institution according to the KWG, see Gehring (1997), § 13

363 See Schwazcz (2002)

transaction, in the latter case the transaction is a "true sale".[364] True sale transactions will also be referred to as "cash-based" transactions in the following section.

The creditworthiness of true sale transactions is often improved through so-called credit enhancements. These are guarantees by a third party (external enhancements) or by the originator (internal enhancements) protecting against the default risks for a part of the asset portfolio. External enhancements such as letters of credit or bond insurances are commonly granted by banks or credit insurers that are interested in investing in credit risks. The originator can improve the credit quality of the assets (internal enhancements) by, e.g., providing a cash collateral to cover initial portfolio losses or through over-collateralization. Over-collateralization means selling the assets under their market value to the SPV so that the repayments from the assets are higher than necessary to serve the issued tranches.[365]

As an alternative to selling the assets, the originator can remain their owner and keep them on its balance sheet. In this case, the originator's creditors can draw on the securities in case of default. Despite not selling the assets physically, however, the originator can use credit derivatives to transfer the asset risks, i.e., payment claims from the assets and/or their appreciation or depreciation, to the SPV. Such a transaction is called synthetic securitization. As shown in chapter 3.2 and particularly in Figure 21, these instruments can also be interpreted as repackaged and tranched derivatives.

The SPV issuing the tranched securities is typically supported by a bank consortium when placing them among investors. The administration of the "original" assets underlying the tranched securities – in particular loan monitoring and collection of claims – is often performed by an external agent.

Payments from the underlying assets (i.e., interest and principal repayments) to investors in the securitized tranches can be made via a so-called "pass-trough" or "pay-through" procedures. In the first case, the payments are directly transferred ("passed through") to the investors.[366] In a pay-through instrument, the SPV manages the cash flows so that investors receive payments according to the respective asset tranche they own.[367]

[364] See Gehring (1997), § 4 for a description of bankruptcy clauses for securitizations under US law as well as § 16 for the respective regulation under German law. For issues related to bankruptcy remote entities and true sales transactions, see also Broome, Markell et al. (2004), § 3.03

[365] See Poppensieker (2002), p. 75 and Anson, Chen et al. (2004), p. 138. Strictly spoken, if the originator takes over default guarantees for the asset portfolio through internal credit enhancements, this is a dilution of the true sale principle

[366] See, e.g., Lowell (2001a) for a comprehensive overview of Mortgage Pass-Through Securities, i.e., tranched pass-through securities which have mortgage loans as their underlying assets

[367] See Hartmann-Wendels, Pfingsten et al. (2004), p. 265 et seq.

Due to the complexity of securitizations, such transactions are only estimated to be profitable if they comprise a sufficient asset volume of at least EUR 25 million.[368]

Depending on the assets underlying a securitization transaction, one can distinguish between three types of securitization instruments:[369]

Although, according to the definition at the beginning of this chapter, the term Asset Backed Securities (ABS) refers to all types of assets, it is typically used for securitizations based on an underlying pool of consumer loans.[370] Mortgage Backed Securities (MBS) have real estate loans as their underlying assets.[371] Collateralized Debt Obligations (CDOs), finally, are instruments, in which the SPV issues securities against an underlying pool of bonds, corporate loans or a mixture of both.[372]

As a wholesale loan portfolio primarily consists of loans to corporations and financial institutions as well as of commercial real estate loans (see above chapter 1.4.1), securitizations referring to consumer loans (ABS in the narrow definition) will not be the focus in the following section.

3.3.2 CDOs

Depending on whether CDOs refer to an underlying loan or bond portfolio, it is differentiated between Collateralized Loan Obligations (CLOs) and Collateralized Bond Obligations (CBOs). Firstly, two types of "traditional" cash-based CDO instruments are introduced before synthetic CDOs, including their advantages over their cash-based counterparts, are described.

3.3.2.1 Cash-based CDOs

Figure 26 describes the typical payment structure of a cash-based CDO transaction. Cash-based CDOs can be structured as balance sheet or arbitrage CDOs.

368 See Ohl (1994), p. 263 et seqq. who also lists typical costs of a securitization transaction

369 See Hartmann-Wendels, Pfingsten et al. (2004), p. 265, table G2-2

370 Depending on the type of underlying claims, it is distinguished between Consumer Loan ABS, Credit Card ABS, Leasing ABS, etc.; see, e.g., Kane (2001)

371 A comprehensive overview of MBS can be found in Hayre (2001) and Fabozzi (2001)

372 See Anson, Chen et al. (2004), p. 132

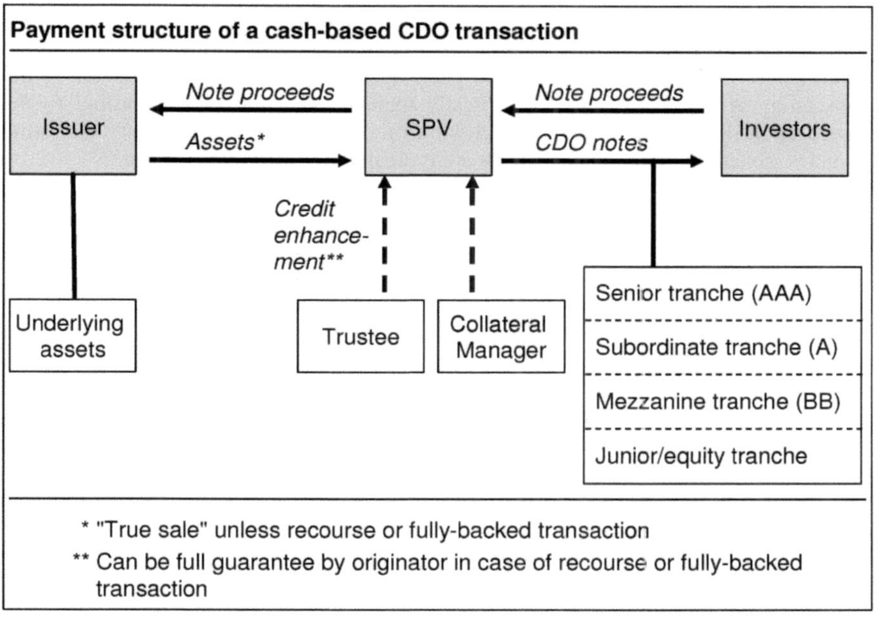

Figure 26: Payment structure of a cash-based CDO transaction[373]

3.3.2.1.1 Balance sheet CDOs

Balance sheet CDOs are typically set up in the form of CLOs. They are designed to remove commercial loans from an originator's balance sheet to an SPV which issues different tranches of securities (notes) that are backed by the loans. Banks and other financial institutions are main issuers of these transactions. Unless the issuer guarantees the underlying assets' payments (recourse or fully-backed transaction), the credit risks associated with the assets are transferred to the holders of the issued notes (true sale transaction). The proceeds from issuing the notes are transferred through the SPV to the originator. Performing such a transaction can help the issuer to increase its return on capital if removing lower-yielding assets from its balance sheet. Furthermore, it can free up lending capacity or reduce regulatory capital requirements.[374]

[373] Source: Own illustration based on Anson, Chen et al. (2004), p. 135 Exhibit 7.2

[374] See Duffie and Garleanu (2001), p. 4

Balance Sheet CDOs are usually designed as cash flow CDOs, i.e., the cash flows generated by the underlying assets are used to pay interest and principal on the issued securities as well as to reimburse third-party agents for their activities related to the transaction. A collateral manager typically manages the portfolio according to the agreed-upon investment guidelines and within the limits required to satisfy the rating agencies. External credit enhancements are typically provided by a Trustee.[375]

The issued securities differ in their external credit ratings. The biggest portion of the issued volume (approximately 90-95%) is usually packaged in a senior note (tranche) which has the highest credit rating. Besides the senior tranche, there are typically several subordinate tranches with accordingly lower credit ratings or without rating. The senior tranche is given preference with regard to cash flows from the underlying assets – no other tranche is granted payments until the senior tranche has been fully paid should there not be sufficient funds available to pay all tranches. After reimbursement of the senior tranche, the subordinate tranches are serviced following a set of compliance tests confirming that the respective tranches have been able to keep their credit rating. The so-called junior or equity tranche bears the greatest credit risk component as it is the first tranche to absorb losses.[376]

3.3.2.1.2 Arbitrage CDOs

While the main purpose of balance sheet CDOs is the removal of assets from an originator's balance sheet, the issuance of arbitrage CDOs aims at exploiting a yield differential between the acquisition cost for the underlying assets and the sale of the associated CDO structure, including management fees. Arbitrage CDOs are often set up in the form of CBOs. Underlying assets are typically lower-rated bonds, commercial bank loans, high-yield debt, and emerging market sovereign bonds.

Regarding asset transfer, notes issuance, payment priority and credit enhancements, arbitrage CDOs usually have the same structure as balance sheet CDOs. Besides being organized as cash flow CDOs, however, they are often organized as market value CDOs and have an actively traded collateral pool whose market value is determined (marked to market) on a daily basis. In the latter case, the quality of the collateral pool, in particular with regard to its weighted average credit rating, concentration, and asset diversity is regularly monitored and, if necessary, adjustments to the portfolio composition are made.[377]

In recent years, arbitrage CDOs have outgrown balance-sheet CDOs.[378]

375 See Anson, Chen et al. (2004), p. 133 and p. 136 as well as McDermott (2001), p. 665

376 See Anson, Chen et al. (2004), p. 136 and p. 137 Exhibit 7.3

377 See Duffie and Garleanu (2001), p. 4

378 See BIS (2003b), p. 12

3.3.2.2 Synthetic CDOs

In contrast to the cash-based CDO structures described above, synthetic CDOs are instruments transferring risks related to an asset pool without physically moving the underlying assets. By means of credit derivatives, the originator (protection buyer) transfers the payment claims and/or value changes from a loan or bond portfolio to an SPV. It is differentiated between multiple- and single-tranche synthetic CDOs.

3.3.2.2.1 Multiple-tranche synthetic CDOs

As in the case of cash-based CDOs, in multiple-tranche synthetic CDOs the SPV issues different tranches of securities based on the synthetically transferred payment streams and possibly additionally secured through credit enhancements.[379]

The type of risks transferred through such a transaction solely depends on the type of credit derivatives used for the deal. While, default risks are transferred, for example, through the use of default instruments such as CDS, the spread instruments enable the transfer of spread risks. By means of TRS, interest rate risks can be transferred. It is because of the counterparty risks inherent in credit derivatives contracts that an additional risk component is inherent in synthetic CDOs.[380]

Depending on the type of credit derivatives applied, multiple-tranche synthetic CDOs can be fully-funded, unfunded or partially-funded.

Fully-funded synthetic CDOs can be regarded as an enhancement of First-to-Default CLNs based on a pool of a large amount of reference assets. They transfer the entire credit risk of the underlying portfolio to an SPV. The SPV, in turn, issues different tranches of notes to the underlying value and invests the proceeds from these notes in risk free assets. These investments are used to compensate for possible losses in the asset portfolio. Yet, fully-funded synthetic CDOs are relatively uncommon.[381]

In unfunded synthetic CDO transactions, risks are exclusively transferred through unfunded derivatives, e.g., CDS. The senior tranches of the transaction are usually acquired by an AAA-rated counterparty. Another counterparty with lower creditworthiness acquires more junior tranches. The originator usually retains a first loss "equity" tranche.[382]

---

379 See Anson, Chen et al. (2004), p. 140. Coleman and Viala (2000) give an introduction to CDOs focusing on synthetic transactions

380 This additional risk component is frequently minimized through credit enhancements or cash reserves within the SPV; see Poppensieker (2002), p. 79. Risks inherent in derivatives transactions will be covered in greater detail in chapter 3.4.3

381 See Anson, Chen et al. (2004), p. 128 et seq, p. 155, p. 156 Exhibit 7.12 and p. 143. Bakalar and Prince (2003), p. 5 Exhibit 5 describe a typical structure of a funded CDO

382 See Anson, Chen et al. (2004), p. 157 Exhibit 7.13

Partially-funded CDO transactions are hybrids between fully-funded and unfunded CDOs. They have become increasingly common in recent years. There are typically two types of derivatives transferring risks in a partially-funded CDO structure: a CDS transfers the most senior tranche – accounting for around 85% of the underlying capital structure – in an unfunded form typically to a single, highly rated investor.[383] The remaining part of the risk is transferred by means of CLNs with different creditworthiness. These notes are typically purchased by various investors. The highest-ranked CLN typically has an AAA credit rating. As the CDS is ranked higher than the CLN – hence having an even lower default probability – it is referred to as a super-senior swap.

The issuance proceeds from the CLNs can either be passed on to the originator or invested in a risk-free collateral pool owned by the SPV. In the first case, the originating institution receives funding for its credit assets. In the second case, the proceeds from the collateral pool are used to cover payments to the notes investors. Thus, the investors are not affected by a possible downgrade or default of the originator; they are protected against the counterparty risks of the transaction. Their exposure is reduced to the credit risks included in the reference assets. The originator pays a credit premium to the super-senior investor as well as through the SPV to the notes investors according to their investment size and the amount of risks they have taken on. The cash flow distribution for the notes investors depends on the creditworthiness of their notes – similar to cash-based CDOs. In the case of a credit event on a reference entity, the originator receives a settlement payment from the CDS protection. The respective losses need to be borne by the investors according to the creditworthiness of their acquired tranche. Figure 27 describes a typical partially-funded synthetic CDO transaction.[384]

383 Typical investors ("super-senior investors") in these tranches are monoline insurance companies; see Bakalar and Prince (2003), p. 8

384 The transaction includes a collateral pool

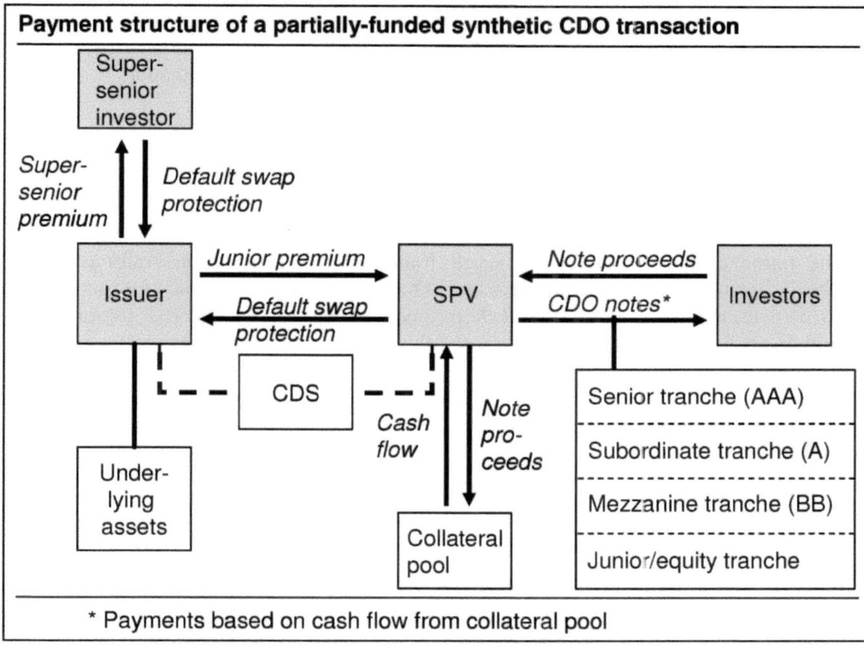

Figure 27: Payment structure of a partially-funded synthetic CDO transaction[385]

The synthetic CDO transactions described so far are typical balance sheet transactions, with the originator collecting interest payments and fees from assets sitting on its balance sheet. Similar to cash-flow CDOs, there is also the possibility to structure synthetic arbitrage CDOs. One way an originator can structure these transactions is through replicating the asset portfolio by means of a CDS instead of having "real" assets as an underlying. In this case, the originator needs to believe that it is more economical to acquire credit risks by selling a portfolio of CDS than by buying and managing a cash asset portfolio. Alternatively, a portfolio of bonds can be bought whose default risk is subsequently mitigated by the CDO. The arbitrage opportunity arises if the spreads on the underlying assets are actually wider than guaranteed by the cost of transferring the portfolio's default risk.[386]

---

[385] Source: own illustration based on Bakalar and Prince (2003), p. 9 Exhibit 5 and Anson, Chen et al. (2004), p. 153 Exhibit 7.10.

[386] See Bakalar and Prince (2003), p. 9 and Goodman (2002), p. 9

The increasingly liquid CDS market has recently led to the emergence of managed synthetic CDOs. These are mostly partly-funded synthetic transactions. Their pool of underlying assets is not static but actively managed by a collateral manager.[387]

3.3.2.2.2 Single-tranche synthetic CDOs

Single-tranche synthetic CDO transactions have been on the market since the beginning of 2003. Their basic structure is very similar to that of multiple-tranche CDOs.[388]

As the name already suggests, in single-tranche CDO transactions only one risk tranche is created and sold to an investor. They are rather individual transactions as investors can customize them around their specific credit views and risk tolerance. In particular, an investor typically determines the desired level of exposure to a certain credit pool of his choice and defines characteristics such as issuance currency, subordination, credit rating, etc. in return for a premium payment. This customization has the advantage that there are no conflicts of interest between senior, mezzanine, and equity investors.[389]

A single-tranche CDO is a multi-layered financial derivative: the tranche itself is a derivative of its underlying reference pool, while the chosen reference pool is a derivative of its underlying asset portfolio.

Similar to multiple-tranche synthetic CDOs, single-tranche synthetic transactions can be structured as funded transactions through CLNs issued by an SPV. Alternatively, these deals can take on an unfunded form by transferring risks through a CDS between the originator and the SPV or directly between the originator and the investor. Despite usually transferring only a part of an originator's portfolio risk, single-tranche transactions often offer higher levels of diversification than multiple-tranche CDOs: they typically refer to around 100-125 credit names compared to approximately 60-100 names in multiple-tranche CDOs. In contrast to multiple-tranche CDOs, however, the issuer of a single-trance CDO is required to hedge (i.e., replicate) the risk transferred to the investor in such a product. This is due to the fact that under single-name CDOs there is no longer a complete set of claims against an asset pool.

387 See Anson, Chen et al. (2004), p. 159 et seqq. who describe characteristics of managed synthetic CDOs in greater detail

388 Whetten and Adelson (2004) give a comprehensive description of single-tranche synthetic CDOs. See also Bakalar and Prince (2003), p. 21 et seq.

389 Multiple-tranche CDOs, which place the risk of an entire capital structure – i.e., across all levels of creditworthiness – to different investors, often face the difficulty that the equity investor exerts strong influence on the choice of the credit assets. This often leads to a riskier, higher-yielding portfolio structure than requested by the other investors; see Bakalar and Prince (2003), p. 21

Consequently, the issuer is confronted with default and default correlation risk as well as the risk that the recovery rate used to value the transaction is not correct.[390]

The most common maturity of single-name CDOs is 5 years, reflecting the most liquid maturity in the CDS market (see again chapter 3.2.4).

The underlyings of most single-tranche synthetic CDOs are static portfolios. It was only in the beginning of 2004 that managed transactions were issued, with the underlying portfolios typically being managed by a third-party asset manager. It is also common that investors use computer models to hedge the impacts of spread changes or changes in the default probability on the value of their single tranche. By means of these models, they can determine, for example, to which extent single-name or index CDS need to be bought in order for the portfolio to be protected against these movements.[391]

It is assumed that single-tranche synthetic CDOs have meanwhile outnumbered their multiple-tranche counterparts.[392]

3.3.2.3 Advantages of synthetic over cash-based CDOs

Synthetic CDOs can have significant advantages over cash-based structures both for originators and investors. They offer the benefit that credit risks related to assets which cannot be removed from an originator's balance sheet – be it due to relationship reasons towards a customer or due to legal restrictions such as in the case of bank guarantees – can nevertheless be transferred. As credit derivatives can be tailored to meet specific needs of the originator, synthetic CDOs offer more flexibility than cash-based transactions. Besides this, under a partially-funded synthetic CDO, the bulge of the credit risks within the reference portfolio is transferred via an AAA-rated CDS derivative which does not need to be funded. This makes the issuance of a synthetic CDO cheaper compared to cash-based CDOs where originators would have to issue

---

390 In particular measuring and managing the default correlation risk requires sophisticated risk management skills, see, e.g., Smithson (2004)

391 Such hedge transactions used to neutralize the impact of spread changes on the value of a tranche are referred to as "delta hedges"

According to a general definition, delta hedging is a hedging scheme designed to make the price of a derivative portfolio insensitive to small changes in the price of the underlying asset. The delta of a derivative is the ratio of the change in its price to the change in the price of the underlying asset. Delta hedges are dynamic hedging schemes, i.e., they need to be adjusted because the delta of an underlying changes following a price movement of the underlying; see Hull (2006), p. 251 et seq. and p. 344 et seqq. Due to the still less-than-perfect liquidity of the CDS market, the hedging of single-tranche CDOs has its limitations, however; see Gibson (2004), p. 20 et seq.

392 See Gibson (2004), p. 19 and BIS (2004b), p. 13

and fund bonds for the entire underlying portfolio. Hence, originators can benefit from saving funding cost and reinvesting the funds into the risk-free collateral pool.[393]

Investors also benefit from entering synthetic over cash-flow CDO transactions as the synthetic structures can be better tailored to provide customized risk-return profiles. Furthermore, investments in the CDS protection of a synthetic CDO yield higher returns than acquiring the underlying cash bonds in a cash-based transaction. This is due to the fact that the spread of the CDS on a certain credit name is typically higher than the respective cash spread.[394]

3.3.3 MBS

As described above, MBS are securities that have real estate assets as their underlying. Before describing MBS, however, it is necessary to introduce Asset-Backed Bonds (ABBs) which share some similarities with MBS. Therefore, the next section gives a brief overview of ABBs and demarcates them from MBS which will be described afterwards.

3.3.3.1 Demarcation of ABBs from MBS

ABBs or covered bonds are bonds whose payments are secured through a collateral asset pool on the originator's balance sheet. In the case of the issuer's bankruptcy, holders of ABBs have a preferential claim to these assets including their cash flows. Apart from the existence of such collateral, ABBs are identical to plain vanilla bonds. Thus, financial institutions can use these instruments as tools to refinance their lending activities. Since the collateral assets as well as related cash flow payments are not transferred to the holders of the ABBs, the issuing institution does not transfer its credit risks related to these assets.[395]

ABBs have a significantly higher credit rating compared to the unsecured debt of the issuing institution; the majority of these instruments are rated AA or AAA. This is due to the fact that regulation allows only mortgages and public debt instruments to be used as collateral. Moreover, in order to minimize mismatches between ABBs and

---

393 See Anson, Chen et al. (2004), p. 147 for a concrete example as well as Exhibit 7.7 for a schematic comparison between a cash flow and a partially-funded synthetic CDO

394 This higher yield, of course, is related to a higher risk. For example, the credit risk typically covered by a CDS includes trigger events such as restructuring of an underlying asset that are not pure default scenarios; see the ISDA definitions for credit events in chapter 3.2.2. Hence, investors run the risk of facing an investment loss for events other than pure default. Anson, Chen et al. (2004), p. 148 list more reasons for the spread differences

On p. 150 – 152, Anson, Chen et al. (2004) discuss advantages of synthetic and cash CDO structures. Bakalar and Prince (2003), p. 11, Exhibit 8 give a comprehensive comparison of a typical cash-based CDO with a typical synthetic CDO

395 See Poppensieker (2002), p. 66 et seq.

their collateral, the structure of the underlying asset pool has to match the structure of the outstanding bonds regarding currency denomination, outstanding amount, interest payments and maturity. Another factor contributing to the high creditworthiness of these instruments is their bankruptcy remoteness: In the case of the issuer's bankruptcy, the bonds, including their corresponding collateral, are removed from the insolvent entity's balance sheet in order to be run as a separate fund.[396]

3.3.3.2 Excursus: German "Pfandbriefe"

German "Pfandbriefe" are the oldest type of ABBs. In Germany, the issuance of these securities was first regulated in 1899 through the introduction of the mortgage banking act "Hypothekenbankgesetz".[397] This act allows mortgage banks[398] to refinance their lending activities to private and commercial real estate borrowers as well as to public debtors through issuance of Pfandbriefe. Thereby, these institutions need to comply to the regulation that the net present value of the collateral needs to be as high as 102% of the net present value of the issued securities. For real estate loans, the ratio of loan to collateral value is limited to 60%.[399] The PfandBG (2005) allows all banks that have successfully acquired a concession from the BaFin to issue Pfandbriefe.[400]

In Germany, Pfandbriefe represent the majority of all bonds issued and have a market share of approximately 35%.[401] Besides Germany, virtually all the major European states have meanwhile enacted laws allowing the issuance of covered bonds similar to the restrictive German standards.[402] However, with a volume share of more than 72%

---

396 See Anhamm (2004)

397 Besides the HypBK regulating the issuance of "Pfandbriefe" for real estate banks, the ship banking act "Schiffsbankgesetz" as of 1927 allowed the issuance of Pfandbriefe for the private ship financing banks. Furthermore, the public covered bond banking law "Öffentliches Pfandbriefgesetz" permitted public banks to issue these securities; see VDH (2004), p. 13 for an overview

Following the abolishment of the the owners' statutory obligation ("Gewährträgerhaftung") and maintenance obligation ("Anstaltslast") for public banks as of July 2005, there was the need to bring the "Öffentliches Pfandbriefgesetz" into accordance with the HypBG (2004). Consequently, a draft for a new act (PfandBG (2005)) has been submitted to the German Ministry of Finance, incorporating the key elements of the HypBG (2004)

398 §§ 1 and 5 HypBG (2004) currently regulate the permitted business activities for mortgage banks

399 See §§ 6 and 11 HypBG (2004)

400 See § 2 PfandBG (2005) as well as N.N (2005a)

401 See VDH (2004), p. 6, table1. Public bonds constitute around 75%, mortgage bonds around 25% of the entire outstanding German Pfandbrief volume

402 See VDH (2004), p. 36 et seqq. for an overview of acts regulating the issuance of covered bonds in Europe. Anhamm (2004), p. 12 sets the volume of German Public and Mortgage Pfandbriefe in relation to the volumes of related covered bonds in Europe

in the EU market, German Pfandbriefe still constitute by far the majority of the covered bond securities issued.[403]

In order to achieve a similarly liquid market for Pfandbriefe as for Government Bonds, the German private mortgage banks brought the so-called "Jumbo-Pfandbriefe" into being, starting in 1995 and 1996. According to the revised standards for Jumbo Pfandbriefe as of May 2004, a Pfandbrief needs to fulfill certain criteria in order to be qualified as a Jumbo Pfandbrief: most importantly, it needs to have a fixed coupon, its nominal volume needs to be at least as high as EUR 1 billion, and at least three consortium banks need to commit themselves to perform market making during fixed trading times, i.e., to quote bid and ask prices for other market participants.[404] Since their introduction, Jumbo Pfandbriefe have been extremely successful, with the German market for these instruments having bid-ask spreads, which are almost as narrow as the ones for Government Bonds.[405] Today, Jumbo Pfandbriefe constitute around 40% of the entire German Pfandbrief volume.[406] Propelled by growing internationalization within Europe, the growth of the Jumbo segment is expected to continue with a two-digit percentage rate per year.[407] German Jumbo Pfandbriefe have a market share of approximately 70% in the EU-wide Jumbo segment.[408]

3.3.3.3 MBS

Like ABBs, MBS can also be used to raise funds in order to refinance the acquisition of real estate assets. As opposed to the covered bonds, however, MBS are suitable to support the management of credit risks as they can also be used to transfer real-estate related credit risks from the originator's balance sheet. Like ABS in general, MBS are repackaged and tranched securities whose most senior tranches, having AAA to AA long-term credit ratings, guarantee a similar risk-free investment as investments in ABBs.

Two types of MBS can be distinguished: on the one hand there are residential MBS (RMBS), typically bundling and securitizing a large number of private real estate loans, each of which having comparably low volumes. Commercial MBS (CMBS), on the other hand, pool a smaller number of commercial real estate loans with comparably higher individual volumes. Underlying collateral of CMBS can be loans on retail and office properties, industrial estate and hotels, for example.[409]

---

403 See VDH (2004), p. 20, figure 1

404 See VDH (2004), p. 41 et seqq. for the requirements for Jumbo Pfandbriefe with a particular focus on market making

405 See VDH (2004), p. 44, Table 2

406 See again VDH (2004), p. 6, table1

407 See Packmohr, Mächtlinger et al. (2003)

408 See VDH (2004), p. 21, Figure 2

409 See Sanders (2001) and Sanders (2001; Wheeler (2001) for a comprehensive overview on CMBS

Transaction structures of MBS are very similar to those of the CDOs mentioned above. Besides securitizing the real estate assets by means of a true sale to an SPV – often supported by credit enhancements – the originator can sell the respective credit risks in a synthetic transaction using credit derivatives. While true sale MBS structures are most common in Europe (> 90% market share), the German MBS market is dominated by synthetic MBS transactions.[410] In the US, it is differentiated between private and agency MBS. While the first ones are issued and/or guaranteed by private financial institutions, it is Government-sponsored Real Estate Agencies such as the Federal National Mortgage Association (Fannie Mae) and the Federal Home Loan Mortgage Corporation (Freddie Mac) which issue agency MBS.[411] Due to their higher liquidity, stronger guarantees, and preferential capital treatment, investors often prefer to hold agency MBS over holding corporate and municipal bonds.[412]

A popular type of agency MBS in the US mortgage market is Collateralized Mortgage Obligations (CMOs).[413] These instruments comprise several classes of bonds (tranches) that are all backed by the same mortgage collateral. The tranches are structured so that each of them has its own risk characteristic and maturity: while all tranches participate in interest payments stemming from the mortgage collateral, they have different ranks regarding timing of the principal repayments. Not before the so-called A-tranche has entirely been paid back, will principal repayments to a B-tranche will be started. In the end, the last principal payments flow to a so-called Z-tranche (or Z-Bond).[414]

410 This is mainly due to the reason that there has an appropriate legal framework for ABS transactions in Germany been established, nor have sophisticated transfer regulations for mortgage assets been passed; see VDH (2002), p. 6

411 See, e.g., Ely and Wallison (2000) who describe these Government-sponsored institutions carrying around 50% of the US residential mortgage risks

412 See Kelman (2002), p. 20 et seq.

413 CMOs were introduced in 1983 by Freddie Mac due to the prepayment uncertainty of MBS structures. The Tax Reform Act as of 1986 permitted CMOs to be issued in the form of Real Estate Mortgage Investment Conduits (REIMCs), providing tax and accounting advantages for issuers and investors; see Bond Market Association (2002), p. 1 and Kelman (2002), p. 22 et seq.

In practice, CMOs are used interchangeably with REMICs. While REMICs differ insignificantly for investors, they have different tax and regulatory characteristics for issuers than CMOs do; see Lehman Brothers (2001), p. 169

414 These instruments are typical pay-through structures (see the above-mentioned differentiation between pass-through and pay-through structures in chapter 3.3.1). While all other tranches are typically structured as bonds with regular interest payments, the Z-tranche is typically issued as a so-called zero-bond whose interest payments are withheld and invested until it is its turn to be repaid. This is why the Z-tranche is often referred to as "Accrued Interest Tranche". The Z-tranche effectively securitizes the equity of the SPV; see Hayre (2001), p. 47 et seq., Lehman Brothers (2001), p. 180 as well as Lowell (2001b) describing Z-Bonds in greater detail

CMOs allow originators to structure the interest and prepayment risks of their underlying mortgage assets.[415] These so-called agency CMOs do not transfer credit risk, however. Hence, agency CMOs can be defined as recourse or fully-backed ABS structures.

Besides agency CMOs, there are also non-agency or whole-loan CMOs which transfer credit risks. Their creditworthiness is typically rated by external rating agencies, with their long-term credit rating depending, e.g., on the type of underlying property, loan size, and purpose of the loan. External or internal credit enhancements are typically used to improve their creditworthiness.[416]

3.3.4 Market development

The regulation of the German Pfandbriefe in the beginning of the 20th century was a cornerstone in the development of securitized assets. In the meantime, Pfandbriefe have not only captured the biggest market share in the German fixed income securities market, they have also been introduced in other European markets through the enactment of legal acts allowing the introduction of covered bonds in German style.[417] While the German Pfandbrief market has seen a consolidation/slight decline in the outstanding volume of the "traditional" Pfandbrief in recent years,[418] the introduction and Europe-wide standardization of the "Jumbo" segment has been the key driver for the strong overall growth in the outstanding volume of 11% CAGR of European Pfandbriefe between 1996 and 2004. See Figure 28 for an illustration of the European securitization market.

---

415 Besides the instruments mentioned so far, there are also other sub-types of ABS allowing the structuring of interest rate and prepayment risk: Pass-through-Certificates directly transfer a share of the entire cash flow of each individual loan within a portfolio on to the investor without structuring the risk in different tranches. Stripped Pass-through-Certificates transfer a share of the interest or repayment claims only. Accordingly, it can be distinguished between Interest-Only Strips transferring participation in the interest claims and Principal-Only Strips transferring participation in the repayment claims. Together with CMOs, these instruments allow the structuring and transfer of interest and prepayment risks; see Hayre, Mohebbi et al. (2001) for a comprehensive description of stripped MBS

416 See Fabozzi, Sanders et al. (2001)

417 See, again, VDH (2004), p. 36 et seq. and Stöcker (2001). In order to create favourable general conditions for the European Covered Bond Market, The European Covered Bond Council was founded at the end of 2004. Having assembled 70 financial institutions as of November 2005, one of the main tasks of the Council is to set preconditions for a generally accepted definition of the Covered Bond supporting the creation of a functioning pan-European secondary market for these instruments; see N.N (2005b)

418 The main driver for this slight decline has been a reduced issuance of public Pfandbriefe; see VDH (2004), p. 6

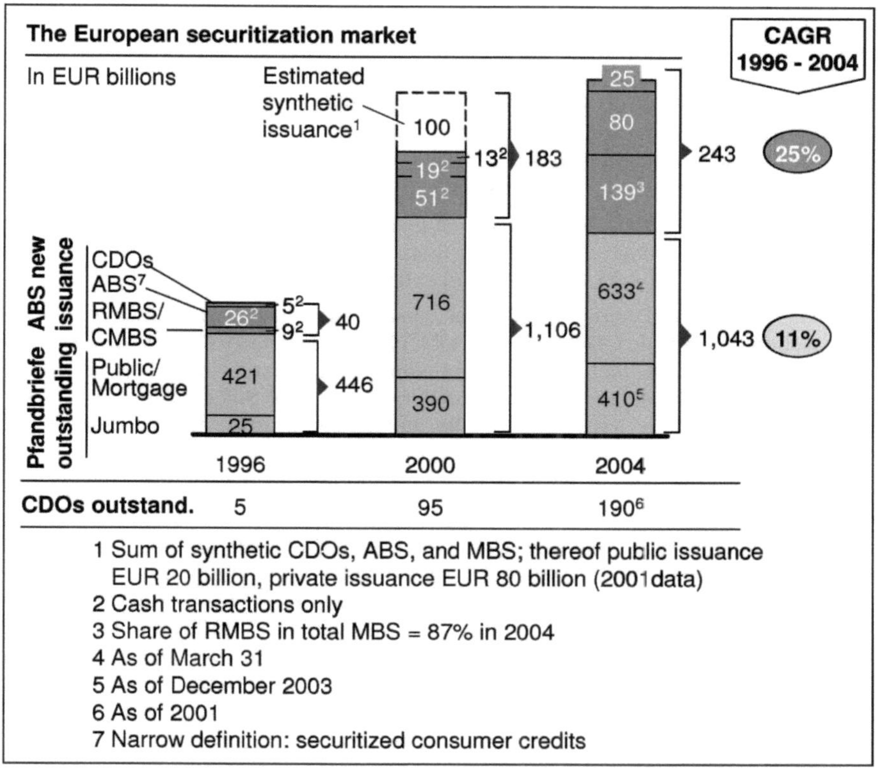

Figure 28: The European securitization market[419]

In the US, securitization was developed in the 1960s in order to facilitate the financing of residential mortgage loans.[420] The establishment and privatization of the above-mentioned Government-sponsored real estate agencies propelled this development.[421]

[419] Source: Own illustration based on VDH (2004), p. 6, table 1, VDH (2001), p. 8, figure 1, ESF (2005), BIS (2003c), p. 8, table 1b, p. 34 and p. 49 and Anson, Chen et al. (2004), p. 141, Exhibit 7.4

It is currently not possible to obtain consistent data on outstanding volumes in the European securitization market. Therefore, Figure 28 shows issuance instead of outstanding volumes for the different securitization instruments with the exception of German Pfandbriefe and CDOs

[420] See VDH (2002), p. 3

[421] See, again, Ely and Wallison (2000) and Hill (1996), Appendix D. These agencies were privatized in 1970 (Fannie Mae) and 1980 (Freddie Mac)

Furthermore, the MBS market was supported through the enactment of the Secondary Mortgage Market Enhancement Act (1984) and the Tax Reform Act (1986), allowing the introduction of Real Estate Mortgage Investment Conduits (REMICs) to facilitate the legal establishment of SPVs.[422] As of today, the outstanding volume of agency MBS has by far exceeded USD 3 trillion. Following the establishment of MBS, the first CMOs were introduced in 1983. Today, CMOs account for around 40% of all fixed-rate MBS outstanding.[423]

Parallel with the development of mortgage loan securitizations, consumer loans have been securitized through ABS transactions since the 1980s. Until today, the outstanding volume of ABS in the US market has risen to over USD 1 trillion.[424]

In 1988, the securitization of corporate loans and bonds was initiated.[425] The introduction of synthetic CDO structures took place in the late 1990s, mainly driven by the goal to circumvent the regulatory and administrative issues related to physically transferring assets by means of a cash-flow securitization.[426] Since its introduction, the synthetic CDO market has grown rapidly and is a key driver for the entire CDO volume augmentation.[427] Along with the continued growth of credit derivatives (see above chapter 3.2.4), this trend is expected to continue. Figure 29 illustrates the US securitization market.

Securitization structures were introduced in Europe in the 1990s but did not gain significant volumes until 1997/1998. Still today, the European market for securitizations is small compared to the world-wide volume.[428] Nevertheless, as can be seen in Figure 28, the issuance volumes in all types of securitization have been strongly growing in past years with a CAGR of 25% between 1996 and 2004 – albeit at comparably low volumes. Strongly growing synthetic securitization transactions

---

422 See Ambrose, LaCour-Little et al. (2003), p. 2

423 See Lehman Brothers (2001), p. 169

424 Securitized credit card and automobile loans have the biggest share in this volume; see and Bond Market Association (2004a)

425 See Anson, Chen et al. (2004), p. 131

426 The first transaction resembling today's synthetic CDO structures was BISTRO 1997-1, issued by JPMorgan; see Das (2000), p. 150 et seq. Before BISTRO 1997-1, there were some synthetic CDOs without a super-senior tranche, merely created to reduce regulatory charges of the issuing institution. An example of these transactions is SBC Glacier Finance Ltd., issued by Swiss Banking Cooperation; see Bakalar and Prince (2003), p. 3 et seq.

427 Not only are synthetic issuance volumes strongly growing (see Gibson (2004), p. 2 Figure 1), synthetic CDOs meanwhile make up the majority of number of transactions in the US, with a share of around two thirds in all CDO transactions (as of 2002; see Bakalar and Prince (2003), p. 5 Exhibit 2)

428 In 2002, the global outstanding volume of ABS transactions (according to the broad definition) was estimated at around USD 7 trillion with merely approximately EUR 550 billion stemming from Europe; see VDH (2002)

have contributed to this increase, with single-tranche CDOs gaining increasing importance.

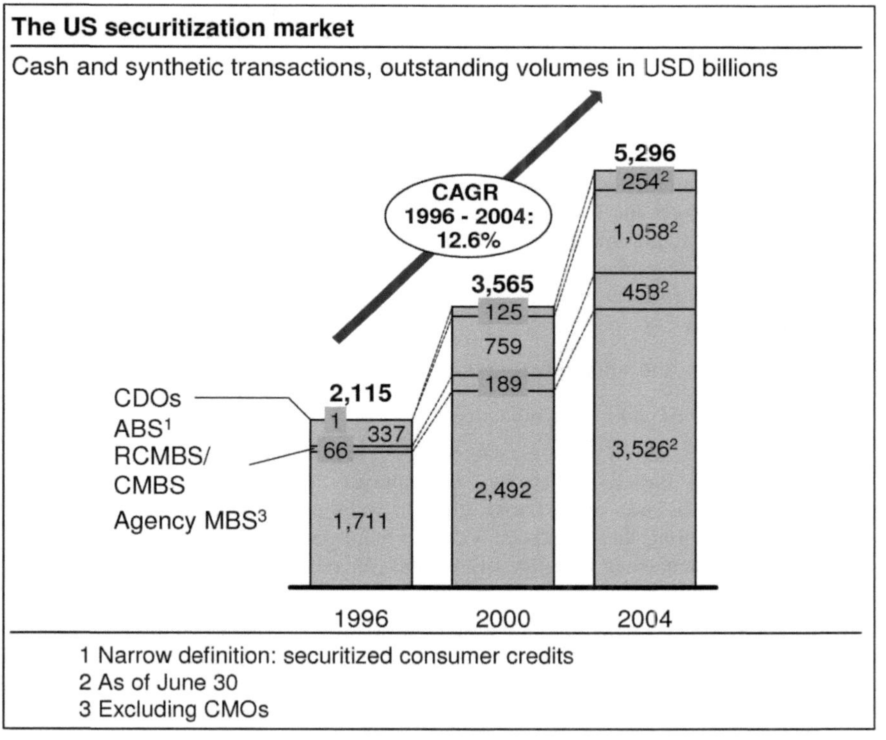

Figure 29: The US securitization market[429]

3.4 Comparison of secondary credit market instruments

The credit instruments introduced above enable an ACPM unit to buy and sell credit risks on the secondary loan markets so that an optimal portfolio composition can be achieved. Performing such secondary market transactions is of particular importance as banks mostly have only limited opportunities to manage their credit portfolios through the primary market side.[430]

[429] Source: Own illustration based on Bond Market Association (2004a) and Bond Market Association (2004b)

[430] See again chapter 2.3.2

As they have different characteristics and limitations regarding their ability to transfer credit risks as well as their quality to serve as refinancing tools, it is necessary to be aware of key differences between these instruments in order to ensure their proper application. It is also essential for portfolio managers to be aware of caveats when applying the instruments introduced before.

Therefore, in the following section a summary and comparison of the different instrument types depicted above will be given. A main focus will be on problems related to asymmetric information, additional risks inherent in these market transactions, and interdependencies between the different subtypes of secondary credit markets. Furthermore, the impact, which the application of these instruments has on regulatory capital requirements, will be briefly described. Figure 30 summarizes the comparison of the secondary credit market instruments by describing their methods of transferring credit risks as well as key issues to be considered when applying the instruments.

3.4.1 Methods and suitability to transfer credit risks

3.4.1.1 Loan sales and loan syndication

Through loan sales, an ACPM unit can transfer (acquire) credit assets together with their related risks directly to (from) other players. Loan syndication allows the distribution of credit risks on its books among several parties besides risk acquisition. A catalyst for enabling these kinds of portfolio management transactions has been the emergence and increasing liquidity of markets on which these instruments can be traded.

As illustrated above, credit derivatives are mostly OTC contracts tailored to fulfill specific requirements of the counterparties. They allow credit risks to be separated and disaggregated from other risk types. Credit derivative contracts are typically closed between the owner of the underlying assets and a third party without this third party acquiring a claim on the underlying assets. Therefore, as opposed to loan sales and loan syndication transactions, they offer a portfolio manager the opportunity to trade credit risks on secondary markets without the knowledge or consent of a particular customer, thus not endangering an existing customer relationship.[431] Besides this, as he is not required to physically sell credit assets, the portfolio manager can avoid a write-off on the asset should its market price have already declined.[432]

431 See Altman, Caouette et al. (1998), p. 305

432 There is the caveat, however, that in some cases hedging of a loan might require writing down the asset to the actual market price as well

Comparison of secondary credit market instruments

Instrument group	Method to transfer credit risks	Key issues to be considered when applying the instruments
Loan sales	• Direct risk transfer between contract parties	• Negative impact on customer relationship • Information asymmetries between seller and acquirer of credit asset • Seller might experience P&L hit due to need to write down assets to be sold
Loan syndication	• Transfer of risk exposures between syndication members	• Information asymmetries between arranger and participating lenders in syndicate
Credit derivatives	• Risk transfer between protection buyer and seller without affection of protection buyer's customer relationship and independent of underlying asset's maturity • Direct and indirect risk transfer also possible in illiquid cash loan markets	• Information asymmetries between – Borrower and lender – Lender and protection seller • Relatively strict requirements need to be fulfilled in order to be considered for regulatory capital relief
Securitization	• Direct and indirect risk transfer (except for covered bonds and recourse structures) • Synthetic transactions allow risk transfer without physical sale of assets	• Information asymmetries between risk shedder and investors • Unfavorable regulatory capital treatment for sub-investment grade tranches expected under "Basle II"

Figure 30: Comparison of secondary credit market instruments

Selling off an asset whose credit quality has surprisingly deteriorated could impede a long-term investment strategy, e.g., given that the long-term outlook is positive despite an expected deterioration in the short run. Therefore, an alternative solution to selling the asset could be to purchase protection for a certain period of time by, e.g., entering into a CDS transaction. In case the credit quality of the underlying deteriorates, the CDS contract gains value and offsets losses on the asset held.

3.4.1.2 Credit derivatives

Chapter 3.2.4 has shown that the importance of credit derivatives as instruments for ACPM is rising. There are several reasons for the increasing relevance of credit derivatives for actively managing loan portfolios:

By means of credit derivatives, it is also possible to gain exposure to a particular sector that does not have a liquid market for bank loans. These instruments can also be used to reduce the risk exposure to entire sectors or gain exposure to sectors an institution cannot or does not want to have a cash exposure to. This can be achieved, for instance, through entering into index derivatives contracts such as index TRS transactions. Given the swap refers to a certain sector, it is possible for the owner of a credit portfolio to gain or reduce credit exposure to this sector.[433]

As they are mostly off-balance sheet instruments,[434] credit derivatives enable a portfolio manager to obtain a credit risk exposure while at the same time avoiding the administrative costs of owning the respective underlying assets. Besides this, these instruments also offer portfolio managers the flexibility with regard to timing of transactions as their maturity is not linked to that of their underlying assets.

Finally, through enabling the market price of credit assets to be determined, e.g., by means of the CDS price curve mentioned above, credit derivatives can help to perform loan sales transactions. In the same way, these instruments can support an origination BU by providing benchmark prices for credit assets to be acquired.[435]

However, there are also pessimistic views on the importance and suitability of credit derivatives to support portfolio management in transferring credit risks. According to an empirical study by Azarchs (2003), credit derivatives have so far not met the expectations that market participants had set in these instruments. She estimates that less than 5% of the entire outstanding notional volume represents a credit risk transfer from banks to other market participants. While it is often believed that commercial banks use credit derivatives in order to hedge their credit risks, in reality these banks act as dealers of credit derivatives like the large investment banks and use credit derivatives to offset positions of protection they had previously bought and sold on behalf of their clients. Azarchs (2003) estimates that there are only 17 institutions

---

433 For a detailed description of applications of credit derivatives see Choudhry (2004a), chapter four, as well as Choudhry (2004b). Anson, Chen et al. (2004), p. 3 et seq. give an overview on the role of credit derivatives in financial markets. BIS (2004b), p. 54 et seqq. describes applications of index credit derivatives

434 As shown above, some credit derivatives, such as CLN, are linked to bonds or other fixed-income instruments. In this case, a part of the instrument has an on-balance sheet element

435 This does not only become relevant when determining prices for originated loans but in particular when setting internal transfer prices for credit assets transferred from origination to ACPM; see Hayt and Smithson (2000b), p. 43. The asset transfer mechanism to ACPM together with the related pricing mechanism will be described in greater detail in chapter 4.4.5.1 of part III

worldwide dominating the credit derivatives business.[436] Furthermore, she finds that the credit risks transferred from the banking system are mainly investment grade, having the effect that the remaining risks on the banks' books increasingly shift towards riskier non-investment grade levels. One reason for this characteristic is that derivatives contracts in the non-investment grade sector are often too expensive compared to acquiring or selling the respective credit asset. Consequently, it is argued that credit derivatives could not really help banks to reduce the massive loan losses they faced in recent years.

3.4.1.3 Securitization

The securitization instruments described above have different features concerning their ability to transfer credit risks:

ABBs/Pfandbriefe and recourse/fully-backed structures do not transfer credit risks at all. They can be used to obtain collateralized refinancing for loan exposures as well as for management of interest and pre-payment risks instead.

The other types of multiple-tranche securitization instruments introduced before (including non-agency CMOs) allow the transfer of credit risks through tranches with unique risk-return characteristics. By deciding which parts of its portfolio are to be sold off, the issuing institution can determine to which extent it wants to shed and transfer credit risks to counterparties. In particular, it is possible to either hold the highest-risk equity tranche or sell it off to another party.

Cash-based securitization structures are similar to loans sales/syndication insofar as they transfer tranches of credit risks in line with transferring the underlying assets from the originator's balance sheet.

Synthetic transactions allow – due their derivatives component – the transfer of risks related to credit assets without the need to physically transfer the assets, thus avoiding the issues related to a physical sale of credit assets. Besides this, synthetic instruments are less expensive to set up and execute than cash-based transactions are.[437] As shown above, it is in particular through partially-funded synthetic structures that originating banks can transfer a big portion of their investment-grade credit risks, which typically generates low returns and is often held or even extended solely for relationship reasons. Furthermore, freeing up high-quality assets allows regulatory arbitrage to be performed. As shown above (see chapter 2.2.2), these assets are characterized by comparably high marginal regulatory capital requirements but contribute only little to economic credit portfolio risks.

---

[436] According to this study, 83% of all CDS are on the books of these 17 European and US commercial and investment banks

[437] See, for example, BIS (2003c), p. 36

While multiple-trance transactions typically transfer credit risks indirectly, i.e., through an SPV, single-tranche securitizations are often characterized by a direct risk transfer. These instruments offer the highest flexibility regarding the ability to arrange a customized credit risk transfer and, hence, are very precise concerning management of individual credit risks.

Credit enhancements limit the extent of credit risk transfers both in cash-based and synthetic securitization transactions.

When applying the secondary credit market instruments depicted above, credit portfolio managers need to consider a number of issues related to these transactions. The remainder of this chapter gives an overview on crucial caveats related to the application of these instruments.

3.4.2 Information asymmetries

3.4.2.1 Loan sales and loan syndication

It has been shown in the beginning of this dissertation that banks can have a competitive advantage in dealing with asymmetries of information between lenders and borrowers through their monitoring activities. The establishment of new instruments and related markets to transfer credit risks has contributed to alleviating these issues related to information asymmetries, while at the same time creating new problems of this kind. This has already been illustrated by the example of the loan sales market (see chapter 1.2). Further to the issues related to loans sales, the loan syndication market gives room for agency problems between the arranging institution(s) and participating lenders in the syndicate.

Adverse selection issues might arise due to the fact that the lead bank possesses private information about the borrower – e.g., regarding prospective performance not disclosed in financial data – which is unavailable to the syndication members. The existence of such "inside information" might be a consequence of a long-term relationship between arranger and borrower. In view of this informational advantage, an arranger has the incentive to retain a larger share of high-quality loans and a lower share of low-quality loans than under the lack of information asymmetries.

There might also be moral hazard problems related to a reduced incentive to monitor loans after they have been sold from the arranger's balance sheet to participating lenders of the syndicate. However, in the case of syndication, this problem is less grave than in the case of loan sales as each participating bank is required to analyze and monitor the borrower in view of its particular share in the transaction. Nevertheless, with regards to loan documentation, e.g., there are monitoring activities which the participating banks delegate to the arranging institution(s), paving the way for potential moral hazard issues.[438]

To this day, though, little empirical evidence for the existence of such agency problems in relation to loan syndication transactions has been found.[439] This might be due to the fact that the arranger has an interest in keeping a good relationship with the participating banks in order to win them again as participants in future syndicated transactions. Also, credit rating agencies increasingly rate syndicated loans so that participants have access to independent assessments on a borrower's credit quality.

3.4.2.2 Credit derivatives

While asymmetric information problems related to loan sales and loan syndication can be overcome through the use of credit derivatives, the contract parties face new problems related to moral hazard and adverse selection. It crucially depends on the ability to minimize these issues, should a successful application of credit derivatives be guaranteed.

3.4.2.2.1 Issues between lender and borrower

Further to Gorton and Pennacchi (1995) who examine moral hazard issues related to loan sales activities, Marrison (2001a) analyzes the issue related to reduced incentives for a lender to monitor a borrower after having purchased credit protection through acquiring a CDS on the derivatives market. He shows that the lender's incentive to pursue monitoring after having purchased credit protection decreases to the extent of the protection acquired. Should the lender's monitoring cost be sufficiently high, he will buy protection for the entire outstanding position and stop monitoring completely.

The purchase of credit protection will send a negative signal about the borrower's creditworthiness. Besides this, as a consequence of the reduced monitoring activity, bank debt will lose the certification value it has due to the lender's monitoring activities.[440] As a consequence of this lost bank certification, the borrower, who so far has been incentivized by the presence of bank lenders to choose first-best projects yielding a higher net present value (NPV)[441] over second-best projects yielding a lower NPV but yielding non-transferable private benefits to the borrower,[442] will issue sub-

---

438 See Dennis and Mullineaux (2000), p. 6 et seq.

439 Simons (1993) finds in an empirical study that the proportion of the syndication which the arranger retains increases with declining credit quality. Jones, Lang et al. (2000) find that agent banks retain a larger part of their low-quality loans. However, banks specializing in origination of low-quality loans seem to retain a smaller proportion of these loans

440 In theory, bank monitoring can be substituted by external providers such as rating agencies. However, this cannot replace bank monitoring entirely; see Marrison (2001a), p. 15 et seq.

441 See, e.g., Brealey and Myers (2003), p. 14 et seqq. for a description of the NPV concept

442 Based on a model by Holmstöm and Tirole (1997) tracing back to an approach first introduced by Fama

investment grade bonds in lieu of taking on bank loans and will increasingly run second-best projects with lower quality.[443] Marrison (2001a) shows that such behavior can reduce the overall welfare in an economy.

A solution to this issue could be that banks are required to give up the opacity of credit derivatives transactions. If they were required to report all credit derivatives trades, they could commit themselves to providing their monitoring services even after having purchased credit protection, thus keeping up the incentives for their borrowers to continue running first-best projects.[444] However, such an approach seems to be unrealistic because market players fear that this would unnecessarily damage the relationship with their borrowers and consequently prevent the sharing of risks entirely. As a matter of fact, banks use CDS and other credit derivatives exactly because they are unobservable by the borrower. Therefore, an alternative solution to this issue could be to add a clause to derivative contracts, requiring banks to continue performing their monitoring activities. It is particularly in non-standardized contracts that such individual clauses can be included relatively easily.[445]

The negative impact that the lender's purchase of credit protection has on the borrower's reputation can also be significantly alleviated if the lender does not fully transfer the credit exposure but only hedges (part of) its credit risks. Alternatively, the lender can retain a first loss tranche on his books.[446]

3.4.2.2.2 Issues between lender and credit protection seller

Another issue related to moral hazard can arise in the relationship between the lender and the seller of credit protection. Once the lender's exposure is fully hedged or transferred, the protection seller cannot or can only at a considerable cost observe whether the lender pursues its monitoring activities. Furthermore, the lender may

(1985), this approach assumes cash-constraint entrepreneurs using debt to finance their projects. They have the choice between two projects: the entrepreneurs have an incentive to select first-best projects, issuing investment grade bonds to finance the projects. Due to the fact that they can access bank loans and benefit from a bank acting as guarantor of the "first-best behavior", they will choose mixed loan and bond financing. However, if this bank now ceases to monitor their borrowers (e.g., after having bought protection on its loan exposure on the credit derivatives market), there is no incentive any more to run the first-best projects. The borrowers know that they will not receive certification benefits any longer. Hence, they cannot pursue their mixed bank/investment-grade bond refinance strategy any more because in the absence of bank certification they cannot credibly run first-best projects. Thus, they choose to issue sub-investment grade bonds and run second-best projects

443 Marrison (2001a), p. 16 asserts that the strongly increasing volume of credit derivatives transactions in Europe has been accompanied by a significantly higher issuance of sub-investment grade bonds

444 Marrison (2001a), p. 17 suggests to impose reporting requirements to banks for the use of CDS

445 See Kiff, Michaud et al. (2002), p. 11

446 See Kiff, Michaud et al. (2002), p. 8 et seq.

prematurely trigger a credit event, hence benefiting from the protection agreed in the contract with the protection seller.

On the side of the protection seller, moral hazard may occur with regards to delay or refusal of payment in the case of a credit event. In this case, a critical feature is whether the secondary market instrument is funded or unfunded: funded instruments prevent this issue from happening as the protection seller must provide funds upfront, before the occurrence of a credit event.[447]

Further to moral hazard-type of agency problems, a lender-protection seller relationship can face adverse selection issues stemming from the fact that lenders have incentives to buy credit protection primarily for their low-quality assets. The relatively high prices for protection on these assets might drive up protection cost for high-quality assets, thus discouraging lenders of high-quality assets from purchasing protection. In case of rated credit names, this issue is less severe as the rating agency has independently evaluated their creditworthiness.[448]

According to Duffee and Zhou (2001), a solution to this issue can be to purchase credit protection at a time when the agency problem is still non-existent (e.g., in the early life of a loan contract). Such a solution would be restricted, however, to instruments exclusively covering the time period in which the agency problem does not exist. Any instrument providing protection until maturity of the contract could not be used. The use of tranched credit derivatives or securitization transactions can also help to mitigate this adverse selection issue: the low-quality assets can be bundled by the protection buyer in the (usually small) first loss tranche. At the same time, a relatively large tranche with more favorable risks can be created and priced at lower cost. This separation of low- and high-risk assets enables to decouple the protection prices of low-risk assets to be decoupled from those bearing higher risks.[449]

3.4.2.3 Securitization

Despite being able to mitigate adverse selection issues, the use of tranched credit derivatives and securitization transactions might also trigger information asymmetries:

For example, a moral hazard problem might arise in the case of the protection buyer having the incentive to use his particular information advantage about the assets he owns by selecting assets of particularly low-quality for certain tranches. Investors or external agencies rating these tranches might not be able to discover the true asset value.[450]

---

447 See Kiff, Michaud et al. (2002), p. 12

448 See Kiff, Michaud et al. (2002), p. 10

449 See DeMarco and Duffie (1999)

450 See, again, DeMarco and Duffie (1999)

3.4.3 Additional risks related to use of secondary credit market instruments

Through transaction structures involving credit derivatives, portfolio managers can shed risks within a credit portfolio. When performing such transactions, though, they also need to consider a range of risks inherent in these transactions.[451]

The key risk arising in consequence of such transactions is related to the fact that these instruments are mostly OTC contracts which are negotiated and closed between two counterparties. Hence, each party faces counterparty risks: while the protection buyer may default on the fee payments agreed in the contract, the protection seller may fail to meet its contingent payout obligation. The establishment of trust accounts or the deposit of collateral as well as the use of funded instead of unfunded instruments can help to mitigate counterparty risks.[452]

However, while funded transactions may reduce or eliminate counterparty risks, they are subject to market risks. Market risks are mainly interest rate and currency risks related to CLNs as well as (synthetic) funded CDO and MBS contracts.[453] These kinds of risks can be alleviated through other specific derivative contracts, such as interest rate and cross-currency swaps.

Legal or documentation risks stem from incomplete credit protection contracts. They very frequently appear in the form of settlement risks when there is too much scope for interpreting the nature of deliverable assets.[454] A proper product standardization, e.g., through the ISDA developing standardized rules for OTC derivatives, can help to minimize these risk types.

Other risks related to secondary credit market instruments include model risks (i.e., loss risks due to errors in mathematical models) and operational risks (i.e., loss risks due to operational deficiencies such as control failures).[455]

3.4.4 Impact on regulatory capital requirements

This section will give a brief description on what the expected impact is following the application of the above-mentioned secondary credit market instruments on regulatory capital to be held. As mentioned above in chapter 2.2.2, the currently valid capital requirements ("Basle I")[456], are expected to be replaced by the "Basle II" guidelines[457]

451 Risks in this context refer to situations where there is no asymmetric information between the counterparties

452 See BIS (2003b), p. 42

453 Liquidity risks are considered a subset of market risks. In the case of MBS, prepayment risk – which is mainly a particular interest rate risk, see chapter 1.4.2.1 – plays an important role

454 See Kiff, Michaud et al. (2002), p. 15

455 Banks (2004), p. 27 et seq. provides an overview on the key risks related to the use of credit derivatives

456 See BIS (1988)

457 See BIS (2004c)

by 2007. Following the final adoption of this new regulation, an EU Directive will be developed which will consequently be converted into national law.[458] During the adaptation procedures in the respective countries, interested parties will be able to hand in additional comments and impact studies on the regulation to national authorities.[459] As, on the one hand, this will most likely result in another adaptation of the proposals – at least, within the boundaries of the EU Directive, on a national level – the current proposal cannot be regarded as final yet. Furthermore, as regulatory capital is rather a surplus than a constraint by most banks at the moment, regulatory issues are considered a side issue of this dissertation.[460] Therefore, this chapter will only give a high-level overview on what the regulatory capital impact following the application of secondary credit market instruments is expected to be.

3.4.4.1 Loan sales and loan syndication

Loan sales transactions imply that the selling institution transfers all claims from the credit asset together with its risks to the acquirer. Consequently, the seller's balance sheet volume shrinks and, accordingly, the regulatory equity required is reduced.[461] Similarly, for syndicated loans, the equity requirement for a participating institution is determined by the amount of risks which the institution accepts through signing the syndicated loan agreement. The arranger's equity requirements are determined by its retained share in the syndicated loan volume.[462]

3.4.4.2 Credit derivatives

If credit derivatives reduce the credit risks of a bank, their application should be reflected in the equity requirements. The currently valid Basle I regulation does not consider derivatives. Therefore, national regulators have subsumed credit derivatives under their equity requirements by interpreting them as third-party guarantees. This so-called substitution approach could result in lower capital requirements since the regulatory equity to be held for guarantees for a credit exposure is determined by the risk weights of the guarantor.[463]

The new Basle II regulation includes credit derivatives by explicitly applying the substitution approach:[464] the regulation assigns the risk weight of the protection seller

[458] See Hartmann-Wendels, Pfingsten et al. (2004), p. 396

[459] See BIS (2004c), p. 1

[460] See, again, Figure 12

[461] As mentioned above, in Germany capital requirements for credit risks are regulated in §§ 10 and 12 KWG (1998) in combination with "Grundsatz I" from the BaFin. Additionally, § 13 KWG (1998) regulates large credit exposures

[462] See Poppensieker (2002), p. 39 describing the regulatory impact of loan sales and syndication transactions according to the current valid German regulation

[463] See, for a summary, Poppensieker (2002), p. 54 et seq.

[464] See BIS (2004c), paragraph 141

to the protected part of a credit exposure. The uncovered portion of the exposure is considered with the risk weight of the underlying counterparty.[465] Thus, protecting an exposure with credit derivatives can lower the required regulatory equity provision should the protection seller have a lower risk weight than the protection buyer.

The explicit consideration of credit derivatives in the new guidelines certainly contributes to making these instruments more attractive for a portfolio manager wishing to reshuffle his credit portfolio. Yet, they need to fulfill certain requirements in order to be recognized as appropriate to reduce regulatory capital requirements:

First of all, the maturity of the derivative needs to be at least as high as the remaining maturity of the underlying asset. If there is a maturity mismatch and the maturity of the derivative is less than a year, it is not recognized for regulatory capital purposes. In the case of a maturity mismatch and a remaining maturity of more than a year, an adjustment to the risk weights is made.[466]

The guarantee provided by the credit derivative must explicitly refer to the underlying exposure(s) to be protected. Besides this, the protection must be unconditional, i.e. there cannot be a clause in the contract preventing the protection seller from performing its duty in some circumstances. Furthermore, the credit events specified in the contract must correspond to certain minimum requirements.[467]

The guidelines name CDS and TRS as the only instruments eligible for recognition and explicitly exclude other types of credit derivatives. First- and Second-to-Default instruments are separately regulated.[468]

3.4.4.3 Securitization

ABBs – hence, in particular, Pfandbriefe – do not transfer credit risks, they merely represent an opportunity to refinance lending activities. Therefore, a financial institution cannot reduce its regulatory capital requirements following the issuance of such a security. An investor in ABBs, however, needs to provide capital for this investment.[469]

---

465 See BIS (2004c), paragraph 196

466 See BIS (2004c), paragraph 143 in combination with paragraph 202 – 205

467 See BIS (2004c), paragraph 189 and 191

468 See BIS (2004c), paragraph 193. In the case of First-to-Default derivatives, banks can achieve regulatory capital relief for the assets included in the basket which have the lowest risk-weighted amount, but only if the notional amount of the asset is less than or equal to the notional amount of the credit derivative. See BIS (2004c), paragraph 207 – 210 for details of the regulation regarding First- and Second-to-Default Credit Derivatives

469 While neither the currently valid Basle I nor the planned Basle II regulation include special requirements for investments in ABBs, the OGAW-Directive of the EU (OGAW (2002)) contains special requirements for covered securities (see OGAW (2002), article 22, paragraph 4)

National regulation (e.g., in Germany § 13 of the BaFin Grundsatz I regulation) refers to this Directive,

ABS are not regulated in the Basle I guidelines. Nevertheless, local regulators have developed a regulation for these instruments.[470]

The Basle II guidelines include a new section regulating the capital requirements for ABS transactions. The key driver for this inclusion was the increasing use of these transactions for the purpose of regulatory capital arbitrage. According to the new guidelines, an originating institution can exclude securitized exposures from the calculation of risk-weighted assets under certain requirements.[471] Against securitization exposures held – be it retention of tranches by the originator or investments in ABS by capital investors – institutions need to hold regulatory capital. Under the standardized approach, the risk-weighted assets of a securitization exposure held are calculated by multiplying the nominal amount of the position with the rating-determined risk weight as shown in the middle column of Figure 31. Obviously, for long-term credit rating categories below investment grade (i.e., below BBB-), the proposed risk weights for securitizations are stricter than the ones for claims on corporations. For the lowest/unrated rating class the securitization exposure must be deducted from regulatory capital.[472]

The explicit consideration of securitizations in the new capital adequacy standards is certainly beneficial with regard to their suitability as risk mitigation instruments for credit portfolio managers. However, due to the obvious discrimination of securitizations against direct asset holdings, this regulation has been met with a lot of criticism. Most importantly, it is feared that the banks' ability to use securitization as a risk management and financial tool will be impaired. From an investor's perspective,

privileging covered securities over uncovered instruments. It is planned to keep such a privilege under the Basle II regulation: German regulation has already decided to determine the risk weight of these instruments based on the respective sovereign risk weight, with their risk weight under the modified standard approach being one level below the respective sovereign risk weight of the same rating class - at a minimum of 10%; see VDH (2004), p. 19 et seqq. as well as Slikker (2004)

470 See Poppensieker (2002), p. 80 et seqq. for a description of the current valid regulatory capital requirements for ABS in Germany

471 This applies for cash-based as well as for synthetic securitizations; see BIS (2004c), paragraph 554 and paragraph 555, respectively. It is important to note that all of the requirements mentioned in these paragraphs need to be met in order to exclude the securitized assets from the calculation of risk-weighted assets. These conditions include, among others, that the assets are legally isolated from the transferor so that, even in the case of its bankruptcy, the exposures are put beyond its reach and that, in the case of cash-based transactions, the transferee is an SPV. Furthermore, in the case of synthetic structures, the instruments used to transfer credit risks must not contain terms or conditions limiting the amount of credit risk transferred

472 According to BIS (2004c), paragraph 561, 50% of the deduction must be taken from Tier-1 and 50% from Tier-2 capital. It is also important to note that the 350% risk weight for tranches with a long-term credit rating between BB+ to BB- is only applicable for investors in ABS structures. Originating institutions must deduct all retained securitization exposures that are rated below investment grade (i.e. below BBB-) from their capital; see BIS (2004c), paragraph 569 and 570

when acquiring non-investment grade securitized tranches, a higher return will be required than when investing in claims on corporations with similar rating. This is because the investor needs to be compensated for the additionally required regulatory capital. Consequently, some securitization transactions may not be completed because paying such high returns would be uneconomic for the originators.[473] Further to comparing capital requirements for securitizations with those for claims on corporations, the authors of BIS (2003c) also assess the capital required for synthetic securitizations. They find that the proposed regulation discriminates against these structures, mainly due to the fact that the capital weights for super-senior positions are too high.[474] Following this critique, the authors of BIS (2003c) suggest lowering the risk weights for securitizations to the level of those for corporate loans (see right-hand column of Figure 31).

473 See BIS (2003c), p. 9. The particularly high regulatory capital requirement for non-investment-grade assets is also shown by means of an empirical example on p. 12, table 2. According to the authors of this paper, there is also no discernible reason why originators should be discriminated against investors with regard to holding sub-investment grade tranches. It is particularly stated that the current US regulation does not follow this discrimination; see Federal Reserve Board (2002) for the respective US regulation

474 See BIS (2003c), p. 36 et seq. in combination with data from Annex A

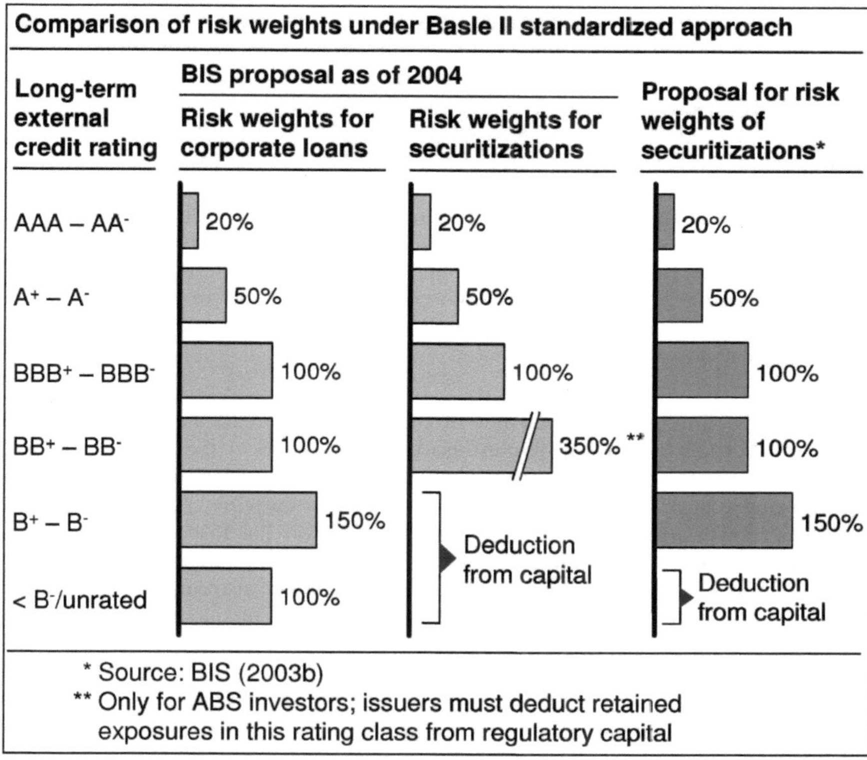

Figure 31: Comparison of risk weights under Basle II standardized approach[475]

3.4.5 Market interdependencies

Besides having to take into consideration product-specific issues, behavioral aspects of market participants as well as regulatory requirements when applying the above-mentioned secondary market instruments, a portfolio manager also has to keep an eye on interdependencies between the different subtypes of secondary credit markets when applying these instruments.

The individual secondary credit market instruments described here have different characteristics. Therefore, they vary in their impact on the underlying loan markets, and their application may influence other secondary credit markets as well.

[475] Source: Own illustration based on BIS (2004c), p. 19 and p. 120 and BIS (2003c), p. 14 Table 3a

Consequently, credit portfolio managers also need to take market interdependencies into consideration when, e.g., pursuing a hedging strategy for their portfolios. Such interdependencies exist, for instance, between the credit derivatives and the loan sales market. Duffee and Zhou (2001) examine the effect which the introduction of a CDS market has for an already existing loan sales market. They find that in some cases the introduction of the CDS market can cause a breakdown of the loan sales market or other markets for loan risk-sharing. If this is the case, a credit derivatives market can promote the risk of bank insolvency.[476] The impact of secondary credit instruments on the underlying reference assets has been subject to a great amount of research. While this subject will not be intensified in the course of this dissertation, it becomes obvious that market interdependencies should not be underestimated or neglected when applying secondary credit market instruments. In particular, such issues become acute in relatively narrow regional credit markets.[477]

* * * * *

In light of the different characteristics of the secondary credit market instruments illustrated above, it is crucial for portfolio managers to select the type of contract fitting best to their strategy to achieve an optimal portfolio composition. Unsurprisingly, there is no single right answer to this question. As the discussion above has shown, a trade-off between a variety of factors has to be evaluated when determining the optimal instrument for a concrete situation.[478] A more formal analysis of the trade-offs between different secondary credit market instruments – especially evaluating their impact on the newly developed regulatory capital standards – would certainly be desirable in supporting such decisions but cannot be provided within the scope of this dissertation.[479]

---

476 In certain cases, the introduction of a CDS market may reduce the amount and quality of traded loans because for those assets which would have been sold before the introduction of the CDS market, the lender now purchases protection through a CDS. However, such a contract typically does not cover the entire maturity of a loan and is usually restricted to the early phases of a loan maturity (see above). Hence, the total amount of credit protection purchased is lower under this scenario than before. Under a different scenario, however, market participants acquire protection for loans which they would not have sold before the introduction of the CDS market. This scenario results in an increase of credit protection. Duffee and Zhou (2001) conclude that the overall welfare effect depends on the relative importance of each scenario

477 See, e.g., Blanco, Brennan et al. (2003) and Hull, Mirela et al. (2004) for two recent empirical analyses on this topic

478 Besides the above-mentioned criteria, it is also necessary to take into consideration the costs related to the use of the secondary credit market instrument. For example, if a CDS transaction is undertaken in order to hedge a credit exposure instead of selling the relevant asset on the secondary loan market, an additional capital charge for the remaining risk-weighted asset and its funding must be taken into account, thus making a CDS transaction more expensive than a secondary loan transaction

479 Another topic that could not be covered within the scope of this dissertation is the pricing and evaluation of secondary credit market instruments. See, for example, Grundke (2003) regarding evaluation and pricing of

* * * * *

After the introductory chapter one, the second chapter has described the recent trends and forces of change that have made it necessary for wholesale banks to rethink their lending business model and that have been key drivers for the development of the ACPM approach. Chapter three has comprehensively described and compared the instruments which can be used by an ACPM unit to reshuffle its portfolio on secondary loan markets.

Before providing empirical evidence on where leading banks stand regarding the active management of their credit portfolios, the theoretical background of the ACPM approach will be illustrated in the next chapter. This illustration will serve as basis for the determination whether, from a theoretical point of view, active management of credit portfolios is at all value-enhancing for an institution's credit business.

credit derivatives, and Gruber, Gruber et al. (2005) regarding pricing of ABS and credit derivatives

4 Theoretical background and value creation potential of the ACPM approach

As already mentioned in chapter 2.3.1, the ACPM approach is based on the principles of classical portfolio theory: The goal is to create a risk-return efficient credit portfolio and to keep this portfolio on the efficient frontier throughout changing economic conditions.

In order to comprehensively understand the theoretical background of the ACPM approach, the principles of classical portfolio theory will be introduced in this chapter. As the theory is founded on certain rather restrictive assumptions, it will also be embedded in a more general context to reflect the specifics of credit assets. Based on this illustration, it will be discussed whether and, if so, under which conditions the ACPM approach can generate additional value for an institution from a theoretical point of view.

4.1 Portfolio selection of individual investors

4.1.1 Risk preferences

An individual rational investor aims at optimally investing his wealth W_0 into a portfolio of financial assets so that, at the end of the investment period, he has a (risky) wealth $\tilde{W}_1$, which maximizes his utility.[480]

When deciding in which portfolio of assets to invest, the investor evaluates the possible asset values $x_1, x_2, ... x_n$, which occur with the probabilities $p_1, p_2, ... p_n$, by means of his individual utility function $U(.)$. Thus, the expected utility $E[U(X)]$ of a portfolio X containing x_n assets can be determined:

$$E[U(X)] = p_1 * u(x_1) + p_2 * u(x_2) + ... p_n * u(x_n)$$

When deciding in which of two alternative portfolios X or Y to invest, the rational investor chooses the one with the higher expected utility.[481]

[480] It is assumed here that the investor has already decided which part of his wealth he wants to invest instead of spending on consumption. The decision on consumption today vs. tomorrow, which is reflected in the risk-free interest rate, can be ignored here as it is not relevant for the remainder of this illustration; see Lintner J. (1965), p. 15 and Poppensieker (2002), p. 105

[481] This decision principle is known as the Bernoulli principle, tracing back to the so-called "Petersburg game"; see Bernoulli (1738) and, e.g., Spremann (2003), pp. 357 – 360.

Von Neumann and Morgenstern (1973) were the first ones to develop axioms proving the Bernoulli principle. If a rational individual bases his preferences on these axioms, the Bernoulli principle holds when deciding between activities with stochastic outcomes; see Von Neumann and Morgenstern (1973), p. 26 et seq.

It can be shown that the expected utility of the risky wealth $\tilde{W}_1$ can be approximated by means of a second-order Taylor series as

$$E\left[U\left(\tilde{W}_1\right)\right]=U\left[E\left(\tilde{W}_1\right)\right]+0{,}5*U''\left[E\left(\tilde{W}_1\right)\right]*\sigma^2\left(\tilde{W}_1\right)+E\left(\tilde{R}_3\right).$$ [482]

If $E(\tilde{R}_3)=0$, the expected utility is only a function of the expected value (mean) and the variance of $\tilde{W}_1$. This is the case under the simplified assumption of a quadratic utility function[483] or if $\tilde{W}_1$ is normally distributed.[484] This simplified risk decision principle is the so-called mean-variance principle.[485]

In the following section, the mean-variance principle will be based on the assumption of normally distributed asset returns. In order to be able to realistically assume normally distributed asset returns, the planning horizon for such investments should be at maximum one year.[486]

The risk aversion of an investor can be determined by his willingness to prefer an investment of his wealth W_0 into risky assets over a risk-free investment. In general, it can be assumed that investors are risk-averse as they usually prefer a risk-free investment over a risky investment yielding the same expected value. Additionally, one can assume that investors prefer more to less. Hence, an investor's utility function

482 $E\left(\tilde{R}_3\right)=\sum_{i=3}^{\infty}\frac{1}{i!}U^i\left[E\left(\tilde{W}_1\right)\right]\sigma^i\left(\tilde{W}_1\right)$; see Poppensieker (2002), p. 105

483 A quadratic utility function is characterized by $U^i(.)=0 \ \forall \ i\geq 3$.

An issue related to the use of quadratic utility functions in this context may be their saturation in the angular point as well as an increasing absolute risk aversion; see Huang and Litzenberger (1988), p. 61. Hence, the types of quadratic utility functions qualifying for a motivation of the mean-variance principle, need to be increasing across the return spectrum of the relevant assets so that the issue of saturation does not occur; see Gonzalez, Litzenberger et al. (1977), p. 177 et seqq.

484 If $\tilde{W}_1$ is normally distributed, $\sigma^i\left(\tilde{W}_1\right)$ and hence $E(\tilde{R}_3)$ is a function of the variance $\sigma^2\left(\tilde{W}_1\right)$.

According to Ingersoll (1987), p. 104 the returns can take on any elliptic distribution function and do not necessarily have to be normally distributed

485 See Rudolph (1979), p. 16

486 For longer investment periods, the deviation of asset returns from the normal distribution would become significantly higher so that the assumption of a normal distribution could not be held any longer; see Spremann (2003), p. 197

is typically monotonically increasing $U^{'}\left(\tilde{W}_1\right) \succ 0$ and – due to his risk aversion – concave (i.e., $U^{''}\left(\tilde{W}_1\right) \prec 0$). The level of risk aversion can be measured by the concavity of the utility function. Based on the work of Arrow (1964), Pratt (1964) suggested measuring the so-called absolute risk aversion through

$$ARAV\left(\tilde{W}_1\right) = -\frac{U^{''}\left(\tilde{W}_1\right)}{U^{'}\left(\tilde{W}_1\right)}.$$

For a constant absolute risk aversion, i.e. $ARAV(W_1) = \alpha_A$, there is an exponential utility function, i.e. $U\left(\tilde{W}_1\right) = -e^{-\alpha_A * w}$.[487] In this case and if $\tilde{W}_1$ is normally distributed, the expected utility of $\tilde{W}_1$ simplifies to

$$E\left[U\left(\tilde{W}_1\right)\right] = U\left[E\left(\tilde{W}_1\right) - 0{,}5 * \alpha_A * \sigma^2\left(\tilde{W}_1\right)\right].$$

Assuming that the utility function $U(.)$ is monotonous, its argument can be directly used as preference function Φ_A over the wealth $\tilde{W}_1$:

$$\Phi_A\left[E\left(\tilde{W}_1\right), \sigma^2\left(\tilde{W}_1\right)\right] = E\left(\tilde{W}_1\right) - 0{,}5 * \alpha_A * \sigma^2\left(\tilde{W}_1\right)$$ [488]

With help of the stochastic return on the investment $\tilde{r}_W$, the wealth at the end of the investment period can be defined as

$$\tilde{W}_1 = W_0 * \left[1 + E\left(\tilde{r}_W\right) + \sigma^2\left(\tilde{r}_W\right)\tilde{\varepsilon}\right].$$ [489]

Linear transformation results in a return-determined preference function Φ_R:

---

[487] See Pratt (1964), p. 130. A constant absolute risk aversion has a particular implication: if an investor disposes of an initial wealth W_0 and has the choice between two lotteries whose outcome will be added to W_0, his choice of the lottery is independent of the level of W_0; see Spremann (2003), p. 365

[488] See Ingersoll (1987), p. 98

[489] $\tilde{\varepsilon}$ is normally distributed

$$\Phi_R\left[E\left(\tilde{r}_w\right),\sigma^2\left(\tilde{r}_w\right)\right]=E\left(\tilde{r}_w\right)-0{,}5*\alpha_r*\sigma^2\left(\tilde{r}_w\right)$$ [490]

4.1.2 Mean-variance efficient portfolios

4.1.2.1 Two-fund separation

In a mean-variance world, when facing a selection of portfolios that consist of n risky assets with the same expected return, a risk-averse investor uses the preference function Φ_R to select the portfolio whose return has the lowest risk, i.e. the lowest standard deviation. Among portfolios with equal risk, he selects the one with the highest expected return. A portfolio for which both conditions are fulfilled is referred to as mean-variance efficient – no other portfolio which is superior regarding risk or return can be composed of the available assets.[491]

An efficient frontier showing the location of these mean-variance efficient portfolios can be determined. In a diagram showing the μ on the vertical and the σ on the horizontal axis, this mean-variance efficient frontier (MVEF) has the shape of a hyperbola open to the right hand side.[492] It can already be determined if two efficient portfolios are known, i.e. if the μ and σ of each portfolio as well as the correlation coefficient between the portfolios is known. Hence, each efficient portfolio can be constructed as a combination of two efficient portfolios. This is the two-fund separation.[493]

The portfolio in the apex of this hyperbola is the so-called minimum-variance portfolio (MVP). The MVP is the efficient portfolio bearing the lowest risk that can be generated with the assets available. All portfolios below the MVP are not efficient as for each of these portfolios another portfolio can be found bearing the same risk but higher return.[494] Hence, all possible mean-variance efficient portfolios are located on the upper half of a hyperbola in the $\mu-\sigma$ diagram. Figure 32 illustrates the MVEF and the MVP in a $\mu-\sigma$ diagram.

---

490 $\alpha_R=W_0*\alpha_A$ is the relative risk aversion; see Poppensieker (2002), p. 106 et seq. and Pratt (1964), p. 133 et seq.

491 See Markowitz (1952), p. 82, Markowitz (1991), p. 129 and Merton (1972), p. 1851 et seq. for a formal illustration of the optimization problem. The term efficient is used in the sense of Pareto efficiency, see again Footnote 25 for a definition

492 The analytic determination of the efficient frontier for a portfolio without risk-free assets traces back to Merton (1972), p. 1851 et seqq. Huang and Litzenberger (1988), p. 66 prove that the efficient frontier has the shape of a hyperbola

493 For a formal evidence of the two-fund separation see Ingersoll (1987), pp. 151 – 165 as well as Spremann (2003), p. 199 et seq.

494 See Jorion (2003), appendix A, p. 77 et seq.

4.1.2.2 Tobin separation

The portfolio selection problem changes if the investor can additionally invest funds in an asset yielding the risk-free return r_f or take a loan at this rate in order to finance an investment into the n risky assets.

The investor invests a share c of his initial wealth W_0 into a portfolio consisting of the n risky assets whose expected return μ_P has a standard deviation of σ_P. The remaining share $1-c$ is invested in the risk-free asset.[495] The expected return of this combined investment is

$$\mu(c) = r_F + c * (\mu_P - r_F),$$

the standard deviation is

$$\sigma(c) = c * \sigma_P.$$

Combining these two equations results in

$$\mu(c) = r_F + b * \sigma(c),$$

which shows that the expected returns of all portfolios that can be generated by combining an investment in the risky portfolio with a risk-free investment are positioned on a cohort of the straight line in the $\mu - \sigma$ diagram. The parameter b , determining the slope of the cohorts, can be regarded as the risk premium over and above the risk-free rate. It is defined as $b = \frac{\mu_P - r_f}{\sigma_P}$. Hence, besides intersecting the abscissa at the level r_F, the cohorts of the straight lines also include the point with the abscissa σ_P and the ordinate μ_P, which is the risk-return coordinate of the risky portfolio the investor chooses.[496]

When deciding on portfolios, a rational investor chooses the straight line with the highest possible gradient because a higher slope means he can achieve a higher return on the assets for the same level of risk. Since the investor aspires to own an efficient portfolio, he chooses the straight line with the highest possible gradient that is tangential to the MVEF. The portfolio, which is positioned in the osculation point, is the so-called market portfolio (M); the tangent to the MVEF in M is the mean-variance capital market line (MVCML); see the schematic illustration in Figure 32.

---

495 It is assumed that $r_f < \mu$

496 See Spremann (2003), p. 209

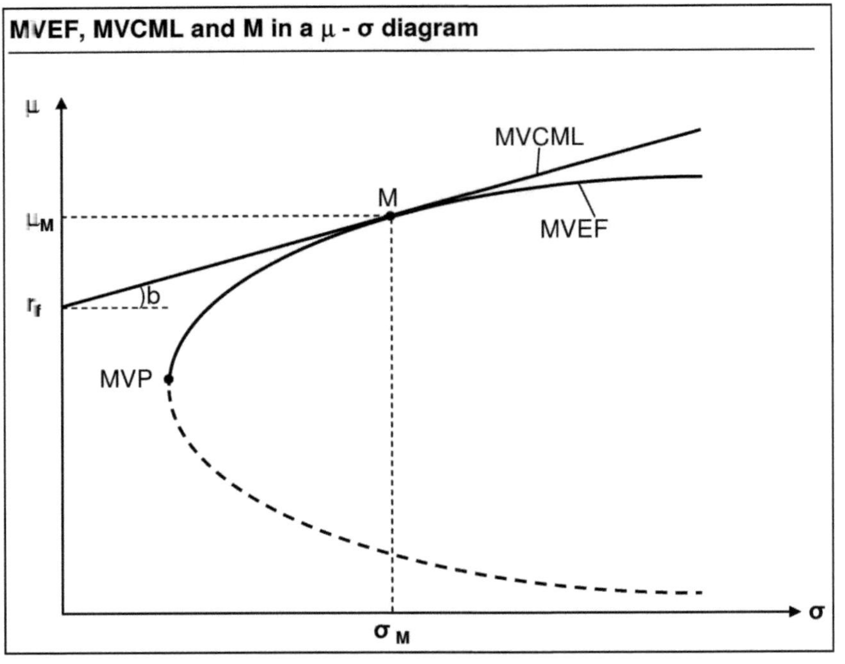

Figure 32: MVEF and MVCML and M in a $\mu - \sigma$ diagram[497]

When comparing the risky portfolios that are located on the MVEF with the MVCML, it becomes obvious that, except for M, each portfolio on the MVEF is dominated by a portfolio on the MVCML, which has the same risk but a higher expected return. In other words, if investors additionally have the opportunity to invest funds in a risk-free asset or take on a loan at the risk-free rate, M is the only remaining efficient portfolio on the MVEF. All other mean-variance efficient portfolios lie on the MVCML.[498] As a consequence, risk-averse investors solely decide on which share of their funds to invest in M and which share to invest risk-free (or to which extent they want to take on a loan at the risk-free rate).

[497] Source: Own illustration based on Spremann (2003), chapter 7

[498] Hence, the MVCML can also be interpreted as the new efficient frontier under the existence of a risk-free investment or lending opportunity. It has the form of a straight line because the covariance between the risk-free and the risky assets is zero; see Rudolf (1994), p. 93

The determination of M's composition can be separated from the investor's decision how to split his funds between an investment in this portfolio and a risk-free investment. This principle is known as the Tobin separation.[499]

As opposed to the two-fund separation, now the ratio between the risky assets remains constant for all investors and is independent of their individual risk preferences. These risk preferences are only relevant for the decision on which percentage of the available funds to invest in M and which percentage to invest risk-free.[500] The composition of M is determined by μ and σ of the risky assets as well as their correlations.[501] Furthermore, r_F needs to be known in order to be able to determine the market portfolio.

4.1.3 Mean-shortfall efficient portfolios

Through using the two parameters standard deviation and mean of the probability distribution in the investor's preference function (Φ_A above), mean-variance efficient portfolios could be determined. When doing so, it needs to be assumed that symmetric risk measures sufficiently describe the risk characteristics of an asset. Yet, as shown before, due to a variety of deficiencies accompanying symmetric risk measures, it seems to be more appropriate to use shortfall risk measures instead.[502] Therefore, it will be examined in the following section in how far the efficient portfolio selection problem changes if an investor defines risk as a deviation below a previously defined target return and consequently includes shortfall risk measures in his preference function in lieu of the hitherto used symmetric standard deviation.

In accordance with chapter 1.4.2.2.3, it will be focused on shortfall probability (κ), defined as the probability that the portfolio's return is below a pre-defined target return (r*). First of all, the assumption that the investor's decision principle is based on normally distributed asset returns will be maintained.[503]

4.1.3.1 Efficient portfolio selection under normally distributed asset returns and shortfall probability

Analogous to the mean-variance optimization introduced above, a risk-averse investor selects the portfolio whose return has the lowest risk. Now, risk is measured not through standard deviation but through shortfall probability. It can be shown that the

[499] See Tobin (1958), p. 83 et seq. and Lintner J. (1965), p. 16 et seqq. See also Merton (1972) p. 1863 et seqq. for an analytic determination of the efficient frontier for a portfolio given the existence of risk-free assets

[500] See also Spremann (2003), p. 212 et seqq.

[501] See Lintner J. (1965), p. 21

[502] See again chapters 1.4.2.2.2 and 1.4.2.2.3 on symmetric and shortfall risk measures, respectively

[503] Normally distributed returns are also assumed by Leibowitz and Henriksson (1989) in this context, for example

optimization problem to be solved in this context is equivalent to the mean-variance optimization problem described before. Analytically, this equivalence is shown by the equation

$$z_k = \frac{\mu_P - r^*}{\sigma_P}.$$

$z_K > 0$ can be regarded as the risk premium over and above the minimum rate of return r*: it is defined as the argument of a standard-normal distribution to the shortfall probability κ: $\phi(z_k) = \kappa$. Consequently, each mean-variance efficient portfolio can be illustrated as a $\mu - \kappa$ portfolio.[504]

The goal is now to find the portfolios which are efficient in a $\mu - \kappa$ context. The relationship between μ and κ can be illustrated in a $\mu - \sigma$ diagram by rearranging the equation of the risk premium to

$$\mu_P = r^* + z_k \sigma_P.$$

This is the equation of a cohort of straight indifference lines which intersect the abscissa at the level of the targeted minimum return. Their slope is determined by the risk premium: a higher risk premium indicates a higher utility, illustrated by a greater gradient.[505] The indifference lines are defined as shortfall lines. All asset portfolios located above such a line fulfill the so-called shortfall restriction that their return is below the pre-defined target at most with the shortfall probability κ.[506]

The shortfall lines represent different shortfall probabilities. The two intersection points between a shortfall line and the MVEF indicate portfolios which are both mean-variance efficient – provided they are located above the MVP – and fulfill the shortfall restriction. However, while both of these points are mean-variance efficient, only the upper one is also mean-shortfall efficient as it has a higher μ than its counterpart at a lower location on the MVEF.

There is one shortfall line for each given r* which is tangential to the MVEF. Its osculation point indicates the asset portfolio which is efficient both in a mean-variance and a mean-shortfall world and has the highest utility as it indicates the lowest probability to achieve a lower return than r*. Therefore, this portfolio is defined as the minimum shortfall portfolio (MSP). All portfolios on or above the MSP on the MVEF are efficient in a $\mu - \kappa$ context for a given r*.[507]

---

504 See Rudolf (1994), p. 89 who, by contrast, defines $z_k < 0$ and interprets it as the standardized target return of a portfolio. It is also proven that there is a monotonous relationship between σ and κ

505 See Kaduff (1996), p. 110

506 See Rudolf (1994), p. 90

507 See Rudolf (1994), p. 90 and Kataoka (1963), p. 182. The tangential criterion is referred to as Roy-criterion,

Figure 33 illustrates schematically the MVEF and the MSP in relation to the MVP in a $\mu-\sigma$ diagram. It can be seen that the MSP is located on the MVEF above the MVP. Therefore, all portfolios that are efficient in a mean-shortfall world are also mean-variance efficient. However, the portfolios on the MVEF between the MVP and the MSP are mean-variance but not mean-shortfall efficient. This is because for a given target minimum rate of return, any shortfall line intersecting the MVEF indicates two possible portfolios of which a rational investor chooses the one yielding the higher μ for the given shortfall risk, hence the one located above the MSP.

As a result, while the same optimization principle as the ones developed in a $\mu-\sigma$ also applies in the more general setting of a $\mu-\kappa$ framework, there are fewer $\mu-\kappa$ efficient portfolios than $\mu-\sigma$ efficient ones.[508]

see Roy (1952)

508 Alternatively, these findings can be illustrated through a mean-shortfall probability efficient frontier (MSPEF) in a $\mu-\kappa$ diagram, see Figure 34 below. A crucial difference between the MSPEF and the MVEF, which has the shape of a hyperbola in the $\mu-\sigma$ diagram, is that the MSPEF has two inflexion points. The inflexion point located above the MSP (I_{EF} in Figure 34) has the following economic implications: if an investor increases his return appetite, he has to accept a higher shortfall probability. Yet, the incremental increase of shortfall probability with an increasing "return unit" gets smaller if the portfolio is located above the expected return determining this inflexion point. Hence, it becomes "cheaper" in terms of additional shortfall risk if an investor desires a higher return. This is a key difference in choosing the variance as risk measure: along the $\mu-\sigma$ efficient frontier, the marginal risk is continuously growing with an additional "unit" of return until the asymptotic area of the efficient frontier is reached, see Rudolf (1994), p. 92 et seq.

Another characteristic of the MSPEF is that it moves to the right, i.e., towards higher shortfall probability if the target rate of return is raised. That is, if an investor increases his target return aspiration level, he cannot expect a higher return from his investment but faces a higher risk that the return falls short of his expectation; see Kaduff and Spremann (1996), p. 786

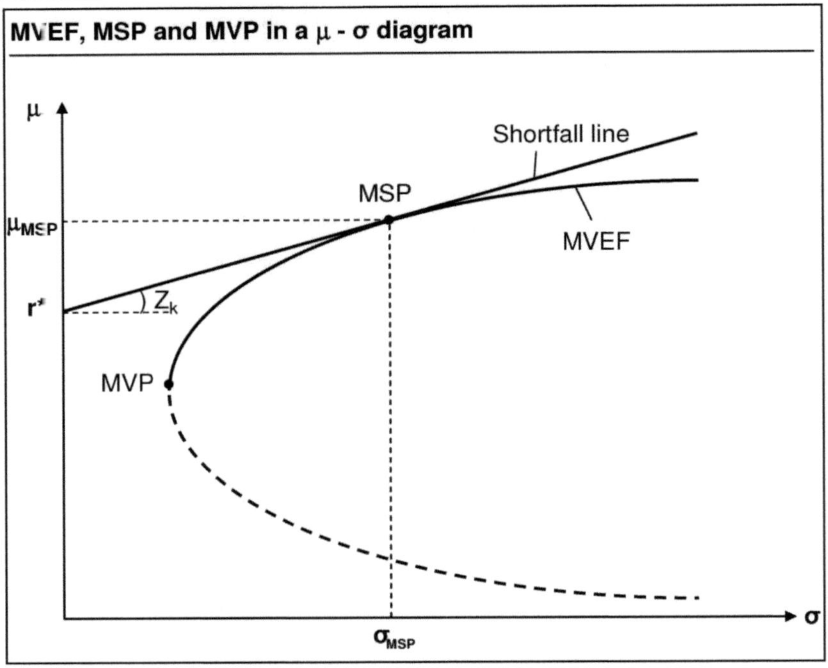

Figure 33: MVEF, MSP and MVP in a $\mu - \sigma$ diagram[509]

4.1.3.2 Generalization of distribution function

So far, normally distributed asset returns have been assumed. However, there are several reasons why this assumption is problematic: firstly, when assuming a normal distribution, the length of the investment period is limited since the extent of a distribution's asymmetry increases with a longer investment horizon.[510] Secondly, there is extensive empirical evidence that returns of financial assets are typically asymmetrically distributed – this holds, in particular, for distribution functions of credit assets.[511]

---

[509] Source: Own illustration based on Rudolf (1994), p. 91 Figure 2

[510] See again Footnote 486

[511] See again chapter 1.4.2.2.1 regarding credit assets. For deviation of stock returns from the normal distribution see, e.g., Marrison (2002), p. 38. The fact that return distributions of stocks deviate from the normal distribution also has an implication on the model-based valuation of derivatives according to Black and Scholes (1973) who, among other things, assume normally distributed returns of the underlyings in their

The question is, in how far the portfolio optimization problem based on mean-shortfall probability optimization changes if the assumption of normally distributed asset returns is relinquished.

This problem has been addressed by Roy (1952): based on Chebyshev's inequality, an upper limit for the shortfall probability can be determined through applying variance as distribution parameter. Moreover, as Chebyshev's inequality can be applied to all types of distributions; this approximation enables to generalize the assumptions on distributions to be generalized; an upper limit, which is based on variance as risk measure, can be given for the risk of any non-normal distribution.[512] This upper limit implies a maximum shortfall probability for all mean-variance combinations on a shortfall line such as the one in Figure 33. Shortfall probabilities of portfolios above this shortfall line are not permitted.[513] As before, the osculation point of the shortfall line and the MVEF determines the location of the MSP.

As a consequence, the findings above, which were based on normally distributed asset returns, may be regarded as a borderline case of the generalization that can be made based on Chebyshev's inequality. This ex-post justification of the limitation on normally distributed asset returns made above allows the further pursuit of this assumption in the following section because the results can be justified in a broader context leading to a generally valid upper limit.

4.1.3.3 Higher-order LPM

So far, the focus has been on shortfall probability as zero-order LPM. It can be shown that an extension of the analysis to higher-order LPM does not provide additional insights and new results over and above the findings on efficient portfolio selection based on shortfall probability. It merely requires higher calculation efforts.[514] Thus, it is sufficient to keep the focus on shortfall probability.

4.2 Capital Market Equilibrium

4.2.1 Mean-variance market equilibrium – the CAPM

Following the research on portfolio selection of individual investors, Sharpe (1964) and Lintner (1965) invented the Capital Asset Pricing Model (CAPM), enabling the behavior of individual investors as well as an evaluation of financial assets' risks in a competitive market equilibrium to be determined. A generalized version of the CAPM was published by Mossin (1966).[515]

---

pricing formula

512 See Roy (1952), p. 434 et seq.

513 See also Kaduff (1996), p. 90 et seq.

514 See Schubert (1996), in particular p. 502 et seqq.

515 While the original CAPM was developed as a one-period model, Merton (1973) has developed a generalized

4.2.1.1 Underlying assumptions

The CAPM is based on the assumption of complete capital markets. A complete capital market has three characteristics: (I) all market participants have unlimited access to the primary capital market on which assets can be issued and also have secondary market access allowing the trading of financial assets. (II) There are no market frictions, i.e., no transaction costs or taxes; in particular, all market participants can invest and borrow capital at the same risk-free rate. (III) There is full information efficiency in the market: all market participants possess the same level of information as well as the same opinions about the stochastic end values of the assets and assume the same probability distributions for the returns on the available assets.[516]

Furthermore, the above-mentioned assumptions on portfolio selection of individual investors underlie the CAPM: investors are risk-averse and aim at maximizing their wealth at the end of the investment period. Hereby, they act according to a quadratic utility function unless asset returns have a normal or at least elliptic distribution.[517] Besides this, market participants need to have the opportunity to take a long or short position of any size in a risk-free asset.

It is the last assumption which differentiates the CAPM developed by Sharpe, Lintner, and Mossin from the so-called "Zero-Beta CAPM" tracing back to Black (1972). Black explores the nature of the capital market equilibrium under the more restrictive assumption that there is neither a risk-free asset nor the opportunity to borrow or lend at a risk-free rate. As the outcome of the model does not change under Black's more restrictive assumption,[518] the following illustration of the CAPM will be focused on the case that a risk-free investment opportunity exists.

4.2.1.2 The model

If a risk-free asset exists in a mean-variance world, the Tobin-separation described above in 4.1.2.2 implies that investors decide on which share of their assets to invest risk-free and which share to invest in the portfolio of risky assets that is tangential to the MVEF. If all investors have homogeneous expectations, they select the same MVEF and consequently choose the same tangential portfolio to this efficient frontier.[519] Hence, all investors have the same mixture of risky assets in their

---

model covering several periods. Breeden (1979) further enhanced the model by including consumption decisions

516 See Sharpe (1964), p. 433 et seq., Lintner (1965), p. 15 and p. 25 as well as Mossin (1966), p. 769 et seq.

517 See again Footnote 483 for the requirement that a quadratic utility function needs to fulfil in this context

518 The function according to which the expected return of an asset in the market equilibrium can be determined has the same form, irrespective of the existence of a risk-free asset. Black replaces the yield of the risk-free asset by the return of a "zero-β portfolio" which is defined as the portfolio with the least σ among all portfolios that are uncorrelated to the market portfolio; see Black (1972), p. 444 and p. 446 et seqq.

519 See Sharpe (1964), S. 434, Lintner (1965), p. 25 and Mossin (1966), p. 775 et seq. A summarized derivation

portfolios. In the equilibrium, the capital market is cleared. This has the consequence that the tangential portfolio must be the market portfolio (M) and that in the market-clearing equilibrium the portfolios of all market participants lie on the MVCML.[520] It has been shown that the MVCML is a straight line in the $\mu-\sigma$ diagram, see again the graphical illustration in Figure 32.

The CAPM describes the relationship between the expected return μ_k and the risk σ_k of each individual asset included in M and of M itself in the capital market equilibrium. Hence, the model gives an answer to the question of how risks of financial assets are rewarded by the market.[521]

According to the CAPM, the risks of an individual asset can be split in two components: one component is the systematic risk, which is determined by the sensitivity of the individual asset towards the market. The other component is the unsystematic risk. The unsystematic risk component can be fully eliminated through diversification – hence, the optimally diversified market portfolio bears no unsystematic risk. As all investors mirror M when structuring their asset portfolio in the market equilibrium, the evaluation of assets is only determined by the systematic risk component. Unsystematic risk is not rewarded by capital markets.[522]

The systematic risk of an individual financial instrument k in relation to M is measured by the so-called Beta (β_k), which is defined as

$$\beta_k = \frac{\sigma_k * \rho_{k,M}}{\sigma_M}$$ [523]

The Beta describes the sensitivity of an asset's return to the return of the market portfolio and allows the security market line (SML) to be determined.[524] The SML shows that the expected return of an individual asset is composed of the risk-free market interest rate r_F and a risk premium over and above the expected return μ_M of M, which is weighted by the asset's β_k The SML has the equation

of the CAPM can, for example, be found in Spremann (2003), p. 273 et seq.

520 See Lintner (1965), p. 592 et seq.

521 See Sharpe (1964), p. 435, Lintner (1965), p. 25 and Mossin (1966), p. 771 et seqq.

522 See Sharpe (1964), p. 439 et seq. and Spremann (2003), p. 255

523 σ_k and σ_M are the risks of the individual asset and the market portfolio, respectively; $\rho_{k,M}$ is the correlation coefficient between the individual asset and the market portfolio. It becomes obvious from the equation that the market portfolio has a Beta of 1.

In practice, the Beta of an asset can, for example, be determined through linear regression of historical data. Already before developing the CAPM, Sharpe (1973) published a regression procedure to determine historical Betas

524 See also Brealey, Myers et al. (2004), p. 294 et seqq.

$$\mu_k = r_f + \beta_k * (r_M - r_f)$$[525]

The returns on an asset indicated by the SML allow the asset's market value to be determined. Provided asset returns are normally distributed or investors follow a quadratic utility function, the SML allows a linear evaluation of asset risks which depends on their individual β_k. In this context, it can be shown that the value of a portfolio of risky assets is the sum of the individual assets' values. The level of diversification between the assets does not influence the portfolio value. Rather, the portfolio value in the CAPM equilibrium is exclusively determined by the additive systematic risk component of the individual assets included in the portfolio.[526]

Since its introduction, the CAPM has been tested in a variety of empirical studies. The pivotal point of these empirical tests was the need to identify a suitable market portfolio. A major point of critique of the CAPM and its testability is related to issues concerning the generation of such a market portfolio.[527] A range of empirical studies testing the CAPM often found contradictions between the model results and real return characteristics.[528] In order to overcome the imperfections of the CAPM, which explains the expected return on an asset based on the Beta as one single factor, more complex multi-factor models were developed. These models measure up to the fact that asset prices are impacted by a variety of different factors.[529] They are not necessarily more precise than the CAPM, however.[530] Therefore, in spite of all the identified weaknesses and deficiencies of the CAPM, it is commonly agreed upon that there is no other model which is superior with regard to both simplicity and accuracy when reproducing and modeling real capital market conditions.[531]

---

525 See Spremann (2003), p. 254 Figure 9.2 for a graphical illustration of the SML in a $\mu_k - \beta_k$ diagram as well as Poppensieker (2002), p. 112 et seqq. for a formal derivation of the SML, referring to Huang and Litzenberger (1988), p. 100 et seqq.

526 See Lintner (1965), p. 26 et seq. and Poppensieker (2002), p. 115 et seq.

527 According to Roll (1977), there are two possible outcomes when empirically testing the CAPM by taking a market index as a proxy for M: one possible outcome is the conclusion that the CAPM is not a suitable model to describe reality. This can be due to the fact, however, that the proxy index does not properly reflect M. Another possibility is that the test concludes that the CAPM can be regarded as a suitable model to describe the real world which, in reality, is due to the fact that a proxy for M has been used which is inadequate to describe reality and leads to this outcome. Following this argument, Roll (1977) infers that the CAPM cannot be tested empirically

528 See, e.g., Campbell, Lo et al. (1997), pp. 182 – 218 for an overview of several empirical tests

529 While most of these models had the character of regression analyses, the Arbitrage-Pricing-Theory (APT) was the first approach to embed them into a theoretical framework; see Ross (1976)

530 See Kruschwitz and Löffler (1997)

531 See, e.g., Steiner and Wallmeier (1997)

4.2.2 Mean-LPM market equilibrium

The CAPM depicted above is based on the classical Tobin separation, underlying mean-variance optimization and foreseeing a straight MVCML in a $\mu - \sigma$ diagram. Further to the remarks on efficient portfolios in a mean-shortfall world made above, it will now be examined what a market equilibrium in a mean-LPM framework looks like. The assumptions on market completeness and investor preferences made above will hold. Analogous to the classical case, it is also assumed in the first instance that investors have the option to invest their funds in a risk-free asset besides selecting risky assets.[532] It will be shown below that in a very general form of a pricing model there is no need to require a risk-free investment opportunity.

The classical MVCML which, in capital market equilibrium, is a tangent to the MVEF at the market portfolio M (see again Figure 32), can be regarded as an efficient frontier itself.[533] In chapter 4.1.3, shortfall lines in a framework where risk is measured not through standard deviation but through shortfall probability have been introduced. When intersecting the MVEF with a cohort of these shortfall lines, a mean-shortfall probability capital market line (MSPCML) can be obtained.[534] In contrast to the MVCML, which has been proven to be a linear in a $\mu - \sigma$ diagram, this MSPCML has an inflection point (I_{CML}) and is left-curved for all $\mu > \mu_{IP}$ and accordingly right-curved for all $\mu < \mu_{IP}$ when illustrated in a $\mu - \kappa$ diagram (see Figure 34). In a more general context with n^{th} order LPM as risk measure, a convex relationship can be found when combining the risk-free asset with any risky portfolio in an LPM_n- μ diagram.[535]

As in the classical case, there is a tangential point between the MSPCML and the MSPEF, indicating M. Consequently, the same fund separation theorem as in the classical case holds: All investors, when applying the decision criteria "mean" and "shortfall probability", solely split their investments between the risk-free asset and M. The lower an individual investor's risk aversion, the higher is the share of M in his individual investment, thus increasing his shortfall risk. Although, as shown before, the total amount of efficient portfolios is smaller in a mean-shortfall risk world than in a mean-variance context, the outcome of the decision problem is the same.[536] Figure 34 gives a graphical schematic illustration of the portfolio separation theorem in a mean-shortfall probability diagram.

---

[532] It is defined that $\mu > r_f$

[533] See again Footnote 498

[534] For an analytical concept regarding the intersection criterion of efficient frontiers consisting of risky assets, see Wolter (1993). See Rudolf (1994), p. 93 Figure 3 for a graphical illustration of this procedure and p. 93 et seq. for an analytical description of the MSPCML

[535] See Harlow and Rao (1989), p. 289 Figure 1 and similarly Bawa and Lindenberg (1977), p. 195 Figure 2

[536] See Rudolf (1994), p. 94 et seq.

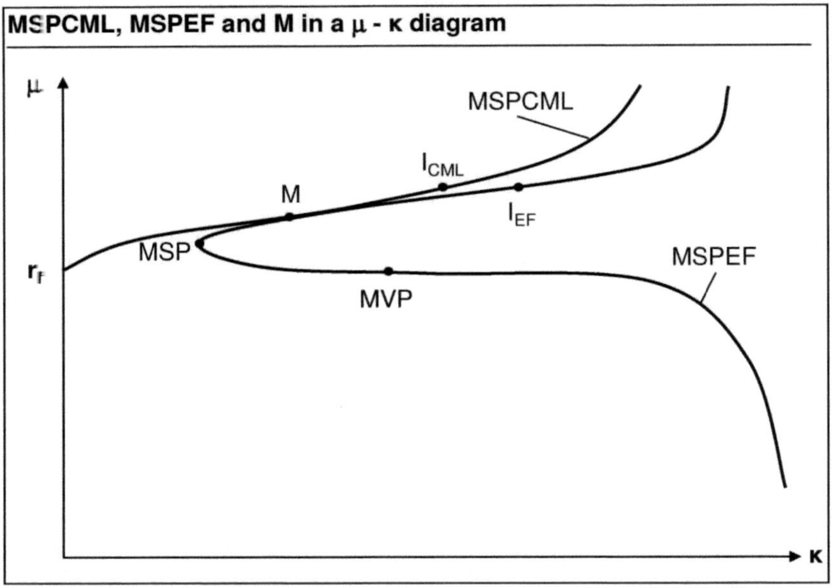

Figure 34: MSPCML, MSPEF and M in a $\mu - \kappa$ diagram[537]

It can be shown that this separation theorem not only holds for the specific mean-shortfall probability case but also in a more general mean- n^{th} order LPM framework with a target rate of return that is arbitrary and does not need to be the risk-free rate.[538]

Based on the result that the "classical" separation theorem also holds in a general mean-LPM context, an equation for an SML can be derived, which is similar to the one of the mean-variance CAPM illustrated above – except for the composition of β as the measure of the assets' systematic risk component. In particular, there is no need to assume normally distributed asset returns for this general pricing model to be valid.[539]

---

537 Source: Own illustration based on Rudolf (1994), p. 95 Figure 3

538 See Harlow and Rao (1989), p. 288 et seq.

539 See Harlow and Rao (1989), p. 289 et seqq., in particular p. 290 equation (6) showing the SML. The Harlow and Rao model is based on the general assumptions of complete markets as stated above (see again chapter 4.2.1.1). Apart from that, investors are required to have homogenous expectations but need to act only according to a very general set utility functions fulfilling the properties of monotonous increase $(U' > 0)$, risk aversion $(U'' < 0)$ and skewness preference $(U''' > 0)$. This implies, in particular, that there is no need any more to assume quadratic utility functions as required in the CAPM world, should the assumption of

This finding has the consequence that a wide range of asset pricing models which include common risk measures such as variance, can be regarded as specialized cases within this very general mean-LPM framework. In particular, the mean-variance CAPM can be regarded as a specialized risk pricing model having the risk-free rate as an implicit target rate of return.[540]

4.3 Value creation of the ACPM approach in complete capital markets

Founded on the complete capital market assumption, Modigliani and Miller (1958) have examined the relation between the way a corporation is financed and its market value. These theories will be introduced in the following as they will serve as a basis for determining whether the active management of credit portfolios can create value over and above the conventional approach towards lending business.

4.3.1 Market value maximization as evaluation criterion

Analogous to the work of Modigliani and Miller (1958), the criterion for value creation to be applied here is the maximization of a firm's market value.

The market value V of a firm is defined as the sum of the market value of its debt D and the market value of its equity E, hence

$$V = D + E$$ [541]

This market value approach has the characteristic that the evaluation of an investment project does not need to take into account the debt and equity holders' preferences because market prices reflect the preferences of the current as well as of all potential future company stakeholders.[542] Furthermore, it has been shown that, independently of the preferences of an individual debt or equity investor, a higher market value of his assets will always increase his utility if he has the opportunity to act on a capital market, which allows him to transform the enhanced asset value into a higher consumption budget according to his time and consumption preferences.[543]

---

normally distributed asset returns be relinquished. Furthermore, the model holds for arbitrary r*

540 The generalized mean-LPM model is reduced to the CAPM if the following assumptions hold: normally distributed asset returns, second-order LPM determining investors with risk-averse utility functions and skewness preference, as well as the requirement that $r^*=r_f$; see Harlow and Rao (1989), p. 291

541 See Modigliani and Miller (1958), p. 268

542 See Modigliani and Miller (1958), p. 264. In particular, assuming that all capital market participants have homogeneous expectations, in the complete capital market of the CAPM, the equity and debt holders of a corporation evaluate the corporation's activities in the same way. There are no information asymmetries between these stakeholders

543 See Makowski and Pepall (1985), p. 1248 and p. 1240 Figure 2. It is shown that an increasing market value of a firm moves the owners' budget constraint in a parallel direction towards higher utility. The secondary market needs to fulfill the following conditions: completeness, competitiveness (i.e. prices are independent

In the following, both financing and investment decisions of corporations will be considered. The key question to be addressed is under which conditions – if at all – they increase the market value of a corporation in the capital market equilibrium of the CAPM.

4.3.2 Irrelevance and separation theorems

Following the assumption that a corporation is financed with debt and equity, the optimal mixture between these two types of capital which leads to a maximization of the corporation's market value is to be determined. Modigliani and Miller (1958) show that in a CAPM world, i.e., under the assumptions of a complete capital market, the finance structure is solely relevant for the split of the corporation's market value among its debt and equity holders but is irrelevant for the market value itself. This is the so-called irrelevance theorem.[544]

In line with the irrelevance theorem, the capital structure is also irrelevant for the market value of a specific investment I which can be financed with debt D or equity E and whose stochastic payoffs $\tilde{I}_1$ at the end of the investment period are distributed among its debt and equity holders. The following equation holds:

$$\tilde{I}_1 = \tilde{D}_1 + \tilde{E}_1$$

It is important to note, however, that the irrelevance theorem only holds under the assumptions if $\tilde{I}_1$, $\tilde{D}_1$ and $\tilde{E}_1$ are normally distributed or if investors follow a quadratic utility function.[545]

An additional investment project is undertaken if its net value creation ΔU_0^{Net} (i.e., the gross value creation ΔU_0^{Gross} minus the initial investment cost ΔI_0) is positive, hence

$$\Delta U_0^{Net} = \Delta U_0^{Gross} - \Delta I_0 .^{546}$$

of single transaction volumes), and lack of transaction costs; see DeAngelo (1981). In a CAPM world, these requirements are fulfilled as the CAPM assumes, among others, unlimited access to the primary and secondary capital market and frictionless issuance and trading of assets on these markets (see section 4.2.1.1)

544 See Modigliani and Miller (1958), p. 268 et seq. The irrelevance theorem can also be formulated in a different way: independently of how a given income stream is split up into different components, the sum of the values of these components equals the value of the original income stream. This is the so-called principle of value additivity; see Haley and Schall (1979), p. 167

545 See again Footnote 483 for the requirements to be fulfilled by quadratic utility functions

546 See Poppensieker (2002), p. 125

It can be shown that this is the case if the project's expected internal rate of return exceeds the expected rate of return that investors can achieve according to the CAPM when acquiring a security on the capital market which has the same risks as the respective project. If this is the case, the investment leads to an increase of the corporation's market value.[547] If there are no synergy effects between the projects, each project can be evaluated individually without having the need to take into consideration diversification effects between already existing investments. This is also due to the assumption that individuals can undertake their own transactions to diversify risks in a corporation's portfolio.[548] As capital costs are also independent of the corporation's capital structure, the decision whether to execute such an investment or not is only determined by the specific, systematic risk of this individual investment and its resulting capital costs.[549]

Consequently, the choice to initiate a new investment can be separated from the question of how to finance this investment. This is the so-called separation theorem.[550]

4.3.3 Value creation of the ACPM approach

As described in chapter 2.3.2, banks only have restricted opportunities to manage a credit portfolio by means of their primary market business. The ACPM approach addresses this issue since the acquisition and distribution of credit assets on secondary markets in order to better achieve a risk-return efficient portfolio composition is foreseen. The execution of secondary credit market transactions is the main difference between the ACPM approach and the conventional "originate and hold" approach towards lending, which is solely focused on primary market credit business.

It is only recommendable to pursue the implementation of an ACPM approach if it creates additional value over the conventional lending approach. Therefore, it will be examined in the following whether, from a theoretical point of view, the market value of a financial institution increases if it pursues an active management of its credit portfolio. As the key difference between the two lending approaches is the execution of secondary credit market transactions, the theoretical argumentation will be narrowed down to the question of whether such transactions are value-adding or not. Hence, based on the theoretical findings illustrated above and by defining value creation as creation of market value according to Modigliani and Miller, it will now be illustrated now, if, given the existence of a complete capital market for debt and equity, secondary credit market transactions can create value.

---

547 See Rubinstein (1973), p. 171 et seq. and p. 172 Figure 3 for a graphical illustration of the acceptance criterion

548 See Rubinstein (1973), p. 173

549 See Rubinstein (1973), p. 177

550 See Modigliani and Miller (1958), p. 288

As shown in chapter three, the use of secondary credit market instruments for the active management of a credit portfolio is motivated by the goals to diversify credit risks, (e.g., with the help of credit derivatives, see chapter 3.2), to perform regulatory arbitrage (e.g., through asset securitizations, see chapter 3.3) or to refinance lending activities (e.g., through issuing instruments, such as ABBs, which are securitized by an underlying pool of credit assets, see chapter 3.3.3.1).

It has been shown before that banks continue to remain the most important participants on secondary credit markets both on the buy- and the sell-side of credit risks despite, e.g., a recently shrinking market share in the credit derivatives market for the benefit of non-bank financial intermediaries such as mutual, pension and hedge funds.[551] This does not rule out, however, that private individuals can act as counterparties in these transactions as well. Consequently, the argumentation in the following section will differentiate between transactions with banks/other financial intermediaries and those with private individuals. In both cases, it needs to be distinguished between complete and incomplete secondary credit markets.[552]

Generally, in a secondary market transaction, a transaction price S_0 to be paid at the beginning of the investment period is exchanged for a stochastic payoff $\tilde{S}_1$ at the end of the period.

In a complete secondary market, an investor pays $-S_0^I$ for a transaction which equals the income S_0^D that his counterparty receives. In return, the investor receives the stochastic pay-off $\tilde{S}_1^I$, paid by his counterparty in the form of $-\tilde{S}_1^D$ at maturity of the investment contract.

Market imperfections in the secondary market can alter these prices, e.g., through transaction costs reducing the value of such deals. As a consequence of these market imperfections, the transaction prices between an investor and his counterparty can differ, i.e.,

$$\Delta S_0 = S_0^D - S_0^I \neq 0 \text{ and } \Delta \tilde{S}_1 = \tilde{S}_1^I - \tilde{S}_1^D \neq 0 .$$

4.3.3.1 Secondary market transactions between intermediaries and private individuals

It is assumed that, as an alternative to refinance its credit portfolio (i.e., its primary market investments in credit assets) through acquisition of debt or equity on the

[551] See again chapters 3.1.3 for loan sales and syndication, 3.2.4 for credit derivatives, and 3.3.4 for securitization transactions

[552] The subsequent argumentation follows Poppensieker (2002), p. 126 et seqq.

complete capital market, a bank can acquire funds through secondary credit market transactions between an intermediaries and private individuals. Hence, a credit investment with the stochastic payoff $\tilde{I}_1$ at the end of the investment period (at maturity of the contract) may not only be financed with debt and equity (having the stochastic payoffs $\tilde{D}_1$ and $\tilde{E}_1$, respectively) but also by means of such secondary credit market transactions.

As a consequence, the following equation holds for the stochastic value of an investment at the end of the investment period:

$$\tilde{I}_1 = \tilde{D}_1 + \tilde{E}_1 + \tilde{S}_1 + \Delta \tilde{S}_1$$

If a complete secondary credit market exists, the value of $\Delta\tilde{S}_1$ is zero. In this case, since $\tilde{S}_1$ can be regarded as an additional segment of the complete capital market, the above-mentioned irrelevance theorem of Modigliani and Miller holds. Accordingly, the changed finance structure following the execution of secondary credit market transactions instead of acquiring debt or equity capital does not influence the market value of a bank. Hence, if the bank decides to finance a credit investment through transactions with private individuals on the secondary credit market instead of or in addition to raising funds on the equity or debt capital market, this does not create additional market value.

As shown above, under the assumption of an incomplete secondary credit market, it might happen that $\Delta S_0 \neq 0$ or $\Delta \tilde{S}_1 \neq 0$ (i.e., there might be payoff changes at the beginning or the end of the investment period). The corresponding market value of these payoff changes at the end of the investment period is $V(\Delta \tilde{S}_1)$. Since it can be assumed that the trading of credit risks on incomplete secondary markets is fraught with transaction costs – in particular following the existence of information asymmetries – the value of the payoff would be lower than the initially paid transaction price; the inequation $\Delta S_0 - V(\Delta \tilde{S}_1) > 0$ holds. Consequently, the transaction costs would reduce the market value of the institution if it pursues secondary credit market transactions as opposed to acquiring refinancing on the complete capital market. Hence, the existence of such an incomplete secondary credit market does not create additional value.[553]

[553] It is theoretically possible that $\Delta S_0 - V(\Delta \tilde{S}_1) < 0$. This is only the case, however, if the secondary credit market is subsidized externally, which is not a realistic assumption

4.3.3.2 Secondary market transactions among intermediaries

If a bank or another financial intermediary enters into secondary credit market transactions with another one, such transactions can be regarded as investments into or divestments of credit risks, with the counterparty performing the respective antipodal transaction. Consequently, following the argumentation which leads to the separation theorem above, such secondary market transactions add value if they have a positive net value creation for the transaction partners involved.

Assuming that a complete secondary credit market exists, the stochastic payoff $\tilde{I}_1$ from such an investment equals the pay-back $\tilde{S}_1$ which the investor gets from the secondary market deal at maturity of the transaction. Accordingly, the divesting counterparty's payoff has the same pay-back with a negative sign, i.e., $-\tilde{S}_1$. As they act in a complete capital market, both parties evaluate the secondary market transaction with identical capital costs, albeit having different signs, i.e. the investor's value of the transaction at maturity of the contract is $V(\Delta\tilde{S}_1)$, his counterparty's is $-V(\Delta\tilde{S}_1)$. The initial investment costs ΔI_0 equal the initial price of the secondary market transaction S_0. As both the investor and his counterparty only execute the transaction if it has a positive net value creation, the following inequations need to be fulfilled:

The investor will execute the transaction if the value he receives at the end of the investment period is greater than the initial transaction price, i.e., if

$$V(\tilde{S}_1) - S_0 > 0$$

The investor's counterparty closes the deal if the initial transaction price that he is paid exceeds the (negative) value at the end of the transaction period, i.e., if

$$S_0 - V(\tilde{S}_1) > 0$$

Since both inequations cannot be fulfilled at the same time, secondary credit market transactions with other intermediaries do not add value in a complete capital market.[554]

If the secondary credit market is incomplete, the transaction prices between an investor and his counterparty can differ, i.e., $\Delta S_0 \neq 0$ and $\Delta\tilde{S}_1 \neq 0$. In this case, a secondary market transaction only adds value if these market imperfections cause a transaction to be value-creating for both parties. This would only be the case if the imperfections were based on external subsidies, which however is not a realistic assumption.[555] As in

554 If value-neutral investment programs were accepted, the in-equations above would include the case that secondary credit market transactions are indifferent with regard to value creation. This would still not justify the existence of a secondary credit market

555 Even if the market was supported by external subsidies, it would additionally be required that the parties manage to split the additional value in a satisfactory manner. In view of existing information asymmetries, this might prove rather difficult

the case of transactions with private individuals, the existence of transaction cost-type of market imperfections would reduce the market value of banks as opposed to a financing of their (credit) investments on the complete capital market. Again there is no economic justification for secondary credit market transactions.

4.3.3.3 Conclusion

Provided that a complete market for equity and debt capital exists, it can be shown that under the assumption of both complete and incomplete secondary credit markets, secondary credit market transactions do not create additional value if external subsidies of these markets are realistically excluded.

The refinancing of credit risk investments has been described above in a very general form, thus enabling the payment flows from all secondary credit market transactions to be subsumed.[556] As a consequence, no transaction that can be performed using the instruments introduced in chapter three – be it transactions to diversify credit risks through selling or acquiring credit assets on secondary loan markets, to refinance lending activities or transactions performed by means of on- or off-balance sheet secondary market instruments – create additional economic value.

Furthermore, following the irrelevance hypothesis according to which the share of equity capital held by a corporation does not influence its market value, the amount of regulatory equity capital held is irrelevant. Hence, transactions that are performed in order to alter the regulatory equity provision do not impact the market value of a corporation.

Founded on the argumentation that the key difference between the conventional "originate and hold" approach towards lending and the ACPM approach is the execution of secondary credit market transactions, it can be concluded that, in view of the lack of ability of these transactions to increase the market value of a corporation, actively managing a loan portfolio by means of secondary market instruments does not generate additional value for an institution. Consequently, the move from an origination-focused "originate and hold" lending approach towards an active management of credit portfolios by means of secondary market transactions does not enhance the market value of an institution, provided it operates in a complete capital market.[557]

---

556 The choice of how to refinance investments through debt and equity according to Modigliani and Miller (1958) has been extended by the payoffs from secondary market transactions. Any secondary market transaction described in chapter 3 triggers a payoff structure of this kind and can therefore be subsumed under the equation $I_1 = D_1 + E_1 + S_1 + \Delta S_1$

557 This argumentation does not take into consideration that the introduction of an ACPM business model might create value through an influence of ACPM on loan origination, e.g., by enforcing a more profitable credit pricing or preventing origination from taking on unprofitable customers. Assuming an optimal loan pricing and customer selection procedure exists under the conventional lending approach, the introduction of an

More generally, this finding leads to the conclusion that in complete capital markets banks can at most generate economic value from their primary market credit business, i.e., through originating credit assets.

As a matter of fact, however, as already shown in the beginning of this dissertation, in complete capital markets resources are allocated in a Pareto-efficient way among market participants. In this case, not even the primary market business of banks creates value. Hence, there is no economic justification for the existence of financial intermediaries. Yet, it has also been shown that such allocation-efficient complete capital markets are an unrealistic assumption. Rather, in reality, despite tendencies towards more complete capital markets, the existence of different types of market incompletions gives banks a right to exist as they can create value through their primary market business.[558]

In view of such market incompletions, it might be possible that, further to the value creation of a bank's primary market business, secondary credit market transactions – and hence the active management of a credit portfolio through applying secondary credit market instruments – can create value.

Therefore, the remainder of this chapter will systematically examine the existence of such incompletions on equity and debt capital markets in greater detail and illustrate the consequences of their existence for firms' finance structures. Based on these findings, it will be elaborated whether secondary credit market transactions can be motivated in incomplete capital markets.

4.4 Incompletions of bank capital markets and implications for value creation of the ACPM approach

Following the discussion in finance theory on the assumptions of complete capital markets underlying the CAPM and the theorems of Modigliani and Miller (see chapter 4.2.1.1), three types of market incompletions can be distinguished whose existence and implications for the active management of credit portfolios through secondary credit market transactions will be described in this chapter: (I) limited market access, (II) market frictions, and (III) information asymmetries. Furthermore, market incompletions arising from involvement of the state or state-owned regulators in banking business will be addressed. The findings are summarized and illustrated in Figure 35.

ACPM approach does not add value. Following this assumption, the introduction of an ACPM approach neither creates additional value on the already optimally set-up primary market side nor, if the unit operates in a complete capital market, through execution of secondary credit market transactions

558 See again chapter 1.2

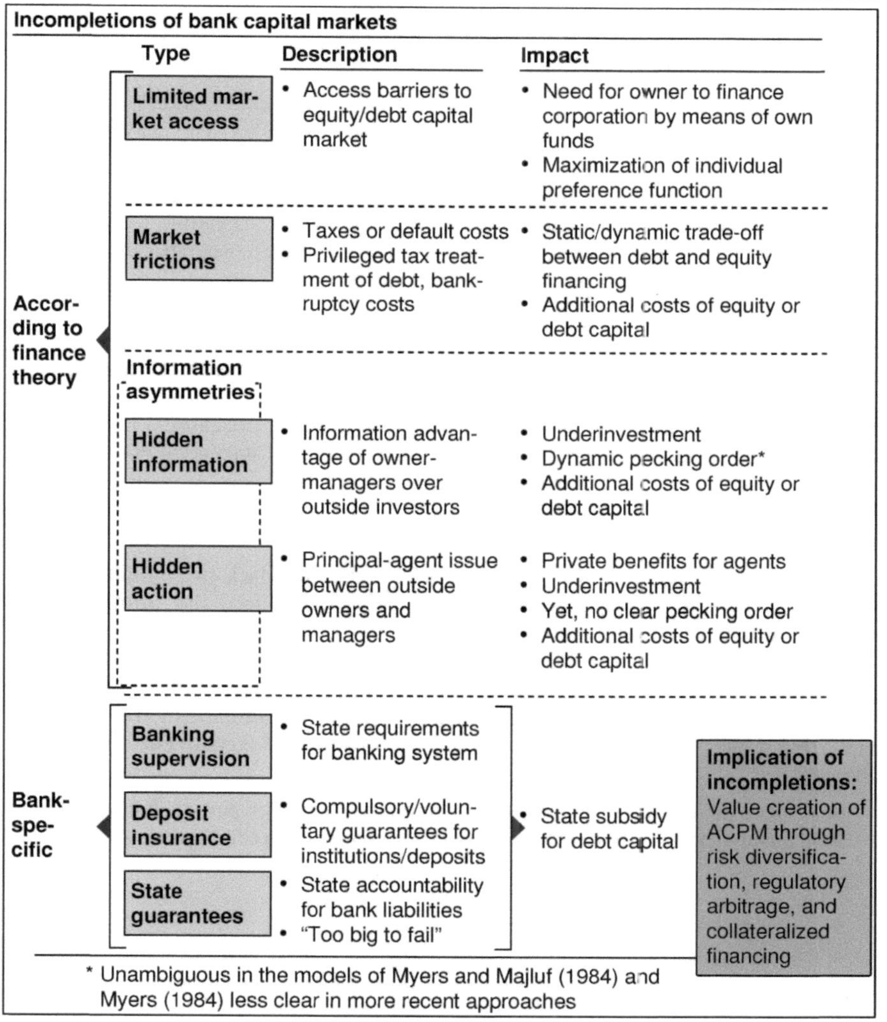

Figure 35: Incompletions of bank capital markets[559]

[559] Source: Own illustration

4.4.1 Market incompletions according to finance theory

4.4.1.1 Limited market access

One characteristic of a complete capital market is the unlimited market access for all participants including free tradability of securities on this market. This may not always be the case.

It has already been shown in the example of the commercial paper market that some sub-segments of the debt capital market are effectively not accessible for all market participants.[560] This might prove particularly grave for these corporations in times of economic downturns which are typically accompanied by a strong limitation of the loan supply through banks.[561]

The ability to access the public equity market has a significant impact on how corporations are financed: it can be shown that privately held, unlisted firms without capital market access may be limited to obtain sufficient equity financing in view of high market frictions such as search costs, for example. Because of the higher illiquidity of private compared to public equity, selling stakes in privately held companies can also be complicated as it may be accompanied by comparably high transaction costs and information asymmetries as opposed to a sale of shares in publicly listed companies.[562]

If issuance and tradability of capital is restricted due to a lack of or limited capital market access, the owner of a corporation needs to finance the firm's business activities through investing his own assets. The lack of possibility to trade financial assets also implies that the owner cannot benefit from an increasing value of his corporation by exchanging this value enhancement into private income on the capital market. Thus, in this case, he will not have the goal of maximizing the firm's market value but rather maximize his own utility according to his individual preference function.[563]

With respect to ACPM, it will be shown in chapter 4.3.2 of part II that the lack of existence and especially insufficient liquidity of secondary credit markets in their field

---

560 See chapter 1.3.3, in particular Footnote 73

561 See Schmidt and Nehls (2004) for an examination whether the recent earnings drop of German banks has resulted in such a so-called "credit crunch". A recent survey by the "Deutscher Industrie- und Handelskammertag" seems to confirm the existence of such a "credit crunch" within the German mid-corps segment: according to the survey, the problems of these corporations to get bank financing were partially even more aggravated at the beginning of 2005 after an already difficult 2004; see DIHK (2005)

562 This is, e.g., shown by Brav (2004) who compares the capital structure of publicly and privately owned firms in the UK

563 See again chapter 4.3.1 regarding market value maximization and chapter 4.1.1 concerning individual utility functions. See Poppensieker (2002), p. 136 for a formal illustration of a finance decision in this context

of activity is seen as a key obstacle by most CPM units on the path to realize their objectives. Therefore, a more detailed examination of the impact that the ability to access secondary credit markets and especially the tradability of credit risks on these markets have on the set-up of CPM units will be provided in chapter 5.2.2 of part III.

4.4.1.2 Market frictions

Market frictions according to finance theory typically occur in the form of taxes and default costs. They lead to a reduced return on a corporation's assets as opposed to the yield such a corporation generates through its investment activities.

The mere introduction of taxes in the model of Modigliani and Miller (1958) does not necessarily impact the irrelevance of the capital structure: if a tax system is in the form that there are unique tax rates for all market participants – i.e., no preferred treatment for a particular type of capital – there is no difference whether it is the corporation which changes its capital structure or whether its investors perform such transactions on a personal level. The after-tax returns for all market participants remain the same.[564]

Yet, if one method of financing enjoys a privileged tax treatment over others, a market value-maximizing corporation will exclusively finance its investment activities through this tax-advantaged type of financing. If, for example, debt financing is more favorable than equity financing because interest payments on debt are tax deductible from a corporation's income, it can be shown that the corporation's market value is a linearly increasing function of the amount of debt used in its capital structure. In this case, provided that the corporation manages to earn and pay for its debt obligation, it will aspire to obtain 100% debt financing.[565] However, using the maximum amount of debt in a firm's capital structure is not a feasible option because it ignores the existence of bankruptcy and its related costs.[566]

Bankruptcy occurs when a firm either fails to pay back the due obligations to its creditors or suffers from over-indebtedness.[567] As a consequence of the insolvency, the firm faces direct and indirect bankruptcy costs: direct bankruptcy costs include, e.g., legal or accounting fees related to the insolvency. Indirect bankruptcy costs relate to opportunity costs resulting, e.g, from disruptions in the relationship of the firm with

---

564 See Modigliani and Miller (1958), p. 239 et seq. and Modigliani and Miller (1963), p. 434 et seq. referring to a deduction of debt capital from the taxable income of a corporation. The impact of personal income taxes for the corporation's owners is not considered. Miller (1977), p. 267 et seq. includes a personal income tax which is structured in a way that even under the existence of this tax, it is not better if the owners finance their firm with tax-deductible debt instead of equity capital

565 See Modigliani and Miller (1963), p. 442. Furthermore, Hirshleifer (1966) shows that further to debt tax shields, any tax minimization procedure enhances a corporation's market value

566 See, e.g., Baxter (1967), p. 395

567 See Haugen and Senbet (1978), p. 384 and, e.g., InsO (1994) for the German bankruptcy regulation: Bankruptcy is caused by a failure to repay debt (§§ 17 and 18) or through indebtedness (§ 19)

suppliers or customers that are related to the transfer of ownership or control after an insolvency.[568]

Bankruptcy costs are solely disadvantageous for debt capital – a company that is purely financed with equity cannot default. Consequently, assuming that there are no other incompletions than bankruptcy costs in a capital market, corporations will finance their activities entirely through taking on equity capital.[569] Hence, debt financing and the associated potential bankruptcy costs can only be explained if there is an offsetting advantage for these costs, e.g., following the above-mentioned tax shield of debt financing.

It can be shown that there is an optimal leverage ratio equalizing the marginal tax benefits from debt financing and the marginal bankruptcy costs.[570] This insight leads to the development of static trade-off theory as a counter-argument to the irrelevance theorem. According to static trade-off theory, a firm sets its target debt-to equity ratio to where the marginal benefits of its debt tax shield equalize the marginal bankruptcy costs.[571]

One critique of this theory is that it does not take into consideration the dynamic process of how to get to this target leverage ratio. Consequently, it has been differentiated between the static single-period trade-off between the tax benefits of debt and bankruptcy costs, on the one hand, and the adjustment behavior of a firm, which has a target level of leverage and gradually removes the deviations from this target over time, on the other hand. This second aspect has recently been addressed through the development of dynamic trade-off theory.[572]

The models developed to examine dynamic trade-off theory include several aspects that have been ignored in static single-period trade-off models. In particular, it is examined which role expectations and adjustment costs play. In a dynamic model, the correct financing decision of a firm usually depends on the financing margin it expects in the following period. Accordingly, there are decisions to be taken regarding whether to pay out or raise funds in the next period and, if funds are raised, whether debt or

---

568 See Haugen and Senbet (1978), p. 385. It is assumed here that there are no positive effects of bankruptcy costs such as tax deductibility. See also Brealey, Myers et al. (2004), p. 407 et seqq. for a description of costs of financial distress

569 This conclusion follows Haugen and Senbet (1978), p. 386 et seq. who argue that the maximal level of direct bankruptcy costs is limited because debt investors can purchase the equity of a firm before a bankruptcy procedure is initiated. Equity investors can similarly avoid direct bankruptcy costs by acquiring the debt of a firm

570 See Kraus and Litzenberger (1973), p. 915 et seqq.

571 See Myers (1984), p. 577 et seqq. as well as Bradley, Jarrell et al. (1984)

572 See Frank and Goyal (2005), p. 9 et seq.

equity capital should be taken on.[573] In this context, it has been shown by Fisher, Henkel et al. (1989), that, if there are transaction costs related to rebalancing the finance structure, a firm might delay changing its capital structure until the structure gets significantly out of balance to justify the payment of such transaction costs. Frank and Goyal (2005) give a comprehensive overview of the recently developed work on dynamic trade-off theory. As most research in this area has only recently arisen, a final evaluation of the variety of the models developed in this context is still pending.[574]

4.4.1.3 Information asymmetries

Besides market frictions, information asymmetries are another source for market incompletions that have an impact on the finance structure of corporations.[575] Their existence has been used to develop pecking order theory as a competing theory to the static trade-off models of finance structure.[576]

---

[573] See Frank and Goyal (2005), p. 14

[574] See Frank and Goyal (2005), p. 17 et seqq. The authors differentiate dynamic trade-off literature according to a set of underlying assumptions:

A key differentiation is the treatment of investments: following the assumptions of Modigliani and Miller (1958) and Kraus and Litzenberger (1973), several models treat a corporation's cash flows as exogenous (e.g., Kane, Marcus et al. (1984), Fisher, Henkel et al. (1989), Goldstein, Ju et al. (2001), and Strebulaev (2004)). Other models assume that investments and with it the corporation's cash flows depend on how the corporation finances its business; hence, they consider investments in line with financing decisions (e.g., Brennan and Schwartz (1984), Mello and Parsons (1992), Mauer and Triantis (1994), Hennessey and Whited (2004) and Titman and Tsyplakov (2004)

If a firm has excess cash, it is typically assumed that this cash is paid out to shareholders. Some models are based on the assumption that all funds are paid out to shareholders (e.g., Brennan and Schwartz (1984) and Titman and Tsyplakov (2004)). Others consider the possibility of keeping some of the excess cash as retained earnings (e.g., Stiglitz (1973) and Hennessey and Whited (2004))

The models developed on dynamic trade-off theory also differ concerning their assumptions of the underlying tax systems. For example, Fisher, Henkel et al. (1989) and Titman and Tsyplakov (2004) do not consider taxes on payouts from corporations to shareholders, whereas Stiglitz (1973) and Hennessey and Whited (2004) assume that taxes are to be paid on distributions from corporations to investors but not on funds which investors provide to corporations. Goldstein, Ju et al. (2001) and Strebulaev (2004) assume that shareholders get a tax rebate when they acquire an equity stake in a corporation

[575] See, again, chapter 1.2, in particular Footnote 32, for introductory comments on information asymmetries

[576] Among others, a motivation for the development of pecking order theory has been the fact that trade-off theory does not always hold in practice: if trade-off theory was empirically valid, this would imply that low profitable growth companies, which have risky and chiefly intangible assets, would aspire to relatively little debt financing, whereas established firms with a solid, tangible asset base and stable cash flows would have the highest leverage ratios. In reality, however, this is often not the case; see Brealey, Myers et al. (2004), p. 412 et seq.

4.4.1.3.1 Hidden information

Following the work of Donaldson (1961), it has been shown by Myers and Majluf (1984) and Myers (1984) that the existence of hidden information can influence the way investment projects are financed. The basic idea behind this theory is that the true value of a corporation and its investment projects as well as its growth opportunities are only known to management of the firm but not to outside investors. A manager uses this information advantage when having to decide about how to finance a new investment project.

Assuming the manager has the opportunity to finance such a new project either through equity issuance or by means of internal funds such as retained earnings or financial slack (i.e., liquid assets or unused credit lines),[577] his knowledge of the true value of both the already existing projects and the new one determines how to finance this new project.[578]

Assuming that the manager acts in the best interest of existing shareholders, he will face two adverse effects when deciding to undertake and finance a new investment: on the one hand, existing shareholders benefit from such an investment if it creates value for the corporation. On the other hand, the issuance of new equity to finance the project will shift value away from existing to new shareholders.[579] Consequently, a new investment will only be undertaken and financed through issuance of new equity if its value-added for existing shareholders is greater than the shift of value from these shareholders to new investors following the issuance of additional equity capital. This will be the case the lower the true value of existing investments, the higher the overvaluation of existing shares through the capital market, the higher the value of the new project, and the lower the need to finance the new project through new shares whose issuance dilutes the share price for existing shareholders.[580]

Yet, investors with rational expectations take the management's behavior into consideration ex-ante. Consequently, they infer from the decision to finance a new project by means of external funds that the true value of the already existing investments must be below their current market value and that the corporation is actually overvalued. Hence, the announcement by a corporation that it is issuing new stock will lower its market value. Therefore, a manager acting in the best interest of

[577] The term financial slack is introduced by Myers (1984), p. 590 who refers to liquid assets or reserve borrowing power

[578] See Myers and Majluf (1984), p. 190 et seq. The existence of debt is not included in their model yet but covered by Myers (1984)

[579] It is assumed that existing shareholders do not adjust their portfolio following the issuance of new equity; see Myers and Majluf (1984), p. 198 et seq.

[580] See Myers and Majluf (1984), p. 200

existing shareholders will be hesitant to undertake new projects – underinvestment is the consequence.[581]

In order to avoid such adverse effects on existing shareholders and to mitigate the underinvestment issue, the manager needs to look for ways of how to finance projects in a way that has a less negative effect on the corporation's market value than the issuance of external equity. Besides retaining internal funds, the issuance of default risk-free debt would be an optimal solution in this context. If these types of financing are not possible, the corporation should issue risky debt before turning towards equity financing.[582]

Obviously, under the existence of such information asymmetries, the irrelevance theorem of Modigliani and Miller does not hold. Theory rather projects a dynamic pecking order depending on historic profitability according to which the most profitable, highest valued firms should have low debt leverage ratios compared to their industry's average as they can better raise external equity without needing to fear a strong share price dilution and will very likely not change this ratio. Unprofitable corporations in the same industry, on the other hand, are expected to have comparably high debt leverage ratios.[583]

More recent research on dynamic pecking order theory has shown that the models developed by Myers and Majluf (1984) and Myers (1984) provide a simplified picture of the issues related to debt vs. equity financing in the case of hidden information-type of asymmetries.[584]

More recent research in this field has shown that corporations frequently face double-sided information asymmetries. If this is the case, there are several equilibriums possible leading to less unanimous solutions regarding the question whether a corporation raise cash through issuing securities or rather pursue internal financing.[585] Viswanath (1993) has developed a multi-period model and concludes that the results with respect to pecking order depend on the relation between the first- and second-

---

581 See Myers and Majluf (1984), p. 203

582 Issuance of default risk-free debt has the advantage that it is virtually uncorrelated to the stock price of a firm, see, Myers (1984), p. 588. Myers also notes that it is unrealistic that a private company can issue debt that is absolutely protected against default. However, he argues that the issuance of highly rated debt securities is a good proxy for such risk-free debt as their impact on the average stock price is relatively small

583 See Myers (1984), p. 589. Myers (1984) concludes that, following this theory, average debt ratios should vary from industry to industry because asset risk, asset types and requirements for external funds vary between industries

584 See Frank and Goyal (2005), p. 23 et seq. as well as Brealey, Myers et al. (2004), p. 413 who state that pecking order theory seems to work best for mature firms but often does not hold for fast growing high-tech firms as these corporations frequently seek for equity issuance to finance their investments

585 See, e.g., Eckbo, Giammarino et al. (1990) dealing with two-sided information asymmetries in merger situations and their implications on the issue whether to finance these transactions through stock or cash

period uncertainties. Halov and Heider (2004) differentiate between information asymmetries regarding the value of a firm and others concerning the risks of a corporation's business activities. In the first case, standard pecking order models apply, i.e., firms prefer to issue debt over equity. In the second case, however, the opposite holds and firms prefer external equity over debt financing. Finally, there have been models developed examining the existence of a pecking order for different methods to issue equity.[586]

4.4.1.3.2 Hidden action

Hidden action related to a corporation's business activities reflects the issue that the corporation's owners (principals) cannot fully observe the actions of its management (agents) with whom they have engaged in a contractual relationship. In particular, assuming that both parties in such a contractual relationship are utility maximizers, there is reason to believe that management – unless sufficiently incentivized through an appropriate contract – will not always act in the best interest of the corporation's owners, to maximize their welfare. With reference to finance decisions, there is the need to design an optimal contract which not only minimizes conflicts of interest between the different parties but also maximizes the corporation's market value and optimizes its capital structure.[587]

A manager who does not own stakes in a corporation has an incentive to undertake expenditures yielding him personal advantages that are unobservable for outside, non-managing shareholders. While such perks are for the exclusive benefit of the manager, they need not or only partly be borne by him – they are (partly) financed by the firm's shareholders. These perks reduce the market value of shareholders' equity. In order to inhibit such managerial behavior, they need to engage in costly monitoring activities. They will pursue such activities until their marginal benefit related to a monitoring of management is equal to the marginal costs they face through these activities.[588]

Such agency costs can be avoided if a sole owner manages the corporation or if investment activities are financed through retained earnings or risk-free debt.[589] A second-best solution is to sell risky debt securities to external bondholders. In order to

---

[586] See, e.g., Eckbo and Masulis (1992) and Eckbo and Norli (2004) showing that adverse selection is a less severe issue if current shareholders are allowed to participate in the issuance of new equity. Accordingly, corporations that expect a lot of their current shareholders to acquire new issuances have low adverse selection issues and consequently prefer to issue uninsured rights while firms with low expected current shareholder participation in new equity offerings are in favor of using firm commitment to such underwriting offerings

[587] See Jensen and Meckling (1976), p. 5 and p. 7

[588] See Jensen and Meckling (1976), p. 11 and p. 17 et seq.

[589] See Jensen and Meckling (1976), p. 34 et seq. and, again, Footnote 582 for restrictions regarding the possibility to issue risk-free debt

limit managerial behavior that reduces the market value of their securities, these bondholders are interested in adding covenants to the debt contracts which impose constraints on certain management decisions. Additionally, debt investors will engage in the monitoring of managerial activities similar to equity investors.[590] Yet, a crucial difference between the interest payments on debt capital and dividends paid out on equity capital is that managers cannot suspend interest payments as easily in order to finance activities that are primarily in their private interests as they can cut down dividends on equity capital.[591] Consequently, debt holders need to perform costly monitoring activities to ensure proper management behavior to a lesser extent than equity holders.[592]

In view of those lower monitoring costs, debt capital is a cheaper and hence preferred external source to finance a corporation than equity capital. It seems as though pecking order theory also holds in the case of hidden action information asymmetries given a separation of management and external financing of a corporation.

So far, incentive issues between management and external financiers of a corporation that are not involved in management activities have been examined. However, it has not been shown yet which are possible incentive issues between outside equity and debt investors if equity investors are involved in management activities of a corporation.

Assuming an owner-manager of a corporation has the opportunity to first issue debt securities and to decide afterwards between two investments of different riskiness, he has the incentive to promise a low-risk project to future debt holders before selling bonds but to undertake a riskier project after having received the funds. He will act like this due to following situation: if both projects solely differ regarding the variance of their output distribution, the riskier project increases the value of the firm's equity and lowers the value of its debt. Thus, the decision to take on the riskier project after having issued debt transfers value from the bondholders to the owner-manager as equity holder.[593]

590 See Jensen and Meckling (1976), p. 45. Covenants can include, e.g., constraints on dividend policy and future debt issues as well as requirements to maintain sufficient working capital. See also Black and Scholes (1973) for a discussion on how dividends and financing policy of a corporation can redistribute wealth between different stakeholders of a corporation

591 See, e.g., Spremann (1996), p. 270 et seqq. for features of equity financing and p. 275 et seqq., in particular p. 276 et seq., for features of long-term debt financing

592 The debt holders do not actually bear the costs of their monitoring activities. They rather take them into account when determining the price they are willing to pay for the debt claim. Hence, it is the owner of the corporation who eventually pays for the monitoring costs; see Jensen and Meckling (1976), p. 46

593 The equity stake in a firm can be regarded as a European call option on the total firm's value (see, e.g., Hull (2006) , p. 181 for a description of European options). It is assumed that the total value of both projects is the same. According to the option pricing model of Black and Scholes (1973), the higher variance of the

Ex ante, rational bondholders anticipate the owner-manager's investment incentives. Hence, they are only willing to pay the (lower) price of debt corresponding to the riskier project. This is equivalent to an increase of the debt capital cost by an agency component. Alternatively, they may engage in costly monitoring activities or add covenants to their debt contracts in order to secure their interests.[594]

Yet, another impact on investment decisions is feasible in this context: since both equity and debt can be regarded as options on the returns of a corporation's investments, the level of a corporation's indebtedness determines to which extent debt and equity holders benefit from returns on such investment projects. It can be shown that the higher the indebtedness of a corporation, the more its debt holders and the less the equity holder/owner-manager benefits from the returns on such new projects. This is because a higher debt ratio implies that risky debt captures a greater share of the investment benefits without bearing the related investment costs which are mostly borne by the owner-manager. The owner-manager has the goal of maximizing the equity value of the firm rather than the firm's total (i.e., equity plus debt) value. Consequently, if a firm has a great amount of debt outstanding, he has an incentive to defer value-maximizing investments. Therefore, ex post, underinvestment may be the consequence of a corporation's high indebtedness.[595]

A clear pecking order following cheaper debt over equity financing is not evident if equity investors are involved in management activities of a corporation.[596]

Yet, it becomes apparent that capital structure matters also under hidden-action type of information asymmetries. In this context, it can be shown that a theoretical optimum, i.e. a Pareto optimal solution is possible, which determines the optimal share of the firm to be held by outsiders as well as the optimal mixture between debt and equity capital depending on the agency costs an owner-manager faces following the inclusion of outside stakeholders.[597]

Recently, dynamic agency models have been developed to provide further theoretical research on issues related to such conflicting investment incentives.[598]

---

high-risk project increases the equity value (i.e., call option) more than the low-risk project does. As the total value of both projects is the same, the value of debt falls if such a riskier project is undertaken

594 While the description above assumes that the corporation is owned by its management, similar incentive problems between equity and debt holders of a corporation can arise if management acts in the interest of the firm's equity owners through a specially designed contract; see Jensen and Meckling (1976) p. 41 et seqq.

595 See Myers (1977), p. 149 et seqq. The owner-manager will particularly defer investments with a long pay-back horizon, see Myers (1977) p. 155 et seq.

596 For a discussion on the existence of an optimal capital structure see Koller, Goedhardt et al. (2005), p. 480 et seqq.

597 See Jensen and Meckling (1976), p. 61 et seq., in particular p. 62 Figure 8

598 See Morellec (2004) and Atkeson and Cole (2005)

Further to theoretical models presented here, a variety of empirical studies examining the practical relevance of capital structure have been developed.[599]

4.4.2 Bank-specific market incompletions

As opposed to the market incompletions brought forward by finance theory, bank-specific market incompletions arise due to interventions of the state or state-owned regulators in banking business. Three types of such interferences can be differentiated and will briefly be described in the following: banking supervision, deposit insurance and state guarantees for banking activities.

4.4.2.1 Banking supervision

Through its supervisory authorities, the state imposes requirements on the banking system, aiming at preventing failures of individual institutions or the entire system.

In Germany, the recently founded BaFin integrates the supervision of banking, insurance and securities trading activities under one umbrella.[600] With respect to banking supervision, the BaFin is supported by the Deutsche Bundesbank.[601]

The overarching goal of the BaFin is to guarantee the functioning, stability, and integrity of the entire German financial system. In order to realize this goal, the authority not only aims at securing the solvency of the financial institutions under its control but also protects customers (in particular deposit holders who provide the main source of debt capital, see chapter 1.4.3) and investors by providing supervision of financial markets and institutions and through combating fraudulent activities.[602] Due to its protective activities for bank customers – especially for deposit holders –, the BaFin absorbs the above-mentioned agency costs related to debt capital. Hence, banking supervision can be regarded as a state subsidy for debt capital.[603]

---

599 A comprehensive summary on recent research undertaken to provide empirical evidence on the relevance of capital structure can be found in Frank and Goyal (2005), chapter 3

600 The BaFin was founded on 1 May 2002 based on the FinDAG (2002)

601 The engagement of the Deutsche Bundesbank in supervisory activities of banking activities is regulated in §7 KWG (1998) as well as in BaFin (2002)

602 See BaFin (2003)

603 The US has established a dual banking supervision system for commercial banks: if these banks are registered as State Banks, they are supervised by State Regulation Agencies; if they are registered as National Banks it is Federal Agencies which provide banking supervision. Federal Agencies include the Office of the Comptroller of the Currency (OCC), the Federal Reserve System, and the Federal Deposit Insurance System (FDIC). It is particularly the task of the OCC to charter, regulate and control all National Banks; see OCC (2004) p. 7 et seqq. for the profile and structure of the OCC

Investment banks are under the supervision of the Securities and Exchange Commission (SEC), see e.g., SEC (2003)

4.4.2.2 Deposit insurance

The existence of deposit insurance schemes can be explained by the need to protect individual customers from losing their bank deposits in the case of an institution's bankruptcy. Furthermore, it is motivated by the goal to promote stability of the financial system since deposit insurance contributes to preventing bank runs.[604]

In Germany, each of the three main bank groups disposes of its own deposit insurance system: while the private banks have an insurance system directly guaranteeing deposits, the insurance system of the savings and cooperative banks primarily guarantees the institutions themselves and hence insures customer deposits in an indirect way.[605]

The deposit insurance system for private banks consists of two components: one component is a compulsory system for all banks protecting 90% of the deposits – at most EUR 20,000 – made by private individuals, limited partnerships, and small incorporated enterprises.[606] The other component is a voluntary insurance system ("Einlagensicherungsfonds"), protecting deposits of each individual customer up to a level of 30% of the liable capital of the respective institution. This scheme is financed by its member banks.[607] The Bundesbank is not allowed to act as so-called "lender of last resort" for the deposit insurance schemes. Rather, in the case of systemic crises, the aim is to find a political solution for the crisis.[608]

604 Concerning bank runs see again, chapter 1.4.3

605 The different set-up of the deposit insurance systems lies in the nature of the different banking types: as private banks are in direct competition with each other, it cannot be in their interest to support competitors that are on the brink of bankruptcy. Savings and cooperative banks, on the other hand, have a rather regional focus and low direct competition; thus, a single institution would not benefit from another's bankruptcy but would rather face reputational damage following the unique public appearance of these institutions. Therefore, an institutional guarantee for savings and cooperative banks is appropriate; see Burghof and Rudolph (1996), p. 73 et seqq. and p. 76 et seqq.

For an overview of the deposit insurance system of savings and cooperative banks see Hartmann-Wendels, Pfingsten et al. (2004), p. 385 et seq.

606 It is required that the deposits are made in Euros; see §4 EinlSG (1998) which implements the EU-wide required minimum protection

607 Each member bank has to pay a yearly premium of 0.03% of its outstanding liabilities towards creditors. Additionally, a premium of 0.09% for new members and, in case the funds are not sufficient, an extraordinary premium of up to 100% of a regular premium needs to be paid. Banks that have paid for more than 20 years and are classified in the lowest of three risk categories (category A) can be exempt from premium payment. Banks in higher risk categories (B or C) can be required to pay up to 250% of the regular premium. See, e.g., Beck (2000), p. 10 et seq.

608 See Bundesbank (1992)

In the US, the FDIC covers deposits up to USD 100,000. Compulsory members in the deposit insurance system are all National Banks and most of the State Banks and Thrifts.[609]

Deposit insurance protects deposits as the main debt capital component of a bank from the institution's bankruptcy. It can be considered a subsidy for this debt capital type if the systematic risk component of a bank's debt capital is higher than the premium it needs to pay to the insurance scheme.[610]

A negative implication of deposit insurance is that the insured deposit holders have lower incentives to monitor actions by bank managers. As a result, bank management has a motivation to take on excessive risks following the introduction of a deposit insurance scheme.[611] Such behavior is also driven by the fact that in practice no sufficiently sophisticated risk-based pricing of these insurance premiums has been established. The moral hazard issue related to deposit insurance might make an already unstable financial system even more fragile.[612]

Advocates of the deposit insurance system often argue that such a moral hazard risk can be confined through prudent regulation and supervision of the banking system.[613] It has also been shown that if deposit insurance replaces a regulation according to which all creditors are fully compensated ("bailed out") if banking institutions fail, it has a positive impact as it can reduce existing moral hazard issues through abolishing the unlimited guarantees and replacing them by the weaker compensation structure of the deposit insurance.[614]

---

[609] See, e.g., Demirguc-Kunt and Sobaci (2000) who give an overview on deposit insurance systems of different countries

[610] The correct risk premium which the bank would be required to pay is determined by the specific risk of the bank's investments, its capital structure, and the split of risk between its equity and debt capital. Yet, in reality, the insurance premium to be paid by banks to the respective schemes is widely insensitive towards the true systematic risk of the deposits and can, therefore, be regarded as constant so that especially for banks with a high systematic risk of their debt, debt insurance is such a subsidy; see again Footnote 607 for the risk categories of the Germany protection system as well as Poppensieker (2002), p. 156

[611] A precondition for such a moral hazard risk is, however, that there are no other costs induced by such a riskier behavior (such as bankruptcy costs, for example), which would offset its advantages; see, e.g., Ritchken, Thomson et al. (1993)

[612] See, e.g., Freixas and Rochet (1997), p. 267 et seq. and p. 270 et seqq., Santomero (1997) and Matutes and Vives (1995)

[613] In an empirical study Demirguc-Kunt and Detragiache (2000) find, among others, that deposit insurance is more harmful to bank stability in countries where the institutional environment is weak. They conclude from this result that in a sound institutional environment an effective system of banking regulation and supervision is in place which offsets the reduced disciplinary incentive that is created by deposit insurance

[614] See Gropp and Vesala (2001), p. 10

4.4.2.3 State guarantees

In July 2005, state guarantees for German savings and state banks ("Landesbanken) together with their "Girozentralen" were abolished. In particular, there is no longer an unlimited state accountability for all current and future liabilities of these institutions. Following the elimination of this subsidy for their debt capital, these institutions are about to receive an external debt rating which will reflect their true riskiness. Still, their creditworthiness is going to benefit from the fact that they have a state as their majority owner.[615]

The US Government-sponsored Real Estate Agencies Fannie Mae and Freddie Mac are privately owned and exchange-listed incorporated companies but enjoy a state guarantee as their activities are considered to serve the public benefit. This guarantee represents a state subsidy of their debt capital.[616]

While the above-mentioned direct deposit insurance schemes for private banks aim at protecting bank customers from suffering losses on their investments, they do not prevent institutions from falling into bankruptcy. If, however, the collapse of an institution and the forced unwinding of its financial contracts in a forced liquidation "would pose unacceptable risks to the ... economy",[617] the state may intervene and rescue the institution in order to avoid more profound implications for the financial system. Such state intervention is known as the "Too-Big-to-Fail" doctrine.[618]

The Too-Big-to-Fail doctrine can be regarded as an implicit state guarantee for the outstanding financial claims against a financial institution. Such a guarantee is in particular for the benefit of deposit holders as the major creditors of a financial institution. Consequently, the doctrine effectively subsidizes debt capital.

615 For the time after the abolishment of state guarantees, external rating agencies have already published "shadow ratings" for savings banks and Landesbanken; see, e.g., N.N. (2004a) and N.N. (2005)

616 See again chapter 3.3.3 and in particular Ely and Wallison (2000) describing these institutions in greater detail

617 McDonough (1998), p. 1051

618 The term "Too Big to Fail" became popular when US regulators decided to permit the economically insolvent Continental Illinois National Bank – then the seventh largest bank in the US and the largest correspondent bank which had inter-bank deposits and Fed funds relationships with over 2,000 other banks – a continuation of its operations under FDIC control instead of closing down the bank. After having permitted the failure of smaller banks before, this rescue activity resulted in sharp criticism from legislators. In a statement in front of the House Banking Committee, the then Comptroller of the Currency declared that it would be unlikely to permit any of the 11 largest multinational banks to fail. An article published in the Wall Street Journal the following day headlined this statement, thus making the term "Too Big to Fail" known and popular; see Carrington (1984) and Kaufman (2003)

4.4.3 Implications for value creation of the ACPM approach

Although there is often not a clear empirical evidence for the validity of the theories developed in connection with capital market incompletions, it becomes evident that the incompletions described above override the irrelevance theorems of Modigliani and Miller (1963) as they make certain types of financing more attractive than others and because investment activities are impacted by the way a corporation is financed.[619]

If, in view of these market incompletions, it could be shown that changes in a credit portfolio composition by means of risk diversification, regulatory arbitrage, and collateralized refinancing transactions using secondary credit market instruments are value-enhancing, it would be proven that the active management of a credit portfolio using these instruments is value-adding compared with the conventional lending approach which does not foresee the execution of such transactions.

The pivotal part in the work of Poppensieker (2002) is to discuss existing and to develop new models to examine the motivation for secondary credit market transactions, given the above-mentioned incompletions in capital markets.

4.4.3.1 Risk diversification and regulatory arbitrage

4.4.3.1.1 Risk preference-based models

Based on the assumption that bank owners only have limited capital market access, the following concepts examined in this context assess investment and financing decisions of a bank based on risk preference functions under the assumption of a constant relative risk aversion.

While the early models developed in this context do not provide a sufficient explanation for secondary credit market transactions, the more simplified approach by Koehn and Santomero (1980) identify risk diversification and regulatory arbitrage as motivation for secondary credit market transactions:[620]

Risk diversification can be achieved through splitting up large credit positions into smaller portions, e.g., through securitization. An arbitrary divisibility of credit risks is precondition for the existence of a continuous efficient frontier in the $\mu-\sigma$ diagram. Furthermore, risk diversification through secondary market investments in imperfectly correlated credit risks that cannot be acquired on the primary loan market, e.g., due to

[619] See, e.g., Poppensieker (2002), p. 160 et seqq. on the empirical relevance of market incompletions showing that there is empirical evidence for the existence of the aforementioned incompletions in markets for debt and equity capital

[620] Early portfolio models include the models developed by Pyle (1971), Hart and Jaffee (1974), Kahane (1977) and Kim (1988). Key feature of these models is that they model debt capital, irrespective of the corporation's investment policy, as a risky asset with stochastic characteristics. In contrast to that, the approach by Koehn and Santomero (1980) assumes constant debt capital cost irrespective of the investment risk

limitations of loan origination BUs, allows a shift of the efficient frontier towards levels of higher utility.[621]

Koehn and Santomero (1980) also motivate regulatory arbitrage not only through substituting low-risk assets having comparably high regulatory capital requirements for those bearing higher economic risks and comparably low regulatory capital requirements but also through specifically designed secondary market transactions binding less regulatory capital without substituting credit risks (direct regulatory arbitrage).[622]

4.4.3.1.2 Market value-based models

Following the critique of Koehn and Santomero (1980)[623] and based on the argument that in view of the development stage of today's capital markets it is not realistic to assume a limited capital market access for banks, the motivation for secondary credit market transactions has been examined using market value-oriented models which are based on the $\mu-\sigma$ principle and the CAPM. They give an endogenous explanation for banks' risk preferences as well as their motivations to perform secondary market transactions. Incentive problems between outside equity and debt investors (see chapter 4.4.1.3.2) are explicitly not considered in this context.

Founded on the assumptions underlying the pecking order theory according to which there are market incompletions in the form of costly financial slack and higher cost of external over internal financing (see chapter 4.4.1.3.1), Froot and Stein (1998) show that secondary credit market transactions can be value-adding both through their ability to diversify risks and through providing the opportunity to perform regulatory arbitrage.

Besides giving a motivation for investments into imperfectly correlated credit risks by means of secondary market transactions, the model proves that the diversification potential from such transactions is higher, the greater the excess return of the respective credit assets over their systematic risk.[624] Yet, as it is assumed that a bank steers its portfolio risks through adapting the volumes of its credit risk position rather than through altering the portfolio composition itself, the motivation to perform regulatory arbitrage can only be explained through direct regulatory arbitrage using

621 See Poppensieker (2002), p. 185 et seqq., in particular Figure 22

622 See Poppensieker (2002), p. 187 et seqq. and in particular Figure 23 which illustrates the value-creation potential of direct regulatory arbitrage

623 In particular, the assumption of constant debt capital cost is not realistic, even given a complete protection of debt capital, e.g., through a deposit contract, see Keeley and Furlong (1990). Rochet (1992) argues that constant risk aversion – and hence constant debt capital costs – can only be assumed for relatively small risks. In case of relatively high risks, however, investors rather behave in a risk-loving way

624 See Poppensieker (2002), p. 201 et seqq., in particular p. 206 et seq.

secondary credit market instruments but not through substituting relatively low-risk by riskier assets.[625]

In view of major points of criticism of the model developed by Froot and Stein (1998), particularly regarding its inability to explain regulatory arbitrage through asset substitution, its assumption that the current size of a bank is a function of its future investments as well as due to the rather low empirical relevance of the pecking order hypothesis,[626] Poppensieker (2002) has developed a model based on the static trade-off hypothesis by assuming the existence of taxes and bankruptcy costs as relevant market incompletions.[627]

The model not only shows a value-creation potential of risk diversification by splitting up large exposures or secondary market investments into uncorrelated credit assets, but it also explains the motivation to perform regulatory arbitrage both through asset substitution and through designing appropriate secondary market transactions.[628]

4.4.3.2 Collateralized refinancing

The bank introduced by Poppensieker (2002) follows the overarching goal of maximizing its overall market value. It aims at generating profits on the capital market by using its position as a specialized player which has transaction cost advantages over other market participants. Like the other market value-oriented models introduced above, this approach ignores possible incentive problems between equity and debt investors. It is the existence of such incentive issues which motivates the use of secondary credit market instruments with the goal of obtaining collateralized refinancing for lending activities.

The underinvestment problem following the refusal of an owner-manager to undertake investment projects whose returns would be primarily beneficial for debt holders (see chapter 4.4.1.3.2) can be addressed by limiting the benefits of such projects for debt compared to equity holders.

Such a limitation can be achieved, e.g., if the corporation finances a new investment project mainly through senior debt which is ideally collateralized by this new project. The newly issued collateralized debt is cheaper than unsecured debt as the latter only has a subordinate claim on the new investment project. In the case of bankruptcy, the new debt investors primarily obtain the proceeds from "their" investment project and,

---

625 See Poppensieker (2002), p. 207 et seqq. Direct regulatory arbitrage is explained by the aspiration of the institution to reduce an overcapitalization, which is triggered by a mismatch of rather unrefined regulatory capital requirements and the optimal EC volume of the institution. Through using secondary credit market instruments, the loss from such an overcapitalization can be reduced

626 See Poppensieker (2002), p. 210 et seqq. for a discussion of the model and again chapter 4.4.1.1 regarding the pecking order hypothesis

627 See Poppensieker (2002), p. 216 et seqq.

628 See Poppensieker (2002), p. 226 et seqq., in particular Figure 25 and p. 228 et seqq., in particular Figure 26

besides this, have the same rights on the liquidation proceeds of the corporation's remaining assets as "normal" debt holders have.

Following the existing debt holders' subordinate rights in the project, they only benefit to a lower extent from the new project's proceeds so that a larger share of these returns remains with the equity owners who will consequently have a higher incentive to pursue the new project. Hence, the issuance of senior collateralized debt can address the underinvestment issue.[629] It can be shown that a similar limitation of existing debt holders' benefits compared to the ones of equity holders can be achieved if banks undertake a collateralized securitization transaction.[630]

Besides reducing the ex-post incentive for managers to defer investments, collateralization can also help to reduce debt refinancing costs ex-ante: debt holders have the incentive to engage in costly monitoring activities or add covenants to contracts in order to secure their interests and the value of their claims. By issuing collateralized debt, such costs could be reduced or avoided.[631]

The argumentation above has shown that the issuance of collateralized debt instruments can reduce incentive issues between a bank's equity and debt holders and hence are value creating for such an institution. This provides a motivation for banks to use secondary credit market instruments such as ABBs or recourse ABS in order to refinance their investment activities.[632]

* * * * *

This illustration has shown that, assuming the existence of incomplete markets for equity and debt capital, the use of secondary market instruments to execute transactions with the objective of diversifying risks, performing regulatory arbitrage and acquiring collateralized refinancing is value enhancing. It has been illustrated before that it is mainly the execution of such transactions which differs the ACPM approach from the conventional "originate and hold" approach towards wholesale lending. As a consequence, following the realistic assumption that banks generally operate in incomplete capital markets – which can be realistically assumed – the implementation of an ACPM approach can create additional value for an institution which has pursued a conventional "originate and hold" lending approach so far.

---

629 See Stulz and Johnson (1985), p. 515 et seqq.

630 See James (1988), p. 641 et seq.

631 See Stulz and Johnson (1985), p. 512 et seq.

632 The approaches to overcome the incentive issue between equity and debt holders introduced here can be summarized as collateralization hypotheses. In this context, the so-called moral-hazard hypothesis has been developed, which however does not give an appropriate motivation for the use of collateralized refinancing instruments to solve the respective issues. Likewise, the models developed by Beneviste and Berger (1987) and Greenbaum and Thakor (1987) do not provide a sufficient motivation for the use of these instruments, either. For a more detailed illustration see Poppensieker (2002), p. 241 et seqq.

4.5 Summary

In this chapter, the principles of classical portfolio theory, which is the theoretical background of the ACPM approach, have been introduced. Furthermore, the theory has been embedded in the more general context including LPM as downside risk measures. Besides this, the value creation potential of the ACPM approach has been examined.

A risk-averse investor, who either acts according to a quadratic utility function or has the opportunity to invest in portfolios whose asset returns follow an elliptic distribution, takes investment decisions according to the mean-variance principle. That is, based on his individual preference function, he selects asset portfolios whose return have the lowest standard deviation or chooses the portfolio with the highest return among such with the same standard deviation. Accordingly, there are no portfolios that are superior to mean-variance efficient portfolios with regard to risk-return characteristics. All mean-variance efficient portfolios are located on the so-called efficient frontier above a so-called MVP.

When additionally given the opportunity to invest funds in a risk-free asset or to take loans at the risk-free rate, the investor's decision problem can be reduced to his choice between what percentage of his funds to invest risk-free and what percentage to invest in the market portfolio which, in this case, is the only remaining efficient portfolio. This is the so-called Tobin separation. The investor's risk preference is merely relevant for his decision regarding how to split his investments between the risk-free asset and the market portfolio.

Yet, shortfall risk measures may be superior risk measures than symmetric ones, especially in the context of credit risks. Therefore, it has been examined in how far the efficient portfolio selection problem changes if risk is measured through shortfall probability instead of through standard deviation. As a result of an equivalent optimization problem, an efficient frontier including a so-called MSP can be determined. All portfolios on the efficient frontier above this portfolio are efficient in a mean-shortfall world. Furthermore, while not all mean-variance efficient portfolios are mean-shortfall efficient, all portfolios that are efficient in a mean-shortfall world are located above the MVP on the mean-variance efficient frontier and, hence, are mean-variance efficient.

The portfolio optimization problems have been based on the assumption of normally distributed asset returns. With the help of Chebyshev's inequality, which can be applied to all types of distributions, an upper limit for shortfall probability can be determined on the basis of variance as a distribution parameter. The possibility of such a generalization allows an ex-post justification of the limitation on normally distributed asset returns. Furthermore, as an extension of the analysis to higher-order LPM does not provide any new insights to the portfolio optimization problem but solely extends calculation efforts, it is sufficient to focus on shortfall probability as a downside risk measure.

Based on the theory of efficient portfolio selection in a mean-variance framework, the CAPM has been developed as a model providing the basis to determine the optimal investor behavior and the return that the holder of an individual risky asset can expect in a competitive market equilibrium. In doing so, the CAPM illustrates the relationship between the expected return and the risks of each individual asset included in the market portfolio. Risks are split into a systematic and an unsystematic component. As unsystematic risks can be entirely eliminated in an optimally diversified portfolio, capital markets only reward the systematic risk component of assets. The systematic risk component of a single asset or an asset portfolio is measured in relation to the optimally diversified market portfolio by means of the asset's or portfolio's β. With help of the β, the SML can be drawn illustrating a linear relationship between the systematic risk – weighted by the β – and the expected return of the respective asset (portfolio).

While the CAPM is based on the classical Tobin separation under mean-variance optimization, a similar market equilibrium can be determined in a mean-LPM world. It can be shown that the two fund separation holds, with investors solely deciding which share of their funds to invest in an asset for which they have predetermined a certain target rate of return and the market portfolio. The target rate of return may be the risk-free rate, but the two fund separation also holds in a general mean-n^{th}-order LPM framework with an arbitrary target return. Based on this generalized two-fund separation, a SML similar to the CAPM can be derived. This allows a generalized asset pricing model to be determined which, among others, does not require the assumption of normally distributed asset returns. In particular, the classical CAPM can be regarded as a specialized risk pricing model in this context, having the risk-free rate as an implicit target rate of return.

The asset pricing models are based on the assumption of complete capital markets, i.e., unlimited market access for all participants, no market frictions, and full information efficiency. Based on this assumption, Modigliani and Miller have shown that the way a corporation or a single investment project is financed does not impact its market value (irrelevance theorem). The decision whether to undertake an investment project can also be separated from the question of how to finance it (separation theorem).

Following the hypothesis of complete markets for debt and equity capital, it has been examined whether transactions on secondary credit markets can create value. This assessment has been split into secondary market transactions between banks and private individuals and those among financial intermediaries. Furthermore, in each case it has been distinguished between the existence of a complete and an incomplete secondary credit market. If external subsidies of the credit market are realistically excluded, it has been shown that, provided a complete market for equity and debt capital exists, secondary credit market transactions do not create additional value – irrespective of whether there are complete secondary credit markets or not.

The main difference between the ACPM and the conventional "originate and hold" approach towards lending business is its aspiration to actively reshuffle the credit portfolio by means of secondary credit market transactions. The main goals in this context are to achieve a higher risk diversification, perform regulatory arbitrage or raise funds through issuing securitized bonds in order to refinance lending activities. As in complete capital markets such transactions are not value enhancing, the ACPM approach cannot be motivated economically under these ideal market conditions.

Yet, the hypothesis of complete capital markets does not appear to hold in reality. Rather, according to finance theory, three different types of market incompletions can be distinguished: limited market access, market frictions and information asymmetries.

If the owner of a corporation is restricted regarding issuance or trading of capital on the capital markets, he is limited to financing his investment activities by means of his own funds. Consequently, he will not follow the goal of maximizing his firm's market value but will rather pursue the maximization of his own utility according to his individual preference function.

Market frictions typically occur in the form of taxes or default costs. In the context of a corporation's finance decision, they invalidate the irrelevance theorem as they typically result in the preferred treatment of one capital form over the other. It can be shown that the tax benefits, which debt financing of a corporation can generate, are typically offset by higher bankruptcy costs. Hence, according to static trade-off theory, a firm sets its market value-maximizing target leverage ratio where the marginal benefit of the debt tax shield equalizes marginal debt-related bankruptcy costs. The recently developed models on dynamic trade-off theory have more closely examined the adjustment behavior of firms towards their target leverage ratio.

Information asymmetries can occur in the form of hidden information and hidden action. If the owner-manager of a corporation has an information advantage over outside investors regarding the true value of his corporation and its investment projects, underinvestment might be the result of this hidden-information type of asymmetry if new projects are supposed to be financed by external equity. The underinvestment issues can be avoided if projects are financed by means of retained earnings or external debt, thus laying the basis for dynamic pecking order theory as a competing theory to the static trade-off models.

If the owners of a corporation cannot or not sufficiently observe the actions of their employed management (hidden action), they need to engage in costly monitoring activities to prevent managers from undertaking activities that yield them personal advantages but do not need to be financed by them. These agency costs can be avoided if a firm is under the management of a sole owner or if investment activities are financed through retained earnings or risk-free debt. A second-best solution is the issuance of risky debt capital because it incurs lower monitoring costs than equity capital.

Yet, under the assumption that a manager also holds an equity stake in the corporation, this seemingly clear pecking order gets blurred. This is due to the fact that an owner-manager has the goal of primarily maximizing the firm's equity rather than its total market value. Consequently, the higher the firm's debt leverage ratio, the lower the incentive for the owner-manager to undertake new projects whose returns would mainly benefit the debt holders – again, underinvestment is the consequence. Rational bondholders will realize this behavior and only pay a lower price for the corporation's debt which is equivalent to higher refinancing costs for the corporation. Thus, debt capital costs are raised by an agency component. Although under the existence of hidden-action type of information asymmetries there is no clear pecking order evident, it becomes obvious that the capital structure of a corporation is not irrelevant under this kind of market incompletion.

Further to market incompletions developed by finance theory, there are bank-specific market incompletions arising due to state intervention in banking business. It can be differentiated between supervision of banking activities through regulators, insurance schemes providing a preferred protection for customer deposits either directly or through granting a guarantee for the deposit issuing institutions, and explicit or implicit state guarantees preventing institutions from falling into bankruptcy. All bank-specific market incompletions have in common that they effectively provide a subsidy for the banks' debt capital, given that bank deposits represent the major type of refinancing.

After having provided evidence that there are different types of incompletions on banking capital markets, it has been shown that these incompletions provide a motivation to perform secondary credit market transactions. Koehn and Santomero (1980) have shown that under the assumption of limited capital market access for bank owners, secondary credit market transactions can be motivated by the goal to achieve a better risk diversification of the portfolio (both through splitting up large concentration risks in smaller portfolios and through secondary market investments in relatively uncorrelated credit assets) and by the aspiration to perform regulatory arbitrage (through adequately substituting credit assets as well as by specifically designing transactions to achieve lower regulatory capital requirements). The same motivation for secondary market transactions can be derived from market value-oriented approaches such as Froot and Stein (1998), following the pecking order hypothesis and Poppensieker (2002) who has based his argumentation on the static trade-off hypothesis. Poppensieker (2002) provides a more extensive explanation for regulatory arbitrage also motivating asset substitution while Froot and Stein (1998) only explain direct regulatory arbitrage. Finally, following Stulz and Johnson (1985) and James (1988), it has been shown that collateralized refinancing can also be a motivation to perform secondary market transactions as it can be used to contain the ex-post underinvestment issue as well as ex-ante agency costs related to debt financing following the existence of information asymmetries on capital markets.

It has been shown that the use of secondary credit market instruments creates value under the realistic assumption of incomplete markets for equity and debt capital. Specifically, a motivation for the three main goals when applying these instruments (i.e., the objectives of risk diversification, regulatory arbitrage and collateralized refinancing) can be given. Consequently, it can be assumed that, from a theoretical point of view, the active management of a bank's credit portfolio by means of such secondary market transactions is value-creating. Assuming that it is the execution of secondary credit market transactions which mainly distinguishes the ACPM approach from the conventional "originate and hold" approach, the implementation of an ACPM approach is value-enhancing over the hitherto predominant "originate and hold" approach.

Part III: Empirical study on ACPM

Part II of this dissertation has provided the fundament for the empirical study: following the introductory chapter one, chapter two has introduced the principles of the ACPM approach. Generic ACPM business models for the implementation of the ACPM approach that have been developed by literature according to the three design criteria (I) mandate for credit functions, (II) asset ownership, and (III) reporting structure within the institution have been presented. Furthermore, determinants for the design of ACPM units have been identified by means of the literature to hand. Chapter three has provided a detailed description of secondary credit market instruments that can be used to actively manage loan portfolios. Chapter 4, then, has described the theoretical background underlying the ACPM approach. This illustration has been used as a basis to show that, from a theoretical point of view, the active management of credit portfolios by means of secondary credit market transactions can generate additional economic value for an institution's credit business.

In order to test the theoretical findings presented and to get profound insights into the relatively unexplored field of ACPM, an empirical study on ACPM has been conducted among leading Western European financial institutions that have been supposed to have established a "best-practice" ACPM approach. This part of the dissertation will describe the results of this empirical study in greater detail, relate the outcomes to the theoretical findings that have been illustrated in part II and depict derived interpretations and conclusions.

The subsequent five chapters comprise the following content: after having introduced the goals and approach of the empirical study in chapter one, the underlying data sample is portrayed in chapter two. The third chapter introduces the methodology applied to raise and analyze the empirical information. The results obtained from the study and their interpretations and conclusions are presented in greater detail in chapters four and five.

1 The goals of the empirical study

Conducting the empirical study was motivated by the following main goals:

1.1 Obtaining empirical evidence on CPM business models

The primary goal was to empirically test the generic ACPM business models that literature on ACPM has developed on the basis of the aforementioned three design criteria.[633] These generic models were tested by closely examining and analyzing a "best-practice" sample of CPM units to be found among the leading European financial institutions which took part in the empirical study.[634]

[633] See also again chapter 2.3.2 of part II for a description of the resulting generic ACPM business models

[634] The more general term "CPM units" instead of "ACPM units" is used here because, as will be shown in chapter 4, not all banks included in the empirical sample examined actively manage their credit portfolios

Literature on ACPM has not described the generic ACPM business models in greater detail. For this reason as well as to get a profound understanding of the currently established "best-practice" approaches towards CPM across Europe, it was the goal to explore the CPM business models differentiated in the empirical sample in greater detail.[635]

The following characteristics were covered by this detailed exploration: it has firstly been aspired to understand characteristic objectives of the CPM business models and related degrees of implementation for the different objectives. Literature on ACPM has described the implementation of an ACPM business model as a multi-step process during which several implementation barriers need to be overcome.[636] Therefore, the empirical study also aimed at exploring typical hurdles the "best-practice" banks face(d) en route to successfully implementing their targeted ACPM business model and especially to achieving related objectives.

Besides getting to know their objectives, related implementation degrees and barriers, the functional competencies of the ACPM business models identified in the empirical sample were explored and described in greater detail. Such a detailed description of the models' functional specifics seemed particularly relevant as this had proven to be a key differentiating factor for the different models and because such an in-depth illustration has not been made publicly available yet.

Chapter 4.4 of part II has proven that actively managing credit portfolios by means of reshuffling their risk-return structure through secondary credit market transactions is value enhancing for an institution's credit business from a theoretical point of view, assuming the institute operates in incomplete secondary credit markets. A further goal of the empirical study was to examine to which extent and along which dimensions participating institutions have actually managed or aspire to create additional economic value for their credit business following the establishment of a particular ACPM business model. Based on this analysis, it has been targeted to identify the value-maximizing ACPM business model.

1.2 Deducting the optimal ACPM business model

It will be shown that the seemingly value-maximizing ACPM business model does not appear to be the optimal target model of all financial institutions. Therefore, a more thorough deduction of the optimal ACPM business model to be implemented by an institution was performed. This deduction was made with help of the external and

yet but still pursue passive portfolio management functions instead. Wherever it will specifically be referred to units that actively manage credit portfolios, the term "ACPM units" will be used in the remainder of this dissertation

[635] In this context, it has also been aspired to draw analogies to previously conducted empirical studies on CPM, especially Rutter Associates LLC (2004)

[636] See again Asarnov (1996) for typical steps and barriers on the path to implementing ACPM units

internal factors determining the design of ACPM business models described in chapter 2.3.3 of part II. Through applying the results of the empirical study, it was examined which specification of the determinants has led the "best-practice" financial institutions covered in the survey to the choice for a particular form of a design criterion and, hence, to the decision to establish a certain ACPM business model. Based on this examination, it has been envisaged to identify the optimal ACPM business model that should be chosen if a certain set of determinants is given. In particular, this analysis has been motivated by the aim to provide advice for decision makers in banks who aim to set up an ACPM unit to help them identify the optimal ACPM business model for their institution, given a range of specific external and internal conditions they face.

Figure 36 illustrates the approach taken to deduct the ACPM business model that should optimally be set up, given certain specifications of external and internal determinants for the design of ACPM units.

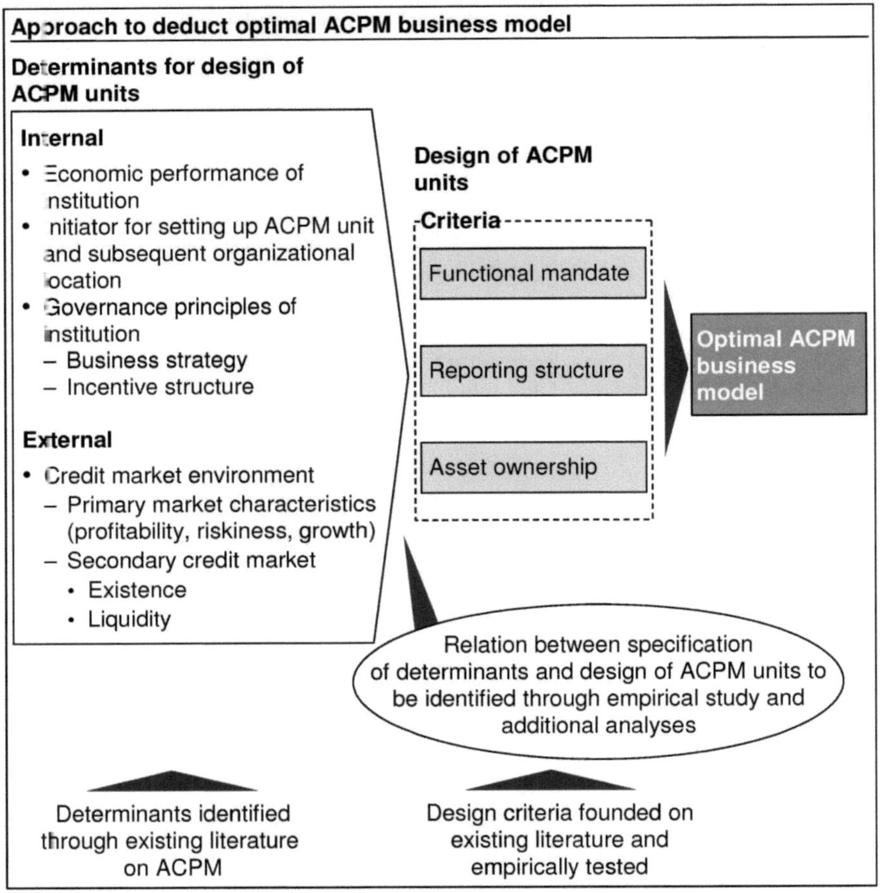

Figure 36: Approach to deduct optimal ACPM business model[637]

[637] Source: Own illustration

2 Data sample

It has been shown before that it is essential for an ACPM unit to be able to perform transactions on secondary credit markets.[638] Thus, the precondition for a financial institution to successfully set up an ACPM unit is to have opportunities as well as the relevant skill-set and infrastructure to perform such deals. It has been for these reasons that the development of the approach to actively manage credit portfolios in thereto dedicated units has in the first place been initiated and driven by players that are active in the most liquid wholesale credit segment and dispose of the required infrastructure to perform secondary credit market transactions.[639]

The goal was to conduct the empirical study among European institutions that are assumed to pursue a "best-practice" approach in the relatively newly established field of ACPM. Consequently, when selecting potential participants in the study, the focus has had to be narrowed down to financial institutions that have a major activity in wholesale credit business and also play an active role on the secondary credit market – if such a market exists in the country in which they mainly operate – since, based on the facts mentioned above, these institutions have been supposed to be leading in terms of ACPM. This has limited the possible scope of the empirical study to the largest and most significant European financial institutions with the business strategy for and access to the relevant credit markets as well as with a sufficient capacity and infrastructure to perform respective transactions. Including a comparably small size of leading financial institutions was also motivated by the goal to obtain an in-depth understanding of the approach taken by these supposedly "best-practice" players in order to get detailed in-depth insights into the previously relatively unexplored field of ACPM.[640]

Eventually, the study included CPM units of 22 of the largest and most considerable European banks and bancassurance groups[641] that can be regarded as market leaders in their domestic country as well as beyond national borders, and that dispose of substantial wholesale lending as well as secondary credit market trading operations.[642] The institutions covered in the study are headquartered in ten different Western

---

638 See again chapter 2.3

639 See again Kuritzkes (1998)

640 Since for this purpose, as will be shown in chapter 3.1, personal interviews were conducted with the participants, including a larger sample size would not have been possible within the scope of this dissertation

641 Regarding the bancassurance concept and its development in Europe see, e.g., Howard (1999)

642 Two banks have participated with two CPM units located in different BUs. Hence, the empirical sample consists of 24 CPM units. It will be shown below that, while the asset focus of the CPM units covered is clearly on wholesale credit assets, there are also some SME-/retail-asset focused CPM units in the sample

European countries.[643] Like this, a broad overview of the development status of ACPM in major European financial markets has been obtained.[644] The study was conducted in the first half of 2005. In Figure 37 the key characteristics of total assets, outstanding loan exposures, market capitalization and headcount of the institutions included in the empirical study on ACPM are illustrated.[645]

The majority of the institutions included in the empirical study are major universal banks or bancassurance groups with a European or global business scope beyond their home market. The primary asset focus of the CPM units surveyed is on wholesale credit assets. A few CPM units included in the sample do not cover their institution's largest multi-national and domestic large cap credit names but primarily focus on loans granted to national SME debtors instead, sometimes also on retail mortgages and consumer loans. This has additionally enabled to get to know how these types of lending assets are typically managed.[646] Other CPM units target the entire loan portfolio of their institution.[647] See Figure 38 on the types of institutions participating in the empirical study as well as the primary asset focus of the CPM units surveyed.

643 The countries include: Austria, Belgium, France, Germany, Ireland, Italy, Netherlands, Spain, Switzerland, and the UK

644 An excerpt of the participating banks in the 2004 Rutter Associates Survey on Credit Portfolio Management Practice shows that the approach to include the largest institutions of a country in an empirical study on ACPM has been successfully applied before; see Rutter Associates LLC (2004), p. 1

645 In order to comply with the information obtained from the empirical study, which was completed by end July 2005, the numbers shown date from 31 July 2005

646 All participating institutions which include these SME-/retail asset-focused CPM units dispose of a separate Investment Banking BU covering the largest multi-national and domestic corporate customers in a separate CPM unit of its own. Two of these institutions have also participated in the empirical study with this Investment Banking BU's CPM unit. The others taking part with their SME-/retail-asset focused CPM units only gave an indication as to where their large corporate-focused counterpart stands in terms of ACPM but have decided not to fill out the detailed questionnaire from the viewpoint of this unit

647 It will be shown in chapter 4 that all CPM units focusing on their institution's entire credit portfolio are not actively managing credit assets yet. They rather perform passive CPM activities from existing risk units. There is no ACPM unit in the empirical sample actively managing its institution's entire credit asset portfolio

Characteristics of institutions included in empirical study on ACPM

Numbers as of July 31, 2005

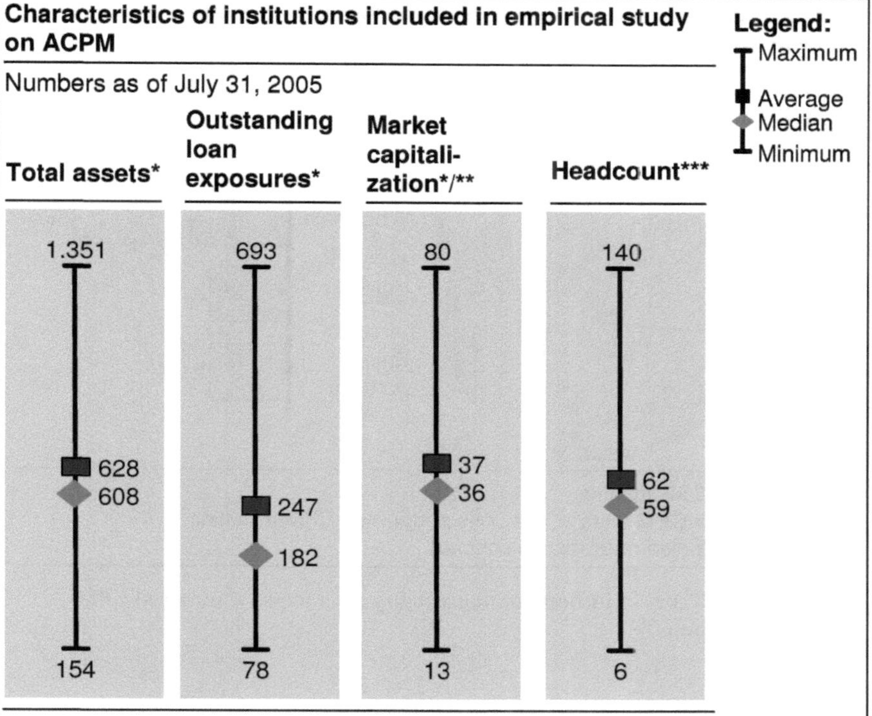

* In EUR billions
** Only 18 institutions included as 4 institutions are either not listed on stock exchange or subsidiary of larger group
*** In thousand employees

Note: Bancassurance groups have been considered without total assets, outstanding loan exposures, and headcount of insurance divisions to avoid distortions

Figure 37: Characteristics of institutions included in empirical study on ACPM[648]

[648] Source: Own illustration partly based on research in annual reports of participating institutions but mostly on research in Datastream and Bloomberg databases

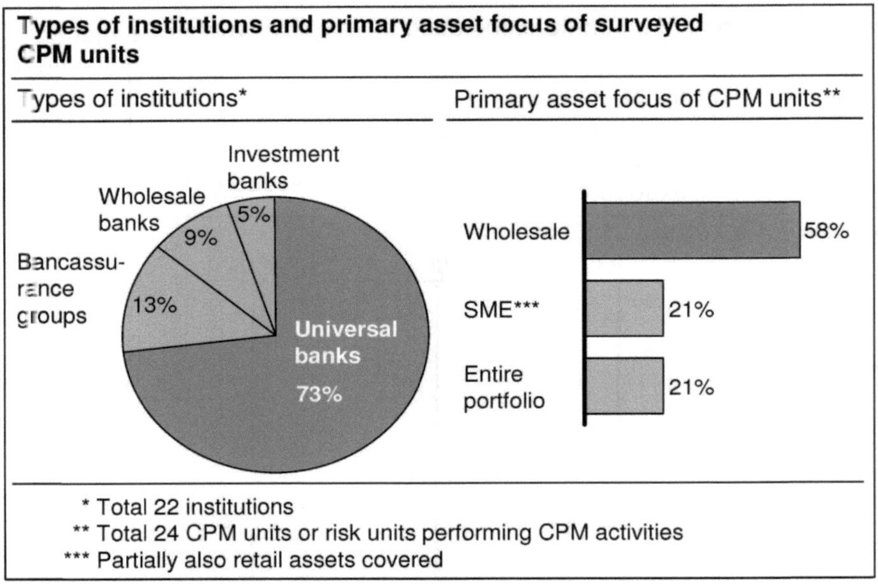

Figure 38: Types of institutions and primary asset focus of surveyed CPM units[649]

[649] Source: Own illustration based on results of empirical study on ACPM

3 Methodology to obtain and analyze empirical information

This chapter describes the methodology applied in the empirical study on ACPM. After a description of the form of data collection that was chosen, the structure and content of the questionnaire that has been used as an instrument to raise the empirical information is described. The chapter concludes with a brief description of the methods used to analyze the information.

3.1 Form of data collection

Generally, four different methods for the collection of data in an empirical study can be differentiated: (I) survey, (II) observation, (III) content analysis and (IV) non-reactive forms of data collection.[650] Following the complexity of the topic to be examined, the comparably small sample size, and especially due to the very limited access to the field of ACPM by means of publicly available sources, collecting the empirical information through a survey was the only feasible method for data collection in the context of the empirical study on ACPM.[651]

Depending on the specific situation in which an empirical study is conducted, it needs to be decided whether a survey is to be conducted through a face-to-face interview, a telephone interview or in a written form through a questionnaire. Each type of questioning has characteristic advantages and disadvantages.[652]

The optimal type of interrogation identified for the empirical study at hand was a face-to-face interview accompanied by a questionnaire as an instrument to raise and retain the information.[653]

The decision to conduct a face-to-face interview was motivated by several reasons: in view of the comparably small sample of 22 banks included in the empirical study, it was important to ensure a 100% return rate of the information requested from each participating institution. In this context, it was especially necessary to find a modus

---

650 See Diekmann (2002), p. 371 et seqq. on survey, p. 456 on observation, p. 481 et seqq. on content analysis and p. 517 et seqq. on non-reactive forms of data collection

651 Collection of empirical data by means of a survey has already been successfully applied in previous academic work with similar goals and sample size; see, e.g., Großpietsch (2003), p. 115 et seqq. and Schulte (2001), p. 165 et seqq.

652 See Diekmann (2002), p. 373 et seqq. and, for a graphical illustration of the advantages and disadvantages of each type of interrogation, Großpietsch (2003), p. 116 Figure 5-1

653 A face-to-face interview accompanied by a written questionnaire is commonly referred to as a structured interview as opposed to an unstructured interview for which the interviewer does not dispose of a questionnaire, see Roth (1993), pp. 152 – 154. In order to keep the interview time in an acceptable time-frame for the interviewees, the questionnaire was mostly sent to participants some weeks before the scheduled interview day so that the addressees could already get an overview of the questions and possibly fill out a first draft of the questionnaire which was subsequently discussed during the following face-to-face meeting that followed

operandi ensuring the avoidance of a non-response bias.[654] The rather complex topic of ACPM has only been described on a relatively high level by literature. Besides this, empirical studies have merely explored it in a rudimentary way. Therefore, it was important to have the opportunity to ask clarifying questions during the interview, exploring certain specifics in greater detail so that a profound understanding of the subject could be obtained. Participants in the empirical study were ensured absolute anonymity and confidentiality of the information provided. Therefore, besides signing a confidentiality agreement with each participating institution, it seemed useful to dispel any remaining doubts regarding anonymity and confidentiality through getting to know each other in person during the interview process.

Besides comparably high costs, a face-to-face interview has the disadvantage that the close contact between interviewer and interviewee may cause a distortion in the answers given by the interviewee. This is in particular due to the fact that the interviewer may subconsciously show non-verbal signals to the interviewee regarding which answer is expected to a certain question. The interviewee may subsequently give an answer which is biased towards the signals of the interviewer.[655]

In order to minimize such distorting effects related to a face-to-face interview, the interviews were not held in an unstructured form but along a questionnaire which contained non-biased questions. Besides this, the author of this dissertation personally conducted all interviews, aspiring to minimize errors when interpreting the results.[656]

The interviews were conducted as expert interviews, with interviewees usually being Heads of the ACPM units of the surveyed banks, located at the 2nd or 3rd management level in their organization. In banks that had not implemented a separate ACPM unit, executives responsible for the supervision and management of their institution's loan portfolios, typically heading the risk unit, were interviewed. The reason for a focus on this person subgroup was that they not only dispose of the broadest know-how on where their institution stands regarding management of credit portfolios but, due to their relatively high hierarchical position, also have a sufficient overview on other functional departments.[657] Sometimes, lower ranked employees from ACPM or related units joined the interviews in order to provide additional specific information on the questions.

---

654 A non-response bias is typically characterized by the fact that results from non-respondents are significantly different from the ones of respondents, causing distortions in the empirical results. For literature on non-response bias see, e.g., Diekmann (2002), p. 359 et seqq. and Roth (1993), p. 170 et seqq. as well as earlier work such as Suchman and McCandless (1940), Kish (1965), and Wagenaar (1972)

655 See Diekmann (2002), p. 375 on neutral behavior in interview situations and p. 382 et seqq. on possible sources of errors in face-to-face interviews. See also Roth (1993), p. 53 regarding interviewer behavior

656 This procedure follows Großpietsch (2003) p. 117

657 Such expert interviews may not be unproblematic. See, e.g., Flick (2002), p. 139 et seqq. and Meuser and Nagel (1991), p. 449 et seq. on issues related to expert interviews

Although mostly conducting the interview along the structure of the questionnaire, the order of the questions asked was held flexible according to the specific interview situation. If necessary, clarifying and specifying questions were asked by the interviewer in the course of the discussion.

3.2 Structure and content of questionnaire

3.2.1 Structure of questionnaire

Generally, when designing a questionnaire, one can choose between including closed- and open-ended questions.[658]

Closed-ended questions provide the interviewee with a range of options for answers to be given. By including closed-ended questions in a questionnaire, a high degree of structuring and standardization can be achieved.[659] This results in a maximum degree of objectivity which is considered a precondition for reliable and valid measurements. A drawback of closed-ended questions is that they do not provide information beyond the predefined options for answers. Therefore, they are typically only recommendable if the interviewer already has sufficient previous knowledge about the situation to be surveyed.[660] Another drawback of closed-ended questions is that the interviewee may choose one of the given answers even if he has not properly thought about which answer best reflects his opinion. In case a high number of such ad-hoc answers is given, the empirical information collected may not be very meaningful and also relatively instable as the interviewee is apt to quickly change his opinion when reconsidering the answers.[661]

Open-ended questions merely confront the interviewee with the questions, and require him to independently formulate his answers. This increases the spectrum of information that can be provided to the interviewer.[662] Open-ended questions entail higher intellectual challenges for the interviewee who not only needs to remember the specific situation he is asked about but also has to adequately formulate his answer. Therefore, a drawback of open-ended questions is that interviewees often refrain from answering open-ended questions or do not know the answer.[663]

658 See Roth (1993), pp. 154 – 156

659 Highly structured interviews including closed-end questions are also referred to as quantitative interviews, see Diekmann (2002), p. 375

660 See Diekmann (2002), p. 374 et seq.

661 See Katz (1972) on the issue of ad-hoc answers related to open-ended questions

662 These less structured interview techniques are also called qualitative interrogation methods; see, again, Diekmann (2002), p. 375

663 See Maccoby and Maccoby (1972) on the issue of insufficient answers given for open-ended questions

In order to unite the goal to have a highly standardized questionnaire with the aspiration to obtain a deep insight into the field of ACPM, which has not been researched in sufficient detail before, a mixture of closed- and open-ended questions were included in the questionnaire. The interviewees were also often asked to first answer a closed-ended question before being required to specify their given answer in greater detail through an open-ended one. Besides this, some questions were set up in a combined closed- and open-ended form by, e.g., giving participants the opportunity to tick a box named "Other, which?" so that they could provide a self-formulated answer other than the predetermined ones.[664] Many closed-ended questions have required participants to rank the importance they ascribe to a certain topic on a five-step ordinal scale with values between 1 and 5.[665] Further to the questions that had to be answered during the interviews, interviewees were asked to provide an organizational chart showing the location of their ACPM unit.

3.2.2 Content of questionnaire

The primary goal of the questionnaire was to explore in detail which CPM business models the institutions taking part in the empirical study have currently established and what are the characteristics of these models.[666] Therefore, in accordance with the aforementioned design criteria for ACPM units, the questions focused on their reporting structure/organizational set-up, their mandate and competencies for key credit functions as well as their approach towards owning and managing credit assets (i.e., asset focus and pursued asset management principles).

Besides this, the objectives pursued with CPM units including perceived implementation degrees and typical barriers faced by participants on the path to successfully implementing these units in general and their specific objectives in

---

664 It is common to use mixtures between closed- and open-ended questions in questionnaires, see again Diekmann (2002), p. 374 et seq. and, for an example of such a mixed questionnaire, Großpietsch (2003), p. 115

665 Rank "1" on this ordinal scale indicates the degree of importance "low/unimportant", rank "5" indicates "high/very important".

Five-step ordinal scales have also been used in earlier academic work, e.g., Schulte (2001). Furthermore, as a five-step ordinal scale between one and five was also chosen in the latest available empirical study on ACPM performed by Rutter Associates LLC (2004), the same scale was applied in the empirical study in question to obtain comparable information.

See Diekmann (2002), p. 249 et seq. for the different types of scales that can be differentiated as well as Diekmann (2002), p. 404 et seq. concerning the optimal number of categories in rating scales. Generally for development of rating scales also see Roth (1993), p. 407

666 As it was initially not clear whether all participating institutions have established an *Active* Credit Portfolio Management (ACPM) unit, the more general term Credit Portfolio Management (CPM) unit was used throughout the questionnaire

particular were surveyed. Participants were also asked which approaches they have taken to successfully overcome these issues.

In order to empirically test the theoretical finding that actively managing loan portfolios creates additional economic value for an institution's credit business, survey participants had to name the economic impact they have achieved with their CPM unit so far.

Last but not least, the institutions' outlook and vision regarding future development of their approach towards managing credit assets was explored.

It has been shown before that it is crucial for ACPM units to closely cooperate with other credit functions of a bank, especially, with origination, secondary market and problem loan management/workout units (see again chapter 2.3.2 in part II). Therefore, it was the goal to get a profound understanding not only of the reporting structure/organizational set-up, functional mandate and competencies of CPM units but also of their embedment within the organization, particularly including their relation to and interfaces with other units. Consequently, the questionnaire included questions related to loan origination – in particular, the objectives, performance evaluation and competencies of origination units as well as their interfaces with CPM units – and secondary market activities. The part on secondary market activities aimed at obtaining information on the secondary market business approach taken by CPM units. Moreover, it was the goal to get to know which instruments are typically applied to perform secondary credit market transactions, for which purpose these instruments are applied, and which typical issues are related to these secondary credit market activities. In this context, participants were also asked details about their secondary market reinvestment strategy pursued.

The goal was to comprise the entire "credit pipeline" in the questionnaire.[667] Therefore , it has also included a section concerning the relation of CPM units towards problem loan management/workout units. However, as it has been learned from the interviews that the CPM units surveyed typically have no specific functional competence for problem loan management/workout, this area will not be in the focus of this dissertation.

By means of a set of open-ended so-called "ice-breaker questions", put at the beginning of the questionnaire, revolving around the overall goals and strategy, current development status and sources of value creation participants see for their CPM unit, it was intended to provide a cooperative interview atmosphere at the beginning of the meetings while obtaining a first overall impression of the CPM approach pursued by the participant.[668]

---

[667] For an illustration of the "credit pipeline concept" see Hammes and Shapiro (2001), p. 105 Figure 6

[668] See Diekmann (2002), p. 410 regarding so-called ice-breaker questions

Figure 39 gives an overview of the content of the questionnaire.[669]

A draft version of the questionnaire was tested and subsequently completed together with the Head of Credit Portfolio Management of a befriended institution in order to ensure the empirical study covered all relevant aspects of this topic in sufficient detail and accuracy.

3.3 Analysis of empirical information

The answers to quantitative questions in the survey were mostly analyzed through univariate statistical analyses such as calculation of averages and relative frequencies as well as through formation of sub-groups. Due to the comparably small data sample, it was not feasible to apply multivariate statistical data analyses. The answers to qualitative questions were interpreted under consideration of additional notes made by the interviewer while conducting the interviews. Often, based on the qualitative results, bivariate relations were formed and illustrated by means of creation of tables and matrices, where appropriate. Furthermore, case examples on selected topics have been generated in a sufficiently sanitized form.[670]

[669] The questionnaire itself can be found in Appendix B

[670] See Diekmann (2002), p. 555 et seqq. for univariate analyses, p. 571 for illustration of bivariate correlations and p. 602 et seqq. for multivariate statistical data analyses

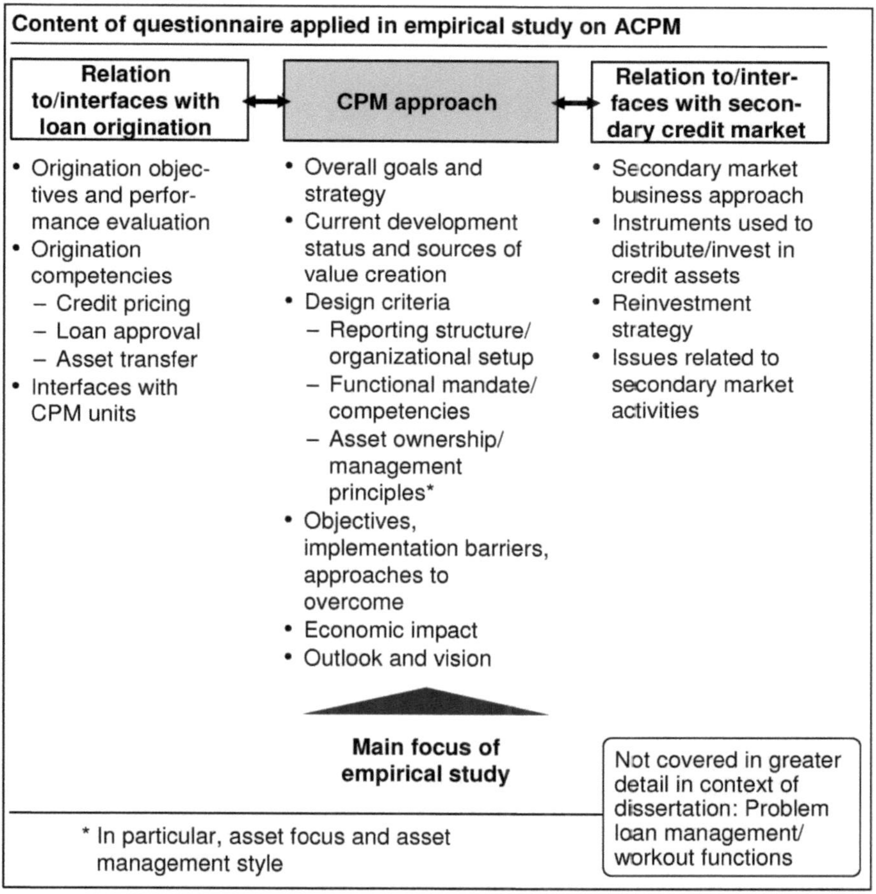

Figure 39: Content of questionnaire applied in empirical study on ACPM[671]

[671] Source: Own illustration

4 Empirical evidence on CPM business models

This chapter aims at describing the different types of CPM business models that have been found in the empirical sample. These business models will be compared to the generic ones developed in literature along the three design criteria (I) mandate for credit functions, (II) asset ownership, and (III) reporting structure within the institution. Subsequently, they will be described in greater detail. Thereby, a particular focus is put on their objectives, related implementation degrees and barriers as well as a detailed description of their characteristic functional competencies. Furthermore, the potential of these business models to create additional value for their institutions' credit business as well as the different value creation dimensions will be portrayed.

4.1 CPM business models identified in empirical sample

4.1.1 Mandate and asset ownership

Participants in the empirical study were asked how they would best describe the functional mandate of their CPM unit.[672] Afterwards, they had to specify their answer in greater detail. When combining the answers to these questions with the findings on asset ownership of the respective units, the following three types of CPM business models have emerged:

4.1.1.1 Risk controllers

Risk controllers pursue the least sophisticated approach towards CPM. They do not actively manage credit exposures, neither through impacting loan origination nor by initiating or actually executing secondary credit market transactions. Rather, they primarily provide risk controlling, reporting, and monitoring functions for the credit assets owned by their customer BUs, thus supporting these BUs' loan monitoring, managing, and servicing activities. Not having set up a dedicated unit for these tasks, risk controllers perform their activities within existing (central or credit) risk units of the institutions. In many of these players, there is a committee of executives with responsibility for credit risk business performing some kind of credit portfolio controlling and monitoring functions, thus effectively acting as risk controllers. Risk controllers dispose of the weakest mandate and competence level towards other units compared to other CPM business models.

[672] In order to test the generic business models described in literature on ACPM, the closed-ended questions were oriented at these theoretical models. Accordingly, participants could choose between four different answers to the question regarding the functional mandate of their CPM unit: (I) risk reporter/controller, (II) advisor on strategic direction of loan portfolio, (III) active portfolio manager with ownership of credit risks and activities on secondary markets, (IV) proprietary investor with asset ownership and full responsibility for credit portfolio

Risk controller CPM business models are typically found among institutions pursuing the conventional "originate and hold" lending approach that has been described in chapter 2.1 and Figure 9 of part II.

More advanced players in terms of CPM have established dedicated units that actively influence the composition of their institutions' loan portfolios on primary and secondary credit markets (hence, referred to as ACPM units in the following sections). An analysis and interpretation of the empirical information allowed two business models to be distinguished:

4.1.1.2 Active advisors

Active advisors provide strategic advice for loan originating BUs regarding acquisition of new and renewal of existing loan contracts. As they typically own the bank's loan pricing model, they also generate transparency for loan origination regarding what would be the "right" risk-adjusted price to charge customers when granting them credit assets. In case a secondary credit market price is available, they also provide market prices as benchmarks for origination.

The mandate of these ACPM units does not foresee taking over credit assets or related risks from origination. Therefore, their enforcement power regarding credit pricing is usually quite low: the price quotation typically has the form of a non-binding advice for originators/relationship managers as to which loan price they should ideally charge their customers. If these recommendations are not implemented, however, e.g., due to the fact that, for relationship reasons, a customer is offered a lower price than required from a risk-return point of view, active advisors typically do not have a sanctioning power over origination. The lower profitability of the loan engagement needs to be borne by the origination BU.

Active advisors do not take over ownership for loan assets or related risks from origination. Nevertheless, they are active in the sense that they aim at optimally structuring the portfolio composition from a risk-return point of view. They do so on the primary market side through impacting origination's decision to conclude new and renew existing credit contracts. On the secondary market side, they perform secondary credit market transactions – often, in coordination and together with the asset-owning BUs. Hereby, they primarily perform risk distribution transactions, in particular hedging of credit risks. Few of these units reinvest the resulting freed-up capital on secondary credit markets.[673]

[673] It will be shown later in chapter 4.4 that it is the conditions of the secondary credit market in which active advisors operate that have a crucial influence on the way they influence their institutions' credit portfolio composition: in particular when operating in rather illiquid markets, these units typically put an exclusive emphasis on actively impacting the origination and renewal of lending relationships on the primary market side as their opportunities to exchange credit risks on secondary loan markets are fairly limited

Typically, active advisors have their own book for the secondary market transactions they execute and bear P&L responsibility for these transactions. The ones actively performing secondary market reinvestments are set up as profit centers, aiming at retrieving the costs related to risk distribution activities through subsequent reinvestments. By contrast, the ones merely focusing on performing risk distribution transactions on secondary markets operate as cost centers, characteristically allocating the risk distribution/hedging costs back to the originating BUs.

4.1.1.3 Proprietary investors

Proprietary investors pursue the most sophisticated approach towards CPM that is currently to be found among leading financial institutions. They are set up as independent profit centers within their institution, acquiring the credit assets fitting into their portfolio structure from the originating BUs at a self-determined, binding settlement price.[674]

Having taken over responsibility for these credit assets and being responsible for the profitability of the overall loan portfolio, they perform transactions on secondary credit markets – having both the goal to distribute and acquire credit risks – in order to optimize its risk-return composition. In a modified form, proprietary investors do not physically acquire the credit assets but only take over their related risks from originating BUs, e.g., through synthetic CDS structures, leaving the assets under the ownership of origination.

* * * * *

So far, the design criterion "reporting structure" has been excluded from the description of the CPM business models identified in the empirical sample. When analyzing and interpreting the empirical information, this was found to be a further differentiating factor for the three ACPM business models identified, in particular regarding their objectives and detailed functional competencies.

4.1.2 Reporting structure

4.1.2.1 Location within organizational hierarchy

As shown before, based on the design criteria mandate and asset ownership, three different CPM business models could be derived from the empirical sample. When additionally considering the design criterion reporting structure, a further refinement of these models can be undertaken.

Some CPM units are located in the (wholesale/markets or SME-/retail asset-focused) BU of their institution while others are centrally located in the bank. Regarding their central location, it can be differentiated between such units whose Head reports

[674] When performing the interviews among proprietary investors, the settlement pricing procedure was explored in greater detail. It will be described in chapter 4.4.5

directly to the group-CEO and others that are located in a central group risk or finance unit, with their Head reporting to the group-CRO or CFO. Often, there are regional sub-portfolio management units in foreign locations, with the Heads of these regional units typically having a dual reporting line both to the global Head of CPM in the institution's headquarters and to the Head of the regional customer BU.

4.1.2.2 Location on private vs. public side

Besides determining the optimal location within the organization's hierarchy, a frequently debated topic among participants in the empirical study is whether their CPM unit is to be optimally located on the private or public side of the institution.

An organizational location on the private side means that the individuals controlling and managing credit portfolios have access to material non-public information about the bank's credit customers.[675] The decision to locate a CPM unit on the private side is typically motivated by the goal to provide its personnel with access to all (material and non-public) information about the risks being managed – in particular, this is information about the internal customer ratings – and to enable a close contact with their colleagues who take the initial lending decisions. The possibility that portfolio management personnel has access to material non-public information requires internal procedures and rules to be organized in a way that prevents them from "insider trading" activities that are based on this information advantage.[676] For example, the institutions' compliance departments need to review, monitor or otherwise control communication between CPM and other public-side units within the organization such as trading desks or trading activities performed by portfolio management itself. Alternatively, the establishment of a "written trading plan" for transactions that will be executed at a later point in time when the respective market participant is expected to possess material non-public information could address the insider-trading issue.[677]

An organizational location on the public side implies that ACPM staff merely possesses publicly known information about their institutions' credit customers. Hence, they should generally be allowed to execute securities transactions without the need to determine on an individual basis whether they possess material non-public information regarding such an individual transaction.[678] What needs to be decided in this case, however, is the maximum amount of proprietary customer information to be provided

675 In line with US insider-trading regulation, material non-public information is defined as information that has not been made available to public investors as there is a substantial likelihood that a "reasonable investor" would consider such information as important in making an investment decision which is "reasonably certain" to have a substantial effect on the market price of an asset; see Joint Market Practices Forum (2003), p. 4

676 See Joint Market Practices Forum (2003), p. 13

677 See Joint Market Practices Forum (2003), p. 14 et seq.

678 See Joint Market Practices Forum (2003), p. 15

to public-side CPM personnel so that they can effectively perform their portfolio management tasks. In this context, procedures need to be established to regulate and determine whether the information provided is material and non-public. Further, it is to be decided in which form to communicate such information. Compliance personnel have a key role in setting up such procedures.[679]

4.1.3 Distribution of CPM business models amongst participants

4.1.3.1 Risk controllers

More than a third of the European banks in the empirical sample (around 37%) manage their credit portfolios as risk controllers, i.e., they perform activities focusing on passive CPM, in particular credit risk controlling, monitoring, and reporting. These tasks are undertaken within existing risk units of the institutions: around two thirds of the risk controllers (or 25% of the total sample of participating institutions) report that they operate from a central bank-wide risk unit. The other risk controllers perform their activities within risk units of the institutions' wholesale/markets or SME-/retail asset-focused BUs. Risk controllers have been subsumed under "model 1" in Figure 40.

4.1.3.2 Active advisors

Characteristics of risk controllers' activities do not differ depending on whether they are performed in a central bank-wide risk/finance unit or in such a function of a bank's BU. When examining active advisory units more closely, however, differing objectives and functional competencies can be observed, depending on whether they are located in a central unit or whether they are located in a BU.

Hence, when additionally considering the reporting structure, it is appropriate to further refine the active advisor business model by distinguishing between active advisors located in BUs (model II a, constituting about 29% of all participants) and others to be found in a central location of their institutions (model II b, making up for 13% of the institutions covered in the sample).[680]

4.1.3.3 Proprietary investors

In particular following their aspiration to have a strong impact on the loan origination side, proprietary investors cannot be located in their institutions' risk units.[681] A

[679] See Joint Market Practices Forum (2003), p. 16 et seq.

[680] See chapters 4.3 and 4.4 for an in-depth description of the objectives and detailed functional competencies of these different models

[681] Due to the regulatory requirement to separate loan origination/credit analysis from credit approval/second vote functions, it is not possible from a regulatory point of view that a proprietary investor, that is strongly involved in loan origination activities, is located within a risk unit where typically credit approval/second vote decisions are taken; see again Footnote 82 for German MaK guidelines as an example for such a regulation

location within the finance unit would not support the goal to strongly execute pricing power towards loan origination and potentially get involved in loan underwriting activities. Consequently, proprietary investors are either situated in customer BUs or have a direct reporting line to the group CEO.[682]

In total, 21% of the institutions taking part in the empirical study have presently implemented a proprietary investor ACPM business model for the management of their credit assets. Except for one proprietary investor acquiring the credit risks related to the assets from origination by means of credit derivatives, these units physically take over the credit assets from origination immediately after the loan contracts have been concluded.[683] One institution has set up such a proprietary investor in its SME-/retail customer BU, taking over loans to SME and retail customers.[684] The other proprietary investors focus their activities on wholesale assets by primarily acquiring and managing lending exposures to large and medium-sized corporate debtors.[685] Proprietary investors have been subsumed under "model III" in Figure 40.

It can be observed that an increasing sophistication of CPM business models from risk controller to proprietary investor is accompanied by a shift in the units' reporting structure within the organization from central risk or finance units towards BUs or, less frequently, towards a direct CEO reporting line.

4.1.3.4 Split of business models in private- vs. public-side location

Around 69% of all CPM units have reported that they are situated on the private side of their institutions, thus having access to material non-public information about the banks' credit customers. Three reasons were named for this decision: firstly, they want their portfolio management to be an integral part of the credit decision-making process by having a strong impact on loan origination and by often actively taking part in credit analysis and underwriting functions. Secondly, CPM units can get a better understanding of their banks' loan portfolio composition if they have access to private customer information. Finally, participants feel that their compliance regulation and processes do not inhibit secondary market trading activities to an extent that would necessitate locating their portfolio management on the public side. It is mainly for the

682 Only one proprietary investor has been found that is centrally located within the organization by directly reporting to the institution's CEO. This ACPM unit does not physically take over credit assets but acquires them in a synthetic form through credit derivatives. See chapter 4.4.5.2 providing a detailed description of this specification of the proprietary investor business model

683 Another ACPM unit, currently set up as an active advisor, is thinking about setting up such a risk transferring proprietary investor model at the moment

684 For reasons that will become obvious in chapter 5, this institution is currently in the process of scaling back its proprietary investor ACPM unit towards an active advisor

685 See also chapter 4.2, describing the asset focus of all CPM business models in greater detail

reason to be able to strongly impact loan origination that all proprietary investors are located entirely or at least partly on the private side of their institution.

Mainly because they do not need to involve compliance departments when communicating portfolio information to other public-sided units and as they are more flexible regarding execution of secondary market transactions, about 21% of all participants have decided to locate their CPM units on the public side. Moreover, these institutions are convinced that knowledge about private information and ability to leverage this information does not add value to their CPM units' activities. Besides this, they often want their CPM units to be as close as possible to secondary credit markets in order to have the opportunity to successfully establish close customer relationships with credit risk investors or distributors on these markets.

Some of the most sophisticated players – around 10% of the participants in the empirical study – have split their CPM units into private- and public-sided units. Aiming at having a strong impact on loan origination while remaining as flexible as possible regarding execution of secondary market transactions, they typically have a loan pricing team situated on the private side while personnel responsible for public portfolio management transactions and secondary market trading activities are located on the public side of the institution. In order to ensure that compliance regulation is adhered to within the CPM unit, some of these institutions have established a control group supervising the information flow between the two sub-functions of their CPM unit.

In Figure 40, the CPM business models identified in the empirical study on ACPM are illustrated in a matrix showing the distribution of the models according to their reporting structure within the organization.

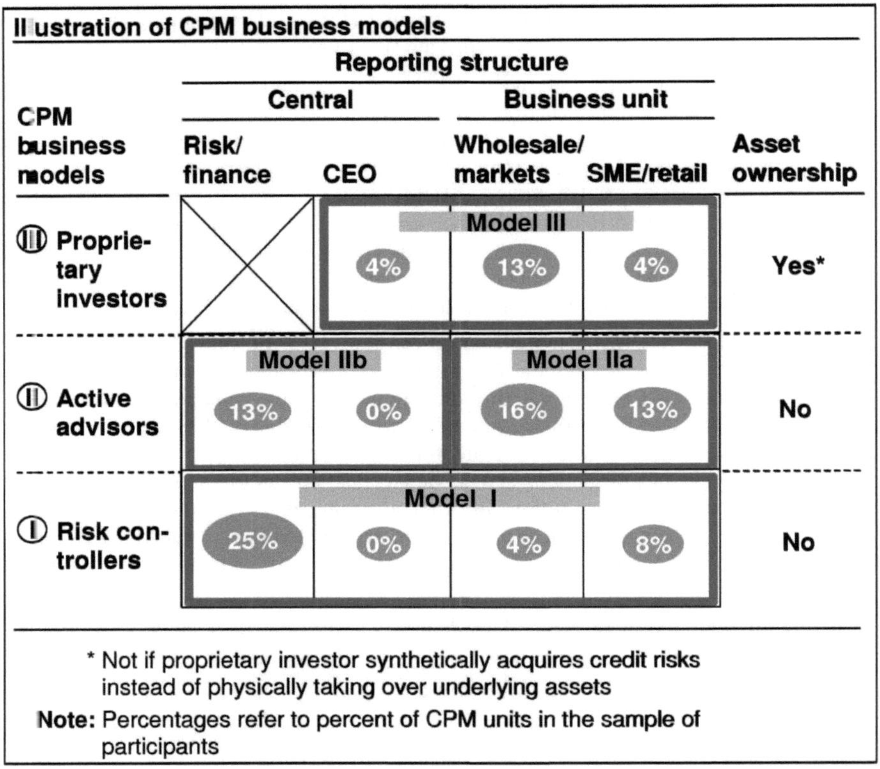

Figure 40: Illustration of CPM business models[686]

4.1.4 Comparison to generic ACPM business models

The empirical results have revealed that the ACPM business models implemented by leading European banks differ from the generic ones developed in literature on ACPM.[687]

The ACPM units which, according to the findings of the empirical study on ACPM, can best be described as "active advisors" have a broader functional mandate than the

[686] Source: Own illustration based on results of the empirical study on ACPM

[687] See again chapter 2.3.2 of part II for the generic ACPM business models described in literature. The risk controller CPM business model identified in the empirical sample complies with the conventional approach towards lending business described in chapter 2.1 of part II

"advisors" described in literature since they not only advise customer BUs regarding how to optimally rebalance their portfolio but – particularly the wholesale asset-focused ones – are also active on secondary credit markets regarding execution of transactions to optimize the risk-return characteristics of their institution's portfolio. Regarding organizational set-up, literature sees advisors located in the risk unit or customer BU of their institution. Yet, the empirical findings have revealed that active advisors can also be located in the finance unit of their institution.

The "active portfolio managers" introduced by literature do not occur in this form in practice. This is mainly due to the reason that there is no ACPM unit acquiring credit assets or related risks from origination while operating as a cost center. All units acquiring credit assets or at least related risks have the responsibility to act as proprietary investors for their institutions' credit assets and unit as profit centers, hence being economically accountable for their transactions instead of passing on costs to other units.

A crucial difference between the proprietary investors described in theory vs. the ones found in practice is their organizational location: only the proprietary investor not physically taking over credit assets but acquiring their risks in a synthetic form through credit derivatives is centrally located within the organization. The ones physically taking over credit assets are situated in wholesale, markets or SME-/retail asset-focused BUs. When conducting the interviews with executives from proprietary investor ACPM units that are currently located in BUs, it was discussed whether they could imagine a central location within their organization as a feasible option. Being able to implement such an organizational set-up seems to be very unrealistic, however, since it would imply shifting revenues related to the credit assets out of the customer BU towards another unit. The executives responsible for the BU are not expected to agree to such a shift of credit revenues from their unit to another department.

* * * * *

Obviously, generic business models developed in literature do not fully correspond to the ACPM business models found among participants in the empirical study. Besides this, there is currently no publication available characterizing the CPM business models – neither the generic ACPM ones nor the ones currently set up in practice – in greater detail. Hence, it seems necessary to fill this gap and to provide a profound description of the approaches towards managing credit portfolios that are presently taken by leading European institutions.

Therefore, based on the findings of the empirical study, the three different CPM business models that have been introduced above will subsequently be described in depth according to the following characteristics: after having portrayed their asset focus, it will be analyzed in detail what the objectives of the different business models are as well as related implementation degrees and main barriers on the path to a successful implementation. The description of the functional mandate of the CPM business models provided above has been on a rather high level as it mainly served to distinguish the different models. As each of these business models has very specific characteristics regarding competence for key credit functions that differentiate it from the other models, their individual functional competencies will be depicted in greater detail. Lastly, it will be examined to what extent and along which dimensions the CPM business models identified above manage to create additional economic value for an institution's credit business.

4.2 Asset focus of CPM business models

As mentioned above, most CPM units have a wholesale asset-focus.[688] This is confirmed by a more detailed view on the asset focus of the three different CPM business models identified (see Figure 41 for an illustration).

Almost all CPM units either own or manage large- and mid-corps "plain vanilla" loans. Fewer CPM units include small-corps and syndicated loans. Structured/leveraged credit products are in the asset focus of about 40% of the active advisors and proprietary investors but are not covered at all by risk controllers. Retail lending assets are mostly managed by ACPM units set up as active advisors. 20% of the proprietary investors assume ownership for these asset classes. Often, a certain "home bias" in the portfolio composition of the CPM units can be perceived, i.e., the majority own or manage domestic credit assets. There is no CPM unit in the empirical sample that currently owns or manages the entire credit asset spectrum of its institution.[689]

---

[688] See again Figure 38

[689] As already mentioned above (see again chapter 2), there are some risk controllers in the empirical sample indicating that they cover the entire asset portfolio of their institution. They merely perform conventional risk controlling and reporting functions, however, and do not actively manage their institutions' loan portfolios.

The result that CPM units only focus on parts of their institutions' credit portfolios, mostly on wholesale assets, corresponds to Hammes and Shapiro (2001), p. 106 who regard this practice as a dangerous shortfall since it may lead to management decisions and strategies that are suboptimal from a bank-wide point of view as they are only based on a partial view on credit risks and fail to consider the mostly high correlations between large corps, SME and consumer lending assets

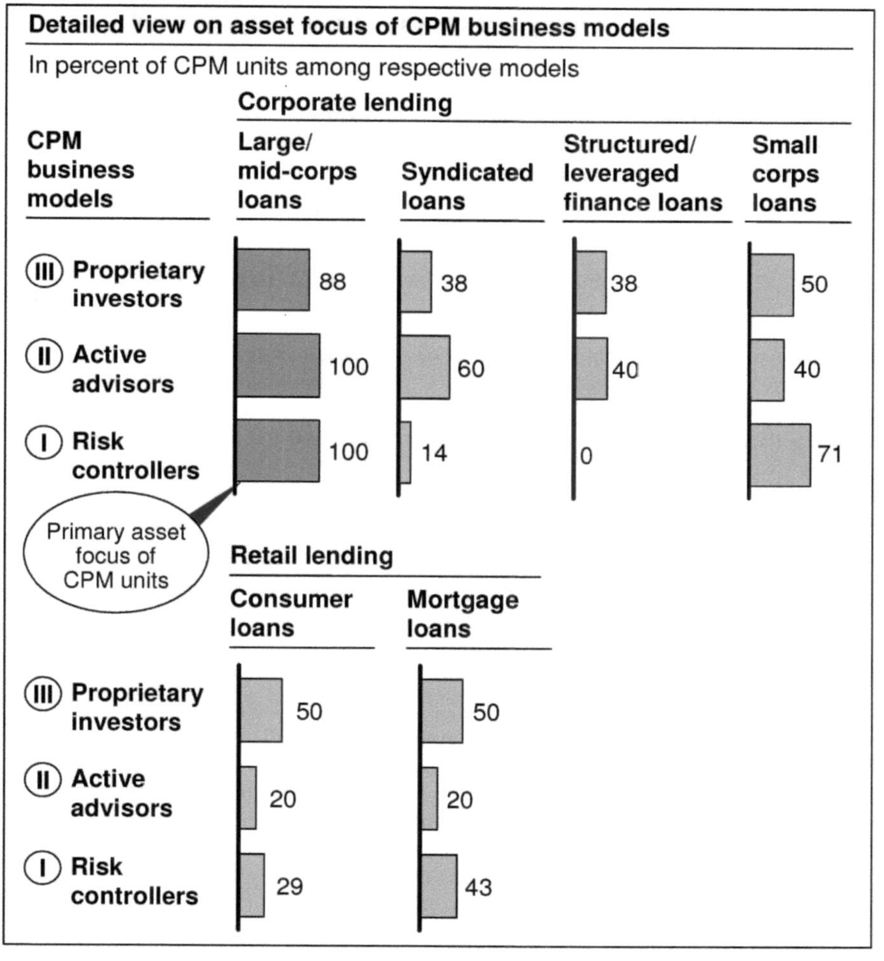

Figure 41: Detailed view on asset focus of CPM business models[690]

[690] Source: Own illustration based on results of empirical study on ACPM

4.3 CPM objectives, degrees of implementation and main implementation barriers

Participants in the empirical study were asked to rank the importance of a selection of objectives they pursue with their CPM unit.[691] Furthermore, they have had to estimate to which percentage they have been able to implement these objectives and to list the typical barriers they face(d) on the way to a successful implementation.

The results often differ significantly across the different CPM business models identified above.

4.3.1 Characteristic objectives of CPM business models and degrees of implementation

From their ranking of the objectives, it can be seen whether the goal of the CPM units is to improve primary market credit business (e.g., through imposing price discipline on loan originating units) or whether they rather put an emphasis on secondary credit market activities. Through subsequent reinvestments of the freed-up capital into higher yielding secondary market assets, ideally in securities with low correlation to the assets on the credit book, an optimization of the earnings from credit investments and a more optimal risk-return structure of the credit portfolio is aspired to be achieved.

Activities on secondary credit markets may include risk distribution transactions which have the goal of diversifying and transferring credit risks in order to limit unexpected credit losses.[692] Besides this, they may aim at reducing economic and regulatory capital bound in credit assets. Furthermore, such activities on secondary markets – especially taking on tradable assets into the loan portfolio – increase the liquidity of the portfolio's asset base.

Also, CPM units may also aim at improving the risk distribution skills of their institution through creating new standardized structured credit products such as CDOs based on the bank's loan book and placing these products on secondary markets. A precondition for a success of such placements is the existence of receptive investors for these products and an understanding of the market receptiveness, also depending on the current position of the credit cycle. Therefore, participants were asked for the importance of their objective to actively manage the credit cycle and to enhance existing or create new markets on which such products can be placed and traded.

When analyzing the results of the empirical study, it became evident that the objectives and the extent to which degree they have been implemented differ significantly depending on the type of CPM business model. Yet, it becomes obvious

---

691 They could rank the importance ascribed to these objectives on an ordinal scale between 1 (lowest importance) and 5 (highest importance)

692 See also again Figure 8 illustrating risk diversification and transfer as major fields of activity of ACPM units

that some goals have a higher-than-average importance across all types of CPM models while others seem to be of particular importance for certain types of the CPM business models introduced above.

Objectives that all banks name as especially important for their CPM are to increase the transparency of their credit portfolios' risk and return characteristics and to reduce the EC bound in credit assets. The latter objective is mainly aspired to through diversification of large concentration risk exposures to single debtors. The goal of reducing regulatory capital consumption has overall importance. This is mainly due to the fact that most institutions report that they do no consider themselves as regulatory capital constrained.[693] It is in particular the active advisors and proprietary investors that have already widely implemented the objective of reducing regulatory capital, reporting an average degree of implementation of about 90% for this goal.

Especially when taking into consideration to what extent participants regard their objectives as implemented, it becomes obvious that there are significant differences between the CPM business models identified. The key results for the individual models are summarized in Figure 42, Figure 43, and Figure 44.

4.3.1.1 Risk controllers

Most important objectives for risk controllers are to increase the transparency of their credit portfolios' risk-return characteristics, to reduce EC, and to actively manage the credit cycle. Despite active advisors having a higher prioritized goal to discipline loan origination, the goals which risk controllers have set for their CPM are not significantly different from the advisors' ones.

What differs tremendously, however, is the degree of implementation across all objectives: while risk controllers estimate they have an average implementation degree of only 15% across all the objectives listed in Figure 42, active advisors feel that they have implemented the same objectives to an average degree of around 50% (see Figure 43). In particular, risk controllers have basically not yet implemented their objectives to perform secondary market reinvestments and to create new secondary credit markets. It seems as though, despite aiming at similar targets as active advisors, risk controllers generally faced significant barriers to sufficiently implement their objectives.

693 On the contrary, as shown in chapter 2.2.4 of part II and especially Figure 12, many institutions currently face a surplus of regulatory capital

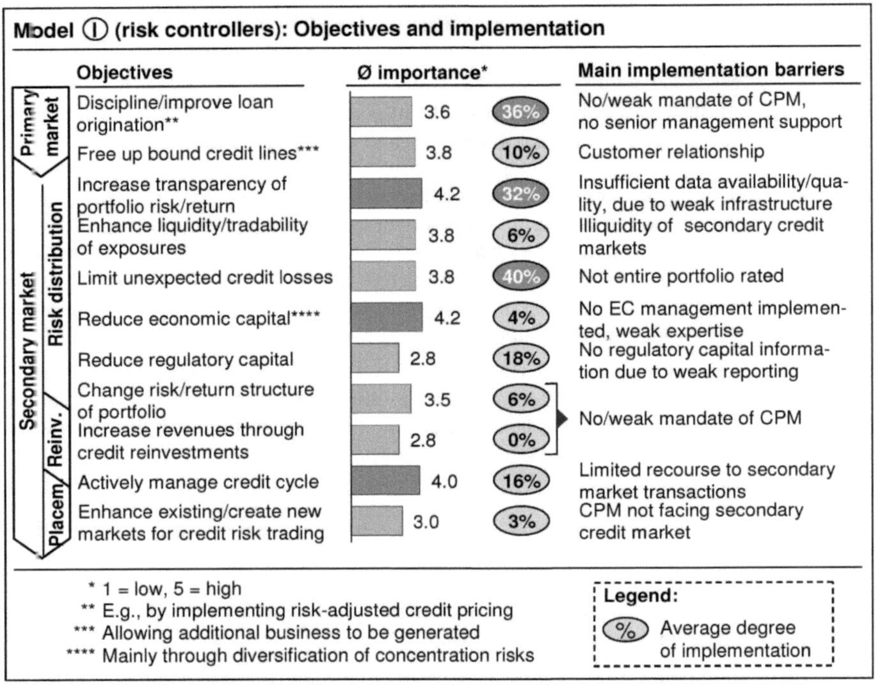

Figure 42: Model I (risk controllers): Objectives and implementation[694]

4.3.1.2 Active advisors

Among active advisors, differences regarding the importance and implementation degree of their objectives can be perceived, depending on whether the units are located in BUs (model II a) or in central risk/finance units (model II b):

The ones located in BUs primarily aim at increasing portfolio transparency, limiting UL and disciplining/improving loan origination. These advisors seem to be able to take advantage of their proximity to loan origination BUs as they not only report a higher average importance for the latter objective but also a greater degree of implementation.

Active advisors situated in a central risk/finance unit primarily focus on limiting their credit portfolio's UL as well as reducing the EL of the portfolio and disciplining loan origination; yet, with a significantly lower average importance for the objectives to

[694] Source: Own illustration based on results of empirical study on ACPM

discipline loan origination than their counterparts located in BUs. Being obviously driven by their proximity to a centralized risk or finance unit, they report their second-highest implementation success after regulatory capital reduction for the objective to limit unexpected credit losses while their weaker mandate towards the origination side is reflected in lower implementation success for the goal of disciplining loan origination.

Except for some of the most sophisticated ones, active advisors mostly do not aspire to perform secondary market reinvestments or to set the basis for actively placing credit assets by enhancing existing or creating new markets for placement and trading of newly created credit products. Accordingly, they have comparably low degrees of implementation for these objectives.

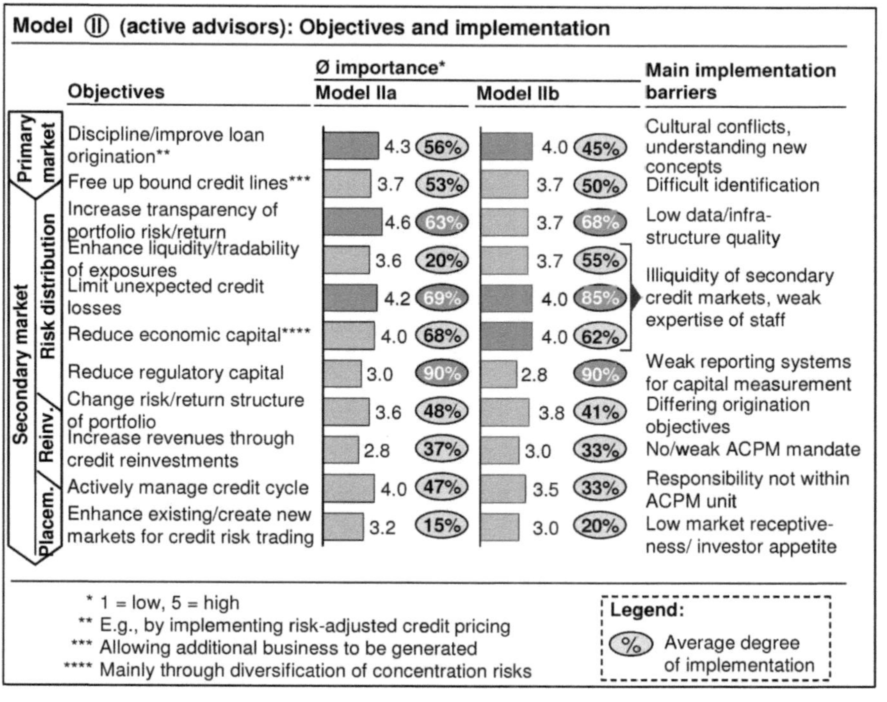

Figure 43: Model II (active advisors): Objectives and implementation[695]

[695] Source: Own illustration based on results of empirical study on ACPM

4.3.1.3 Proprietary investors

Proprietary investors have a clear priority to discipline and improve loan origination, followed by the goal to increase portfolio transparency and to change the risk-return structure of their loan portfolio. Having an average implementation degree of more than 70% for their main objectives, they seem to have found a way to successfully overcome major implementation hurdles. In particular, their main goal of disciplining and improving origination has been implemented to 90%. Also, as opposed to active advisors and particularly to risk controllers, proprietary investors have been able to achieve implementation degrees in the range of 50-60% for their objectives to perform secondary market reinvestments and lay the foundation for successful placements of newly structured products on secondary markets, e.g., through engaging in efforts to create markets/an investor base for these products (see Figure 44).

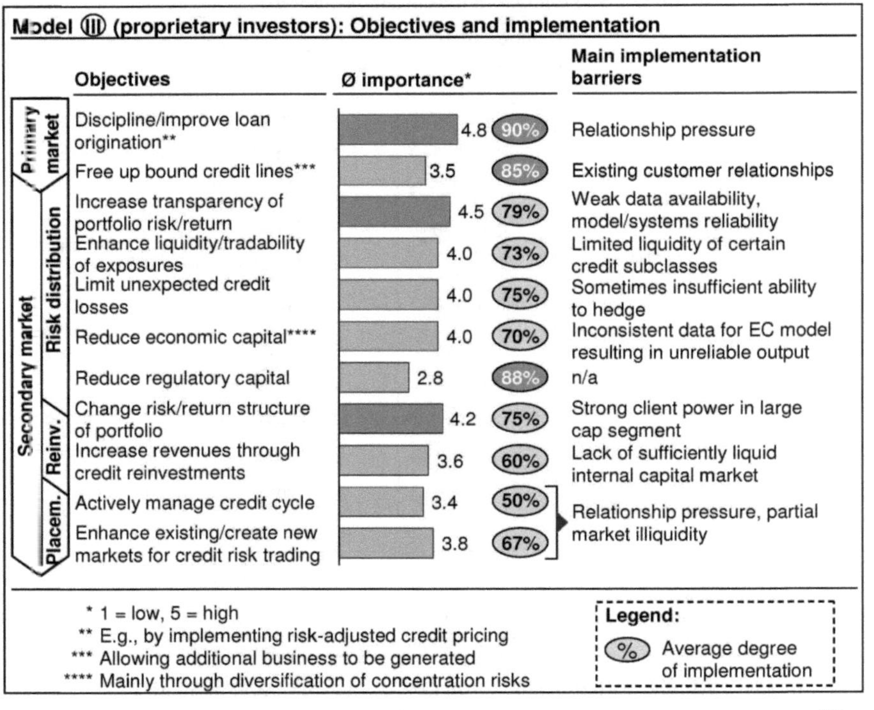

Figure 44: Model III (proprietary investors): Objectives and implementation[696]

[696] Source: Own illustration based on results of empirical study on ACPM

4.3.2 Main implementation barriers

The varying degrees of implementation success for the key objectives shown above can be traced back to barriers that participants face on the path to a successful implementation of their objectives. While some of the barriers identified are faced by all CPM business models, there are also typical model-specific ones. The implementation hurdles identified with the help of the empirical study shall be described in the following sections.

4.3.2.1 Risk controllers

Risk controllers feel their business model does not allow them to satisfactorily implement their goals with respect to impacting primary market credit business or changing the credit portfolio structure by means of secondary market transactions. The main reason named for these low implementation degrees is that following their location in existing risk units, risk controllers do not have a (sufficient) organizational mandate and the assertiveness to do so.

Besides an inadequate location within the organization to achieve this objective, their weak mandate can particularly be traced back to the lack of senior executives supporting and pushing forward an enhancement of their approach towards CPM.[697] Furthermore, due to insufficient coordination with other units of the institution, secondary credit market transactions are often performed in other units (e.g., markets BUs or ALM units) without the knowledge and agreement of CPM.

Often facing a deficient reporting systems infrastructure, they are not very successful in generating transparency about their portfolio structure. Risk controllers are also frequently opposed to the issue that the quality, reliability and consistency of their loan portfolio data is rather poor. Furthermore, they mostly have not yet implemented an EC-based loan pricing tool to set a "true" risk-adjusted price for origination. Some risk controllers have named the low expertise of employees or the insufficient availability of a skilled workforce on the labor market a hurdle on the path to implementing an EC management system.

The major obstacle that risk controllers see on the path to achieving a higher implementation degree for their main objectives as well as for a further enhancement and sophistication of their business model, however, is the lack of existence or widespread illiquidity of secondary credit markets in their field of activity. They have typically not yet developed clear concepts and approaches on how to address and overcome this issue.

[697] It will be shown in chapter five that risk controllers are typically located in rather benign market environments e.g., regarding profitability of primary lending business. Therefore, there is no strong incentive and urge for senior executives to push forward an enhancement of their CPM activities

4.3.2.2 Active advisors

Similar to reactive controllers, many active advisors also regard the lack of existence and illiquidity of secondary markets for credit assets as the main obstacle to achieving higher degrees of implementation success, especially for their important objectives of limiting unexpected credit losses and reducing EC consumption. Some of them have also named the issue as a crucial reason why they cannot successfully move towards a proprietary investor business model.

They also perceive the lack of availability of skilled staff with secondary credit market expertise as a major hurdle on the path to achieving higher implementation degrees for the latter two objectives. Besides this, they consider cultural conflicts towards origination BUs as a major implementation hurdle, in particular for their objective of imposing pricing discipline on origination. Such conflicts are primarily rooted in the fact that incentives for originators/relationship managers are mainly driven by profit contribution and customer volumes while active advisor ACPM units are managed an incentivized by risk-driven performance metrics and incentives such as RAROC-improvement (see left-hand side of Figure 45, illustrating the importance of key performance indicators for origination BUs).[698]

Another major implementation hurdle typically faced by active advisors is an unclear communication of the newly established ACPM business model within the organization, with the consequence that the approach is often not properly understood and supported outside the ACPM unit, especially in loan origination BUs.

Further, similar to risk controllers, active advisors struggle with issues related to insufficient availability and consistency of loan portfolio data. Following the higher degree of sophistication of their business model, they typically regard these issues as even graver than risk controllers do.

4.3.2.3 Proprietary investors

Proprietary investors have managed to widely overcome the typical implementation hurdles faced by the two other CPM business models. As a major reason for this high implementation success, they name a senior executive strongly supporting and driving their approach towards managing credit assets.

The major issue that proprietary investors are still struggling with is an often unsatisfactory liquidity of the secondary credit market environment in which they operate. This issue limits the players' ability to execute secondary credit market transactions to an optimal extent. Besides this, the matter is perceived as grave since the proprietary business model foresees determining a "fair", ideally market-based settlement price for assets to be transferred to their unit after the loan origination

[698] The relevance that a clearly defined incentive structure aligned with the goals of ACPM and other units has for the establishment of an ACPM unit will be described in greater detail in chapter 5.1.3.2 of part III

process has been concluded. Some players have successfully developed approaches to circumvent this problem for the largest non-tradable names in their portfolio.[699] However, the illiquidity issue becomes particularly acute for these ACPM units when aiming at expanding their asset coverage beyond the largest credit names towards mid- or even small corps credit asset classes.

Illiquidity of secondary credit markets is held responsible for the fact that most proprietary investors typically have not satisfactorily implemented their objective to implement strategies regarding actively managing the credit cycle to be better protected against future downturns. Further, since they have not perceived a receptive market environment, not all of these ACPM units have been successful in generating new types of securities based on their loan book and placing them among investors.

Typically, proprietary investors have already accomplished high implementation degrees regarding disciplining and improving loan origination. Yet, in particular following their goal to increase profitability of primary market business, they see a difficulty in the way to impose an even higher achievement of this objective related to the fact that, for the sake of acquiring and maintaining customer relationships, loan origination/relationship management BUs face pressure to grant a price to clients which is lower than the optimal price they are supposed to charge according to the requirements and demands of ACPM units. In large cap credit segments especially, primary market units face clients with strong pricing power, not allowing them to charge the "true" credit price as determined by secondary credit markets or internal bank pricing models.[700]

In particular when aiming at performing secondary market reinvestments in credit risks, proprietary investors are opposed to the issue that there is often no optimal bank-internal capital flow established yet, enabling EC to be easily allocated towards more profitable credit segments.

Cultural conflicts between ACPM and origination are not explicitly named an issue by these proprietary investors: although the ACPM units place an emphasis on different performance metrics than loan origination BUs (see the right-hand side of Figure 45 for an illustration), it seems as though the stronger mandate which these ACPM units have over origination BUs combined with a strong senior management supporting the establishment of such a business model have crucially contributed to solving these potential conflicts of interest.

[699] See in particular chapter 4.4.5.1.1 for an approach developed by some proprietary investors to determine a "fair" transfer price for non-tradable credit names based on the "universe" of tradable names on the secondary markets

[700] See Footnote 754 for empirical evidence from the empirical study regarding loans closed by relationship management below their "true" value

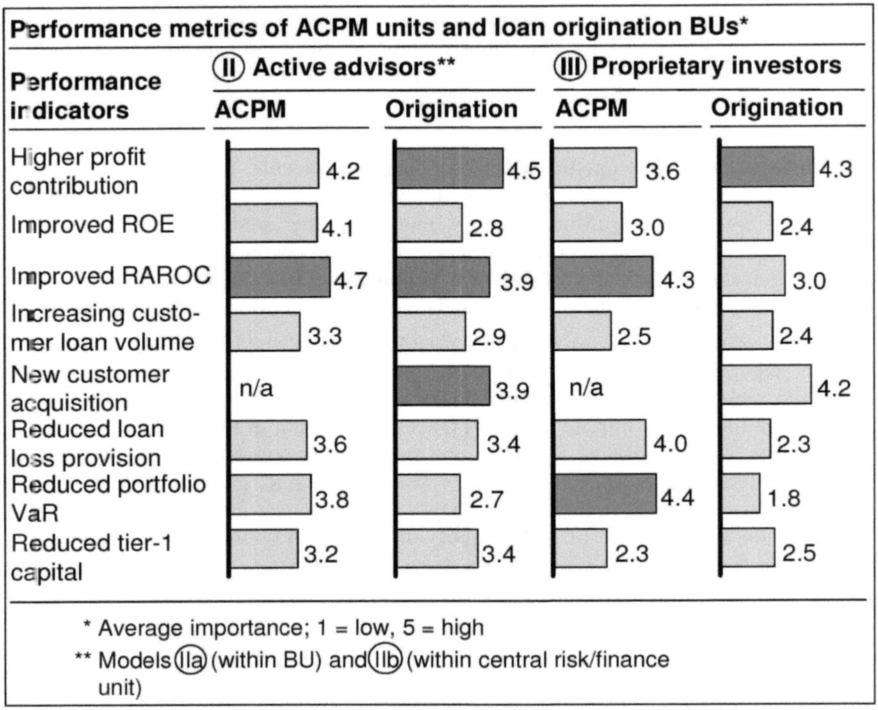

Figure 45: Performance metrics of ACPM units and loan origination BUs[701]

* * * * *

The analysis of the objectives pursued by the different CPM business models, perceived implementation degrees related to these objectives as well as barriers on the path to a successful implementation has revealed specific characteristics of the different models. Conducting the interviews revealed, however, that participants in the empirical study – irrespective of the CPM business model currently implemented – regard limited tradability of assets on secondary credit markets due to partially the lack of existence and insufficient liquidity of these markets as the most severe barrier on the path to achieving a higher implementation success for several of their key objectives.

701 Source: Own illustration based on results of the empirical study on ACPM. A similar picture arises when comparing the importance of key performance indicators between reactive controllers and origination BUs

This often lack of existence and insufficient liquidity of secondary credit markets is strong evidence that the CPM units examined seem to operate in an incomplete secondary credit market environment.[702]. Furthermore, the fact that a further development and sophistication of CPM business models appears to be inhibited through the conditions on secondary credit markets faced by CPM units can be regarded as a confirmation for the aforementioned finding that the credit market environment in which an institution operates is a key determinant for the design of its CPM unit.[703]

In a separate question included in the empirical study, participants were asked to determine the typical approaches they have taken to overcome the most severe issues on the path to implementing their CPM unit.

As shown in Figure 46, the most advanced institutions, having established the most advanced and successfully implemented ACPM units, have found effective ways to solve the majority of these issues. For example, they have achieved the improvement of the availability and quality of their loan portfolio data, thus gaining a better transparency of their credit portfolio composition through setting up dedicated projects or a committed task force to solve this issue. By initially developing and rolling out a relatively simple internal portfolio model that has been refined and sophisticated at a later stage, some players have taken a relatively pragmatic approach to ensuring such a model is available early on and implemented within the organization. Others have decided to acquire and implement an external portfolio model at an early stage.[704] A key approach for successfully implementing an ACPM business model has been to set up a well-defined incentive framework for the different units engaged in activities around managing credit portfolios that is aligned with the objectives of ACPM. Clearly defining and communicating the functioning of the asset transfer process – in particular the shortfall compensation procedure – has helped proprietary investors to successfully set up their asset transfer model. Good communication of the newly established ACPM approach across all levels in the banking organization together with ensuring that senior management supports and drives forward the implementation of

702 See again in part II chapter 4.2.1.1 on the assumptions of complete capital markets underlying the CAPM as well as chapter 4.4 on incompletions of bank capital market and especially chapter 4.4.1.1 on limited ability of market participants to access capital markets including free tradability of securities

The view that incomplete markets for credit capital are a major obstacle for the successful implementation of ACPM business models is also shared by Asarnov (1996) who regards limited loan market liquidity as a main constraint to overcome once a bank has decided to adopt the goals of ACPM

703 See again chapter 2.3.3.2 introducing the credit market environment as external determinant for the design of ACPM units. A detailed analysis of the impact the credit market environment has had on the design of the best-practice institutions' CPM units included in the empirical study on ACPM will be performed in chapter 5.2 of part III

704 See again Figure 11 showing which types of credit portfolio models are currently used by banks

the aspired business model have been crucial for overcoming issues related to a cultural change within the organization. In order to obtain sufficient attention and support from senior management as well as BUs within the organization, it has proven essential to develop a business plan clearly showing the economic benefits and value creation of the aspired ACPM business model.[705] Further, engaging senior management early on in the design process of an ACPM unit and jointly agreeing on goals have proven to be crucial for obtaining sufficient support. Finally, issues related to the low availability of skilled employees have been addressed through combining the targeted recruiting of experienced hires with effectively "training on the job" newly recruited staff and setting up dedicated training programs.

When exploring the approaches taken to overcome problems relating to the existence and liquidity of secondary credit markets, however, it has been revealed that even the most advanced institutions in terms of ACPM still have significant improvement potential regarding this issue. Some ideas regarding how to improve tradability of credit assets and exchange of related risks have already been developed: besides the concept of developing CDS proxy curves allowing the determination of a "fair" internal settlement price for non-tradable assets to be transferred to ACPM[706] and the market-making activities for CDS prices of particular debtors,[707] the ideas mentioned by participating institutions include enhancing the standardization of credit assets as well as swapping parts of the credit portfolio directly with other CPM units instead of trying to exchange the risks on secondary credit markets. Yet, apart from a few institutions calculating CDS proxy curves and quoting market prices, the implementation of these ideas has not been pushed yet.

705 See chapter 4.5 for a detailed description of the value-creation potential of the different CPM business models

706 See chapter 4.4.5.1.1 for a description of this concept which has already been implemented by some proprietary investors in the sample

707 For an example of the market-making efforts see again Footnote 357 describing the activities in this field performed by HypoVereinsbank

Approaches taken by most advanced institutions to overcome main implementation issues

Key issues	Approaches taken to overcome implementation Issues by most advanced players
Data • Insufficient data availability • Low consistency/ cleanness of data	• Solved issues related to availability and quality of data during implementation of Basel II guidelines • Set up dedicated project/task force to clean up data and achieve higher consistency
Tools/processes • Difficult to implement portfolio models • Unclear incentives origination vs. ACPM • Asset transfer pro-cess hard to set up	• Rolled out preliminary internal model early and improved/sophisticated at later stage; acquired external models • Set up clear incentive framework aligned with ACPM objectives for all units engaged in CPM activities • Clearly defined and communicated asset transferal process (e.g., introducing shortfall compensation)
Culture • Issues related to cultural change	• Made sure senior management supports and drives new approach towards CPM • Communicated approach across all hierarchies of banking organization
Senior mgmt. support • Lacking board/ CRO involvement • Weak divisional support	• Developed business plan early clearly showing benefits of new approach to gain support within organization • Engaged senior management early on in process to gain strong support and jointly agree on goals
Staff • Weak staff expertise • Insufficient availa-bility of skilled staff	• Combined recruiting of experienced staff with "training on-the-job" of new hires • Established dedicated training programs
Existence/liquidity of credit markets • Insufficient ability to trade credit assets	• Initial approaches/ideas to improve status quo – Develop CDS proxy curves to determine "fair" internal settlement price – Perform own market-making for credit names – Better standardize credit assets – Swap credit exposures directly with other players

Figure 46: Approaches taken by most advanced institutions to overcome main implementation issues[708]

[708] Source: Own illustration based on results of empirical study on ACPM

Obviously, the major issue faced by CPM units on the path to further completing and advancing their business model is the lack of existence and insufficient liquidity of the credit markets they operate in. As it is of central importance for the successful set-up and effective functioning of an ACPM unit to have the opportunity to perform secondary credit market transactions,[709] this dissertation tries to make a contribution to overcoming this key issue on the path to successfully establishing an effective ACPM unit. Therefore, in addition to the ideas already envisaged by some of the participants in the empirical study, food for thought for further research on how to possibly circumvent this issue will be developed in part IV of this dissertation. This will contribute to an enhanced tradability of credit risks, aiding a more effective functioning of CPM units, an improved implementation success for their key objectives and providing the basis for a further sophistication of the approaches towards actively managing credit risk exposures.

4.4 Functional competencies of CPM business models

The participants' CPM units differ significantly with regard to their competencies for major credit functions. In the following section, a detailed description of the CPM business models identified in the empirical sample will be provided. It will focus on their functional competence for setting credit policies, performing loan origination and underwriting tasks and controlling the credit portfolio as well as for arranging and executing transactions on secondary credit markets to reshuffle the credit portfolio composition.[710] Afterwards, the specific functional features that differentiate proprietary investors from the other CPM business models identified in the empirical sample will be described in greater detail.

---

709 See also again chapter 2.3 of part II

710 In order to get such an overview of CPM units' functional competence, participants in the empirical study were given a range of closed-ended questions referring to a broad set of credit functions. First of all, they had to answer to which degree these functions are the responsibility of their CPM units by estimating the percentage of involvement of their units in performing the functions. Furthermore, they had to reveal to which percentage other units than CPM have a major involvement in these functions. In an open-ended amendment to the questions, the institutions could also name other credit functions that are the responsibility of their CPM units.

Besides estimating the percentage of involvement in the credit functions, the level of competence that CPM units have for the various functions had to be chosen from a list of the following five competence levels for each function: No competence, informational role/competence, advisory power, veto power and decision-making right. Figure 47, Figure 48 and Figure 49 aim at illustrating the average competence levels which the different CPM models have reported for the most important credit functions and which other units besides CPM typically were named to dispose of competence for these functions.

As it has been found out that the CPM units included in the empirical study typically do not have a functional competence for problem loan management/workout function, this part of the "credit pipeline" will not be covered further in this section

Generally speaking, as can be seen in Figure 47, Figure 48 and Figure 49, an increasing sophistication of CPM units from risk controllers over active advisors towards proprietary investors is accompanied by an expansion of the units' functional competence, in particular in the field of loan pricing and secondary credit market transactions.

4.4.1 Credit policy setting

Participants had to answer which competence their CPM units have to define policies for their institutions' target credit portfolio. Risk controllers have an advisory competence for this function on average; in these institutions this task is often under the responsibility of the group CRO. Being supported by the central risk management or the bank's credit risk committee, active advisors and proprietary investors have on average slightly higher competence levels for this function.

Concerning guideline-setting for loan underwriting as well as regarding provision of loan pricing standards, risk controllers clearly have the weakest competence. Active advisors report a weak advisory competence on average. It is due to their strong mandate for loan pricing that proprietary investors have the highest impact on these units, in particular on setting pricing standards together with loan origination BUs.

Active advisors located in BUs have the highest competence levels regarding setting policies for determination of concentration risk limits. This above-average competence is driven by the advisors located in SME-/retail asset-focused BUs: operating in a rather illiquid market environment not allowing the distribution of concentration risks very easily, these players are particularly prone to inhibit the acquisition of concentration risks through impacting primary market transactions. While this type of active advisors reports a strong advisory competence for policy setting of concentration risks on average, their counterparts in central units (having a wholesale asset-focus), as well as on average the proprietary investors and risk controllers merely have weak advisory power for this function.

4.4.2 Loan origination and underwriting

Except for proprietary investors' strong competence for loan pricing, other CPM units have rather weak average competence levels for loan origination and underwriting functions.

The task of performing analysis and rating for prospective credit customers is mostly under the responsibility of loan origination BUs instead of being a competence of CPM units. It is typically risk management units that provide an internal rating for credit assets. There is only one proprietary investor in the empirical sample which has decision-making power for credit analysis and credit rating, which drives the average competence for the proprietary investor group towards a weak advisory power. Apart from that, it is only the active advisors located in BUs that have a (rather weak) informational role/competence for these functions.

Active advisors typically assume ownership for credit pricing models and, hence, determine a risk-adjusted model-based price for loans to be granted. This price is given as a recommendation to origination BUs.[711] The final decision about the customer price lies in the hands of sales/relationship managers on the loan origination side. Active advisors typically do not have the power to impose sanctions on sales/relationship managers if they charge their customers a price differing from the one they have quoted. Still, they dispose of different competence levels towards origination regarding loan pricing. It seems as though their organizational location had a major influence on their pricing impact: the active advisors located in BUs (model IIa) have on average an advisory competence regarding credit pricing. The most empowered ones for credit pricing – despite not aspiring to set up an asset transferal procedure – are currently thinking about setting up a shortfall compensation system for their origination BUs analogous to the one found among proprietary investors.[712] Their counterparts located in central risk or finance units (model IIb) see weaker enforcement power towards origination, reporting at most an informational role for loan pricing.[713] As proprietary investors acquire credit assets or related risks from originating BUs at a self-determined, binding settlement price, all these units report a decision-making right or at least a strong veto power for loan pricing. Risk controllers virtually do not have such a pricing mandate at all.

All portfolio management units generally have low competence levels for first- and second vote loan approval decisions as well as concerning credit control and loan documentation. The highest average competence for these functions have active advisors situated in central risk units which act as weak advisors for credit approval

711 If there is a liquid market price for credit assets available, they also base their recommendation on this comparable market price instead of the model-based price

712 See in particular chapter 4.4.5 for the specific features – also shortfall compensation among others – related to the asset transferral process established among the proprietary investor business models

713 One reason why active advisors that are located in BUs have a stronger competence for credit pricing is their organizational location enabling a stronger impact on primary market credit business.

The other reason is the fact that the SME-/retail asset-focused active advisors are located in BUs rather than in central units of their organizations. Induced by insufficient market liquidity, these units typically do not dispose of strong competencies to perform transactions on secondary credit markets (see also later in chapter 4.4.4). Therefore, they place emphasis on actively managing the composition of their institution's credit portfolio through influencing origination regarding issuance and pricing of new as well as renewals of existing credit business. This particularly has the goal of ensuring that the "right" credit assets are acquired at an appropriate price once their distribution on secondary markets is rather difficult due to the insufficiently liquid market environment they face. As a consequence, they are equipped with a particularly strong competence for credit policy setting (see also again chapter 4.4.1) as well as for loan origination and underwriting functions, in particular pricing (second vote) and credit control decisions. Following the requirement that credit approval must be organizationally separated from loan origination,[714] such a task can only be assumed by CPM units located in separate risk units but not by ones located in origination BUs. Risk controllers as well as some active advisors and proprietary investors typically take part in credit control and documentation functions by acting as a weak advisor. It is particularly legal departments of the institutions that are responsible for these functions.

Figure 47 gives a graphical illustration of the average competence the different CPM units have for credit policy setting as well as for loan origination and underwriting functions.

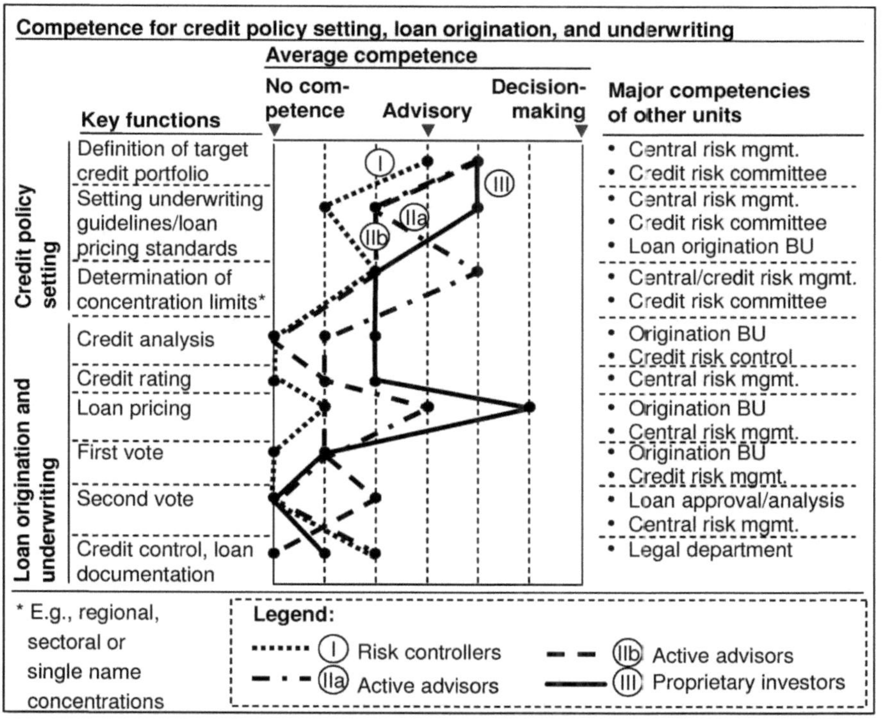

Figure 47: Competence for credit policy setting, loan origination, and underwriting[715]

[714] See again Footnote 78

[715] Source: Own illustration based on results of empirical study on ACPM

4.4.3 Credit portfolio controlling and management

4.4.3.1 Credit portfolio controlling

As a general finding it has been discerned that except for an average veto power which risk controllers and the active advisors located in BUs have concerning development of concepts and models/tools to support the controlling of credit portfolios, CPM units typically act as advisors for credit portfolio controlling tasks and share their competence in this field mostly with central- or more specialized credit risk management units. It would be wrong to infer from proprietary investors' low competence for concept and model/tool development that developing such concepts and models is not important for these units. Rather, the most sophisticated participants indicated that they already dispose of these means and do not need to develop them any more as opposed to their less sophisticated counterparts.

A frequently debated topic is the question whether CPM units should dispose of a credit research function or not. Around 64% of all participating institutions perform some kind of credit research. The following reasons were mentioned why such a function should be included: portfolio management needs to have its own perspective on trends in credit markets and in the economy as a whole. Therefore, it is essential that it has a credit research team of its own. Besides this, as credit research in portfolio management offers the value-enhancing opportunity to combine insights from market- and credit industry-oriented functions, it should ideally be located there.[716] The 36% of the participants not having a credit research function included in their CPM unit believe that such a function would only be a duplication of already existing ones and would therefore not create additional value. Managers of CPM units that dispose of credit research competence typically report they have an advisory competence for this function.

Active advisors located in central risk units underline their risk affiliation by disposing of an above-average competence to monitor the quality of outstanding loan positions. Their counterparts in BUs as well as risk controllers and proprietary investors report a significantly weaker competence for this function.

Regarding controlling of credit limits and exposures, proprietary investors have the highest competence, acting as an active advisor for this function on average. The other CPM units report weaker competence levels for this function which is mainly due to the fact that they do not assume ownership for credit assets. Risk management and origination BUs typically have the primary responsibility for controlling credit limits and exposures.

[716] It is due to the latter reason that research functions within CPM units typically do not focus on (publicly available) individual name research but emphasize research on credit markets and overall economic developments

Setting loan loss provisions is typically not a strong responsibility for ACPM units. The fact that risk controllers have reported higher levels of competence for this function is due to their location in risk management units: characteristically, it is central risk management and loan workout units which have a leading role regarding setting loan loss provisions.

As with controlling of credit limits and exposures, it is not the typical competence of CPM units to perform controlling activities for the performance of the institutions' credit portfolios.

Figure 48 illustrates the competence that participants reported for credit portfolio controlling functions.

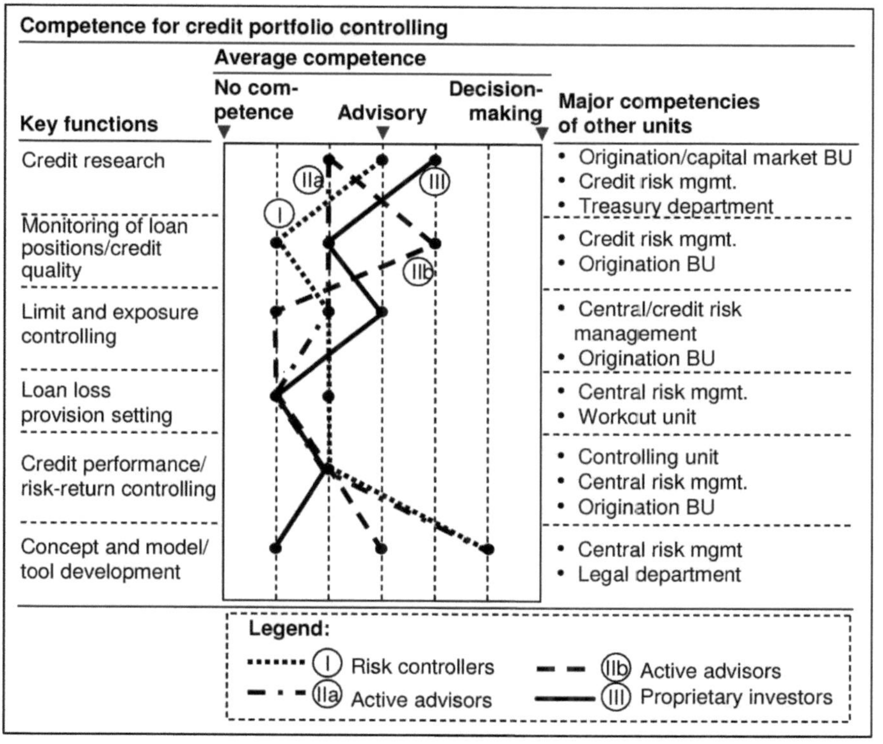

Figure 48: Competence for credit portfolio controlling[717]

[717] Source: Own illustration based on results of empirical study on ACPM

4.4.3.2 Portfolio management styles

Participants were asked according to which style they manage their credit portfolios. Most institutions still clearly pursue a "originate and hold" management style, in particular for less liquid asset classes: while 47% of all banks in the empirical sample manage their large- and medium-sized assets like this, about 57% manage their small-cap credit assets according to the principle "originate and hold". Banks with a consumer asset credit portfolio – except for some of the most sophisticated players – almost exclusively hold their assets until maturity or default after having acquired them. It is the most advanced active advisors and proprietary investors which describe their management style as "selectively hedge and invest" or at least as a mixture between "selectively hedge and invest" and "originate and hold".[718] A pure "originate and trade" approach to managing credit assets can only be found among three proprietary investors and one sophisticated active advisor for the syndicated lending or leveraged finance assets included in their credit portfolios.[719]

4.4.4 Secondary credit market transactions

4.4.4.1 Competence of CPM business models

Risk controllers do not have a mandate to initiate, structure or execute transactions on secondary credit markets, nor do they assume controlling tasks for these deals. At most, they report an informational competence for such transactions.

By contrast, active advisors as well as proprietary investors report their highest average competence for these functions. A closer examination of these players' secondary market competence levels reveals, however, that they are driven by the wholesale-focused ACPM units in the empirical sample. ACPM units set up in SME-/retail credit markets do not perceive that they have the opportunity to operate in a secondary credit market environment strongly supporting the exchange of credit risks. Therefore, these units have reported that they typically dispose of low functional competencies for secondary market transactions but emphasize their activities on the primary market side instead (see again in particular chapter 4.4.2). Consequently, the following illustration on competence for secondary credit market transactions – in particular Figure 49 – displays the responses given by wholesale asset-focused ACPM units.

---

718 For example, 42% of all banks in the sample including all proprietary investors name that they pursue a "selectively hedge and invest" management style or a mixture between "selectively hedge and invest" and "originate and hold". No bank manages its consumer credit assets exclusively according to "selectively hedge and invest"; at most, as a mixture between "originate and hold" and "selectively hedge and invest"

719 Three players in the sample report a management style between "selectively hedge and invest" and "originate and trade"

Active advisors, irrespective of whether they are located in BUs or central risk/finance units, on average have a strong advisory or even veto power to initiate, structure, and price secondary market transactions as well as to negotiate such deals with other counterparties. They also have advisory competence to allocate limits to certain counterparties involved in the transactions. By indicating a decision-making right, proprietary investors report even higher competence levels for these functions. Typical other units involved in such secondary credit market activities besides ACPM units are capital markets BUs, finance and treasury departments, the central risk or credit risk unit of the institution or its Asset-Liability-Committee (ALCO).[720]

With respect to the final decision concerning which secondary credit market transactions to execute as well as regarding their actual execution and subsequent controlling, competence levels for active advisors and proprietary investors are generally pretty similar. On average, they are in the range of strong advisory/veto power. When comparing the active advisors' competence to execute and control secondary market transactions, it becomes obvious that there is a difference as to whether the advisors are located in BUs or in central risk/finance units: following their proximity to secondary credit markets, advisors located in BUs have a higher competence to execute such transactions, whereas their counterparts in risk or finance units, which are more remote from secondary markets, have an accordingly lower competence level. It is typically secondary market trading desks within capital markets or Investment Banking BUs or, less frequently, Treasury units that are strongly involved in the execution of secondary market transactions. Active advisors located in risk units report the highest average competence for controlling of secondary market transactions, having a significantly higher competence level for this credit function than their counterparts in BUs and proprietary investors. Still, however, central risk management and finance departments have the major competence for controlling these deals. An overview of participants' competence for secondary credit market transactions is given in Figure 49.

---

720 An ALCO is a functional department whose main task is to initiate measures aiming at adjusting a bank's balance sheet structure according to developments and changes on the money and capital markets such as shifts of yield curves, for example. Following its far-reaching impact, the ALCO is typically attended by senior executives; see, e.g., Schierenbeck (2003), p. 9 and Schüller (1984)

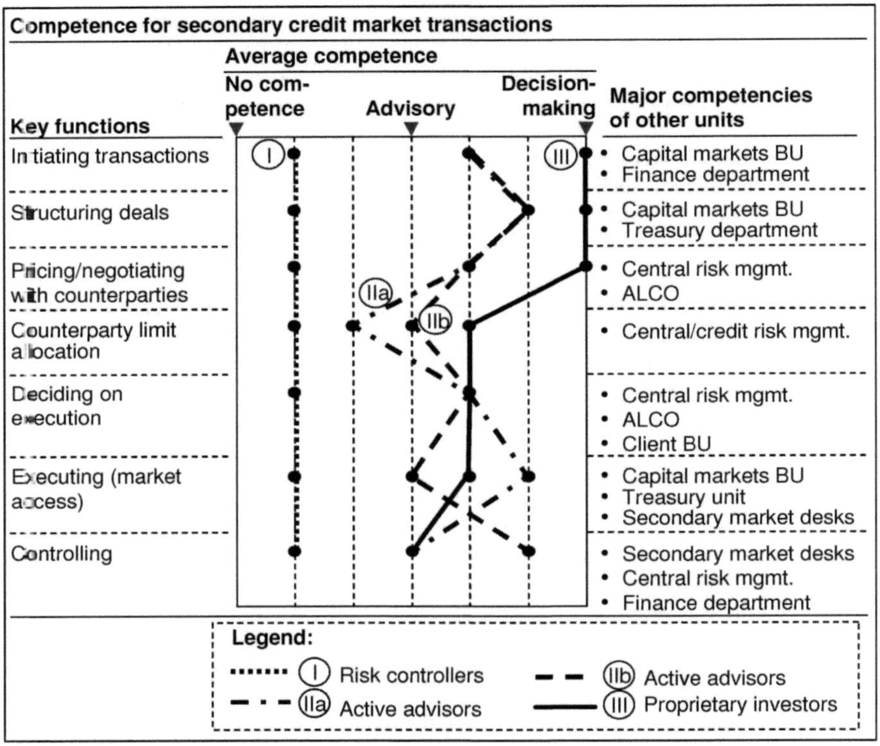

Figure 49: Competence for secondary credit market transactions[721]

After having described the competence levels of the CPM business models for performing transactions on secondary credit markets, it will now be examined what the motives are to perform these transactions and which the characteristic instruments are that CPM units use to execute such deals. Furthermore, it will be shown to which extent CPM units aspire to have direct access to secondary loan markets. Since it has become evident that reactive controllers do not have a mandate to perform secondary credit market transactions, the following illustration will focus on active advisors and proprietary investors.

[721] Source: Own illustration based on results of empirical study on ACPM

4.4.4.2 Motives for secondary credit market transactions

Participants in the survey were asked to rank the importance of the three motives for secondary credit market transactions: risk distribution, credit risk investments, and trading of credit risks. In general, as illustrated in Figure 50, of highest importance both for active advisors and proprietary investors to perform such deals is the motive to distribute credit risks. Participants stated that they mainly perform these risk distribution transactions in order to reduce and hedge single-name concentration risks so that bound EC in such bulk risks can be released and unexpected credit losses that may occur during market downturns can be diminished. Few proprietary investors also aspire to actively distribute credit risks through newly created structured products such as CDOs based on an underlying pool of credit assets on their books.

Secondary credit market investments are generally regarded as less important than risk distribution both for active advisors and proprietary investors. Yet, while the former rank investments as medium important only (average importance level 3.0), the latter still regard them as highly important (average importance level 4.4).[722] There are three main reasons why secondary market investments in credit risks are undertaken: firstly, after having freed up EC through risk distribution transactions, ACPM units aim at reinvesting the capital into more profitable asset classes on secondary markets. Secondly, by generating yields on the invested assets, ACPM units can cover the costs related to risk distribution.[723] Thirdly, targeted secondary market investments into asset classes with low correlation to the existing credit portfolio are performed as a means to move the loan portfolio closer to the risk-return optimal efficient frontier.

The least important motive for secondary market transactions is the intention to trade credit risks. Figure 50 illustrates the importance of participants' motives to perform secondary credit market transactions.[724]

[722] In this context, only secondary credit market investments driven by ACPM units with the goal of changing the risk-return structure of their credit portfolios have been considered. Credit investments performed by other units within the institution (e.g., by markets or Investment Banking BUs) that are not initiated by ACPM units have not been taken into account

[723] Such costs occur, for example, if an ACPM unit purchases CDS protection on a certain credit exposure which requires paying an insurance premium to the protection seller. See again Figure 22 for the payment structure of a CDS contract

[724] This illustration includes the entire sample of ACPM units, i.e., also SME-/retail-focused units. This is because irrespective of their competence levels for secondary credit market transactions and actually executed deals, the SME-/retail-focused units also stated the importance they ascribe to the execution of secondary market transactions

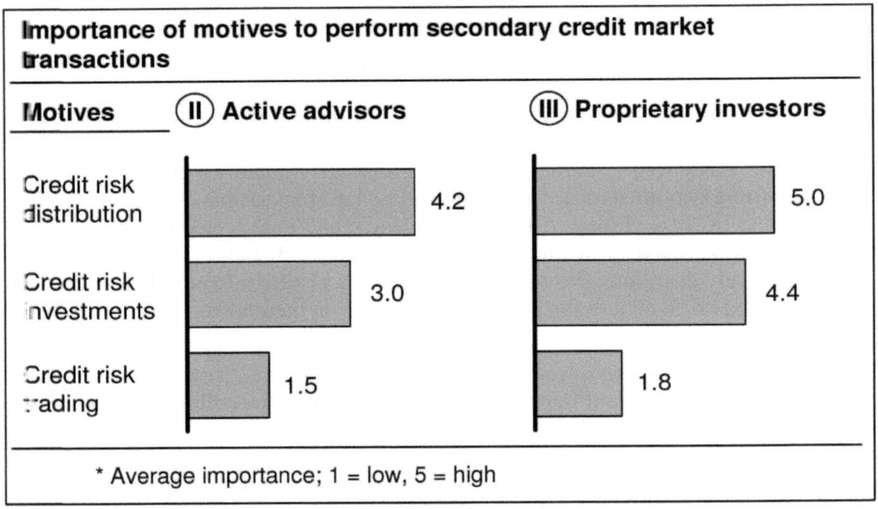

Figure 50: Importance of motives to perform secondary credit market transactions[725]

4.4.4.3 Secondary credit market instruments used

Figure 51 illustrates which credit instruments are typically used by active advisors and proprietary investors to distribute credit risks on secondary markets and shows the average importance these instruments have for the ACPM units concerning risk distribution.[726]

---

725 Source: Own illustration based on results of empirical study on ACPM

726 The average importance ascribed to the different instruments used for credit risk distribution and investments is taken from the viewpoint of all active advisors and proprietary investors. This is because even the ones not actually performing transactions by applying these instruments – mainly, because they face a non-supportive market environment for such deals – ranked the importance they ascribe to such transactions. The description of the secondary credit market instruments actually used by active advisors and proprietary investors, however, reflects the answers given by the wholesale asset-focused units in the sample.

The proprietary investor focusing on SME and retail assets, for example, considers insufficient secondary market liquidity as a key issue on the path to a more effectively use of secondary credit market instruments. While also regarding loan sales and CDS transactions as important for distribution of credit risks, the only types of deals this unit has effectively performed so far have been six synthetic CDOs structured on the basis of its loan book. A similar picture emerges for the SME-/retail asset-focused active advisors: lacking opportunities on secondary credit markets have at most enabled these units to initiate and structure CDO transactions. Often, performing these deals has been motivated by the goal of obtaining regulatory capital relief. There is no SME-/retail asset-focused ACPM unit in the sample which has managed to use these types

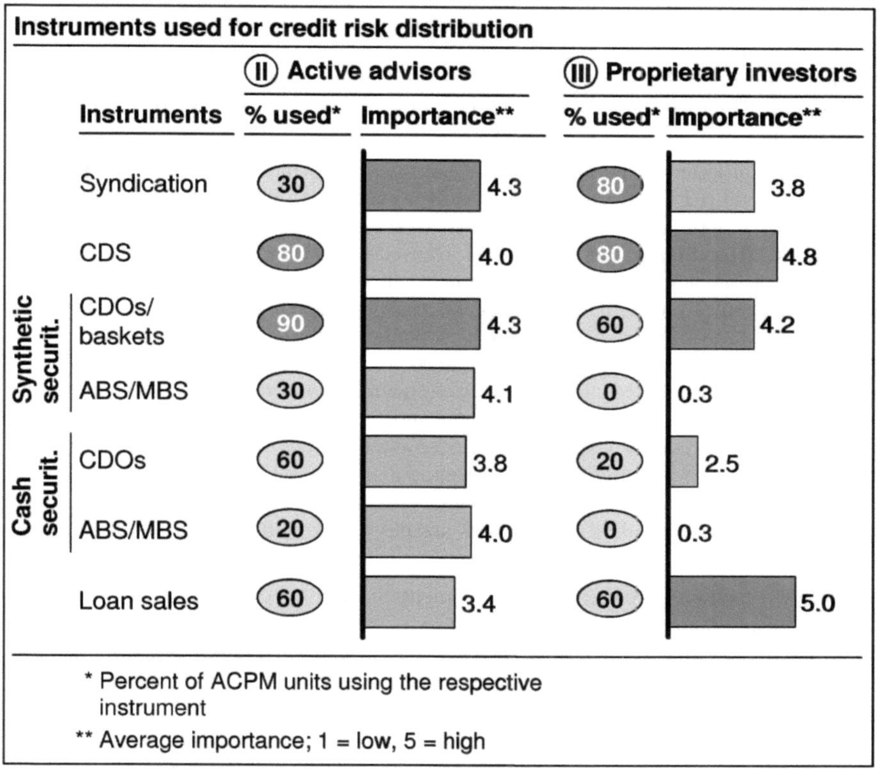

Figure 51: Instruments used for credit risk distribution[727]

CDS are among the most frequently used instruments to distribute credit risks both for active advisors and proprietary investors. Synthetic CDOs/basket structures are more frequently used by active advisors than by proprietary investors. Most proprietary investors also use loan syndication to distribute credit risks, an instrument rather rarely applied by active advisors for this purpose. Loan sales transactions to distribute credit risks are undertaken by around 60% of all CPM units. The least frequently used instruments for risk distribution are ABS/MBS transactions as well as cash CDOs for proprietary investors.

of transactions as a channel to place economic credit risks in the form of standardized tradable tranched securities among investors

[727] Source: Own illustration based on results of empirical study on ACPM

Active advisors consider loan syndication and synthetic CDOs/basket structures as the most important instruments to distribute credit risks. The application of CDS as well as synthetic and cash ABS/MBS transactions are ranked with a slightly lower average importance. The least important instrument for active advisors to distribute credit risks are loan sales transactions.

By contrast, proprietary investors regard loan sales as the most important instrument to distribute credit risks, followed by risk distribution through CDS. This is mainly due to the fact that proprietary investors as owners of the assets do not require the consent of origination BUs to perform loan sales transactions. Hence, as confirmed by the interviews, wherever the market environment allows it, they prefer selling credit risks through loan sales rather than by means of more expensive synthetic risk distribution transactions. Accordingly, products such as synthetic CDOs/baskets are ranked with a lower average degree of importance by these ACPM units. Loan syndication has a lower priority despite being used very frequently for credit risk distribution by proprietary investors. The reason why these units perform less loan sales transactions than synthetic CDS deals despite ascribing a higher degree of importance to the former type of transactions is either due to the limited availability of tradable credit names on the loan sales market or strong customer relationships which are feared to be endangered if corresponding credit assets are physically sold off from the institution's loan book.

Generally, secondary credit market investments have a lower average importance for active advisors than for proprietary investors (see again Figure 50). Besides this, the study has shown that significantly fewer advisors than proprietary investors actually perform credit investments on secondary markets: Only 60% of all advisors in the empirical sample perform some kind of secondary market investments into credit risks, whereas all proprietary investors perform such transactions.

The active advisors undertaking credit risk investments mostly do so through investing their capital in structured credit products such as (synthetic or true sale) CDO structures and CDS, followed by investments in syndicated loans.[728] They least frequently acquire credit risks through ABS/MBS structures as well as by means of investments in traded loans, bonds or macro investments such as iTraxx indices, although they consider these products as equally important for credit risk investments.

Surprisingly, the secondary market investment behavior of proprietary investors has a somewhat different pattern: all wholesale asset-focused proprietary investors acquire credit risks on secondary markets by means of loan syndication and CDS investments,

728 Credit investments by means of loan syndication refer to investments in secondary syndications – i.e., investments in existing syndicated loans – as opposed to primary syndications which are not performed by ACPM units but through loan origination teams on the primary market side. For a distinction between primary and secondary syndications see again chapter 3.1.2 of part II and, in particular, Footnote 265

as well as acquisitions of bonds traded on secondary credit markets and macro investments are also undertaken. Similar to advisors, around 40% of the proprietary investors perform investments in structured credit products such as synthetic or true sale CDOs, while ABS and MBS investments are currently only performed by 20% of these ACPM units. The wholesale proprietary investors' main focus of importance lies on acquisitions of credit risks through investments syndicated loans and single-name CDS.[729] So far, the proprietary investor owning and managing SME-/retail credit assets has not yet performed secondary market investment transactions. Figure 52 illustrates the instruments that participants use for credit risk investments on secondary markets as well as their average importance for the different ACPM business models.

Among all ACPM units pursuing secondary credit market investments, there are 36% pursuing these investments along an explicitly defined strategy, i.e., having defined a target investment portfolio composition and a migration path from the current portfolio composition towards this target by means of credit investments.

About 50% of the active advisors and proprietary investors that perform secondary credit market investments undertake efforts to actively structure and manage their investment portfolios in order to maximize the profitability of these investments. They use different tactics to do so (see Figure 53 for an illustration): almost all ACPM units that actively manage their investments (83%) aim at picking the single names for their portfolio which seem to fit best to their portfolio composition. Market timing, i.e., the goal of generating higher returns by actively shifting exposures across different credit risk classes within a defined segment, is performed by 67% of the credit investors.[730]

---

729 The proprietary investor performing secondary market investments in credit risks through synthetic and cash-based ABS/MBS transactions ranked these transactions with a degree of importance of "5". The other proprietary investors in the sample refrained from rating their degree of importance for this investment product. Therefore, the high degree of importance for this investment instrument is not representative

730 In general, market timing is a major investment strategy applied both by equity and fixed income fund managers.

It is still unclear whether the market-timing approach promises an over-performance compared to index investing in fixed-income markets. This is because, as opposed to an extensive examination of equity funds' market timing ability, only little academic research has been done examining the market timing ability of fixed income funds and the over-performance of this strategy compared to mere index investing. Comer, Boney et al. (2005) try to fill this gap with a study examining the market timing ability of a sample of high-quality corporate bond funds. They find only weak evidence for over-performance of actively managed bond funds according to the market-timing approach, mainly due to the reason that forecasting future bond returns appears more difficult than forecasting stock returns

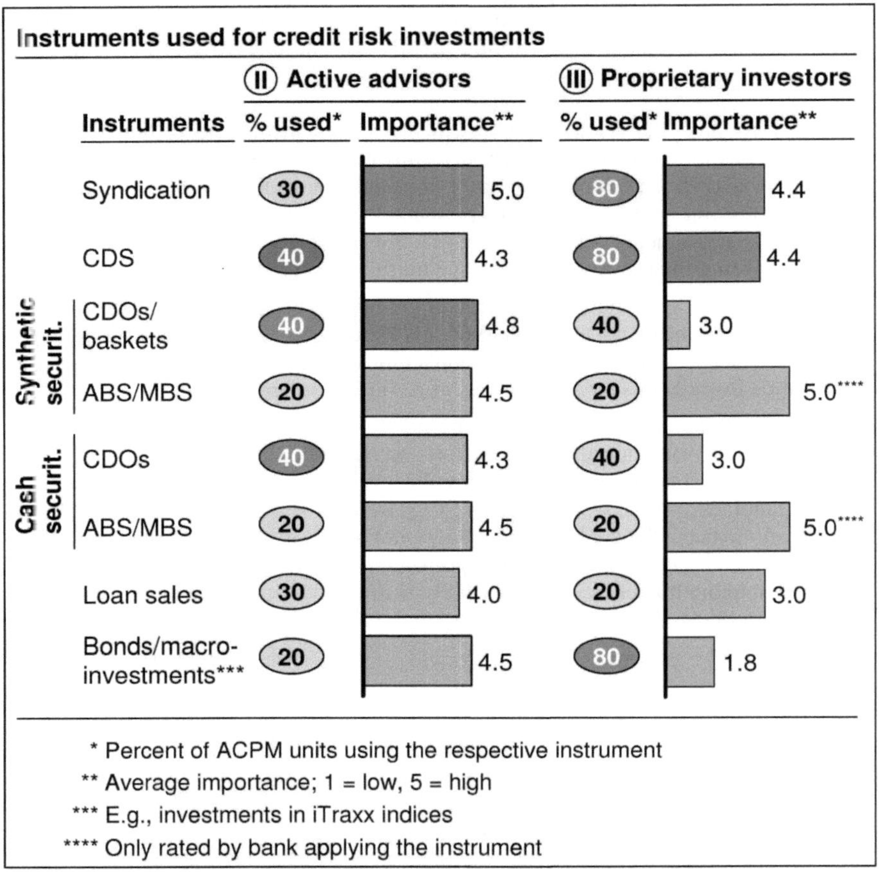

Figure 52: Instruments used for credit risk investments[731]

Fewer investors aim at actively varying their investments between different industries/sectors to boost yields ("sector plays") or try to create value through reinvesting capital in higher yielding transactions than the ones in which their capital has been bound before (so-called "leveraged plays").[732]

[731] Source: Own illustration based on results of empirical study on ACPM

[732] Regarding types of such capital reinvestments on secondary credit markets, acquisitions of structured credit products appear to be a higher yielding investment opportunity than "plain vanilla" instruments such as

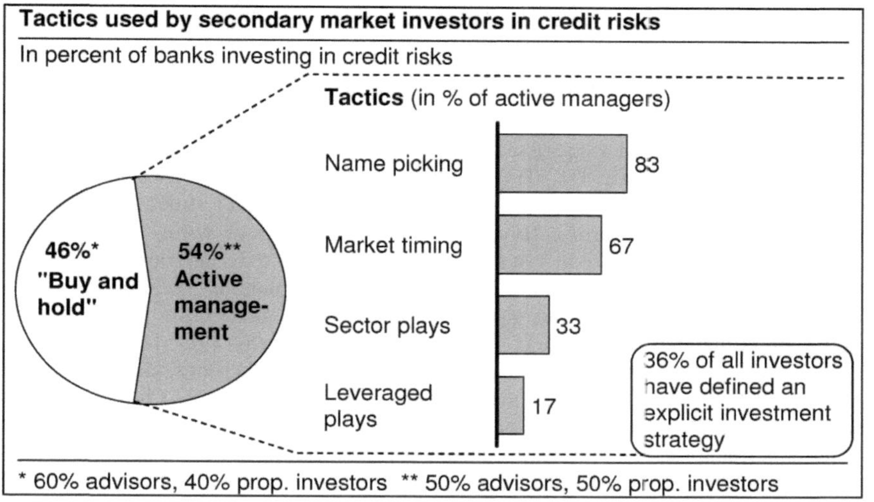

Figure 53: Tactics used by secondary market investors in credit risks[733]

standard bank loans. This is shown in Figure 78 in Appendix A displaying the credit spreads to Euribor (respectively Libor) of four different tradable structured credit products: AAA-rated tranches of UK CMBS, AAA-rated tranches of UK RMBS and AAA-rated tranches of Eurozone consumer loan ABS. These spreads are compared with the ones for AA-rated banks bonds.

Euribor is taken as proxy for the risk-free market interest rate, effectively representing the credit risk of AA-rated European financial institutions; see also again Footnote 315. If an institution's credit rating is below AA, however, it may not obtain funding for its investments at Euribor and is, thus, required to borrow funds at a higher interest rate than Euribor. This may subsequently lead to lower profits of an investment in the products described in Figure 78 than indicated by the spreads of the product yields to Euribor.

Libor is an international money market interest rate representing the average rate offered by banks for the interbank placements of Eurodollars, i.e., of deposits in financial institutions outside the US denominated in USD; see American Bankers Association (1999), p. 149 and p. 226

The illustration shows that in the time period between July 2002 and July 2005, an investment in structured products, particularly in CMBS and consumer loan tranches would have yielded significantly higher returns than an investment in bank bonds with comparable creditworthiness

What needs to be taken into account when investing in such structured products, however, is the greater volatility of such an investment as also illustrated in Figure 78 by displaying the standard deviation of the spreads during the three year period covered. The CMBS and consumer loan spreads are significantly more volatile than the bank loan spreads

733 Source: Own illustration based on results of empirical study on ACPM

4.4.4.4 Direct secondary credit market access

There are different rationales behind the decision of active advisors and proprietary investors as to which extent they should have direct access to secondary credit markets.

Most ACPM units regard a direct secondary market access as essential only for some product categories, mostly for OTC products such as CDS transactions on rarely traded, illiquid underlying credit assets or placements of CDO structures requiring direct contact to counterparties. However, they shy away from setting up their own trading infrastructure, e.g., loan syndication, loan sales or credit derivatives desks for two key reasons: on the one hand, setting up and maintaining such desks would involve upfront investments and significant fixed costs, mainly for personnel and trading infrastructure. Despite the opportunity to achieve a better price for transactions than by trading them through existing internal or external facilities, these costs are hardly expected to be amortized, in particular, if the desks operated in comparably narrow regional European markets not allowing them to trade large enough volumes. On the other hand, many players, especially the ones that have a separate Investment Banking BU, already dispose of extensive credit trading facilities so that they regard the establishment of a trading infrastructure within their ACPM unit as an unnecessary and costly duplication of activities.

There are only a few ACPM units that have set up or are about to set up a fully-fledged secondary market trading infrastructure. These units mostly cannot fall back on an extensive secondary market trading infrastructure in their institution which they may use to execute their transactions and for which they might even act as a competitor on the secondary credit markets. Therefore, they believe that they can achieve better prices through direct market access than by using external brokers as intermediaries for these transactions. Another motive to establish such a trading infrastructure is the aspiration of these ACPM units to be able to easier place new credit assets on the secondary market and achieve better trading opportunities through establishing their own clientele such as hedge fund investors, for example.

4.4.5 Excursus: Specific features of proprietary investor business model

The transfer of credit assets from origination to ACPM is the key characteristic differentiating the proprietary investor from other ACPM business models.[734] Therefore, when interviewing proprietary investors, the interview partners were asked

[734] As mentioned above, there is one bank in the empirical sample that has implemented a modified proprietary investor model and foresees the transfer of credit risks in synthetic form to ACPM while the assets remain under ownership of origination. This modified proprietary investor approach will be described and discussed in greater detail in the following chapter 4.4.5.2. For the moment, the depiction will focus on the "typical" asset transferring proprietary investor business model

some additional open-ended questions to get a profound knowledge of the functioning of the asset transfer and related settlement pricing methodology.[735] Besides this, further specific implications which establishing a proprietary investor business unit will have on an organization will be illustrated in the following section.

4.4.5.1 Asset transfer and settlement pricing methodology

The proprietary investor business model foresees the transfer of loans including their related revenues and costs from origination to ACPM's book immediately after the origination process has been concluded.

A crucial procedure in this context is the determination of an individual settlement price between ACPM and origination for each loan to be taken over by ACPM. It is typically the ACPM unit that has the mandate to determine this settlement price. Thereby, it ideally takes as a benchmark the "true" price at which the asset, a risk-equivalent credit or a derivative based on the asset, is traded on the secondary loan market. The typical settlement pricing methodology found amongst proprietary investors will now be outlined in greater detail. Figure 54 provides a graphical illustration.

4.4.5.1.1 Computation of settlement margin

The settlement pricing methodology foresees to compute a settlement margin for the credit assets to be transferred as difference between the expected customer income margin on the asset and a transfer margin, which is determined by the asset's "true" market price (see left-hand side of Figure 54).

For fully drawn loans, the customer income margin is the product of the outstanding exposure and the net interest margin obtained from holding the asset. For credit lines that may not be fully drawn,[736] the expected average usage of the credit line needs to be additionally taken into consideration: the customer margin from a credit line is calculated as the sum of the expected average usage over the maturity of the credit line[737] times the net interest margin and the expected unused part times a commitment fee[738] (see Figure 71 in Appendix A for an illustration).

---

[735] An in-depth understanding of this specification was of particular importance for the discussion regarding the optimal ACPM business model, see chapter five

[736] A credit line is an agreement by a bank to make a specific amount of funds available to a certain borrower when required, see American Bankers Association (1999), p. 101

[737] Typically, the usage of credit lines increases with the deteriorating creditworthiness of debtors, see Schiller and Tytko (2001), p. 110. Therefore, regular updates of the expected usage taking into consideration the latest customer ratings are necessary

[738] Banks typically charge customers a commitment fee for providing credit lines. This fee is lower than the interest rate that customers need to pay if they actually decide to draw the line, see American Bankers Association (1999), p. 79

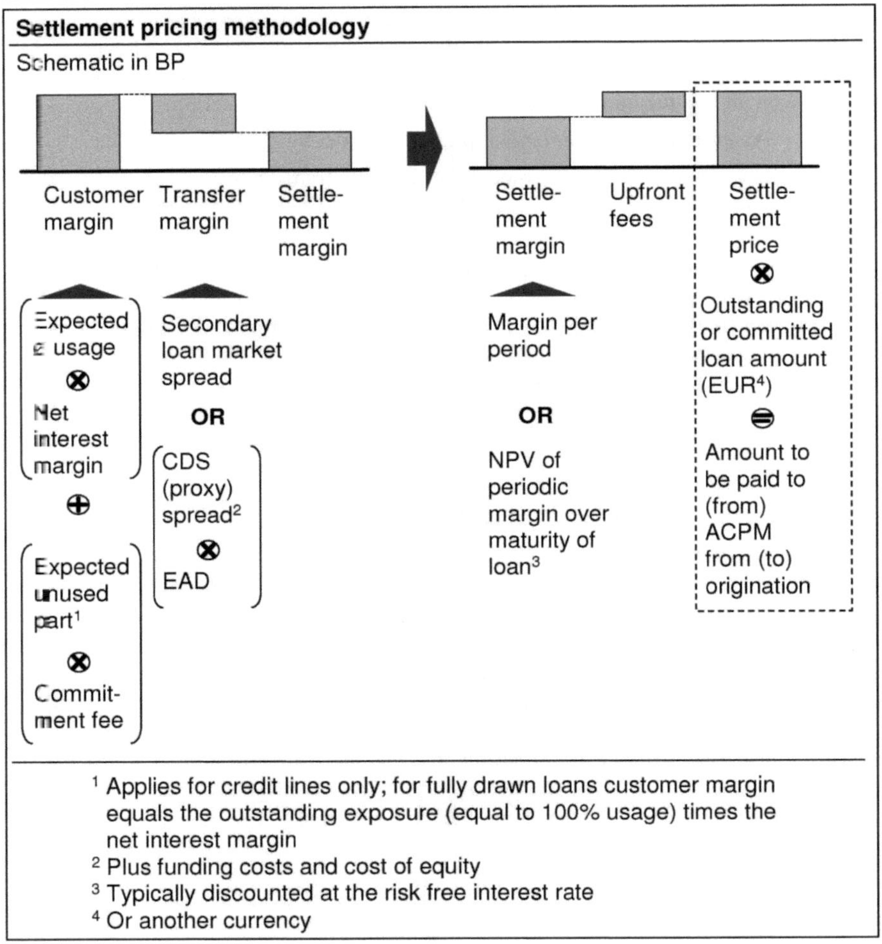

Figure 54: Settlement pricing methodology[739]

The transfer margin represents the actual costs for ACPM to transfer the risks of a credit asset to the secondary loan market. It can also be regarded as opportunity costs to buy the same amount of credit risks in the secondary market. The transfer margin is

[739] Source: Own illustration based on results of empirical study on ACPM

made up of two components: the transfer price and credit exposure to be transferred (see Figure 72 in Appendix A for an illustration).

If an asset is traded on secondary loan markets and provided there are no restrictions concerning selling the asset, the transfer price is determined by the asset's secondary loan market price which is typically measured as spread over the risk-free interest rate.

If a credit cannot be sold on secondary markets because there is no such price or in case such a placement is prohibited by contract clauses or preferences of origination BUs, the fair transfer price is typically determined by the spread over the risk-free interest rate of a CDS contract having the respective credit name as its underlying. In this case, the asset remains on ACPM's book. Consequently, an additional charge for funding the asset and for costs of the underlying equity that needs to be held to, e.g., cover the counterparty risk of the CDS transaction, must be considered when determining the transfer price.

In case there is no secondary loan market price or CDS quote obtainable for a credit asset, the most advanced players in the empirical sample have developed a workaround for determining a "fair" transfer price: based on the universe of quoted CDS names worldwide, a median spread curve split in different industries is determined showing the median CDS spread of different credit rating categories for each industry.[740] If a loan customer has an external credit rating, a proxy CDS spread for his credit asset is determined through the CDS price indicated by the respective industry spread curve at the corresponding customer rating class. If no external credit rating is available for a debtor, the institutions typically match the default probability of their internal credit rating for this client on external rating classes in order to be able to determine the CDS proxy spread.[741]

Besides the transfer price, the relevant credit exposure to be transferred is to be determined for a calculation of the transfer margin. This exposure is typically set at the EAD. The reason behind this approach is that the EAD is the amount that will be lost if the customer defaults; hence, protection needs to be bought for exactly this amount.

---

740 The median is defined as the value separating the upper 50% from the lower 50% of a distribution, see, e.g., Diekmann (2002), p. 252

741 There are two proprietary investors in the empirical sample determining settlement prices based on CDS proxy curves as described here.

It is only for illiquid credit names with a low sub-investment grade long-term credit rating (typically being in the single-B range) that these institutions determine individual hedging costs for each transaction instead of proxy CDS prices. This is because they have found that existing CDS spreads in these rating classes are usually broadly scattered around the median which would make a CDS proxy curve relatively inaccurate.

The SME-/retail asset-focused proprietary investor in the empirical sample mostly uses an internal loan pricing model to determine a "fair" price for the credit asset which is to be transferred to ACPM. This is because comparable market prices are only available for very few credit names in its portfolio

Similar to the determination of the customer income margin, the type of loan commitment determines the EAD: fully drawn loans are usually considered with 100% of the outstanding loan amount as they are fully used by the customer in the case of default.

Credit lines are typically not fully used if a debtor defaults, although their usage normally increases significantly following deterioration in his credit quality.[742] The proprietary investors that have implemented an asset transfer business model reported that they typically reduce the EAD of a credit line by a certain percentage if covenants have been agreed with a customer since such agreements reduce the customer's incentive to draw a line.

If a customer has provided eligible collateral for a loan, the corresponding EAD is reduced by the collateral value. Accordingly, the equity costs are decreased because lower economic and regulatory capital needs to be held for the outstanding volume.[743] In a similar way, the EAD is usually reduced if outstanding exposures have been secured by guarantees.[744]

4.4.5.1.2 Margin- vs. NPV-based settlement price

With the help of the procedure described above, the settlement margin is determined as the difference between customer and transfer margin for one time period of a loan contract, usually a year. The crucial question is how to determine the settlement price for assets transferred to ACPM that have a multi-period maturity. Two options on how to determine this settlement price have been developed (see right-hand side of Figure 54):

The first option is to calculate the settlement price on a margin basis. That is, at the end of each time period during the lifetime of a loan, the settlement margin for the transferred asset is exchanged as a periodically recurrent settlement price between ACPM and origination.

This margin-based price calculation has the advantage that it is consistent with the accrual accounting logic according to which banks are typically managed in general and the performance of loan portfolios is usually measured in particular.[745] Furthermore, it provides an incentive for origination to close loan contracts yielding a positive settlement margin in each single period because otherwise there would be a negative impact on origination's P&L account due to a negative margin in a certain

742 See again Schiller and Tytko (2001), p. 110

743 For a comparison see BIS (2004c), paragraph 296 et seqq. describing the methodology for treatment of collateral under the new Basle II capital accord

744 For a definition of guarantees see Grill and Perczynski (2003), p. 353. Types of guarantees are described in Grill and Perczynski (2003), p. 498

745 See, e.g., Kimmel, Weygandt et al. (2004), chapter 4 for a description of the accrual accounting concept

period. The margin-based settlement price calculation has the major disadvantage that it implies a rather complicated booking procedure for each individual loan. Particularly, issues may arise if a customer exercises special loan features such as a prepayment option on his contract. In this case, the basis for the regular settlement payments ceases to exist and a reverse posting has to be booked to amortize future claims between ACPM and origination that have already been booked in the accounting system. Moreover, the periodic payment streams provide an incentive for origination to negotiate loan contracts foreseeing higher customer payments in early phases of their maturity.

As an alternative to the margin-based price calculation, the settlement price for a loan to be taken over by ACPM can be calculated as NPV of all periodical settlement margin payments over the asset's maturity.[746] At the moment the loan is transferred to ACPM, the NPV of the settlement margin is exchanged between ACPM and origination. Hence, there are no recurrent payments streams between these units related to the transferred asset.

Compared to the margin-based settlement price calculation, the NPV approach has the advantage that it provides transparency of a loan engagement's "true" profitability at the time the asset is transferred. The profitability impact is immediately P&L effective instead of being spread over the lifetime of the loan. Therefore, there is a strong incentive for origination to select lucrative credit business, hence minimizing the incentive for unprofitable relationship investments. Furthermore, the NPV approach allows origination to fully focus its activities on new business since all payments related to legacy business are accounted for by ACPM upon acquisition of the assets. Besides this, there is no incentive for origination to negotiate loan contracts with irregular payment schemes because they would not be reflected in the NPV. The NPV-based settlement calculation is simpler than the margin-based approach regarding booking of special loan features: For example, if a customer decides to exercise a prepayment option at some future point in time, a new NPV-based settlement price between ACPM and origination will be computed considering the prepayment as if a new customer transaction had taken place. The difference to the originally performed transaction is accordingly booked. There is no need to perform reverse posting of several future periodical claims that have already been booked in the accounting system as is the case under the margin-based calculation.

Following its advantages over the margin-based calculation approach, all proprietary investors in the empirical sample but one determine their settlement price on a NPV basis.

---

746 In this context, the payment streams are typically discounted with the risk-free interest rate. The NPV approach is referenced in Footnote 441

Further to regular customer payments from the loan contract, potential one-time upfront fees that origination demands from customers when closing the transaction need to be considered when calculating the settlement price.

Typically, the settlement price is calculated in BP as a spread over the risk-free interest rate. By multiplying it with the outstanding (or committed) loan amount, the payments to be exchanged between ACPM and origination are determined.[747]

4.4.5.2 Risk transfer as possible alternative

In view of some issues related to the establishment of an asset transferring proprietary investor business model, a risk transfer model, foreseeing that ACPM takes over credit risks in a synthetic form instead of physically acquiring the underlying assets has been developed. Such a business model has currently been established by one institution in the empirical sample. Another one – at the moment still set up as an active advisor – is currently in the process of setting it up. The potential issues seen in relation to an asset transfer that have been named by some survey participants will briefly be discussed before the characteristics of the risk transferring proprietary investor business model are depicted.[748]

4.4.5.2.1 Potential issues related to asset transfer

The acquisition of credit assets through the proprietary investor is accompanied by a transfer of the assets' interest revenues from origination to ACPM. Especially if the proprietary investor is to be organizationally located outside the customer BU, setting up such an ACPM unit implies a loss of the BU's revenue base. As shown in chapter 5.1.2 and illustrated in Figure 59, such a location outside the BU can particularly be expected if the initiator/sponsor of the ACPM unit is organizationally located in a central unit of the institution. According to survey participants evaluating setting up a proprietary investor, senior managers of the respective customer BUs would heavily oppose such a loss of revenues for their units. This issue is one of the main reasons why all asset transferring proprietary investors in the empirical sample are located in a customer BU. In this case, the credit assets, while still being transferred from the loan book of origination to the one of ACPM, remain at least within the sphere of the same BU, including their revenue streams and the additional benefits ACPM creates when optimizing the portfolio structure.[749]

747 See next chapter regarding direction of these payment streams

748 The issues depicted in the following were mostly voiced by a few active advisors that do not regard the move towards an asset transferring proprietary investor business model as advantageous for their institution

749 The major caveat following the location of a proprietary investor in a certain BU instead of being centrally located within the institution is the lack of opportunity to tap the full diversification potential of its institution's entire credit portfolio as its field of activities is typically narrowed down to the asset base within its BU

Another major concern voiced in relation to the establishment of an asset transferring proprietary investor business model is a possibly lacking incentive of customer BUs to monitor and particularly service credit customers once ownership of the assets including their revenues has been transferred to ACPM.[750] As a consequence, an insufficient monitoring and servicing of loans and, due to that, a negative impact on existing customer relationships is feared. Less intense customer contacts may also imply a loss of information about credit customers, making it more difficult to evaluate and rate loan contracts.

However, some participants in the empirical study also put forward arguments as to why such concerns related to a lack of monitoring and servicing of customers following the asset transfer are baseless:

Since relationship managers have a strong incentive to conclude follow-up business with existing profitable borrowers besides acquiring new customer relationships, they are sufficiently incentivized to take care of their lending customers even after the corresponding credit assets have been transferred to an ACPM unit. Besides this, the empirical study has shown that central risk or credit risk management units typically carry out activities to monitor the credit quality of outstanding loan positions in addition to origination BUs.[751] Consequently, it is argued that even if there is a reduced incentive for customer relationship managers to look after credit assets as a result of their acquisition through a proprietary investor, monitoring of debtors will still be ensured by risk management units. Finally, discussions with senior managers of customer BUs and risk management units have shown that, instead of merely focusing on information based on direct customer contacts through relationship managers and due to existing customer relationships, they increasingly rely on market and other publicly available information when performing an evaluation and rating of potential loan customers.[752] Thereby, an increasing importance when taking such decisions is ascribed both to credit research functions which combine insights from specific customer information with market information and to debt capital markets BUs. Hence, should incentive issues of customer relationship managers result in less "inside" information about credit customers, this issue would not weigh that gravely.

[750] See again chapter 1.4.1 of part II describing typical activities related to loan origination, approval and monitoring

[751] See again Figure 48

[752] This view is empirically supported: all proprietary investors reported that they use market data and other public information as the main information source for the evaluation and rating of loan customers, while information from customer contact is not regarded as a primary information source; see Figure 76 in Appendix A for an illustration

4.4.5.2.2 Characteristics of risk transferring proprietary investor business model

The potential issues named by critics of the asset transferring proprietary investor business model – resistance to a shift of revenues from origination to ACPM and lacking incentives to monitor and service customer relationships – have led to the development of an ACPM business model foreseeing that assets remain under the physical ownership of origination BUs. Although it could be shown above that several fruitful counterarguments against the potential issues and concerns seen in consequence of a credit asset transfer from origination to ACPM were put forward, it seems appropriate to briefly introduce specifics of the risk transferring proprietary investor as an alternative proprietary investor business model.

This business model foresees that the ACPM unit is to be set up as a proprietary investor having the functional competencies as described in chapter 4.4 as well as the specific characteristics outlined in chapter 4.4.5. Instead of physically taking over credit assets from origination, however, ACPM synthetically acquires their related credit risks by means of credit derivatives (typically CDS) and subsequently manages and optimally structures this credit risk portfolio by means of secondary market transactions. Like its asset owning counterpart, the proprietary investor is set at "zero profitability", hence being forced to create value through actively managing the risk portfolio. The settlement price origination needs to pay ACPM for ceding the credit risks of its assets related to the risks to be transferred is determined by the spread at which the corresponding credit derivatives are traded in secondary credit markets. Analogous to the settlement pricing methodology outlined in chapter 4.4.5.1, the payments can be made either on an NPV or a margin basis. Should revenues from a loan contract fall short of the asset's true risks as determined by the secondary credit market, the corresponding negative shortfall is booked on origination's P&L account.

Besides not facing the drawbacks of its asset transferring counterpart mentioned before, a main advantage for setting up a risk transferring proprietary investor is the higher simplicity and easier implementation of such a model compared to its asset transferring counterpart.

Still, however, this version of a proprietary investor business model requires the existence of sufficiently liquid secondary credit markets as it is foreseen to transfer credit risks at their "fair" price or at least a suitable proxy based on comparable market-based quotes. Furthermore, a major disadvantage of this model arises from ACPM's restricted flexibility to reshuffle risks on secondary credit markets at its discretion since assets are physically owned by origination. For example, this business model does not enable ACPM to independently perform true sale transactions of credit risks.[753]

---

753 See also chapter 5.3 drawing a conclusion regarding which is the optimal ACPM business model that should be implemented by a financial institution depending on certain constellations of determining factors

4.4.5.3 Impact of proprietary investor business model on profitability of origination and ACPM

The introduction of a proprietary investor business model implies the establishment of separate P&L accounts for origination and ACPM. The basic thought behind the business model is that the asset-or risk-owning ACPM unit should be set as if it had bought the asset directly on the capital markets instead of acquiring it from origination. This procedure effectively sets the ACPM unit at "zero profitability", forcing it to create value-added, thus justifying its existence by means of actively managing its loan portfolio.

The direction of the payment streams between origination and ACPM induced by the asset transfer is determined by the arithmetic sign of the settlement price: a positive settlement price indicates that origination has concluded a loan contract yielding a higher income for the bank than when buying the same or a similarly risky asset on the secondary credit market. As this implies that ACPM acquires an asset whose income stream exceeds the costs of its risk transfer, ACPM needs to pay the positive settlement price to origination in order for it to be set as if it had acquired the asset on capital markets. This settlement price is either paid on a margin basis at the end of each period or as NPV over all expected periodic payment streams at the time of the asset transfer. In the case of a negative settlement price, corresponding payments flow from origination to ACPM. Such payments are typically referred to as "shortfall compensations".

The proprietary investor business model still allows origination, which is expected to be profitable on a stand-alone basis as well, to offer a single loan at a price below the asset's "true" value.[754] However, in this case origination is required to pay the shortfall compensation to ACPM. Having to pay this shortfall compensation has an immediate negative impact on origination's P&L account and specifically on the performance and incentive schemes of the credit relationship manager who is ultimately responsible for the profitability of the entire customer relationship.[755]

---

[754] It is remarkable that most of the loan contracts closed by the institutions that have established a proprietary investor ACPM unit are actually closed below their "true" value as determined by secondary credit markets or bank internal pricing models. On average, these institutions have reported in the survey that 59% of their loan contracts are concluded at a price below their market or model-value benchmarks.

Thereby, significant differences between the retail and wholesale lending segment become obvious: the institution in the sample that has implemented a proprietary investor unit in its retail lending segments reports that only 10% of all loans are closed below the benchmark hurdle, while as many as 40% of these contracts are even closed at a price above the hurdle. By contrast, among the institutions that have set up wholesale-focused proprietary investors, on average 75% of all loan contracts are concluded below the hurdle rate. This observation confirms the statement of banks operating in the large corporate lending segment that their lending customers dispose of significant pricing power

[755] As shown with the help of the empirical study, the high responsibility of credit relationship managers for the

As the shortfall compensation directly lowers the profitability of the customer relationship, it provides a strong motivation for relationship managers to reduce pure relationship investments. At the same time, there is a strong encouragement to look for profitable niches instead. Furthermore, origination is incentivized to close deals that require the payment of shortfall compensations only if these transactions are expected to provide the foundation for more profitable follow-on business with the same customer. Such business is typically concluded in other BUs and the income stream from these new deals is supposed to overcompensate the losses incurred by loan engagement so that the total customer relationship is profitable.[756]

When deciding whether to engage in a loan transaction or not, the relationship manager in charge as the ultimate person responsible typically evaluates the overall profitability of the customer relationship by taking into consideration the cross-selling potential anticipated in other BUs as a result of the pending loan transaction. Furthermore, the other BUs need to commit themselves to make a certain contribution to origination to cover the shortfall. Based on a weighing of the shortfall payments against the committed contributions, the relationship manager decides whether the lending transaction will be performed because it has the potential to contribute to an overall increase in the profitability of a customer relationship or whether it is rather to be declined.[757]

---

profitability of their customers' overall relationship is expressed in the basis for their performance evaluation: The criterion "Profitability of overall customer relationship including all credit and non-credit products" is by far the highest ranked criterion based on which relationship managers' performance and hence their compensation is determined; see Figure 73 in Appendix A

756 In particular the universal banks in the empirical sample mentioned during the interviews that they enjoy a considerably higher success rate in gaining underwriting mandates for equity and debt (especially high-yield debt) securities from loan customers than from customers with whom they have no lending business relationship. Hence, it is mostly Debt and Equity Capital Markets BUs that are interested in origination to initiate a loan transaction despite it potentially not being profitable on a stand-alone basis.

Further to a higher customer revenue potential of intensified cross-selling activities, it has been shown that the combination of commercial banking lending with securities underwriting activities can result in significant efficiency gains for a universal bank, not only due to an enhancement of the bank-customer relationship but especially following economies of scope in the production of such financial services; see, e.g., Santos (1998)

757 Survey participants were asked for the decision mechanisms in their institution if a pending loan transaction does not meet the required profitability hurdle rate. Typically, it depends on the extent of the shortfall compensation to be paid who has the authority to decide whether to perform such a transaction or not: for comparably low shortfall compensations, the competence to take such decisions usually rests with the relationship manager responsible as he is ultimately responsible for the profitability of the customer account. For larger shortfall amounts or in the case of disagreement within the origination BU whether to grant the loan or not, the decision is usually escalated towards senior management of the origination BUs. Mostly, investment or other executive committees attended by senior BU managers decide on whether to perform a transaction in this case

Following the asset transfer, ACPM receives all cash flows related to a credit contract, particularly including interest margins, commitment, and upfront fees. A frequently debated topic is the allocation of hedging costs as well as benefits stemming from a better credit risk diversification in ACPM's portfolio due to secondary market transactions. Proprietary investors bear costs for hedging the assets on their books as well as the EL and UL related to these loans. Accordingly, they keep benefits from a better diversified credit portfolio within their unit as well as additional income, e.g., from capital reinvestment transactions or structuring and placements of new credit products.[758]

4.4.5.4 Required adjustments of processes and committee structure

The establishment of a proprietary investor ACPM business model requires the adjustment of existing credit processes. In particular, details regarding determination of the settlement price quotation need to be clarified. The typical approach found amongst participants foresees that origination completes a standardized term sheet in which details of a pending credit transaction are recorded.[759] Based on this information, ACPM quotes an initial settlement price at which it is willing to take over the asset (or related risks). Following this quotation, origination decides whether it should close the respective contract by weighting the potential shortfall compensation against the cross-selling income possibly induced by the transaction. If the contract is concluded, the final settlement price is fixed at closure date of the loan contract.

4.4.5.5 Required infrastructure adaptations

The requirement to adjust existing credit processes also entails changes in the existing IT system infrastructure. Furthermore, in order to meet the demands of a market-based credit pricing, existing loan pricing models have to be updated or new ones need to be developed.[760] Besides this, adaptations in the institution's accounting and performance

[758] As opposed to the proprietary investors, not all active advisors have developed a clear procedure for allocation of hedging costs and diversification benefits yet.

Regarding allocation of hedging costs, advisors typically report that they allocate them to origination BUs if the hedging activities are in direct relation to a contract closed by origination. If, by contrast, they have their own book and P&L for hedging and capital reinvestment transactions, they keep the costs related to hedging deals initiated at their own initiative within their unit and do not charge origination. Often, active advisors do not measure and allocate the benefits from better asset diversification. If so, such generated benefits are kept within ACPM and are not added back to origination's P&L account

[759] See Kimber (2004), chapter 2.5, in particular p. 96 Table 2.1 for an example of a term sheet of a European corporate borrower

[760] Loan pricing models of active advisors and proprietary investors usually differ with respect to their input parameters: all active advisors consider PD and LGD estimates from their internal credit rating as well as the maturity of the pending loan transaction when determining its price. Costs that are incurred when hedging the asset on secondary markets are only considered by 15% of the active advisors. By contrast, all proprietary investors consider such market-based hedging costs in their pricing model. PD and LGD

measurement logic, especially regarding allocation of hedging costs and diversification benefits after having implemented an asset-owning ACPM unit, entail the modification of relevant systems.

As described in chapter 4.4.4.2, it is especially proprietary investors that regard credit risk investments on secondary markets as an integral part of their business model. These investment activities may collide with primary market customer business, e.g., regarding concentration risk limits. The rule typically established in this context is that primary market customer business has priority over investment transactions of the ACPM unit. This can have the following implications:

Given an existing customer relationship for which a concentration risk limit has been set that is not fully exploited, the ACPM unit can perform secondary market investments in this customer's assets until the limit is fully exhausted.[761] Yet, should origination close additional business with this customer thereafter, the customer business is given primacy and must be taken on by ACPM against a settlement price. As a consequence, in order to comply with the previously agreed-upon concentration risk limits, ACPM needs to reduce the amount of credit risk exceeding the concentration risk limit through appropriate risk distribution transactions.

In case the proprietary investor intends to perform secondary market investments in credit assets of debtors with whom the institution has not established a customer relationship including defined concentration risk limits yet, it needs to apply for internal credit lines and concentration risk limits before concluding such investment transactions. Should origination decide to engage in business activities with this customer thereafter, ACPM needs to distribute potentially limit-exceeding credit risks according to the procedure for existing loan customers described above.

Typically, proprietary investors have established an investment committee attended by senior executives from loan origination BUs and the ACPM unit. This committee

---

estimates from internal credit ratings are only taken into account by 60% of the proprietary investors. See Figure 75 in Appendix A illustrating the different input parameters considered in loan pricing models of active advisors and proprietary investors.

Furthermore, active advisors are typically different from proprietary investors with regard to the data sources they use to determine the input parameters for their pricing models: active advisors place the highest importance on historical portfolio default rates when determining PDs and LGDs for their pricing models as well as correlations between default rates and LGDs. The only market data active advisors regard as significantly important for their input parameters are equity prices. Proprietary investors, on the other hand, consider market data, especially bond prices, as significantly more important data sources for input parameters of their loan pricing models than active advisors do. Accordingly, historical portfolio default rates are of lower importance for proprietary investors than for active advisors. See Figure 76 in Appendix A for an illustration

761 While some institutions have only set up a bank-wide concentration risk limit for their customers, others report that they have additionally established sub-limits for certain BUs which must not be exceeded

holds regular meetings, primarily with the goal of deciding on credit applications for secondary market investment transactions of ACPM by taking into consideration concentration risk limits. Following the consent of the investment committee, these deals need to undergo an approval process by risk management or, usually for large credit volumes, by a senior executive credit committee.

4.5 Value creation potential of CPM business models

Chapters 4.3 and 4.4 of part II have shown that, from a theoretical point of view, the ACPM approach is creating value over the conventional "originate and hold" approach towards lending business, provided that banks operate in incomplete capital markets.

This evidence has been based on the observation that a key difference between the ACPM and the conventional approach towards lending business is the execution of secondary credit market transactions. Since it could be shown that such transactions create value in incomplete capital markets, it has been concluded that actively managing a credit portfolio through performing secondary market transactions must be value-enhancing compared to the conventional static approach towards lending business which does not foresee such a reshuffling of credit portfolios. In this context, it has been assumed that the establishment of an ACPM approach does not change the way in which banks carry out their primary market credit business.

4.5.1 Value creation dimensions identified in empirical sample

In order to empirically test the theoretical finding that the ACPM approach creates additional value for an institution's credit business,[762] participants in the empirical study were asked to report the economic impact which the implementation of their CPM unit has had on their credit business activities or which impact they expect from an implementation of their target CPM business model.[763] Surprisingly, none of the interviewees were able to exactly quantify such an economic impact in "hard" numbers.

Two main explanations why this is currently not possible were given: most interviewees stated that their current data and (reporting) systems infrastructure does not allow isolating and hence quantifying the exact value-added that has been created

[762] Given the existence of incomplete capital markets which needs to be realistically assumed, see again chapter 4.4.3 and in particular Footnote 619, it has been concluded that actively managing loan portfolios enhances the economic value of an institution from a theoretical point of view

[763] Specifically, the participants were asked to quantify the economic impact they have achieved with their CPM unit according to the four categories (I) performance (net profit, ROE, RAROC/RORAC and returns compared to a benchmark), (II) volume (customer loan volume and risk assets), (III) risk (credit risk costs and volatility of their P&L) and (IV) capital (regulatory and economic capital). The interviewees were also able to name other performance figures that have been improved following the establishment of their CPM unit

through the activities of their CPM units on primary and especially on secondary credit markets. Another frequently named reason why such an accurate quantification has not been possible yet is the relatively short time period since completed implementation of the active advisor and especially the proprietary investor ACPM business models.[764] Consequently, the extent to which an ACPM approach creates value for an institution's credit business – thus justifying its existence – had to be explored in a different way.

As opposed to an exact quantification of the economic impact generated, the interviewees provided a qualitative judgment of the ways in which their CPM units create additional value for their institutions' credit business or promise to do so once they have been established. During interviews conducted, it has been explored that a CPM unit can potentially create additional value for an institution's existing credit business according to four different major dimensions. These dimensions can be clustered along the flow of credit assets from their origination to placement on secondary credit markets: improvement of primary market business, risk distribution on secondary credit markets, subsequent reinvestments of the capital released into higher yielding assets as well as secondary market placements of new credit assets that have been structured and repackaged on the basis of the institution's loan book.

Chapter 4.3 has shown the main objectives on which participating banks in the empirical study focus. These objectives can be categorized according to the four value creation dimensions of CPM units that have been explored during the interview process.[765] Consequently, the importance banks ascribe to the objectives for their CPM units enables an indication according to which dimensions the three CPM business models identified in the empirical sample aspire to create additional economic value for their institutions' credit business. Furthermore, through considering the implementation degrees of these objectives, it is possible to determine the extent to which the institutions perceive that their targeted value creation has actually been put into effect.

In the following section, the four dimensions named by participants as the dimensions according to which a CPM unit can enhance the value of their institutions' credit business as well as the extent to which they have been realized by the three different CPM business models shall be described in greater detail. With the help of this description, the value creation potential of the business models will be determined with the goal of identifying the value-maximizing approach towards managing credit assets.

[764] Most of the ACPM business models came into existence at most five years ago. 40% of the proprietary investors were even set up only less than one year ago, see Figure 77 in Appendix A

[765] See also again the left-hand side of Figure 42, Figure 43, and Figure 44

4.5.1.1 Improvement of primary market credit business

It has become evident from the empirical study that loan origination staff/customer relationship managers are primarily driven and incentivized by new customer acquisition and generation of a higher profit contribution (see again Figure 45). This view may imply that loan prices charged to customers are too low, specifically because the risks inherent in lending contracts are not in the main focus of relationship managers and may, therefore, not be appropriately taken into account. Hereby, the tendency to under-price credit assets may be enforced by the fact that origination faces pressure to acquire and maintain customer relationships in increasingly competitive loan markets and with clients – particularly large corporations – having a growing pricing power due to their opportunity to acquire financing on capital markets instead of through taking on bank loans.[766]

In this context, survey participants have stated that a CPM unit can contribute to achieving higher margins for credit transactions, e.g., through creating transparency for origination concerning which should be the "right" price to charge credit customers. Such a price may be a risk-adjusted price derived from a loan pricing model. It can also be the price at which a similar loan exposure of a prospective customer or a derivative on already outstanding debt is traded on the secondary loan or CDS markets, for example. Following this higher transparency created by CPM, origination becomes conscious of forgiven revenue potential in an individual loan engagement.

It needs to be noted, however, that such price increases are often not possible due to significant pricing power especially of large corporate customers.[767] Obviously, enforcing higher margins may also result in the loss of some business volume. However, survey participants reporting the highest success rates regarding origination price discipline have stated that the types of loan contracts typically turned down in consequence of higher margin requirements are the ones that are unprofitable on a stand-alone basis so that they should not be concluded anyway or pursued any further unless more profitable follow-on business from such relationships is expected. Besides

---

[766] See again Footnote 73 for opportunities of large corporations to acquire financing from other sources other than bank loans.

The importance of customer relationships in growingly competitive loan markets is reflected in the results of the empirical study. Participants were asked what the most important reasons are why the loan prices they actually charge to customers do not correspond to the market- or model-based prices for these credit assets that reflect their "true" value. It is the importance of their customer relationship that is regarded as a highly important motive for these deviations, in particular in the large corporate segment: the importance of the customer relationship as a motive to under-price loans in the large corporate segment is ranked with an average degree of importance of 3.7. For SME customers, participants rank the same motive with an average importance of 3.1 (scale indicating 1 as least important and 5 as most important)

[767] See also Footnote 754

this, higher transparency on the "true" prices to be asked for loans is seen to provide a motivation for origination to search for more profitable, higher margin customer segments.

Furthermore, survey participants operating in sufficiently liquid secondary credit markets have reported that establishing an ACPM unit has enabled their origination BUs to increase loan volumes in selected profitable customer segments and, in accordance with origination, has offered them the opportunity to exceed pre-set concentration limits on certain credit names because ACPM has managed to hedge or distribute the above-limit risks on secondary markets.[768]

Following its ambitions to trade the loans acquired by origination on secondary credit markets, an ACPM unit is interested in origination to achieve a high standardization of its loan structures so that a high tradability and potential ability to repackage and tranche them in securitization instruments is achieved. Participants have reported that they expect decreasing operational costs related to origination and management of loans in consequence of such an enhanced structuring.

The disciplinary effects which a CPM unit has on origination BUs are enhanced with an increasing enforcement power of CPM over origination BUs. In particular, if CPM units are mandated to set a binding settlement price for origination at which they are willing to take over loans from origination, they dispose of the highest disciplinary competence. Such mandates have been found among proprietary investor ACPM units requiring origination to bear responsibility for the difference between the price set by CPM and the one charged to a customer in the case of a difference.[769]

4.5.1.2 Risk distribution

Further to improving primary market credit business, CPM units perceive that they can enhance the profitability of their institutions' credit business through transactions on secondary credit markets aiming at hedging and distributing credit risks. It is only participants operating in a sufficiently liquid secondary market environment, however, that see a value creation potential for their CPM units through executing such deals.

Risk distribution transactions are mainly performed to protect an institution from losses on loan engagements – particularly, loan losses to large single name debtors, to industries or countries – should default rates of these debtor categories increase as a consequence of an economic downturn or a crisis in a specific industry or country. Besides this, it is aspired to create value through improving the loan portfolio diversification and to reduce the share of EC bound in certain credit assets to free up capacity for additional, ideally more profitable lending business. Another motivation

---

768 See again chapter 4.4.5.4 regarding treatment of concentration risk limits in the context of a proprietary investor business model

769 See again chapter 4.4.5.1 for a detailed description of the settlement pricing methodology typically found among proprietary investors

named for these transactions is to perform regulatory capital arbitrage.[770] Furthermore, in the context of a lending strategy aiming at actively managing the credit cycle, i.e., aiming at foreseeing downturns in order to take appropriate actions, some institutions see a key value creation potential of their ACPM activities through performing strategic hedging. That is, following an opinion that a specific industry may experience a downturn in the near future, for example, the ACPM unit initiates appropriate hedging transactions to be protected against such a possible decline.[771]

However, while risk distribution transactions may prove particularly beneficial through protecting institutions in times of economic downturns, participants have also been aware of their drawbacks as they typically have a negative impact on current income from credit business. This is mainly for two reasons: on the one hand, if credit risks are distributed through sale of assets, the credit revenue base of the institution is diminished. On the other hand, insuring credit exposures against losses with the help of credit derivatives such as, e.g., CDS transactions requires the payment of insurance premiums to the protection seller.[772]

4.5.1.3 Reinvestments in credit assets

Two alternatives regarding treatment of the capital that has been freed up through risk distribution transactions have been reported: on the one hand, it can be returned to shareholders. On the other hand, reinvestments in different types of credit assets can be performed to optimize the institution's capital allocation and maximize its earnings from lending business.

---

770 Although regulatory capital arbitrage has recently become more important since most institutions are currently not subject to regulatory capital constraint; see again Figure 12 for RWA changes of major European institutions over the past few years

771 In the context of such strategic hedging activities, participants currently see a major issue regarding the need to obtain qualification of respective contracts as a hedge for accounting purposes. It is important that these hedging contracts need to be recognized as a hedge for accounting purposes because only in this case gains and losses from the instrument are recognized in the same period in which gains and losses from the item being hedged are recognized. If such a matching recognition is not achieved, an increased volatility of the institution's P&L may result after having initiated a hedge. Currently, FASB Statement number 133 ("FAS 133") determines what the requirements of derivatives are to be accepted for hedge accounting. With "IAS 39" a similar standard has been developed. See, e.g., Hull (2006), p. 39 for an overview on hedge accounting standards

772 These payments make the establishment of strategic hedges, e.g., on exposures towards a certain industry in order to be protected against potential downturns, particularly problematic. Credit portfolio manager typically aim at initiating such hedges with a long-term perspective, requiring the corresponding financing of the transactions over the entire period. In particular if the downward movement of their protected underlying does initially not occur, their protective value-added does not materialize. The financing requirements make it difficult for the managers to justify the existence of these contracts and their required funding, especially towards executives from the finance departments

Participants in the empirical study see a value creation potential if the previously freed-up capital of their CPM unit is reinvested by origination on the primary market into new, higher yielding credit assets than the ones in which it was originally bound.

Alternatively, CPM units can perform such capital reinvestments on the secondary credit market themselves. Like this, they not only have the possibility to offset costs related to previously executed risk distribution transactions,[773] but they can also contribute to increasing lending income by performing reinvestments in credit assets yielding higher revenues than the ones having been distributed before.[774] Furthermore, knowing the composition of their institution's credit portfolio, CPM can undertake investments in such credit assets whose risk characteristics support the effort to optimize the risk-return structure of their portfolio. Some participants have stated that capital reinvestments in liquid, tradable secondary credit market instruments are advantageous over similar transactions on the primary market side as they increase the overall liquidity of their credit portfolio.

4.5.1.4 Repackaging and placements of credit risks

The risk distribution activities described above are primarily motivated by goals to protect an institution against unexpected credit losses and to release economic or regulatory capital. Some survey participants disposing of a strong product-/capital market orientation have reported that it is their goal to use credit assets on ACPM's book as a basis for creating structured products such as CDOs in which the loans on their books are repackaged, tranched, and subsequently sold to investors.[775]

While supporting the efforts to distribute credit risks and release capital, setting up such securitizations entail transaction costs for the initiating institution. Yet, these expenses are typically overcompensated by the income stream generated from placing the newly generated securities tranches among the investor community. As such instruments are often sold to retail investors, they bring along the advantage that the issuing institution, especially if it operates in a wholesale credit segment, can open up new markets by generating income from a different investor base than their "typical" primary market customers. Furthermore, some players have voiced the idea of generating additional fees from leveraging their product platform by offering

[773] As mentioned before, all CPM units independently performing capital reinvestment transactions are set up as profit centers. As they are held responsible for their profitability on a stand-alone basis, they are incentivized to seek the optimal reinvestment opportunities for their freed-up capital

[774] See again Footnote 732 on possible types of secondary market transactions that can be initiated to reinvest freed-up capital in a more profitable way than before

[775] This does not include the SME-/retail focused ACPM units in the empirical sample which have performed few structured transactions that have not primarily been motivated by goals to generate additional income but above all by the motive to perform regulatory capital arbitrage; see again chapter 4.4.4 as well as Footnote 726 for the issues these units face regarding secondary credit market transactions in view of the incomplete markets in which they operate

structuring services to other institutions that are willing to set up such instruments but do not dispose of the skill-set, infrastructure or investor base of critical size to structure and place such transactions.

4.5.2 Value-maximizing CPM business model

When examining the value creation potential of an ACPM approach from a theoretical point of view in chapters 4.3 and 4.4 of part II, the execution of secondary market transactions has been focused on, assuming that an institution's primary market business is not affected by the introduction of an ACPM business model. By contrast, the empirical study has surprisingly shown that banks also see a significant improvement potential for their loan origination business that can be realized in particular if a strong CPM unit is introduced which not only creates transparency concerning the "right" price to be charged to primary market customers and the true profitability of customer relationships but also enforces loan origination to have greater pricing discipline, especially if quoting binding settlement prices. Consequently, although the aforementioned restrictions regarding actively influencing primary market credit business might still be faced,[776] an additional value creation potential for CPM units by improving primary market lending business activities is perceived.

The CPM business models introduced in chapter 4.1 put a different emphasis on the above-mentioned four dimensions identified during the survey interviews with participating institutions according to which a CPM unit can create additional value for its bank's credit business. Which value creation dimensions the different CPM business models put an emphasis on and to what extent they typically manage to capture and, hence, materialize the related value creation potential can be seen from the importance they ascribe to the related objectives and their corresponding degrees of implementation.[777]

Improvement of primary market credit business has a clear priority for proprietary investors – each of the ACPM units attributes an importance of between 4.5 and 5.0 to the objective to discipline loan origination. Furthermore, these units achieve the highest success among all CPM business models regarding implementing this goal, reporting an average implementation degree of about 90%.[778] Active advisors consider improvement of primary market business as medium to highly important, naming an average importance in the range of 4.0 for the corresponding objective. However, mainly due to cultural conflicts with origination BUs, they only achieve an

776 See especially again Footnote 243 for such possible restrictions

777 See again Figure 42, Figure 43, and Figure 44 illustrating the average importance that CPM units assign to a selection of objectives including corresponding implementation degrees

778 See again Figure 44

implementation success of about 50%. Reactive controllers see the lowest potential to create additional value through enhancing loan origination.

Most CPM units aim at creating value by means of credit risk distribution on secondary markets. Thereby, they see a major value creation potential through the limitation of unexpected credit losses and EC reduction. Lowering regulatory capital consumption is typically not in their primary focus. Again, it is proprietary investors and active advisors that mostly aim at creating value in this way, also reporting the highest implementation degrees of all CPM units. Reactive controllers ascribe similarly high importance to risk distribution activities. However, mainly because they do not have a mandate to perform secondary market transactions, they only manage to realize the potential from limiting unexpected credit losses to a somewhat significant extent by reaching an average implementation degree of about 40%. To achieve this goal, such distribution transactions have been executed by other units within their organization, e.g., ALM units.

Chapters 4.4.4.2 and 4.4.4.3 have already shown that secondary credit market investments to accommodate freed-up capital in a more profitable way are generally of lower importance than risk distribution transactions both for active advisors and proprietary investors, while reactive controllers do not perform such transactions at all. Furthermore, only 60% of the active advisors perform these transactions. By contrast, all proprietary investors aim at increasing their revenues through such secondary market reinvestments and also achieve the highest implementation degrees for this objective.

In the European sample, it is currently only the two most advanced proprietary investors that have established an asset transferring version of this business model that create structured products based on their loan portfolio with the goal of placing credit risks among investors in the form of standardized, tradable securities, earning fees related to structuring these transactions and potentially expanding their product platform to other players. This is possible because they have had the opportunity to operate in a market environment receptive to the products generated by their distribution platform and encompassing an accessible investor base. Equally important for successfully engaging in these activities, however, is the fact that their credit asset ownership provides them with sufficient flexibility to independently structure and execute such transactions based on their loan book. The other units in the empirical study – both proprietary investors and active advisors – currently do not engage in structuring and placing new credit products. At most, they have expressed potential interest to do so in the future and, therefore, aim at enhancing their internal infrastructure and the conditions of their underlying markets as well as assembling a potential investor base for such transactions in the future.[779] As they are not active on secondary credit markets, reactive controllers do not engage in these activities at all.

Figure 55 illustrates the four dimensions along which a CPM unit can create additional value for its institution's credit activities and shows to which extent the different CPM business models manage to exploit the corresponding value creation potential.

Value creation through CPM business models

CPM business models	Dimensions of value creation: Improved primary market business	Risk distribution	Reinvestments	Repackaging/placements of credit risks
(III) Proprietary investors	✓	✓	✓	(✓)
(II) Active advisors	(✓)	✓	(✓)	–
(I) Risk controllers	(✓)	(✓)*	–	–

* No transactions but at most laying the foundation for execution of secondary credit market transactions in other units

Legend: Value-creation potential exploited: ✓ Fully; (✓) Partially; – Not at all

Figure 55: Value creation through CPM business models[780]

Although not having been able to exactly quantify the ACPM value creation potential, it has been shown with the help of the empirical study that not all CPM business models foresee creating additional value for their institution's credit business along all the four possible dimensions identified above. Besides this, the different business models manage to realize their foreseen value creation potential to a different extent as

[779] In this context it becomes evident that a major obstacle on the path to realizing these plans is the lack of asset ownership of most of these units, requiring them to get an agreement with asset-owning loan origination BUs regarding which assets to securitize

[780] Source: Own illustration based on results of empirical study on ACPM

they vary regarding implementation success of the objectives related to the various value creation dimensions.

Proprietary investors – at least the longest established and furthest developed ones covered in the empirical sample – not only focus on creating value along all four identified dimensions but have also achieved the highest implementation degrees for the related objectives.[781] Consequently, this ACPM business model seemingly promises to generate the highest additional economic value for an institution's existing credit business.

This may lead to the conclusion that setting up a proprietary investor is the optimal target business model whose implementation should be aspired in all cases. However, when asked about their goals to further develop their ACPM unit, participants in the empirical study did not convey such an unanimous picture.

All institutions that have currently set up a risk controller aim at further developing their CPM towards an ACPM unit. They mostly have not specified, however, whether they aim at establishing an active advisory unit or whether they rather aspire to directly move towards a proprietary investor ACPM business model.

The active advisors in the sample have provided a different picture regarding goals to further develop their ACPM unit: not all, i.e., only around 71% of the advisors which primarily manage wholesale credit assets (i.e., the ones in the empirical sample located in wholesale/markets BUs or in central risk/finance units) have a strong intention to further develop their units towards a proprietary investor model. Some of these units are currently in the transformation process. Among the SME-/retail asset-focused active advisors, by contrast, there is currently no unit considering the move towards a proprietary investor business model as an advantageous one.[782]

This lends reason to the supposition that the question regarding the optimal target ACPM business model an institution should implement is more complex and depends on more factors than the mere goal of setting up the model promising to create additional value according to most dimensions. There must be other components determining the optimal ACPM business model an institution should implement besides the potential additional economic value that establishing a certain ACPM approach promises to create for an institution's credit business.

---

781 See again Figure 77 in Appendix A showing how long ACPM units have existed in the participants' organizations. It is the 60% of the proprietary investors which were established at least 2 years ago which report the highest implementation degrees for the objectives related to the four value creation dimensions identified

782 The institutions not aiming at establishing a proprietary investor business model cite different motives why they do not regard such a move as advantageous. See the following chapter 5 for details

Therefore, it seems necessary to perform a more thorough derivation of the optimal target ACPM model by taking into account a broader range of determining factors. This will be goal of chapter five.

The examinations performed there are founded on the external and internal determinants for the design criteria of ACPM business models that have been identified in chapter 2.3.3 of part II. It will be examined what is the relation between the specification of these determinants and the CPM business models implemented by the "best-practice" institutions covered in the empirical study. The goals these institutions have for further developing their CPM units will also be taken into account.

With the help of this in-depth analysis examining the impact which these determining factors have had on the design of the "best-practice" players' CPM business models, it is aspired to support the decision-making process of institutions reflecting on the optimal approach they should take towards managing their loan exposures.

4.6 Summary: empirical evidence on CPM business models and comparison to previous empirical research

In the following section, a brief summary of the empirical findings on the different CPM business models presented above will be given. Where possible, a comparison to previous empirical research will also be provided.

4.6.1 Summary of empirical findings on CPM business models

Based on the three design criteria (I) mandate for credit functions, (II) asset ownership and (III) reporting structure within the institution, three generic ACPM business models have been developed by literature on ACPM: "Advisors" are seen to be located within the risk unit or customer BU, primarily performing credit risk measurement functions and giving recommendations to customer BUs how to reshuffle the credit portfolio composition. "Active portfolio managers", centrally located within the organization according to literature, assume asset ownership and sell off credit risks on secondary markets while operating as cost centers. "Proprietary investors" are also regarded as centrally located within the banking organization and take over credit assets from origination as well. However, they have full P&L responsibility for this acquired credit portfolio and are entitled to independently take positions on secondary credit markets based on their views regarding future market developments.

A comparison between theory and practice has shown that the business models set up by leading European institutions to manage their loan portfolios differ from the generic ACPM models portrayed in literature. Three main types of CPM business models have been differentiated among these financial institutions. Two of them foresee the establishment of a dedicated ACPM unit whose task is to actively manage and optimize loan portfolios through transactions on primary and secondary credit markets.

4.6.1.1 Risk controllers

More than one third of all participants currently do not actively manage their credit portfolios yet. Instead, they perform passive CPM functions within existing risk units, supporting the loan monitoring, managing, and servicing activities of their customer BUs. Overall, these "risk controllers" pursue a conventional "originate and hold" management style for the assets under their control. Risk controllers aspire to the same objectives when managing their credit portfolios as active advisors do. However, they report significantly lower degrees of implementation for these objectives than their actively managing counterparts. This is mainly due to the fact that they do not perform their activities from a separate, dedicated unit yet and typically face major implementation barriers, such as lack of senior management support regarding developing a clear ACPM strategy and further development of their CPM approach as well as insufficient data quality, model and reporting infrastructure. Furthermore, they have mostly faced issues related to lacking existence and illiquidity of credit markets.

The main tasks of risk controllers are to influence the definition of target credit portfolios, to develop concepts and tools for measurement of credit risks, and to perform credit research functions. They typically neither impact origination BUs regarding pricing of credit assets nor do they independently perform transactions on secondary credit markets to actively reshuffle their banks' credit portfolio composition.

4.6.1.2 Active advisors

Most of the European institutions surveyed (42% in the empirical sample) have established a dedicated ACPM unit which can best be described as "active advisor". Two sub-groups of active advisors have been distinguished which partially differ, in particular regarding objectives and related implementation success as well as concerning functional competencies. The smaller share of active advisors in the empirical sample is located either in their institutions' central risk or finance unit. The greater share of these units is situated in wholesale or SME-/retail asset-focused BUs. None of them has been established independently within the organization, e.g., directly reporting to the group CEO.

Active advisors aim at optimizing their institutions' credit portfolio structure by impacting origination regarding acquisition and renewal of loan contracts. If finding supporting conditions, they perform transactions on secondary loan markets, mainly having the aspiration to hedge or sell off concentration risks by means of CDS and synthetic structured derivatives. Through using synthetic instruments, they can circumvent the need to get consent from asset-owning customer BUs when wanting to sell credit assets on these markets. Only a few active advisors operate as profit centers and reinvest their freed-up capital in higher yielding asset classes on secondary credit markets. The ones doing so mainly invest in CDO and CDS instruments as well as in syndicated loans.

Active advisors do not assume ownership for their banks' credit assets or risks. Yet, they characteristically dispose of a mandate to exert influence on primary market lending business by giving non-binding advice to loan originating BUs as to what the right price should be to charge their customers when granting a loan. Often, this advice is given through recommendations in the form of setting pricing guidelines. The advisors with a stronger pricing competence typically assume ownership of the bank's loan pricing model, hence providing origination with the "correct" model-based risk-adjusted price. It is within the sole competence of sales managers, however, to deviate from such a price, e.g., for the sake of maintaining a customer relationship.

In particular regarding their impact on the primary market side, functional competencies of active advisors differ depending on whether they are located in central risk or finance units or in BUs of their institutions. This is because the ones located in central units, especially the ones located in risk units, have stronger risk management-related competencies than the ones situated in BUs. Advisors in BUs typically have a significantly stronger competence and enforcement power towards the primary market side than their counterparts in central locations have, with some of them thinking about further enhancing their impact by setting up a shortfall compensation mechanism towards origination. This mechanism is aspired to prove particularly beneficial regarding overcoming existing cultural differences between sales staff, who are primarily driven and incentivized by generation of new customer loan volumes on the one hand, and active advisor units that try to impose a risk view towards lending business on the other hand. These conflicts of interest typically inhibit a stronger impact of advisors on primary market business.

4.6.1.3 Proprietary investors

The smallest share of participating institutions in the empirical sample (21%) has currently implemented a proprietary investor ACPM unit. Most of these proprietary investors are located in wholesale or market BUs and focus their activities on the most liquid credit names.

Proprietary investors take over credit assets or related risks from loan originating BUs and have the competence to set binding price recommendations towards origination for these assets or risks. They mainly owe their strong primary market competence to the existence of a shortfall compensation mechanism for the asset- or risk-transfer whose establishment has been facilitated by a strong senior management as the driving force for their business model.

On secondary credit markets, proprietary investors sell credit risks in order to hedge exposures and release capital bound in concentration risks. A few proprietary investors also use their loan books as a basis to create newly structured credit products and subsequently actively distribute credit risks on secondary loan markets through these structures. Besides this, by means of selective secondary market (re-)investments, they try to cover hedging costs, optimize their portfolios' risk-return profile, and profitably reallocate capital that has been freed-up before.

The longest established proprietary investors focus on creating economic value along the four dimensions: (I) improvement of primary market credit business, (II) distribution of credit risks on secondary loan markets, (III) subsequent reinvestments of the freed-up capital into higher yielding credit assets, and (IV) repackaging and structuring credit risks and subsequently placing them among secondary market investors. Hence, this ACPM business model promises to create highest additional economic value for an institution's credit business.

However, by far not all institutions covered in the empirical study aim at developing their ACPM unit towards a proprietary investor business model. This raises doubts as to whether a proprietary investor model is the optimal ACPM business model whose implementation should be pursued in all cases. Therefore, it will be examined in chapter 5, which specification of a range of determinants has led the "best-practice" institutions included in the empirical study on ACPM to the decision for implementing a certain CPM business model. This best-practice exemplification will enable the specification in greater detail of which is the optimal target ACPM model an institution should choose if it faces a certain constellation of pre-defined determinants for the design of its unit.

4.6.2 Comparison to previous empirical research on CPM

As mentioned at the onset of this dissertation, the 2004 version of a biannual survey on ACPM performed by Rutter Associates LLC (Rutter Associates LLC (2004)) is the latest publicly available empirical study in this field.

However, there is only a limited comparability possible to the results of the empirical study at hand since merely parts of this survey have been published. Besides this, the results released do not differentiate between ACPM business models but rather provide average results of the entire empirical sample covering 44 institutions worldwide. Still, however, it seems worth drawing a brief comparison to the empirical study at hand to find out whether there is some common ground between the empirical results.

4.6.2.1 Asset focus and types of CPM units

Similar to the participants in the empirical study at hand, the institutions surveyed by Rutter Associates LLC (2004) primarily focus their credit portfolio management activities on large- and mid-corps loans and less frequently on exposures to retail customers.[783]

[783] On average, 39% of the obligors of responding institutions were large corporates, 19% medium-sized corporates, and 10-14% retail customers and financial institutions; see Rutter Associates LLC (2004), p. 2

About 91% of the respondents report that they have a formal CPM unit without further specifying the type of unit. If the term "formal CPM unit" can be understood as a unit that is actively managing its institution's loan portfolio rather than merely performing risk controlling functions, this would mean that there are more dedicated ACPM units in the international data sample of Rutter Associates LLC (2004) than in the Europe-focused empirical study at hand, which only includes about 63% institutions actively managing loan exposures through a dedicated unit.

About 14% of all respondents and 15% of the institutions that have established a formal CPM unit report that this unit exclusively owns the economics of credit assets. If these units can be interpreted as "proprietary investors", their share would be lower than in the empirical study at hand, which includes 21% proprietary investors in the total sample of participating institutions or 33% of the banks having established a dedicated ACPM unit.

About 33% of the respondents in Rutter Associates LLC (2004) report that a line unit/CPM partnership assumes ownership for their institution's credit assets. What this partnership looks like is not further specified, unfortunately. Yet, an obvious conclusion to draw seems that parts of these institutions' credit portfolios, most likely the most liquid large corporate exposures for which a "fair" settlement price can easily be determined due to existing secondary market prices, are transferred to a CPM unit possibly acting as a proprietary investor while rather illiquid exposures remain under the ownership of the line unit. If this is the case, the share of institutions that have established an asset-owning ACPM unit for at least parts of their portfolio would increase to about 52% of all respondents or 58% of all institutions reporting that they have a formal CPM unit which would be a significantly higher share of proprietary investors than in the European empirical study on ACPM.

Approximately 39% of all respondents or about 43% of all institutions that have set up a formal CPM unit report that the line unit remains the owner of the credit asset economics. Assuming that the corresponding CPM units operate as "active advisors", this would compare to 42% active advisors among all participants in the empirical study at hand or about 66% of all participants having established a formal ACPM unit in their organization.[784]

4.6.2.2 Objectives of CPM units

Rutter Associates LLC (2004) publish a question asking for the average importance that participants ascribe to a selection of five objectives for their CPM units.[785]

[784] See again Rutter Associates LLC (2004), p. 2. See also again Figure 40 on the results of the empirical study on ACPM conducted in the context of this dissertation

[785] The objectives provided include reduction of regulatory capital, management of concentration risks, protection against risk deterioration, reduction of EC and portfolio risk/reward optimization, see Rutter Associates LLC (2004), p. 3

Unfortunately, the answers are not differentiated according to CPM business models but are merely provided as an average across all participants. Besides this, there is no indication as to implementation degrees and barriers of the respective goals.

Most of the ratings do not seem to be in disagreement with the ones obtained by the empirical study on ACPM at hand: while the objective to manage concentration risks and to protect against risk deterioration is ranked as most important,[786] least importance is ascribed to the goal to reduce regulatory capital. It seems, however, as though the objective to change (optimize) the risk-return structure of the credit portfolio has lower importance for the banks included in the empirical sample of Rutter Associates LLC (2004) than for the ones in the empirical study on ACPM conducted for the purpose of this dissertation. The objective to discipline loan origination, one of the most important ones especially for active advisors and proprietary investors, is included in the results of Rutter Associates LLC (2004).

4.6.2.3 Instruments applied to manage credit portfolios

The survey results released by Rutter Associates LLC (2004) also contain a ranking of the importance that participants ascribe to instruments used to manage their credit portfolios on primary and secondary credit markets. Like the information released on the objectives of CPM, the published results on instruments are relatively unspecific: with respect to secondary market instruments, they are only clustered into the four buckets "loan sales and trading", "single name CDS", "portfolio CDS", and "securitizations". Besides this, the results do not differentiate between the importance of the instruments for risk distribution and investments in credit risks.

Generally, an impact of CPM units on the primary market side, e.g., through decisions regarding approval of new or renewal of existing business, is regarded as more important than execution of secondary market transactions. The most important instruments supporting the reshuffle of a credit portfolio on secondary credit markets are single name CDS. The second-highest importance is ascribed to loan sales and trading activities, while securitizations and portfolio CDS are less important for the responding institutions.

These answers cannot be exactly compared to the results of the empirical study conducted in the context of this dissertation. Yet, there is no obvious contradiction between the results discernible: the European institutions rank single-name CDS and loan sales among the most important instruments to distribute or invest into credit risks. While not being of significantly lower importance for active advisors, synthetic and cash securitization transactions are of noticeably lower importance for proprietary investors than the aforementioned instruments. Hence, across the average of all

[786] As equivalents in the empirical study on ACPM can be considered the objectives "reduce EC mainly through diversification of concentration risks" and "limit unexpected credit losses". These objectives rank among the most important ones across all CPM business models

participating institutions, these instruments have a lower degree of importance than CDS and loan sales and trading activities which is in line with the results of Rutter Associates LLC (2004).[787]

[787] See, in particular, Rutter Associates LLC (2004), p. 6

5 Optimal ACPM business model

In chapter four, the generic ACPM business models described in literature have been tested with the help of the empirical study on ACPM. The empirically identified business models have subsequently been characterized in greater detail regarding their objectives and related degrees of implementation, their detailed competencies for key credit functions as well as their potential to generate additional value for their institutions' credit business. The latter analysis has also had the goal of identifying the value-maximizing ACPM business model.

In particular since it does not appear to be a unanimous view among participants in the empirical study that the apparently value-maximizing proprietary investor ACPM business model is the optimal target model that should be implemented in all situations (see again chapter 4.5.2), it seems necessary to perform a more thorough derivation of the optimal ACPM business model an institution should establish if it faces certain specifications of determining factors. Therefore, it is the goal of this chapter to examine which specifications of the internal and external determinants for the design criteria of ACPM business models (see again chapter 2.3.3 of part II as well as Figure 36 for an illustration of the determinants identified with help of existing literature) have motivated the "best-practice" participants in the empirical study to implement a particular type of ACPM unit. Based on these analyses, conclusions regarding which promises to be the optimal ACPM business model depending on an institution's specific situation will be drawn.

In the following section, for each determinant identified before, the relation between its specifications and the CPM business models established will be examined. Figure 56 illustrates the different determinants, their specifications and which analyses have been performed to measure these specifications.[788]

[788] In view of the fact that risk controllers represent the least sophisticated way to manage credit portfolios in a reactive style and since all institutions covered in the empirical sample want to move towards actively managing credit portfolios, the argumentation will primarily focus on the business models foreseeing the active management of credit assets that can potentially be implemented

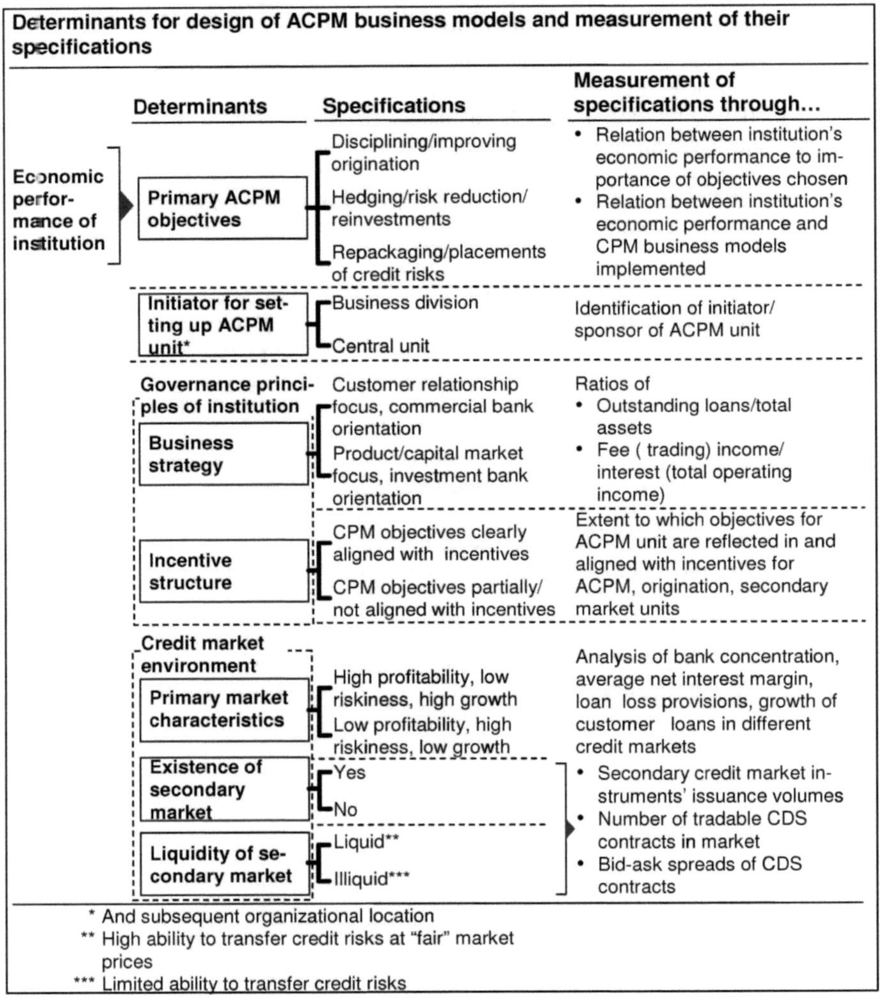

Figure 56: Determinants for design of ACPM business models and measurement of their specifications[789]

[789] Source: Own illustration

At first, the relation between the specifications of the internal determinants and the thereby induced CPM business models that have been established by the "best-practice" institutions covered in the empirical sample will be examined.

5.1 Relation between specifications of internal determinants and established CPM business models

5.1.1 Economic performance of institution

It has been shown before that the historical economic performance of a financial institution not only has an impact on the overall banking strategy in general but also on the objectives for the institution's approach towards lending business.[790] Therefore, the relation between the survey participants' economic performance and the importance they ascribe to the objectives for their CPM units has been examined.

This analysis already indicates differences in the focus of the CPM objectives, suggesting the implementation of a particular CPM business model that promises to best reap the benefits from a successful realization of these pre-set goals. Moreover, this indication has been fortified by a direct comparison of the institutions' economic performance with the types of models that have been implemented to manage credit portfolios. To measure the survey participants' economic performance, a set of performance indicators has been defined and analyzed.

5.1.1.1 Relation between institutions' performance indicators and CPM objectives

The 22 institutions participating in the empirical study on ACPM have been clustered according to their historical profitability, indicated by their average ROE, as well as according to the riskiness and growth of their loan books which have been determined by analyzing their LLP to RWA ratio and their RWA growth, respectively.[791] These indicators for their historical performance have been juxtaposed to the importance the institutions ascribe to the objectives for their CPM units. Thereby, emphasis has been put on objectives whose analysis allows a classification of the CPM goals into the three categories (I) disciplining/improving origination business, (II) hedging/minimizing credit risks and optimizing the portfolio composition as well as

[790] See again, in particular, Footnote 232

[791] The analysis of these indicators has been performed with the help of historical annual data over the 7 year horizon between 1998 and 2004. In order to avoid distorting effects caused by BUs that have no relation to the CPM unit considered, the analysis has focused on corresponding data from the BU in which the CPM unit is located, wherever the information has been published by the institutions.

Due to insufficient availability of data on outstanding customer loans over this time period, the analysis has focused on largely available RWA volumes instead, which can be regarded as a suitable proxy for outstanding customer loans as RWAs are strongly driven by outstanding loan volumes (see again chapter 2.2.2.1 of part II on derivation of RWAs from outstanding loan volumes through risk weighting of different types of loans)

(III) distributing credit risks through repackaging and placements on secondary credit markets.[792] In particular when generating sub-groups of the best and worst five institutions in each performance cluster, it becomes obvious that the economic performance of an institution seems to impact the objectives it pursues with its CPM unit. This gives an indication of the CPM business model to be ideally chosen in order to ensure the most successful implementation of the objectives that have been induced by a particular economic situation.

The relation between the institutions' performance indicators and the importance they have ascribed to the objectives for their CPM units are illustrated in Figure 57. Following key differences can be observed:

The least profitable institutions in the sample – as indicated by the lowest ROE levels – place higher emphasis on disciplining loan origination than the most profitable survey participants do. Low profitability also seems to be a trigger for a greater aspiration to limit the UL of a credit portfolio, as can be seen at the higher importance for the objective to limit a credit portfolio's UL named by institutions at the lower end of the ROE spectrum. Survey participants with the highest LLP put greater emphasis on disciplining loan origination than players with a less risky portfolio composition do. Differences between the importance to discipline loan origination become even more apparent when clustering survey participants according to their RWA growth: institutions with the lowest growing (actually declining) RWAs over the past few years have a significantly stronger aspiration to increase origination discipline than their counterparts that have recently enjoyed a high RWA growth.[793] The opposite holds regarding the players' objective to limit the UL of a credit portfolio.

---

792 These categories are oriented at the value-creation dimensions of ACPM units identified in chapter 4.5. For the purpose of this analysis, the value creation levers "risk distribution" and "reinvestments in credit risks" have been aggregated into one cluster "hedging/minimizing credit risks and optimizing the portfolio composition"

793 Historically growing RWAs seem to be related to high profitability: While four of the five banks whose RWAs have recently grown most strongly are among the 50% of the most profitable players, 2 of these banks are even among the five players having enjoyed the highest ROEs over the past few years. The opposite holds for institutions with slowly growing RWAs

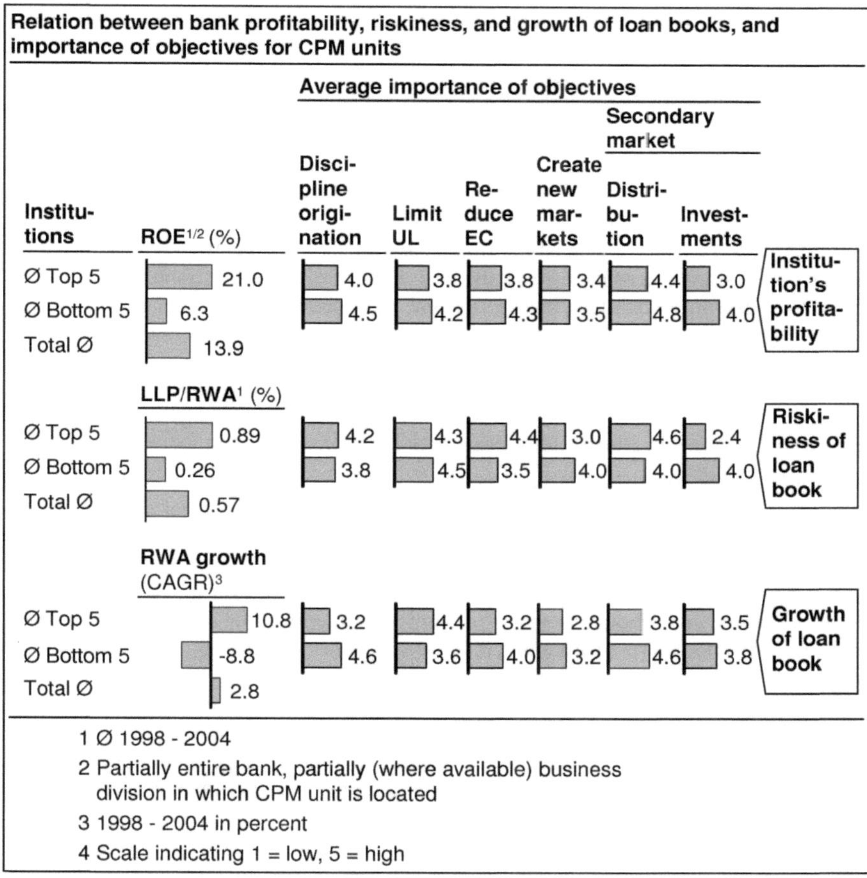

Figure 57: Relation between bank profitability, riskiness and growth of loan books, and importance of objectives for CPM units[794]

These findings may be interpreted as follows:

Institutions that have lately been under strong profitability pressure – in particular following a low quality of their loan books as shown by above-average LLP[795] – try to

[794] Source: Own illustration. Information on importance of objectives based on results of empirical study on ACPM, bank ROE, LLP, and RWA derived from Datastream and Bloomberg databases

[795] Most of the low profitability banks are among the institutions with the highest loan losses: Three out of the

increase the profitability of their lending business through establishing a CPM unit that strongly impacts the origination side in order to ensure origination concludes profitable lending business. Low profitable banks may also aspire to avoid further negative impacts on their profitability by engaging in activities to limit the UL of their loan portfolio.[796]

The significantly higher goal to discipline origination activities reported by financial service providers that have experienced the lowest – actually negative – RWA growth over the past years can be interpreted as follows: institutions opposed to a sluggish credit demand regard it as crucial to strongly impact origination BUs in order to drive the credit business activities towards the most profitable segments, having the intention to maximize lending income. At the same time, they seek to switch to new areas of growth e.g., on secondary credit markets through redistributing the assets acquired on the primary market side. By contrast, institutions that have recently experienced a strong growth of their lending exposures seem to primarily focus on activities limiting the UL of their portfolio in order to avoid or at least minimize a profitability squeeze in case of an increasing defaulting rate of debtors.[797]

When relating the performance indicators of survey participants to their aspiration to reduce a credit portfolio's EC by means of their ACPM activities, clear parallels to the objective to discipline loan origination arise: the least profitable players, required to bear the highest LLP, report a significantly stronger objective to reduce the EC of their loan portfolio than their more profitable counterparts do. It seems as though the CPM units of these institutions aimed at freeing up capital to subsequently enable engagements into more profitable credit assets. Furthermore, those having credit portfolios with a comparably low debtor quality, i.e., the ones characterized by high LLP, have a strong aspiration to release the RWAs related to these risks at the initiative of their CPM units. Since EC reduction transactions are typically performed through secondary credit market instruments, the participants' importance of the objective to distribute credit risks on secondary credit markets moves in line with the significance of EC reduction.

Five banks that have the lowest average ROE are in the cluster with the highest LLP to RWA ratio

796 The relation between an institution's profitability and its aspiration to limit the UL of its credit portfolio becomes obvious from a comparison between its ROE and the importance ascribed to UL limitation rather than from comparing its LLP over RWA ratio with the goal to limit its UL, however. Institutions facing the lowest LLP compared to their RWA volumes place a slightly higher importance on the objective to limit their portfolio's UL than their counterparts that have a riskier credit portfolio composition. This may be due to the fact that, given a rather "healthy" loan portfolio, they engage in measures to be protected against potentially harmful future downturns

797 Also compare these findings with an illustration of the RWA changes of major European institutions outlined in chapter 2.2.4.1 of part II and Figure 12

Three of the five institutions with the highest LLP to RWA ratio are among the five players in the sample having recently faced the slowest growing RWA base. Such a weak RWA growth may have been consequence of these institutions' goal to scale down the unprofitable parts of their loan book by releasing the corresponding RWAs and related bound capital on secondary credit markets. This may have been a motivation for ascribing an above-average degree of importance to the objective to perform secondary market distribution transactions. Secondary market distribution transactions can also be explained with these institutions' aim to get rid of their unprofitable credits in order to generate capacity for more profitable business on the primary market side and to open up new fields of growth through active redistribution of credit assets on these markets.

When comparing the degrees of importance that institutions with different profitability and riskiness of their loan books ascribe to the goal to perform secondary credit market investments, it becomes obvious that the least profitable players ascribe a significantly higher importance to such investment transactions than their more profitable counterparts do. These deals may be regarded as important by these comparably low profitable players since they provide them with the opportunity to redeploy their freed-up capital – previously bound in less profitable business – into higher yielding credit assets.[798] The fact that players with the lowest LLP to RWA ratios regard credit investments as significantly more important than institutions with the highest riskiness of their loan books seems surprising, especially in view of the fact that the opposite holds regarding importance for risk distributions. However, this particular finding needs to be interpreted with caution as there are only two of the five players enjoying the lowest LLP that have ranked the importance of their objective to perform credit investments.

Survey participants with different profitability characteristics do not significantly diverge regarding their objective to create new loan markets by generating new credit products. The subgroup ascribing highest degree of importance to the objective to create new credit markets are the institutions with lowest LLP to RWA ratios. They may pursue the development of appropriate credit products and new markets for credit risk trading mainly following a motivation to have the preconditions for protection of their loan book against potential future defaults in place.

It could be shown that the importance which participants in the empirical study assign to the different objectives of their CPM units appears to be determined by the economic conditions of their institution. Therefore, in order to ensure these situation-specific targets can best be met, it needs to be determined which CPM business model promises the most successful implementation of these objectives.

798 It needs to be noted, however, that only four of the five least profitable banks have ranked the importance of their objective to perform secondary credit market investment transactions. Only three players actually perform such transactions at the moment

5.1.1.2 Business model promising highest implementation success for CPM objectives

Based on the findings that the CPM business models identified in the empirical sample not only put various weights on a set of objectives but also achieve diverse implementation degrees for these goals (see again chapter 4.3 and particularly Figure 42, Figure 43, Figure 44 and Figure 50), the CPM business model which should ideally be implemented to best enable the realization of an institution's objectives that are induced by its specific economic situation is to be identified. As risk controllers have been found to achieve the lowest implementation degrees for the different goals and since all participants aspire to move to some type of CPM unit which actively manages their loan portfolios, this business model cannot be a recommendable aspiration.

It has been found out above that proprietary investors are the types of CPM business models placing highest importance on the goal of disciplining and improving loan origination while at the same time achieving the highest implementation degrees for this objective. This implies that a financial institution facing low profitability and sluggish growth of its RWA (e.g., due to low customer demand for its credit assets) can best achieve the objective to enhance its primary market business through implementing a proprietary investor business model. When intending to set up an active advisor model instead, this ACPM unit should ideally be located in the institution's customer BU that owns the assets to be managed since this promises to achieve a higher implementation degree of the objective to discipline and improve loan origination.

Active advisors – both the ones located in BUs and the ones in central locations of their institutions – put similar emphasis on the objective to reduce EC and also achieve comparable implementation degrees for this goal as proprietary investors do. They are less eager than proprietary investors regarding secondary market reinvestment transactions, however, since they are often set up as cost centers. Hence, if particular emphasis is not only placed on successfully realizing the objectives to distribute credit risks on secondary credit markets but also on subsequently reinvesting the freed-up capital into higher yielding credit assets, it appears to be more recommendable to implement a proprietary investor instead of setting up an active advisor business model. Again, it is the survey participants with the lowest ROEs, highest LLP to RWA ratios, and lowest RWA growth that primarily focus on these objectives. This confirms that institutions facing these economic situations should ideally implement a proprietary investor business model as this model not only promises to impose the highest impact on the origination side but also promises the most successful realization of objectives aimed at executing transactions on secondary credit markets. If it was decided to implement an active advisor instead, these units should ideally be set up as profit centers having P&L responsibility for their own investment books since this enables the execution of secondary market investment transactions.[799]

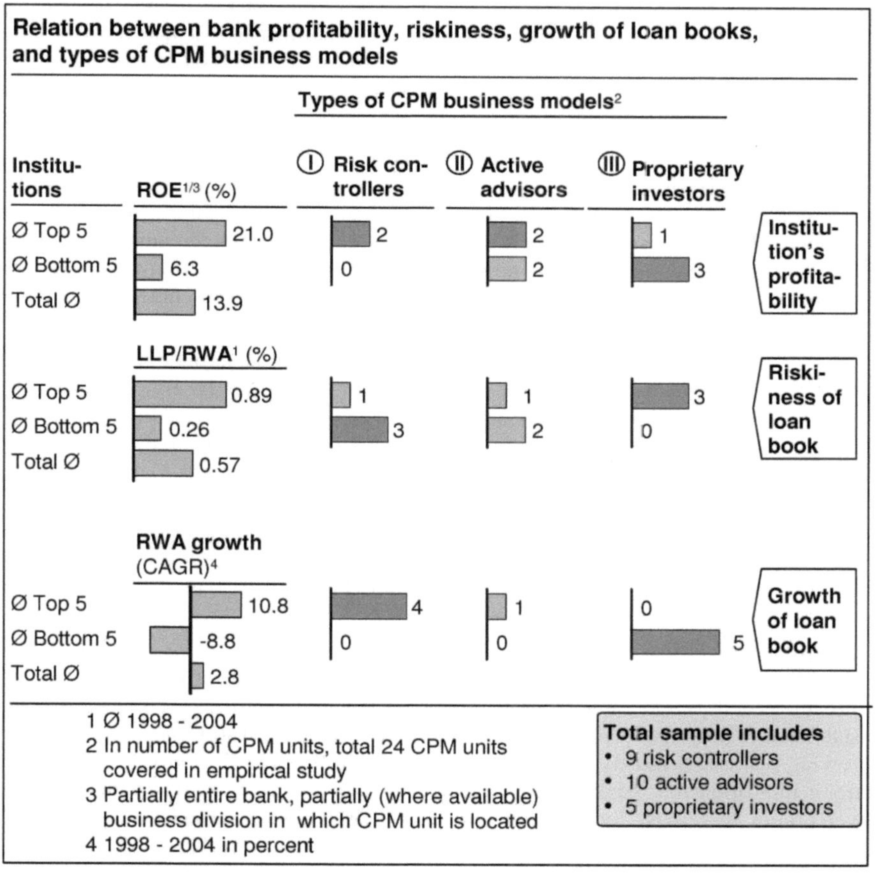

Figure 58: Relation between bank profitability, riskiness and growth of loan books and types of CPM business models[800]

---

[799] See also again chapter 4.1.1.2

[800] Source: Own illustration. Information on CPM business models based on results of empirical study on ACPM. Data on ROE, LLP and RWA derived from Datastream and Bloomberg databases

Institutions that have recently experienced a comparably high growth of their loan exposures and, therefore, primarily aim at being protected against unexpected credit losses during the next downturn could successfully achieve this target by implementing an active advisor business model. Having recently managed to strongly and profitably grow their credit asset base and thus often enjoying above-average profitability, these institutions may not feel a particular need to enhance their origination business activities. Hence, setting up an active advisor business model may meet these institutions' requirements for managing loan portfolios.

Relating the performance indicators of the participants in the empirical study to the importance they ascribe to different objectives has enabled conclusions to be drawn as to which CPM business model promises the most successful implementation of these objectives. These conclusions can be confirmed by a direct comparison of the institutions' performance indicators with the CPM business model chosen (see Figure 58 for an illustration):

Among the five survey participants with the lowest average ROE and the highest LLP per RWA ratios, there are three proprietary investors, respectively. By contrast, there is only one proprietary investor among the five most profitable players in the empirical sample. The five institutions with the lowest LLP per RWA ratio have set up their CPM units either as reactive controllers or active advisors. This leads to the conclusion that the decision to implement a proprietary investor business model may have been strongly driven by pressure on an institution's profitability. More profitable institutions seem to be more apt to implement an active advisor or have not yet felt a strong urge and support to establish an ACPM unit at all, hence still managing their credit portfolios in a conventional way as risk controllers.[801]

The differences between the business models become even more apparent when clustering the participants according to their RWA growth: the five banks with the lowest – actually negative – RWA growth over the past years are the ones that have established a proprietary investor ACPM unit. By contrast, institutions with strongly growing risk assets mostly manage their credit portfolios as risk controllers. This is a strong indication that banks facing a slow growing primary market business aim at overcoming this issue by implementing an ACPM business model that not only enables them to have maximum impact on the primary market side regarding acquisition of the most profitable and fastest growing credit segments but also puts them in the best position to open up new additional revenue and growth opportunities on the secondary market side. This is aspired to be achieved, e.g., through actively placing structured credit assets on secondary markets, providing the institutions with

801 Although, when conducting interviews with risk controllers, all participants expressed their intention to pursue an active management of their loan portfolios in the future

additional fee income, or through more profitable investments into credit risks on these markets should growth perspectives on the primary market side be limited.[802]

5.1.2 Initiator for setting up an ACPM unit

The initiator for setting up an ACPM unit has been identified as a crucial influencing factor on its eventual location within the banking organization.[803] This finding has been confirmed by the empirical study on ACPM: as shown in Figure 59, the senior manager/board member acting as initiator and sponsor of an ACPM unit strongly determines its eventual location within the organization.[804] The unit's organizational location, in turn, determines the possible ACPM business model that can be pursued.

---

802 The observation that banks with the slowest RWA growth put the highest emphasis on both disciplining loan origination and distributing assets on secondary credit markets (see again Figure 57) and that all five banks with the lowest RWA growth have established proprietary investor ACPM units (see again Figure 58) can also be interpreted in a different way:

One might argue that these institutions have not established a proprietary investor ACPM unit in order to encounter sluggish growth of credit assets through increased impact on the primary market side and to open up new business opportunities on the secondary credit market. Rather, the argument could be put forward that these institutions have set up a proprietary investor in order to support their aspiration to change their overall business strategy from a strong customer relationship orientation, aspiring to "run" a large loan book towards a more product-/capital market orientation aiming at primarily using the credit assets on their books as a basis to generate fee-based follow-on business on secondary markets, e.g., through creating and distributing structured credit products. If this argument was true, the on average negative RWA growth of proprietary investors would be a consequence rather than a cause of this business model.

The relationship between the overall business strategy of participating institutions in the empirical study and the ACPM business model they have implemented will be analyzed in greater detail in chapter 5.1.3.1. At this point, the argument that a negative RWA growth is actually a consequence rather than a cause of establishing a proprietary investor ACPM unit does not seem to be unrealistic – albeit only seeming feasible for long enough established ACPM units: As shown in Figure 77 in appendix A, 40% of all proprietary investors were set up less than a year ago (taking beginning of 2005 as a reference point), another 20% only between two and five years ago. In view of the fact that the analysis on RWA growth shown in Figure 59 has been performed by taking an average of data over the time horizon from 1998 to 2004, with the negative RWA growth being a trend over the entire time spectrum and not only over the last few years considered, such an argument may at most hold for the 40% of the proprietary investors set up more than five years ago, i.e., before the year 2000

803 See again chapter 2.3.3.1.2 of part II

804 Risk controllers have not been considered in this analysis: on the one hand, their organizational location within the institution's risk unit is obvious. On the other hand, while all executives of risk units that have been interviewed in the course of the empirical study stated that they aspire to move towards a business model foreseeing the active management of credit risks, in most cases they have not yet been able to name a senior executive outside their risk unit who would drive the project to set up an ACPM unit. Therefore, the analysis where active advisors and proprietary investors stand in terms of senior management support for establishing their ACPM business model aims at providing a guidance for risk controllers who should be the optimal executives to convince as initiators and sponsors for the establishment of an ACPM unit

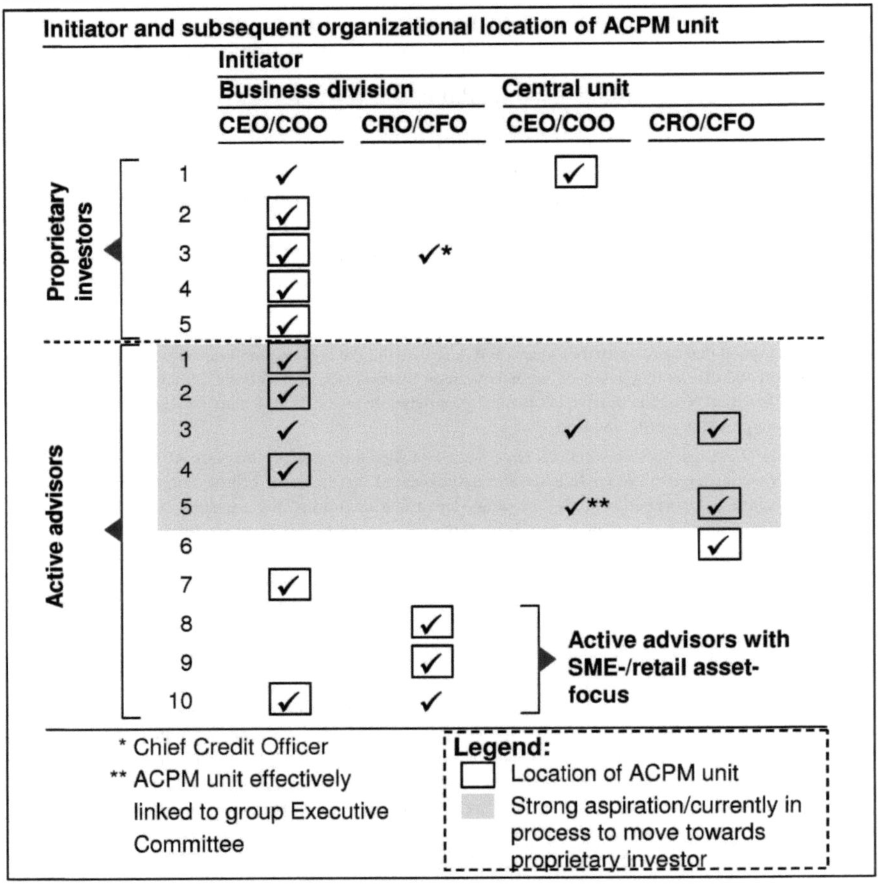

Figure 59: Initiator and subsequent organizational location of ACPM unit[805]

The empirical study has revealed that all proprietary investors but one are situated within a BU of their institution. A main reason for this organizational location is the fact that the implementation has been driven by the CEO or COO of this BU, in one case strongly supported by the BU's Chief Credit Officer. The establishment of the proprietary investor that is centrally located within its organization reporting directly to the CEO has been initiated and strongly driven by the institution's CEO. Focusing

805 Source: Own illustration based on results of empirical study on ACPM

on the acquisition of wholesale asset-related credit risks, however, this participant has reported that it has also been a crucial criterion for a successful implementation to obtain support from the CEO of the wholesale BU.

A somewhat different picture emerges for active advisors:

Three of the five active advisors aspiring to further develop their business model towards a proprietary investor or just being in the process of doing so are located in their institution's BU, with the CEO or COO of this unit supporting the further development of these units.

Another institution is currently significantly changing its approach towards managing credit assets: having set up an active advisor ACPM unit which has historically been located within the central finance unit of the institution, it is aspired to set up two different ACPM units at the initiative of the group CEO and strongly driven by the group CFO – being owner of the current ACPM unit – as well as by the CEO of the wholesale BU: Besides a proprietary investor located in the wholesale BU focusing on the management of this unit's credit exposures, it is planned to equip the active advisor in the CFO unit with the competence to manage the institution's credit exposures on an aggregated level, mainly to grasp benefits from a group-wide diversification of credit exposures. Hence, like the other advisors aiming at moving towards a proprietary investor business model, it is the Head of the BU in which the newly set-up proprietary investor unit is to be located who is driving its development.

There is one active advisor in the empirical sample focusing on management of wholesale credit assets and located in the central finance unit of its institution. So far, the main aspiration of the ACPM unit has been to optimize the risk/return profile of its institution's loan portfolio, in particular through reduction of single name concentration risks. Accordingly, the functional focus has been on advising, initiating and pricing of secondary credit market transactions which have subsequently been executed through trading desks in the institution's wholesale BU. When interviewing the Head of ACPM, a strong interest was expressed to develop the unit towards a proprietary investor business model. In this context, it became clear that a crucial next step will be an organizational relocation of the unit. Being convinced that setting up a proprietary investor requires a move from the central finance unit closer to the primary market side of the institution, it is aspired to have the newly set-up ACPM unit located in the institution's wholesale BU. Therefore, it is seen as a crucial next step to get the buy-in and support of the wholesale BU's CEO to realize these plans.

Two wholesale asset-focused active advisors do not aspire to move further towards a proprietary investor any time soon:

One of them has been set up at the initiative of the group CRO within the institution's central risk unit, with a major goal being the hedging and reduction of single name concentration risks through initiation of corresponding secondary credit market transactions. To support that functional focus, the central risk unit is seen as the optimal organizational location for this ACPM unit. As there is currently no intention to develop the unit towards an asset transferring proprietary investor – neither by the Head of ACPM nor by the CRO as the ultimate responsible for the ACPM unit –, the central risk unit is seen as the ideal organizational location for the unit.

The other wholesale-oriented active advisor not aspiring to move towards a proprietary investor has been set up by the COO of the institution's wholesale banking BU. The main reason it is not aspired to develop this unit towards a proprietary investor is the strong conviction – especially of the ACPM Head – that a thereby induced stronger product/capital market business strategy of the institution would result in sustainable harm to customer relationships. Having traditionally followed a relationship banking approach and regarding credit as a core business that provides a stable interest income stream, sound credit-based customer relationships are seen as crucial for the institution's business activities. Therefore, it has been argued that the implementation of a proprietary investor business model according to which ACPM takes over credit assets in order to manage the credit portfolio at its discretion might have an adverse effect on customer relationships. Furthermore, in view of the more distribution-focused approach proprietary investors take towards managing credit assets, it is reasoned that such a business model might cause major conflicts within the banking organization. Hence, despite having the organizational set-up which, according to a comparison with the established proprietary investors, would enable the successful implementation of a proprietary investor ACPM unit, such a development is not aspired to.[806]

The three SME-/retail asset-focused active advisors in the empirical sample do not regard a move towards proprietary investor as beneficial. The set-up of two of these units has been driven by the BU's CRO, one of them has been established at the initiative of the BU's CEO. It is mainly for reasons that are primarily seen in the credit market environment, however,[807] that there is no aspiration to develop these units towards a proprietary investor business model.[808]

---

806 In this context see chapter 5.1.3.1 discussing an impact of the institutions' business strategy as a determinant for the set-up of their ACPM units

807 In this context also see chapter 5.2 illustrating the credit market environment as a determinant for the set-up of an ACPM unit

808 Resentment against a move of these institutions' active advisors towards proprietary investor business models has also been expressed by senior managers of customer BUs: these executives have voiced the concern that a proprietary investor ACPM unit quoting binding prices towards origination through its own pricing model based on which it subsequently takes over credit assets, may have an incentive to exploit its pricing power in order to obtain arbitrage benefits. Such arbitrage benefits are feared to be possible due to the lack of comparable market prices in these rather illiquid credit markets with which the model-based prices set by ACPM can be compared. As a consequence of these arbitrage incentives for ACPM, origination may be confronted with a binding settlement price for a particular credit asset that is above its true value, potentially inducing an inflated shortfall compensation payment. Cultural conflicts between origination, typically primarily driven and incentivized by generation of customer revenues, and ACPM, typically taking on a risk

This analysis has been performed to explore from which unit within an institution the establishment of a targeted ACPM business model should be ideally driven to ensure its successful implementation. It has been confirmed that the initiator and sponsor of an ACPM unit seems to be a major determinant for its eventual organizational location. In particular, as shown by all proprietary investors in the empirical sample, the strong support of the business BU's CEO, whose assets are to be acquired by the proprietary investor, is a crucial success factor for the implementation of such a business model. This typically leads to its actual location in the respective BU.[809] By contrast, if driven from a central level within the institution, mostly at the initiative of the group CRO or CFO, ACPM units are characteristically set up as active advisors located in these central units with a primary functional focus on secondary market transactions, chiefly reducing (single name concentration) credit risks.[810] It has become clear that the transformation of such an advisory business model towards a proprietary investor requires a strong commitment from the BU's CEO and, ultimately, an organizational relocation of the unit.

This analysis has shown that the set-up of an ACPM business model appears to be determined by its initiator and sponsor at senior management/board level. It has also been proven, however, that there may be other determinants that are weighted more strongly for the decision on the specification of an ACPM business model than the question who actually is the initiator and sponsor of the ACPM unit: although disposing of the organizational prerequisites to develop its unit towards a proprietary investor, the Head of ACPM of the above-mentioned active advisor located in the COO unit of its institutions' wholesale BU is convinced that the move towards such a business model would have significantly adverse effects on the institution's customer relationship-oriented business strategy and imply a negative impact on existing customer relationships. Similarly, the SME-/retail asset-focused active advisors, which, judging from their organizational location and senior management sponsorship might be well positioned to move towards a proprietary investor see the credit market conditions they operate in as a major hurdle for the further development of their unit

view when pricing credit assets, may aggravate such a discrepancy between these units

What is considered by some advisors aiming at increasing their empowerment towards the primary market side, however, is to establish a shortfall compensation system foreseeing that origination's account is charged with a shortfall compensation should it close transactions that are below the risk-adjusted model price quoted by ACPM. As ACPM does not receive the shortfall compensation payments, there would not be an incentive to generate arbitrage benefits

809 The only proprietary investor not located in the institution's BU is the one acquiring risks of the institution's largest credit customers in a synthetic form from the wholesale BU. It has not been regarded as feasible by this institution to establish a physical transfer of the credit assets from their originating wholesale BU to the centrally located ACPM unit

810 See again chapter 4.4 regarding the functional competence of active advisors and especially Footnote 713 on particular characteristics of SME-/retail-focused advisors

towards such a business model. The determinants of the business strategy of an institution and credit market environment will be discussed in greater detail below.

5.1.3 Governance principles of institution

Existing literature on ACPM describes the redefinition of a bank's business strategy from a primary customer relationship focus towards a higher degree of product-/capital market orientation as an essential precondition for setting up a proprietary investor ACPM unit.[811] Therefore, it has been examined with the help of the empirical study to what extent the implementation of a specific CPM business model is related to the overall business strategy of an institution. Besides this, the relation between the existence of an aligned incentive structure and the implementation of a specific ACPM business model has been analyzed.

5.1.3.1 Business strategy

Most of the participants in the empirical study are universal banks (see again Figure 37). Yet, when examining a set of financial ratios, it becomes obvious that the institutions covered seem to differ with regard to their business strategy:

It can be differentiated between institutions primarily focusing on commercial banking activities, on the one hand, and others being rather set up as investment banks on the other hand. The former types of banks are characterized by an emphasis of their business activities on accepting deposits and granting loans, thus regarding strong and stable relationships with their lending customers as crucial for their business activities. The latter types of banks primarily focus on underwriting and trading of securities, consequently having a higher product-/capital market orientation.[812]

Accordingly, commercial banking-oriented institutions dispose of a higher share of customer loans in their total asset base than their investment banking-oriented counterparts do. Commercial banking business activities related to taking on deposits and granting loans primarily yield interest income. By contrast, through performing investment banking business, an institution mainly earns fee and trading income.[813]

Based on these typical characteristics, the 22 participants in the empirical study on ACPM have been clustered according to their ratio of outstanding loans to total assets, their relations of fee and trading income to interest income as well as their relation between fee and total operating income.[814] The thereby indicated primary business

811 See again chapter 2.3.3.1.3 of part II

812 See also again chapter 1.3 of part II on the different types of banks

813 See, for example, Hartmann-Wendels, Pfingsten et al. (2004), p. 780 et seqq. on the different types of income into which the P&L statement of a financial institution can be subdivided

814 Unfortunately, due to mostly insufficient segment information, it has not been possible to isolate the ratios for the BUs that include the CPM units of the surveyed institutions. However, when analyzing the data of the bancassurance groups included in the empirical sample, it has been possible to retrieve data from the

strategy of the institutions has been compared with their currently pursued CPM business models in order to find out whether, as suggested by literature, a certain CPM business model requires a particular business strategy.

Figure 60 illustrates a ranking of the survey participants according to their ratio of outstanding customer loans to total assets, indicating clear differences between the institutions. The banks that have most of their total assets bound in customer loans – including five players whose customer loan book constitutes more than two thirds of their total asset base – can be regarded as commercial banking-focused institutions putting a strong emphasis on stable customer relationships. By contrast, there are seven players in the sample with a ratio of outstanding customer loans to total assets of less than a third. Apparently, these banks do not regard holding a large loan book, which is a major source for generating interest income and also constituting a strong customer focus, as their core business activity but primarily pursue a product/capital market business strategy.

In contrast to what has been described by literature on ACPM, however, not all the proprietary investor ACPM units in the empirical sample are to be found among the more investment banking-oriented institutions putting a major emphasis on product/and capital market business. Rather, 40% of the proprietary investors are set up in the group of 11 participants whose outstanding customer loans constitute about 65% of their total asset base. This group of primarily customer relationship-focused institutions also includes 30% of the active advisors and 66% of the risk controllers.

A similar picture emerges when clustering the participating institutions according to their ratios of fee to interest income (see Figure 61) as well as according to trading to interest income (see Figure 62) and relating the observations to the types of CPM business models established: among the 11 institutions with the lowest ratios of fee and trading to interest income – indicating a business strategy focusing on interest income-generating lending business and a subsequently strong customer orientation – there are 60% proprietary investors. The cluster of the 11 institutions with the lowest fee to interest income ratio also includes 60% of the active advisors and 33% of the risk controllers. The 11 participants with the lowest trading to interest income ratios include 40% of all active advisors and 55% of the risk controllers.[815]

These analyses show that there does not seem to be an unambiguous relation between the business strategy of a financial institution and its decision to implement a certain ACPM business model. In particular, the statement put forward by literature on ACPM that the move towards a proprietary investor business model requires the development of an institution's business strategy towards a greater level of capital market

banking BUs only in order to avoid distorting effects from the institutions' insurance BUs

815 A similar picture emerges from a comparison of the survey participants' ratio between fee and total operating income with their chosen ACPM business model, see Figure 79 in Appendix A

orientation cannot be confirmed by the empirical results given that there are some strongly customer relationship-focused institutions which have also successfully implemented such an ACPM business model.[816] Consequently, there must be other factors influencing the specification of an ACPM business model that weigh more strongly than the institution's overall business strategy.

816 However, as already shown before (see again chapter 5.1.2 outlining the example of an active advisor that does not intend to move towards a proprietary investor for reasons of aspiring to maintain strong customer relationships), a different opinion among strongly relationship-focused institutions also exists: Although often disposing of the organizational prerequisites to successfully develop the existing advisory ACPM unit into a proprietary investor, it is refrained from going this way mainly for fear of a significant deterioration in strong relationships to key lending customers

Still, the findings presented in this chapter are no contradiction to the argumentation brought forward in Footnote 802 that the establishment of a particular ACPM unit (in this case a proprietary investor) has been undertaken to support the change of an institution's overall business strategy

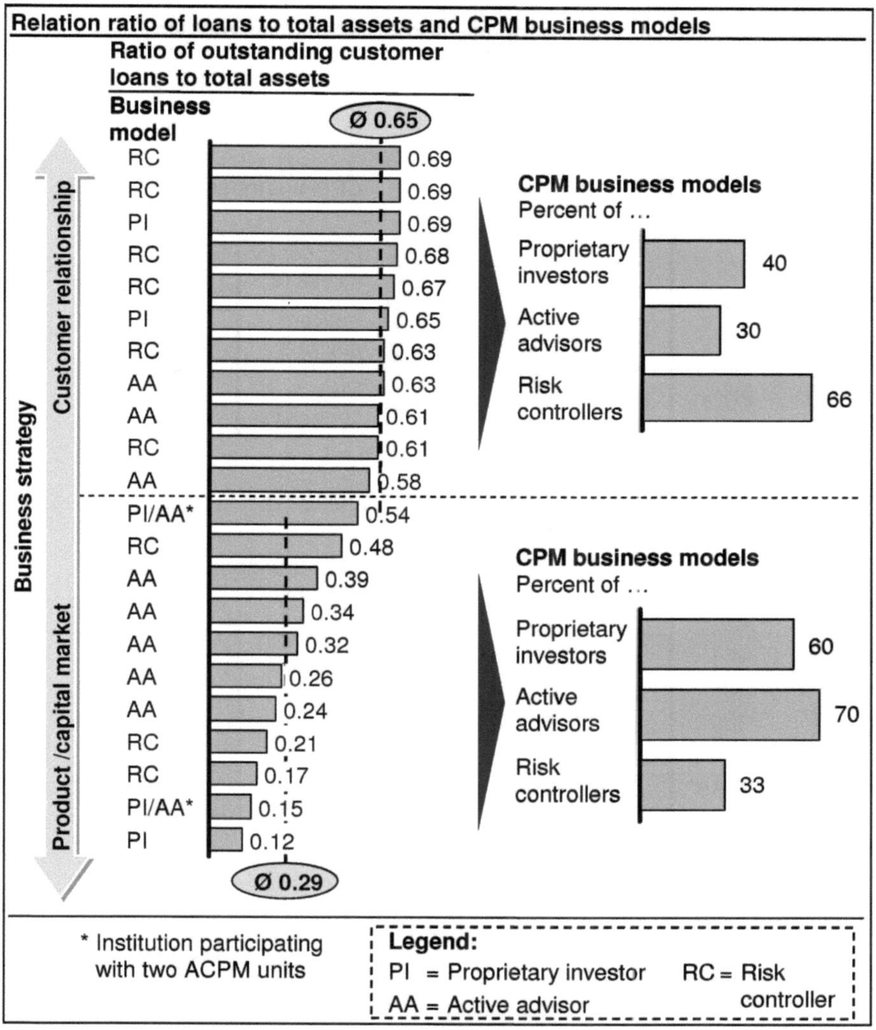

Figure 60: Relation ratio of loans to total assets and CPM business models[817]

[817] Source: Own illustration. Information on CPM business models based on results of empirical study on ACPM. Ratio of loans to total assets based on research in Datastream and Bloomberg databases and derived

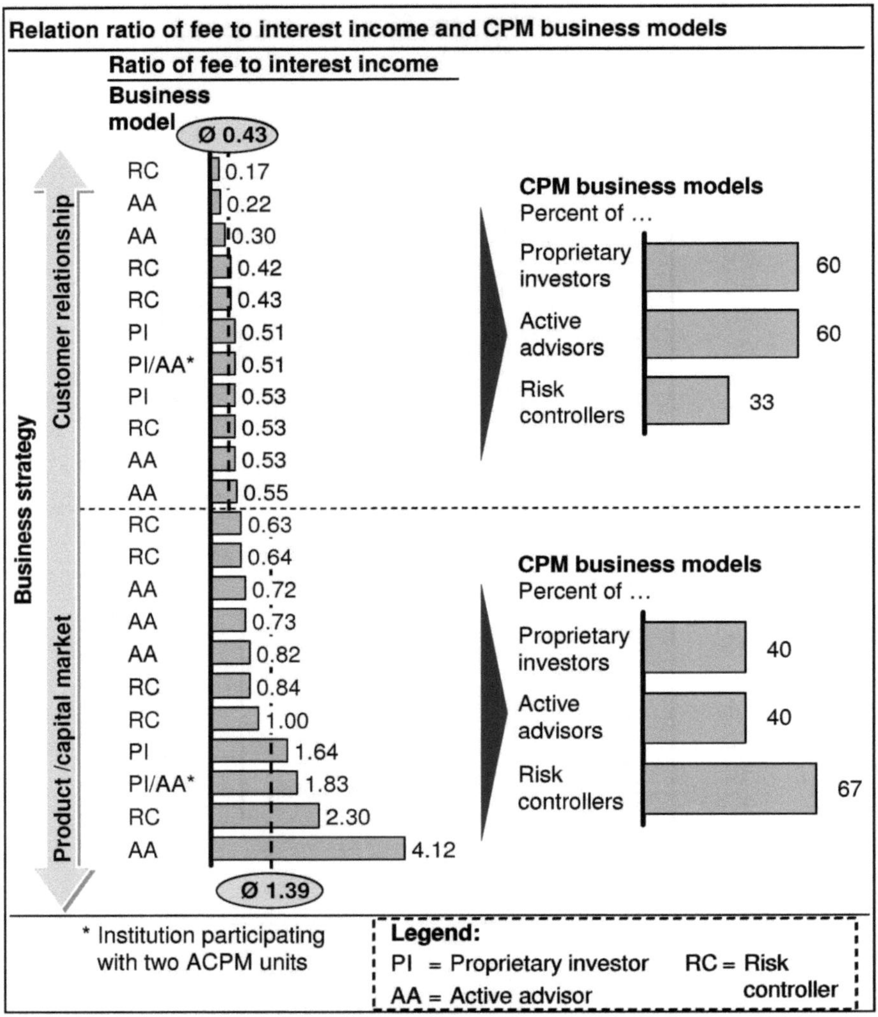

Figure 61: Relation ratio of fee to interest income and CPM business models[818]

from annual reports

818 Source: Analogous to Figure 60

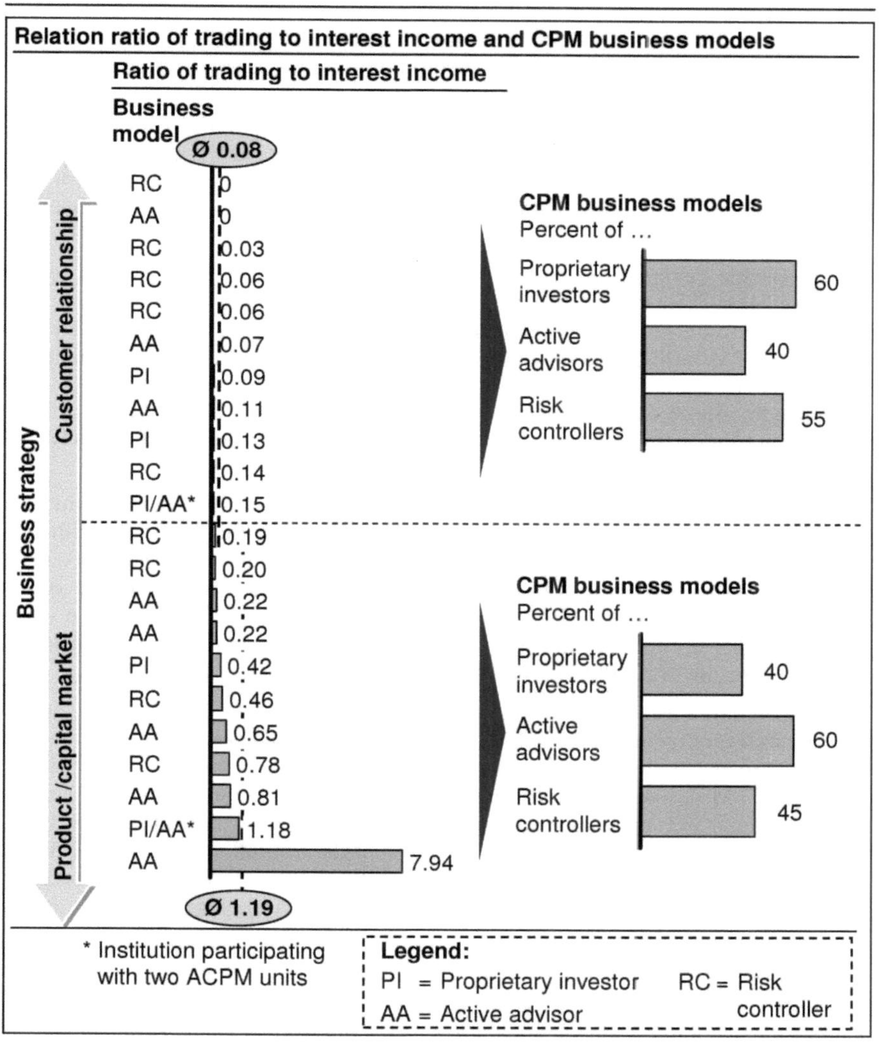

Figure 62: Relation ratio of trading to interest income and CPM business models[819]

[819] Source: Analogous to Figure 60

5.1.3.2 Incentive structure

In view of the significant changes of an institution's approach towards lending business that are induced by the implementation of an ACPM business model, it is necessary to have clearly defined incentives in place that are aligned with the goals of the different units affected by ACPM activities.[820] Particularly, it is necessary to sufficiently motivate staff – besides ACPM employees, this applies especially for staff of origination and secondary credit market units – to act according to the goals of the newly-set up ACPM unit.[821]

Since specific exigencies are expected to be required for the successful implementation of the different ACPM business models identified, it was examined whether there is a relation between institutions' incentive system structures and the types of ACPM business models implemented. For this purpose, survey participants were asked to name to which extent an alignment of their CPM objectives with corresponding incentives for their own and for other units has been achieved. Figure 63 illustrates the analysis of the responses to this question provided by active advisors and proprietary investors.

Not all participants that have implemented an active advisor or proprietary investor ACPM unit consider the objectives set for this unit to be fully reflected either in ACPM's own incentives or in the ones for origination or secondary market units. Only 60% of the proprietary investors and active advisors report a full alignment of the objectives set for ACPM with their own incentive structure. There are even some institutions that do not consider their ACPM units' objectives to be reflected in the incentive structure of ACPM, origination, and secondary market units at all.[822]

The biggest difference between the two types of ACPM business models seems to exist regarding alignment of ACPM objectives and incentives for origination and secondary market units: 60% of all institutions that have established a proprietary investor ACPM business model regard the objectives of this unit to be fully aligned with origination and secondary market units, while another 20% consider this as being at least partially fulfilled. By contrast, only 10% of the institutions that have set up an active advisor business model consider the goals of their ACPM unit to be fully reflected in origination's incentives; 90% of the active advisors regard this as partially

820 See also again chapter 2.3.3.1.3 of part II

821 Sufficient motivation of staff through providing incentives for the employees to act in accordance to the objectives set for ACPM is especially required in view of the cultural conflicts existing between ACPM and origination. These conflicts are typically based on the fact that originators/relationship managers are incentivized by different performance metrics than portfolio managers; see again Figure 45

822 The proprietary investor reporting that the objectives for ACPM are not clearly reflected in the incentives of ACPM, origination, and secondary market units is the one whose unit has most recently been established. Accordingly, it is the longest established proprietary investors in the sample reporting a full reflection of objectives in related incentives

given. 40% of the active advisors consider their ACPM objectives to be clearly aligned with the incentives of secondary market units, 30% see such an alignment as partially fulfilled.

Extent of clearly defined and aligned incentive structure

"Are the objectives for your ACPM unit clearly reflected in and aligned with the incentives for management and staff in ACPM and other units?"

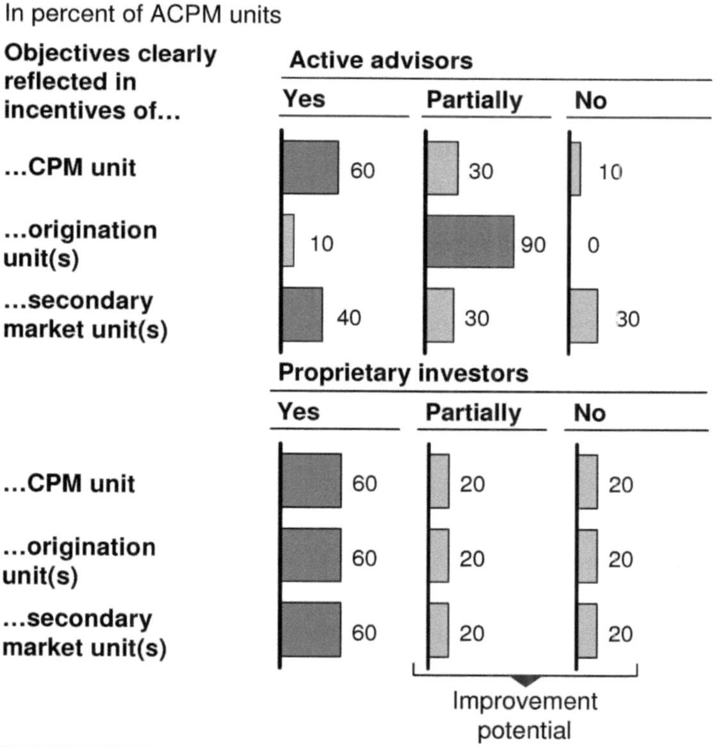

Figure 63: Extent of clearly defined and aligned incentive structure[823]

Clearly, both for proprietary investors and active advisors there seems to be room for improvement regarding a clear reflection of these ACPM units' objectives in their own

[823] Source: Own illustration based on results of empirical study on ACPM

incentive structure as well as in the ones of origination and secondary credit market units. Nevertheless, it is particularly the longest established and most effectively functioning proprietary investors which report a full alignment between such objectives and incentive structures. This indicates that a well-defined, aligned and implemented incentive structure seems to be a crucial enabler and precondition for the successful implementation of a value-maximizing proprietary investor business model.[824]

Further to analyzing the impact of internal determinants on the approaches to managing credit portfolios taken by financial institutions, in the following section, the relation between specifications of external determinants and implemented CPM business models will be examined.

5.2 Relation between specifications of external determinants and established CPM business models

Chapter 5.1.1 has examined the impact of a financial institution's historical economic performance on its primary CPM objectives and its chosen business model. Further to its individual economic situation, the credit market environment in which an institution operates is seen as a key determinant for the design of its approach towards managing credit portfolios.[825] Hence, it will be examined in the following section which characteristics of primary and secondary credit markets have led participants in the empirical study to the choice for a particular CPM business model.[826]

---

[824] The proprietary investors reporting a full alignment between objectives and incentive structure are the ones generating additional economic value for their institutions' credit business along all four dimensions described in chapter 4.5 and Figure 55

The fact that most of the active advisors appear to struggle with getting the incentives of their origination BUs well aligned with their ACPM goals may also be a result of the typical cultural conflicts between these units that have been mentioned before. These cultural differences between origination and ACPM have been perceived as a major hurdle on the path to successfully establishing an ACPM business model (see again 4.3.2 and Figure 45). Proprietary investors have best overcome cultural differences towards origination, mainly due to a dedicated senior management involvement and support for the ACPM business model

[825] See again chapter 2.3.3.2 of part II introducing the credit market environment as an external determinant for the design of CPM business models.

The analysis of typical implementation barriers faced by the different CPM business models identified in the empirical study on ACPM has confirmed that the credit market environment in which institutions operate crucially determines their ability and hence their possible approach towards actively managing loan portfolios; see again chapter 4.3.2

[826] One could argue that an institution's individual profitability already reflects the impact the credit market environment has on its approach to managing loan portfolios. It seems obvious that the credit market environment determines a bank's individual economic performance, which, in turn, is a determinant for the objectives it has for its CPM unit and the chosen type of CPM business model. Yet, there are other factors than the market environment influencing the performance of an institution's credit business: for example, the performance is impacted by a managerial decision on which types/segments of credit assets to focus the

With help of these analyses, it is aspired to support the decision-making process regarding which type of CPM business model should best be implemented if an institution faces a certain market environment.

5.2.1 Primary market characteristics

Figure 64 illustrates the credit market conditions of the seven countries in which most of the institutions surveyed are located and puts them in relation to the types of CPM business models found in the different markets.[827] The markets have been characterized along four dimensions: (I) Level of competition, measured by banking concentration as the ratio of "number of banks per million inhabitants", (II) Profitability, indicated by the average net interest margin,[828] (III) Riskiness, measured by the ratio of "average LLP divided by average customer loans" and (IV) Market growth, i.e., growth of customer loans over the past few years.[829] The market conditions have been compared with the types and numbers of ACPM units that have been set up in the respective markets.[830]

---

institution's credit business. Therefore, an institution's individual profitability does not give a pure picture of the market conditions faced and their impact on the lending approach. As a consequence, it appears necessary to perform a separate analysis mapping the economic conditions of different credit markets on the approach towards managing credit portfolios chosen by players that operate in these markets

827 Austria, Belgium, and Ireland have not been covered by the analysis for the main reason being that each of these countries merely includes one of the ACPM units covered in the empirical sample

When illustrating the CPM business models found in the different countries, some nations have been aggregated where possible without negatively influencing the explanatory power of the analysis. The reason for this aggregation has be the goal to preserve confidentiality of the empirical information provided by the survey participants

828 The net interest margin has been calculated as net interest income in percent of total average assets; see, e.g., Hartmann-Wendels, Pfingsten et al. (2004), p. 781

829 It has been aspired to perform the analysis of the credit markets' economic situations analogous to the analysis of the individual banks' (BUs') economics illustrated in Figure 57 and Figure 58, which has been performed along the criteria profitability of the institutions as well as the riskiness and growth of their loan books.

However, as opposed to the analysis of individual banks or, where data available, the BUs in which their CPM unit is located, better data availability for the aggregated credit markets has enabled the use of information which more closely reflects credit business activities: net interest margin gives a more exact picture of the credit business profitability than the ROE figure used before. Taking LLP as a percentage of customer loans instead of as percentage of RWA and growth of customer loans instead of RWA growth more accurately reflects the riskiness and growth characteristics of credit markets

The latest available data on number of banks per million inhabitants in the different countries stems from 2003. The average net interest margins have been calculated based on data between 2001 and 2004, for Switzerland between 2001 and 2003. The ratios of LLP to customer loans as well as growth of customer loans are based on average data between 1999 and 2003

830 In view of the relative small sample of ACPM units included in the empirical study, the anonymity and

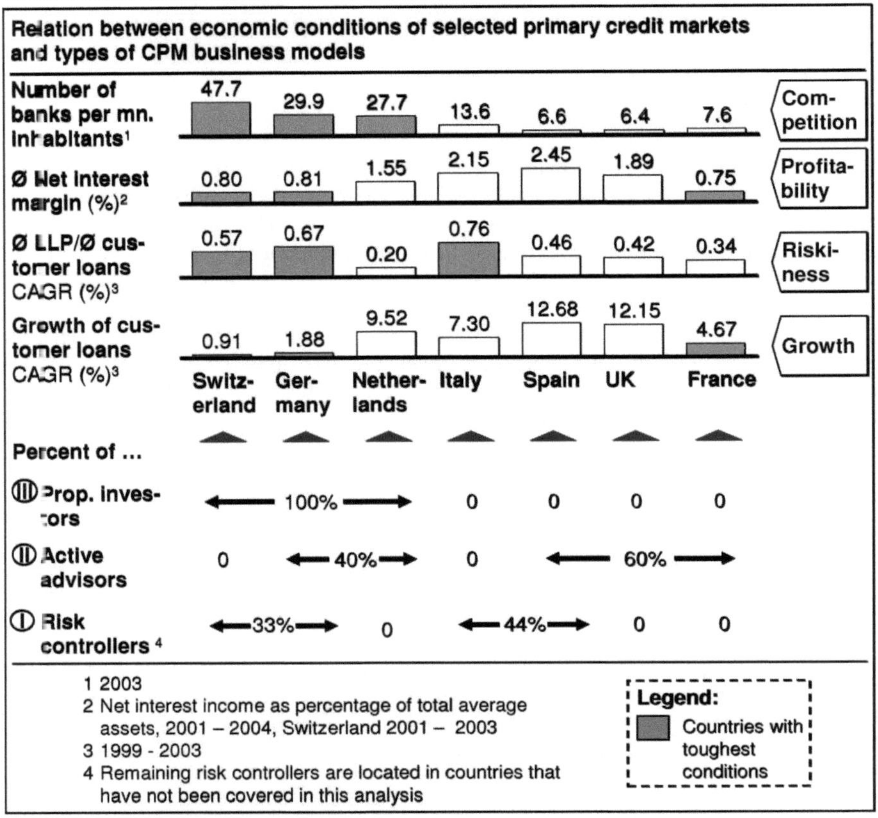

Figure 64: Relation between economic conditions of selected primary credit markets and types of CPM business models[831]

confidentiality of the information provided by the participating institutions might not be guaranteed any longer if the exact number of the CPM business models to be found in each country was displayed. Therefore, Figure 64 illustrates percentage ranges of the types of CPM units that have been set up in the seven credit markets considered for this analysis

[831] Source: Own illustration

Information on CPM business models based on results of empirical study on ACPM

Statistics on number of banks per million inhabitants, LLP, and customer loans derived from following sources:

Information for Germany derived from Bundesbank (2005b), Bundesbank (2005a), Bundesbank (2003b) and

The analysis has revealed that the economic conditions of the credit markets covered in the empirical study differ substantially:

The highest banking concentration can be found in Switzerland, Germany, and the Netherlands, indicating that these are the markets with the highest level of competition among financial institutions. By contrast, the UK, Spain, France, and also Italy are countries with a significantly lower number of banks per inhabitants.

High competition among financial institutions in Switzerland and Germany may also be a main reason for the fact that credit business in these countries is the least profitable, as indicated by historical average net interest margins. France seems to have a similarly unprofitable credit market, while the other countries, especially Spain, Italy, and the UK enjoy considerably higher average net interest margins.

It is Switzerland and Germany whose credit markets are characterized by the highest average LLP, followed by Italy. A clearly less risky credit market environment can be found in the Netherlands, France, the UK, and Spain.

Besides apparently having the riskiest credit markets, Switzerland and Germany also dispose of the markets characterized by the most sluggish credit demand. All other countries covered in the analysis have seen a much higher average growth of customer loans in recent years, with Spain, the UK, and the Netherlands at the forefront of market growth.

When comparing the CPM business models found in the empirical sample to the different credit markets analyzed, a relation between the economic conditions of the markets and the types of CPM business models becomes apparent: Proprietary investor ACPM units are to be found in countries with the toughest credit market conditions, with most of these units having been set up in Switzerland and Germany. By contrast, in countries enjoying the most comfortable credit market environment – above all in

---

Bundesbank (2004)

Information on Dutch credit market based on DNB (2005), DNB (2004), DNB (2003), DNB (2002), DNB (2001), and DNB (2000)

Information on French credit market derived from CECI (2005) and Banque de France (2004)

Information on Swiss credit market derived from Schweizerische Nationalbank (2004) and Schweizerische Nationalbank (2003)

Information on Spanish credit market based on CECA (2004), CECA (2003) and CECA (2002) for savings banks and based on AEB (2004), AEB (2003), AEB (2002) as well as AEB (2001) for other Spanish banks

Information on UK banks have been derived from Bankscope database covering about 98% of all UK-based institutions with a business focus on the UK. This procedure has been taken to avoid distortions from a large share of global banks (especially Investment Banks) which have their headquarters in the UK but performing global instead of UK-focused business

Data on net interest margins for all countries except for Switzerland have been obtained in an aggregated form from BIS (2004a), p. 123 Table VII.1 and ECB (2005) p. 51 et seq. Table 14

Spain, the UK and, except for their high LLP, in Italy, the banks have set up their CPM units as active advisors or risk controllers.

Interpreting these findings shows that they are in line with the results of the comparison between the institutions' individual profitability and their primary objectives, and, accordingly, the CPM business models they focus on: players operating in the toughest credit market environments, spearheaded by German and Swiss institutions, have had to find ways how to make their credit business more profitable. They have also had to open up new fields of growth in light of sluggish credit demand on the primary market side which they have aspired to achieve, e.g., through reinvesting freed-up capital on secondary credit markets. As these objectives could best be realized through implementing a proprietary investor ACPM unit, these business models can currently be found in the least profitable and slowest growing credit markets. By contrast, institutions, which have not faced such a strong pressure on their lending margins but have rather been able to enjoy a benign market environment that is characterized by high profitability and growing credit demand of debtors, have typically not faced pressure to significantly change their approach towards bank lending to improve the profitability of credit business, which would strongly suggest the implementation of a proprietary investor business model. As a consequence, these institutions – mainly located in Southern European countries and the UK – have at most set up an active advisor ACPM unit. Many of them still pursue the conventional originate and hold approach towards bank lending. The characteristic main focus of these players' CPM units is to protect their loan book against possibly future downturns in the credit cycle to avoid or at least minimize loan losses.

Apparently, the economic conditions of the primary credit market in which an institution operates crucially determine the set-up of its CPM unit. Further to the primary market conditions, it has been shown before that the existence and sufficient liquidity of a secondary credit market is essential for successfully setting up an ACPM unit.[832] Besides this, it has already been revealed that favorable credit market conditions are pivotal for successfully enabling the realization of CPM objectives.[833]

In order to obtain a systematic derivation of the optimal approach towards lending business that should be implemented given specific conditions of secondary credit markets, it will be examined in the following section to which extent the design of the surveyed participants' CPM units has been determined by the secondary credit market environment they face.

[832] See again chapter 2.3.3.2 of part II

[833] See again chapter 4.3.2 displaying that secondary credit market illiquidity is regarded as the main implementation barrier on the path to a more successful realization of CPM units' objectives

5.2.2 Existence and liquidity of secondary credit market

5.2.2.1 Existence of secondary credit market

Further to the illustration of recent developments on markets for loan sales and syndication, credit derivatives as well as for asset securitization provided in chapter three of part II, analyses have been performed aiming at determining in which of the seven countries that include most of the CPM units covered by the empirical study one can best assume the existence of a significant secondary credit market that can be accessed to exchange credit risks. Afterwards, a comparison with the types of CPM business models to be found in the respective markets has been provided.[834]

Figure 65 illustrates in which countries the lead arrangers that have issued syndicated loans in 2004 are located. The goal of this analysis has been to find out which of the European countries under consideration dispose of the most significant syndicated loan markets, thus providing the institutions with the best opportunities to exchange credit risks on these markets.[835] UK institutions issued most of the syndicated loans in 2004 (29% of the entire European issuance volume), followed by French and German banks (having a 19% and 15% share in the total volume, respectively). Significantly smaller volumes have been issued by Dutch, Spanish, Italian and Swiss institutions. US players took a 13% share in the 2004 European syndicated loan issuance volume. As these players mostly operate from a London-based location when serving the European market,[836] their issuance volumes can effectively be assigned to the UK syndicated loan market.

In terms of outstanding volumes, the global credit derivatives market has experienced soaring growth in recent years, with CDS constituting the bulk of the outstanding contracts. Still, however, sufficiently liquid CDS markets which are characterized by a sufficient number of publicly quoted CDS prices on the reference entities' debt as well

[834] This analysis has in particular been motivated by the fact that the lack of markets on which credit risks can be exchanged has been named as a key implementation barrier for the objectives of ACPM units, see again chapter 4.3.2. As this implies the existence of incomplete markets (see again chapter 4.4.1.1 of part II), it has been aspired to find out which of the European secondary credit markets under examination in the empirical study can be considered the most complete ones. Furthermore, the goal has been to draw a comparison between the development stage of secondary credit markets and the typical types of CPM business models implemented

[835] This analysis has the weakness that the lead arranger may issue a syndicated loan which is eventually not placed in its home market. This might particularly be the case for UK-based investment banks that are frequently engaged in syndicated loan transactions outside the UK. Still, if it is assumed that the bulk of the syndicated loan volumes is eventually placed in the issuing institutions' national markets, the analysis gives an indication of the existence and significance of syndicated loan markets in these countries

[836] The largest US players in terms of European syndicated loan issuance that operate through a London-based subsidiary are Citigroup Inc., J.P. Morgan plc., Goldman, Sachs International Ltd. and Bank of America Securities Ltd.

as by actually traded CDS contracts mainly exist for the largest, typically investment grade-rated borrowers. Most of these contracts have a maturity between 1 and 5 years (see again chapter 3.2.4 of part II).

The goal has been to understand the magnitude of the market for credit derivative contracts in the individual countries covered by the empirical study on ACPM. Therefore, an analysis has been performed to explore how many reference entities on whose outstanding debt there are publicly quoted CDS prices are located in the different European markets. In a second step, then, the liquidity of the CDS markets in the different countries has been examined. This has followed the goal to find out in which European nations it is potentially easiest for an ACPM unit to exchange credit risks by means of CDS.

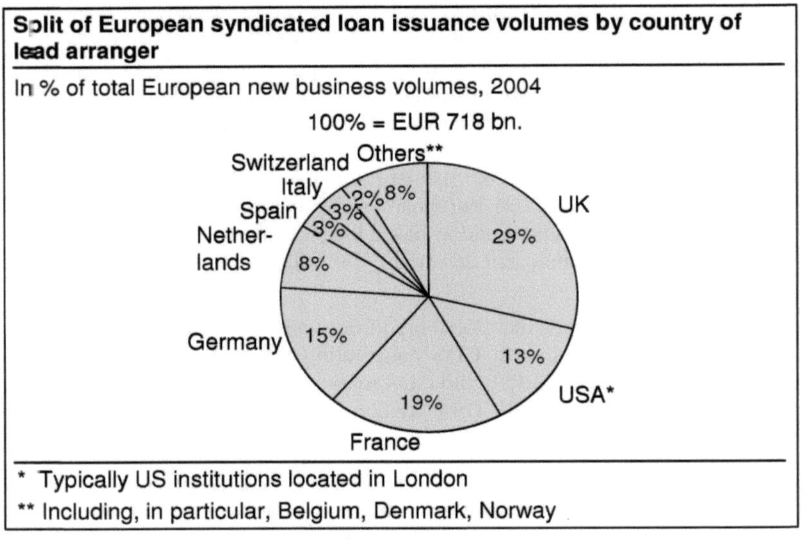

Figure 65: Split of European syndicated loan issuance volumes by country of lead arranger[837]

[837] Source: Own illustration based on research in Dealogic Loanware database

Number of European reference entities with publicly priced CDS contracts

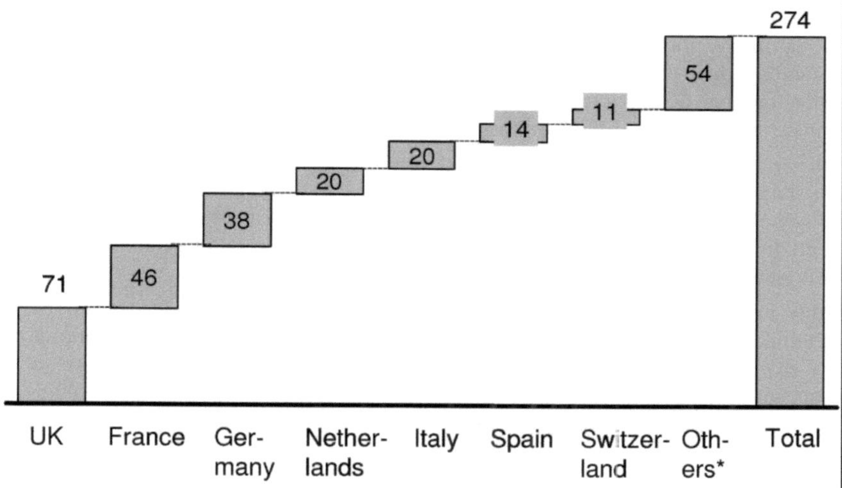

* Austria, Belgium, Denmark, Finland, Greece, Ireland, Luxemburg, Poland, Portugal, Sweden

Figure 66: Number of European reference entities with publicly priced CDS contracts[838]

Figure 66 shows the number of European reference entities on whose outstanding debt there are publicly quoted CDS contracts available having a maturity of 1, 3 or 5 years.[839] According to their origin, the reference entities have been subdivided into the

---

[838] Source: Own illustration based on research in Bloomberg database

[839] The analysis is based on information retrieved from the Bloomberg database. It covers all Euro-denominated CDS contracts on European reference entities. Except for the CDS contracts that are based on Government Bonds issued by Belgium, France, Germany, Greece, Italy, Portugal and Spain, the reference entities for the derivatives are corporations and financial institutions.

The maturity of the derivative contracts is 1, 3 or 5 years, hence, covering most of the CDS spectrum (see again BBA (2003/2004), p. 24 stating that around 75% of all publicly traded credit derivatives are in the maturity spectrum between 1 and 5 years). The maturity split of these contracts is illustrated in Figure 80 and Figure 81 in Appendix A. The prices of these contracts are quoted by Bloomberg based on an aggregation and averaging of individual prices quotes for these contracts provided by different financial institutions. Therefore, this list of CDS contracts does not only consider exchange traded CDS but also

seven nations in which most of the CPM units covered by the empirical study are located.

Based on this analysis, it has been found that countries differ significantly regarding number of contracts with outstanding publicly priced CDS names: followed by France and Germany, the UK is the nation housing most reference entities on whose outstanding debt there are publicly quoted CDS contracts available. A significantly smaller number of publicly priced CDS contracts exists for credits of Dutch, Italian, Spanish, and especially Swiss debtors.

A closer examination of the types of underlying reference entities has revealed that it is the largest corporations in these nations whose outstanding credit exposures can be exchanged by means of such derivatives.[840] This is another clear indication that it is the credit segment of wholesale banks for which there is a functioning secondary credit market.

Further to examining the market size for syndicated loans and credit derivatives, the magnitude of the asset securitization market in the different European countries has been explored. Therefore, based on the description of the developments in the European securitization market (see again chapter 3.3.4), the total volume of securitized instruments that were issued in 2004 has been split into the countries in which the instruments' underlying collateral is located.[841] The findings are illustrated in Figure 67.

Driven by the highest issuance volumes of Pfandbriefe in Europe, Germany is the country with the largest volumes of newly issued securitized instruments, constituting more than one third of the entire European securitization issuance volume in 2004. While the German market is insignificant in terms of ABS issuance, the opposite holds for the UK: with a 43% share in the European ABS market, which is primarily driven by MBS issuances, the UK is the second largest European market for total issuance of securitized products. Spain ranks second in terms of issuing Pfandbriefe and third regarding ABS issuances, which makes it the third-largest European securitization

covers all non-exchange traded CDS contracts in the respective maturity spectrum for which there is a publicly quoted price. It may be possible that some of the price quotes are "synthetic" in the sense that there are prices quoted for the contracts without the derivatives actually being traded

840 Typically, most of the corporations and financial institutions included in the analysis are represented in the countries' large cap stock indices. For example, 23 of the 38 German reference indices are represented in the Dax™ index representing the 30 exchange-listed German corporations with the highest market capitalization. Another five reference entities are represented in the MDax™ index representing the next 50 listed Germany corporations in terms of market capitalization. See, e.g., Börsenzeitung (2005), p. 16 for an overview of the corporations included in the Dax™ and MDax™ indices

841 The analysis was composed of the European ABS new issuance volumes (with ABS being broadly defined, i.e., including MBS, CDOs as well as ABS according to a narrow definition, i.e., securitized consumer credits) and the new issuance volumes of European Pfandbriefe

market.[842] Italy, France and the Netherlands have smaller market shares. Switzerland is an even tinier market for issuance of securitized products.

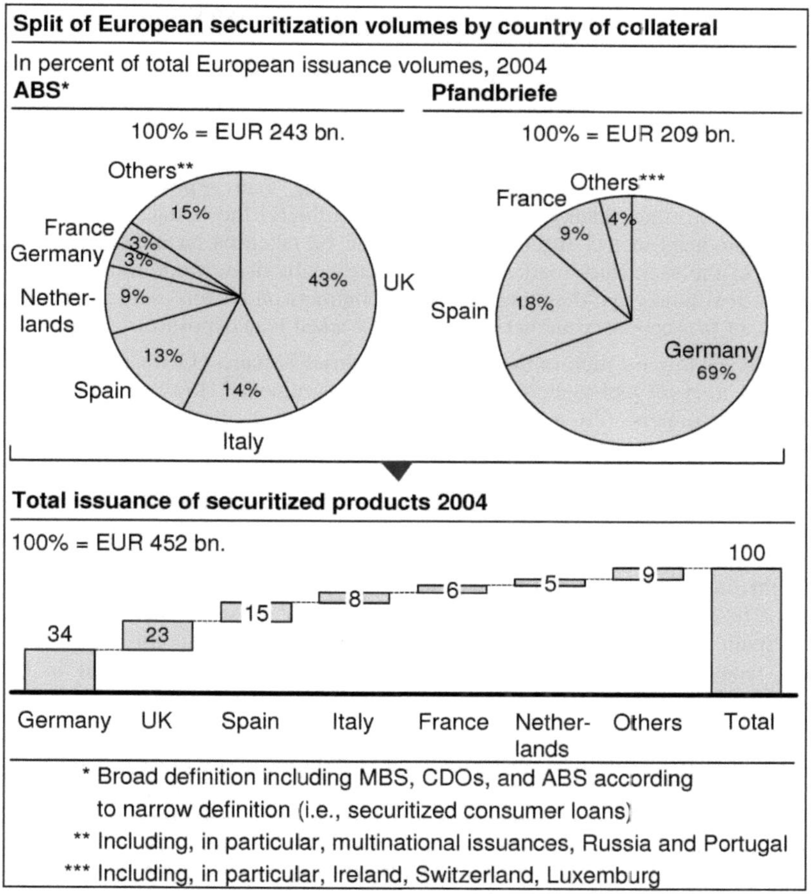

Figure 67: Split of European securitization issuance volumes by country of collateral[843]

[842] In the UK, MBS issuances constituted almost three quarters of the newly issued ABS in 2004, while Spanish MBS issuances had a share of nearly 60% in the newly issued ABS instruments in the same time period; see ESF (2005), p. 3

[843] Source: Own illustration based on information derived from ESF (2005)

Clearly, the European securitization market is characterized by real estate-related instruments: not only has almost half of the newly issued securitization volume in 2004 consisted of Pfandbriefe, nearly 60% of the ABS have been issued in the form of MBS, which has particularly been driven by the UK.[844]

With help of the analyses illustrated in Figure 65, Figure 66 and Figure 67, assumptions about the existence of secondary credit markets in the surveyed countries can be made. It has been shown that the European securitized instruments are mainly based on loan exposures towards real estate assets. Syndicated loans and CDS contracts, by contrast, are typically applied to trade loan exposures granted to corporations and other financial institutions. Accordingly, the issuance volumes of securitized products in the different countries can be taken as an indication of the magnitude of the secondary market for real estate credit risks, while the syndicated loan issuance volumes and the number of CDS contracts on lenders' debt assets point out the size of the secondary market for non asset-backed loan exposures.

Owing to its leading position in the field of Pfandbrief issuance, Germany represents the largest market for real estate-based securitized instruments. However, Pfandbriefe refinancing instruments do not enable the transfer of credit risks.[845] Therefore, Pfandbriefe do not constitute a secondary market allowing the exchange of credit risks. Consequently, as Germany only plays an insignificant role regarding issuance of ABS in general and MBS in particular, one cannot assume the existence of a secondary market for real estate-related credit risks in Germany. The UK, by contrast, is the largest European country in terms of ABS issuance, with MBS constituting the major share in this instrument group. This indicates that the UK is the European country in which it is best possible to trade real estate-related credit risks. Compared to the UK, in Italy, Spain, and the Netherlands, there are much smaller markets for the exchange of these types of risk. The French and Swiss markets are insignificant in this context.[846]

As the nation with the highest syndicated loan issuance volumes as indicated by the origin of the European lead arrangers as well as housing most European reference entities with publicly quoted CDS contracts on their debt, the UK can also be supposed to dispose of a significant secondary market for non asset-backed credit risks. France and Germany rank second and third in this context, respectively. The Netherlands, Italy, and particularly Spain and Switzerland seem to have a far less significant secondary market for these types of credit risks.

844 See also again Figure 28 for the European ABS issuance volumes over the past few years and their split in different securitization instruments

845 See again chapter 3.4.1.3 of part II

846 Again, as in the case of Germany, the comparably high Pfandbrief issuance volumes in the Spanish and French market do not indicate the existence of a secondary market for real estate credit risks

5.2.2.2 Liquidity of secondary credit market

The existence of an adequate secondary credit market is essential for an ACPM unit to be able to swap credit risks with other players. To what extent and at which costs exchanging such risks is possible, however, is determined by the liquidity of this market.[847]

It has been shown that the primary asset focus of most CPM units is on large- and mid-corps lending securities. Fewer units own or manage syndicated loans, small-corps, and retail lending assets or mortgage loans (see again Figure 41). From their major focus on loans granted to large- and mid-corps debtors, it can be implied that the ability of most CPM units is crucially dependent on the existence of secondary markets for this asset class. CDS play a significant role as instruments used to exchange these types of credit risks.[848] Therefore, by examining the liquidity of the national CDS markets in the seven countries in which most of the ACPM units included in the empirical study are located, it has been intended to discover the most supportive environment for an exchange of the most important credit risk class on which ACPM units focus.

A key determinant for the liquidity of a securities market is the so-called bid-ask spread of the assets traded on this market.[849] Small bid-ask spreads are an indication of high market liquidity.[850] Consequently, in order to understand the liquidity of their credit markets, the relative bid-ask spreads, i.e., the relations between the ask and bid prices of the CDS contracts in the seven countries analyzed above have been calculated. As illustrated in Figure 68, the individual relative bid-ask spreads have been averaged over the seven countries and maturities of the contracts.[851]

---

847 Since high secondary market liquidity facilitates the exchange of credit risks on these markets, it is an indication for their completeness, see again chapter 4.4 of part II

See also Gallati (2003), p. 431 for the role that market liquidity plays regarding transaction costs to be borne when exchanging credit risks

848 See also again Figure 51 and Figure 52 for the instruments used by ACPM units for risk distribution and investments

849 The bid price is the price at which a market maker is prepared to buy a security. Accordingly, the ask (or offer) price is the price at which he is prepared to sell the asset. The bid-ask spread is the amount by which the ask exceeds the bid price; see Hull (2006), p. 192

850 See Gallati (2003), p. 433

It is differentiated between exogenous and endogenous market liquidity. The former is a result of market characteristics; it is common to all market participants and cannot be influenced by the actions of one individual player. Besides the width of the bid-ask spreads of securities, the stability of the spreads as well as trading volumes of the securities are an indicator for market liquidity. Endogenous market liquidity, by contrast, is determined by the size of the position held: holding a larger position in an asset implies a higher endogenous liquidity

851 See again Figure 80 and Figure 81 for the number of contracts included in the analysis and their maturity

The analysis has revealed that judging from their average relative bid-ask spreads, markets for CDS contracts with a five-year maturity have the highest liquidity across all countries, followed by the ones for three-year maturity instruments.[852]

Interestingly, depending on the instruments' maturity, the countries considered rank differently regarding liquidity of their CDS markets: in the one-year maturity segment, the most liquid markets judging from the bid-ask spreads seem to be Spain, the Netherlands, Germany, and Italy. By far the highest spread between bid and ask prices exist for CDS contracts on Swiss debtors. Comparably illiquid markets for contracts with a maturity of one year also seem to be France and particularly the UK. A different picture emerges in the three- and five-year maturity segments, in which the UK and German markets are the most liquid ones.[853] Italy ranks third in terms of market liquidity for three-year CDS contracts but disposes of the least liquid market for five year instruments. The French market tends to be more liquid compared to other countries with an increasing contract maturity, while the opposite holds true for the Spanish market. The Dutch market is a comparably illiquid market for CDS contracts with a maturity of three years, while ranking in the midfield for five year instruments. Similarly, in the one-year segment, Switzerland has a relatively illiquid CDS market for higher maturities.

split. In order to avoid distortions related to different levels of CDS prices, the relative instead of the absolute bid-ask spread has been calculated

852 On average, the relation between ask and bid prices of five-year contracts is 1.21, i.e., the institutions quoting prices for these instruments are willing to sell them to investors at a price that is 21% higher on average than the price they agree to pay when purchasing the contracts. The average relation between ask and bid prices of three-year contracts is 1.34, while one-year contracts are significantly less liquid, having an average relative bid-ask spread of as high as 1.94

853 The fact that Germany is among the countries with the most liquid CDS markets seems to reflect successful efforts of German institutions to act as a market maker for CDS prices on this market, see again Johannsen (2005)

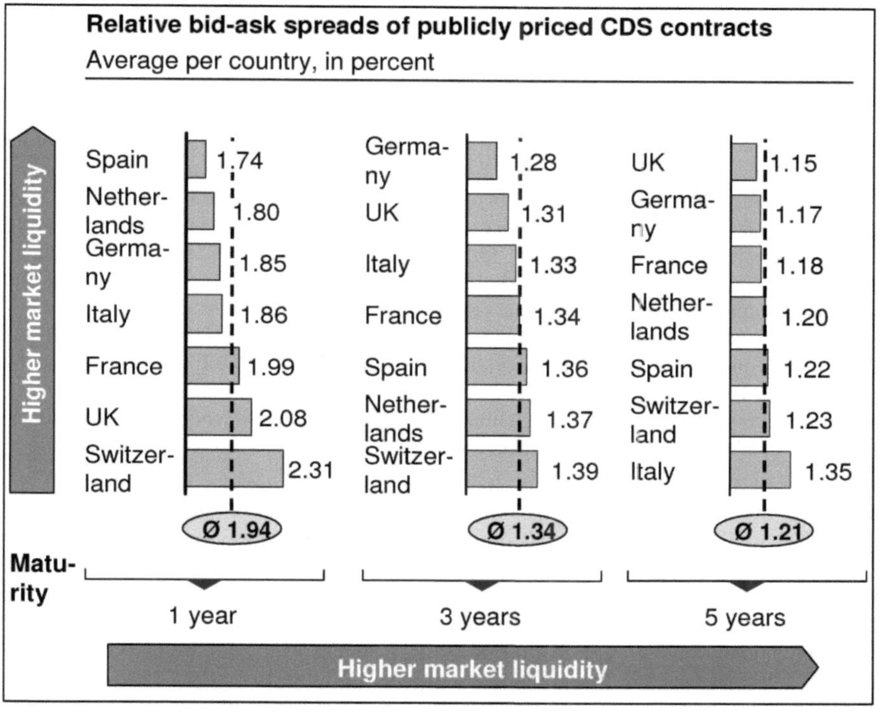

Figure 68: Relative bid-ask spreads of publicly priced CDS contracts[854]

5.2.2.3 Relation between secondary credit market conditions and established CPM units

Figure 64 has illustrated that the proprietary investor ACPM units included in the empirical sample are located in Germany, the Netherlands, and Switzerland, i.e., obviously in countries with the toughest primary market conditions. Most of the active advisors and reactive controllers, by contrast, are to be found in comparably benign primary credit markets such as France, the UK and Spain, but also Italy.

While disposing of a fairly low developed market for real estate-related credit risks, Germany seems to have a quite advanced secondary market for non-asset-backed lending assets. Besides this, German secondary credit markets appear to be fairly liquid, at least in the segment for wholesale credit assets. This is an indication that the

[854] Source: Own illustration based on research in Bloomberg database; see also Footnote 839 for further annotations

existence and sufficient liquidity of secondary credit markets has driven the implementation of proprietary investor business models in German financial institutions.[855]

The fact that the proprietary investor business model is also to be found among Swiss institutions, identified as a country with a virtually non-existent secondary credit market, seems to be contrary to the findings for the German market at first sight. However, interviews with Swiss players that have implemented such an ACPM business model have revealed that there are thoughts to scale the proprietary investor down towards an active advisor. One of the main reasons for that intended restructuring is the Swiss credit market environment that has not allowed the ACPM units to execute secondary credit market transactions to the extent originally planned when the proprietary investor business model was established. Hence, this confirms that the secondary credit market conditions faced by an ACPM unit are a crucial determinant for the specification of its business model and that it is in particular secondary credit market liquidity which crucially determines whether a proprietary investor ACPM unit can be successfully set up.

It is especially the evidence from Italian and Spanish markets indicating that an advanced ACPM approach foreseeing active management of credit risks through secondary market transactions is not perceived possible without the existence and sufficient liquidity of a secondary market for the assets on which an ACPM unit focuses: compared to the UK, France, and Germany, these nations dispose of a relatively low developed secondary credit market judging from issuance volumes of syndicated loans and securitized products as well as from the number of publicly priced CDS contracts and their liquidity – especially in the five-year CDS segment.[856] There is currently no Italian participant in the empirical study which has implemented

---

855 In this context, it is important to note that these German proprietary investors have a wholesale credit asset-focus, thus being able to capture the opportunities presented by the liquid secondary credit market in Germany

Some of the other German ACPM units that are set up as active advisors or risk controllers target the management of SME and retail credit assets, thus operating in a segment for which there is no liquid secondary credit market. This secondary market illiquidity is a main reason why they do not regard the move towards a proprietary investor business model as beneficial. Therefore, as already shown in chapter 4.4, they pursue an active advisory model whose functional competencies are mainly focused on the primary market side. The active advisors among this group aim at actively managing their institutions' credit exposures particularly by exerting influence on loan origination BUs to ensure the "right" credit risks are taken on the institutions' loan books at a price which corresponds to their riskiness. Some of these units are currently evaluating setting up a shortfall compensation system analogous to the one which can be found among proprietary investors

856 Although – somewhat surprisingly – the relative spreads between ask and bid prices of Italian and Spanish CDS contracts are not among the lowest ones in Europe for one and three years maturity

a CPM unit actively managing its institution's credit portfolio.[857] All Spanish participants in the empirical study have currently set up dedicated ACPM units operating as active advisors. Facing very limited national secondary market conditions, however, their business models foresee a primary focus on actively managing their credit portfolios through impacting the primary market side.[858] A further enhancement of their ACPM approach is regarded as crucially impeded by the secondary market conditions they encounter in their domestic credit market.[859]

Apparently facing a similarly insufficiently developed credit market, Dutch institutions should be expected to pursue identical approaches towards CPM as their Spanish or Italian counterparts. However, there are more sophisticated ACPM business models to be found in the Netherlands than in the Southern European countries. It is the more competitive credit market environment in the Netherlands compared to Spain and Italy which seems to have propelled Dutch players to obtain a competitive advantage over contestants by changing their approach early on to managing loan portfolios.[860]

If the existence and liquidity of secondary credit markets propelled the establishment of a proprietary investor ACPM business model, these types of ACPM units should especially be found in the UK. This is because the UK has not only been found to be the most significant market for syndicated loan and securitization issuances as well as for publicly priced CDS contracts, but since it also ranks among the top liquid CDS markets in Europe, at least for the most frequently designed three- and five-year maturity contracts. However, the UK institutions included in the empirical study – despite mostly having wholesale asset-focused ACPM units – have exclusively set up these units as risk controllers or active advisors. This finding indicates there must be determinants influencing the decision for implementing a specific ACPM business model to a greater extent than the existence and liquidity of secondary credit markets. Interviews with credit portfolio managers of the UK-based institutions revealed that

---

857 Italian participants in the empirical study stated a lack of opportunity to capture the value creation potential from an ACPM business model due to unsatisfactory secondary credit market conditions as a major reason why they have not yet moved towards some type of CPM unit aiming at actively managing its institutions' credit portfolio. The second major reason perceived why Italian institutions have not yet moved towards implementing ACPM units seems to be the lack of competitive pressure to change their approach towards bank lending in view of the comparably complacent credit market environment they operate in

858 Accordingly, the ACPM approach taken by the Spanish institutions resembles the SME-/retail asset-focused German active advisors, see again Footnote 855

859 The credit portfolio manager of a Spanish active advisor disposing of a large lending exposure to domestic debtors has particularly voiced his discontent about the secondary credit market in his country and especially considers both the insufficient number of CDS contracts on Spanish credit names as well as the low tradability of the contracts as a key obstacle for being able to actively manage his credit risks more effectively and for moving towards a more advanced ACPM approach

860 See again Figure 64 showing the significantly higher banking density and lower average net interest margin in the Dutch credit market compared to Spanish and Italian markets

the very complacent primary credit market environment – low competition and riskiness of the credit market paired with a profitably growing customer loan base (see also again Figure 64) – has apparently neither caused the need nor provided an incentive for the institutions to move towards proprietary investor units.[861]

Similar to UK institutions, there is no French player that has currently implemented a proprietary investor ACPM unit – despite France disposing of a fairly liquid secondary market in the non-securitized wholesale credit segment, judging from the number and liquidity of CDS contracts outstanding in the French market.

Yet, while some of wholesale asset-focused participants that operate in liquid credit market environments are currently evaluating moving their ACPM unit towards a proprietary investor, there is especially one of these players that is convinced that such a reorganization of its approach towards ACPM would have overall negative implications for the institution. The portfolio manager of this institution states that for the sake of maintaining existing or acquiring new wholesale customer relationships, the majority of new lending contracts is currently closed at a price below the "true" price as determined by market or bank-internal pricing models with the deficits in this field being recaptured through successful cross-selling activities.[862] In particular due to the establishment of a shortfall compensation scheme, setting up a proprietary investor business model is expected to put pressure on relationship managers to renounce concluding loan contracts at such an unprofitable price just for the sake of customer relationships. Therefore, it is feared that such an enhanced pricing discipline may have a negative impact on customer relationships and overall lending volumes of this institution.

---

[861] Interviews conducted with credit portfolio managers of UK-based institutions revealed that they typically regard the secondary market conditions in which they operate as strongly supportive for an advancement of their CPM unit towards a proprietary investor. However, the portfolio managers regard it as the main goal of their CPM activities to protect their loan book against downturns in the credit cycle. Consequently, they take advantage of the relatively liquid secondary credit market environment by primarily engaging in hedging activities on these markets. Facing sufficiently profitable lending margins on the primary credit market, they do not feel the urgent need to discipline and improve their origination business. Moreover, in view of their profitably growing customer loan base, they do not regard it as necessary to engage in secondary market transactions to invest their risk assets in a more profitable way. While a focus on disciplining origination and performing secondary market investments to increase profitability of credit business would strongly suggest the implementation of a proprietary investor business unit, the UK credit portfolio managers feel that they can satisfactorily perform their risk distribution-focused portfolio management activities with the help of an active advisor approach to CPM or even from risk management units with their CPM units effectively operating as risk controllers

[862] See again Footnote 754

5.3 Conclusion: Optimal ACPM business model

Based on an examination of the dimensions according to which the different CPM business models established by participants in the empirical study promise to create additional economic value for their institutions' credit business, the proprietary investor business model has been identified as the seemingly value-maximizing approach towards managing loan portfolios. However, it has also been observed that the move towards proprietary investor is apparently not a common goal of all players (see again chapter 4.5.2). This finding has questioned whether this business model is the optimal approach towards managing loan portfolios that should be implemented in all situations.

Consequently, the specifications of internal and external factors that have been found to be determinants for the design criteria of CPM units have been put in relation to the types of CPM business models established by participants in the empirical study on ACPM. Based on these relations, it has been aspired to discover the preconditions that have motivated the "best-practice" players in the empirical sample to implement a certain CPM business model. From this finding, it has been intended to derive the optimal approach towards managing loan portfolios to be pursued by an institution depending on the specific determining factors it faces.

As a general conclusion from the analyses whose results have been illustrated above and confirmed by the interviews conducted among survey participants, it has become obvious that the active management of loan portfolios can create significant additional value for an institution's credit business. Yet, "the" optimal ACPM business model does not seem to exist. Instead, the optimal approach according to which loan portfolios are to be managed is to a great extent dependent on each institution's specific situation, how it manages to overcome typical implementation barriers as well as which individual importance and preferences decision makers ascribe to the different determinants. Therefore, a general recommendation as to which is the overall optimal ACPM business model to be implemented would not appropriately reflect reality.

Nevertheless, when analyzing the approach towards managing loan portfolios taken by the "best-practice" players in the empirical study, it could be found that there are specific constellations of determining factors which, if faced by a financial institution, make the implementation of a certain type of ACPM business model particularly advisable.

5.3.1 Asset transferring proprietary investor

The asset transferring proprietary investor business model has been identified as the approach towards actively managing lending assets that promises the creation of the highest economic value for an institution's credit business.[863] Yet, in order for an institution to be able to successfully implement such a business model allowing this value-creation potential to be best exploited, certain preconditions need to be given:

A crucial precondition for the successful implementation of such a business model is the opportunity to determine a settlement price for the credit assets to be transferred which is perceived as "fair" by all units involved in the transferal procedure.[864] In this context, the most suitable "fair" price is the price at which a loan itself or a derivative issued on the asset is traded on the secondary credit market as this price appropriately reflects the riskiness of the loan engagement.[865] This requires the institution to operate in an existing and sufficiently liquid secondary credit market.

However, it is not only for the requirement to determine a "fair" settlement price that the existence of such a secondary market environment is essential for successfully establishing a proprietary investor ACPM unit. In order to ensure an effective functioning of the proprietary investor and for the maximum of the value-creation potential to be captured, it is essential that the unit be able to perform risk distribution transactions as well as subsequent reinvestments of the freed-up capital in credit assets on secondary markets.

It is for these reasons that most proprietary investors covered by the empirical sample are responsible for managing the most liquid wholesale credit assets of the markets they operate in. Not being able to match their model-based transfer prices against market quotes and being significantly restricted regarding tradability of credit assets on secondary credit markets seem to be main reasons why proprietary investor business models set up in SME-/retail asset segments apparently do not live up to their expectations regarding creation of additional value for their institutions' lending business. Asset transfers founded on model- instead of market-based prices often lead to discussions regarding which is the fair price for assets to be taken on ACPM's loan book. Consequently, proprietary investors in this setting have aspired to a refocusing towards active advisor business models. Instead of physically taking over credit assets and focusing on secondary market transactions, it is intended that these refocused ACPM units will emphasize their future activities on impacting loan origination. In particular, it is aspired to ensure that sales units perform a risk-adjusted pricing of loans so that deals are closed in a profitable way on the primary market side.

---

863 This finding is also in line with existing literature on ACPM, which regards the move towards a proprietary investor not as a question of "whether" but rather of "when"; see again Kuritzkes (1998), p. 3

864 Weighting the advantages against the disadvantages of the two types of settlement prices quotations that have been identified, an NPV-based settlement price determination appears to be advantageous compared to a margin-based price quotation, see again chapter 4.4.5.1.2

865 Alternatively, a suitable proxy for the "fair" price of a security which is based on market prices of comparable assets can be taken as the second-best alternative promising high acceptance as "fair" among involved parties; see again chapter 4.4.5.1.1 for the principle to determine CDS proxy curves

Hence, it can be concluded that a crucial determining factor for successfully setting up an ACPM unit as proprietary investor is an environment in which there are sufficient secondary market prices quoted for the assets on which its lending activities focus. In this case, it can maximize the value creation of its institutions' credit business activities. In Europe, such market environments have been proven to exist in the UK, France, and Germany, albeit to the greatest extent for the largest credit names in each country. Hence, it appears to prove most promising to set up a proprietary investor ACPM unit in the wholesale credit segment of these nations.

Making use of a proprietary investor's value creation potential becomes particularly essential for institutions that see themselves confronted with a strong profitability pressure – often following high LLP on their lending exposures or through operating in highly competitive credit market environments – and exposed to a sluggish credit demand. This business model is especially beneficial in those situations as it not only ascribes the highest importance to the goals of disciplining and improving loan origination – thus preventing the acquisition of further "bad risks" – but also supports opening up new growth opportunities through performing secondary market investments in credit risks. Besides this, it also achieves highest implementation successes for these objectives. The fact that many German "best-practice" wholesale credit asset-focused players, which face relatively tough conditions in their domestic credit market compared to their Western European counterparts, have set up such a type of ACPM unit is an indication of the advantages entailed by establishing a proprietary investor in such situations.

However, establishing a proprietary investor business model also appears to be the most recommendable option for institutions operating in a more benign credit market environment. Specifically, setting up such a business model may be particularly value-enhancing for the credit business activities of UK-based banks, which, according to the analysis performed above, seem to operate in the most liquid secondary credit market environment among the markets examined. Moving towards such a business model could enhance the value of their already comparably profitable lending business even further. In particular, such a business model would best enable them to take measures against potential downswings in their present favorable market surroundings.

In order to ensure the successful implementation of a proprietary investor business model, it is essential that its establishment is primarily driven by the BU whose assets or related risks are subsequently to be taken over by the ACPM unit. As there must be expected resistance within an organization if credit assets are to be transferred from the BUs in which loan origination takes place towards a centrally located ACPM unit, an asset transferring proprietary investor is required to be eventually located within the respective customer BU of its institution.

Furthermore, the significant organizational changes induced by a proprietary investor business model make it essential for its successful implementation that the incentives for ACPM and the units affected by its activities – in particular origination BUs – are very well aligned with ACPM's goals to minimize cultural clashes within the organization. This can be derived from the finding that the most effectively functioning proprietary investors report the best alignment between their objectives and their incentive structure as well as the one for other units involved in ACPM activities.

There are some primarily customer relationship-focused institutions to be found in the empirical sample reporting that they have managed to successfully implement a proprietary investor ACPM unit. As opposed to statements made in literature on ACPM, this is evidence that the reorientation of a financial institution's overall business strategy towards higher degrees of product-/capital market orientation is not essential for setting up a proprietary investor. Furthermore, it weakens the argument of some participants in the empirical study that setting up such an ACPM business model may be harmful for their strong lending customer relationships.[866] In particular, this indicates that even the primarily customer relationship-focused institutions in the empirical sample operating in a wholesale asset segment might be able to significantly create additional value for their lending business by moving towards a proprietary investor business model if other relevant determinants are fulfilled.

5.3.2 Risk transferring proprietary investor

The risk transferring proprietary investor business model foreseeing the transfer of credit risks in a synthetic form from origination to ACPM can be regarded as an intermediate business model between asset transferring proprietary investor and active advisor. Since credit assets and, hence, their revenues are not physically transferred to ACPM, potential issues regarding this transferal procedure as potentially occurring when setting up an asset transferring proprietary investor can be avoided.[867] In particular, this opens up the opportunity to establish the ACPM unit in another BU of the organization than the one in which loan assets are originated. For example, it can potentially be set up at a central location within the organization, having the advantage of being in a better position to realize bank-wide diversification benefits than its counterparts that are located in certain BUs.

[866] Specifically, some participants in the empirical sample that have successfully implemented a proprietary investor business model cited counterarguments for the conviction of these institutions that the obligation to price credit assets according to their "true" value may be harmful for lending business. It was reported that after having established a proprietary investor, relationship managers have had a higher incentive and put an increased effort into building up client relationships in more profitable segments while reducing exposures in unprofitable ones. Searching for such profitable "niches" is seen as particularly relevant and rewarding in low-margin wholesale lending markets; see also again chapter 4.4.5.3

[867] See especially again chapter 4.4.5.2.1 on these possible issues

However, the fact that ACPM does not assume ownership for credit assets under this business model entails the disadvantage that it has significantly lower flexibility to operate on secondary credit markets in order to optimally structure the credit portfolio. Besides this, not having the assets on its books appears to make it more difficult for ACPM to get transparency over the composition of its institution's outstanding loan portfolio than when owning the assets.

Also, alike its asset transferring counterpart, it is essential that the unit operates in a sufficiently liquid secondary credit market environment. This is in particular because the credit risks need to be transferred at a "fair" market price, typically through CDS contracts issued on the borrower's debt. Also, the implementation of a well-defined and aligned incentive structure appears to be a crucial determinant for successfully setting up this business model.

It needs to be decided individually and depending on the specific situation and preferences of an institution and its decision makers whether the possible advantages of the risk transferring proprietary investor business model outweigh the disadvantages of its asset-owning counterpart.

5.3.3 Active advisor

Especially when having the opportunity to operate in sufficiently liquid secondary credit markets, the proprietary investor business model has proven to be the approach to managing credit portfolios promising the highest economic value creation for an institution's credit business. Particularly due to its significantly lower flexibility regarding secondary credit market transactions, an active advisor would give away a large part of this possible value creation potential in such a market environment. In this case, refraining from establishing a proprietary investor seems like a lost value-creation opportunity.

Still, the individual situation of an institution and convictions or preferences of the executives responsible may lead to the decision that an active advisor business model is the superior solution despite a set of conditions in favor of a proprietary investor.[868] In this case – should the other crucial determining factors mentioned before also be fulfilled – it should be ensured that ACPM nevertheless has a significant influence on loan origination and pricing decisions. Ideally, it should quote a market-based price to origination, ensuring the assets' riskiness is appropriately reflected in the price requirement charged to customers. Furthermore, it appears recommendable to set up a

[868] This may be the case, for example, if the potential issues related to an asset transfer from origination to ACPM mentioned in chapter 4.4.5.2.1 are regarded as particularly grave. The required efforts related to adjustments of processes (see again chapter 4.4.5.4) and infrastructure (see again chapter 4.4.5.5) following the establishment of a proprietary investor business model may also be considered as not feasible in a specific situation

shortfall compensation mechanism analogous to the one typically established among proprietary investors. This may serve as a strong and influential incentive mechanism for origination to act according to the guidelines of ACPM. Although assets or related risks are not intended to be transferred to ACPM, this mechanism might foresee a negative charge for origination's P&L account, should the eventual customer price be lower than the one set by ACPM.[869]

It has been shown that setting up an ACPM unit as an active advisor seems to be the preferred alternative for participants in the empirical study if favorable secondary credit market conditions enabling the exchange of risks on these markets do not exist.[870] Again, the active advisor should ideally be equipped with strong empowerment towards loan origination. Since comparable market prices may not be widely available, it should be active on the primary market side by quoting model-based hurdle prices to origination for concluding new or renewing existing loan contracts. To have maximum impact, it should ideally be empowered to set price quotations that have a binding character rather than merely being recommendable opportunity prices without sanctions for origination BUs if relationship managers deviate from these guidelines, e.g., for the sake of customer relationships. Combined with a clearly defined and aligned incentive structure, a shortfall compensation mechanism may serve to place sufficient incentives on origination to act in accordance with the requirements of ACPM. Through operating as such an "empowered advisor", it can be ensured that the ACPM approach creates the highest possible value on the primary market side, even without acquiring credit assets or related risks.

Although extensive trading activities on the secondary credit market side may be limited due to unfavorable market prerequisites, the active advisor facing these conditions should nevertheless be equipped with the skill-set to perform such transactions. For example, even if active trading of positions or related risks is severely limited, it may still be possible to open up a new risk distribution and additional income channel by creating synthetic structured products (e.g., CDOs) on the basis of the institution's loan book.[871] While only the two most established proprietary investors momentarily initiate these types of transactions to distribute

869 Some of the most advanced advisors which also intend to stick to this business model in the future, are currently evaluating to set up such a shortfall compensation mechanism

870 For another argument why an asset transferring proprietary investor may not be advantageous in an illiquid market environment see also again Footnote 808: An asset-owning ACPM unit may have an incentive to exploit its empowerment towards origination to obtain arbitrage benefits in view of the lack of comparable market prices for the lending assets taken over

871 Moreover, setting the basis for secondary credit market transactions preserves potential opportunities to actively change the loan portfolio composition on the secondary credit market should restrictions regarding impacting the loan portfolio composition through the primary market side such as the ones mentioned in Footnote 243 be faced

credit risks and generate additional revenues, this may be a way for SME-/retail asset-focused ACPM units to open up new opportunities for business with SME- and especially retail customers but also other institutional investors looking for investment opportunities in transparent credit asset classes.

Ideally, an active advisor should be set up as a profit center instead of a cost center since this provides an incentive for the unit to be profitable on a stand-alone basis.

It has been shown above that setting up an asset transferring proprietary investor business model is only feasible should the unit be eventually situated in asset-owning customer BUs of an institution. Conversely, if the establishment of an ACPM business model is initiated and driven from a central unit within the organization, either a risk transferring proprietary investor or, preferably in comparably illiquid secondary credit markets, an active advisor business model seems to be the most feasible option.

An active advisor located in a central unit may also be part of an ACPM target business model foreseeing the establishment of two ACPM units in an institution: a proprietary investor in the wholesale banking BU and another ACPM unit, set up as an active advisor, in a central unit of the organization.

While the proprietary investor may be dedicated to optimizing the portfolio composition in the wholesale BU, the active advisor may have the responsibility of managing the outstanding credit risk exposures on a group-wide level without physically taking over credit assets or related risks. Its central location may enable the advisor to have an overall perspective on the group-wide credit exposures and risk structure, thus being able to realize diversification benefits that would most likely not be captured if it was located in a certain BU. On the secondary market side, the advisor may perform synthetic derivatives trades to selectively distribute or invest capital in credit risks besides initiating structured credit transactions driven by the goal to divest concentration risk exposures, for example.

Such an ACPM target business model could combine the benefits of having a strong impact on the primary market side, especially in the wholesale credit segment – which is typically accountable for the highest loan loss provisions should origination business not be properly managed – with an overall view on the credit risk positions of the institution allowing the realization of maximum diversification benefits to be achieved.[872]

[872] There is one survey participant currently in the process of initiating such an ACPM target model. It names an effective coordination between these two different ACPM units as a key challenge for successfully setting up this model. In particular, a close alignment and coordination regarding execution of secondary credit market transactions is considered as indispensable. In order to avoid issues regarding questions of authority, it is aspired to anchor both units in the institution's Executive Committee

Part IV: Summary, critical evaluation, and further research requirements

Part IV concludes the dissertation by summarizing the discussed topics and key results. Furthermore, a critical evaluation of the approach taken to address the research questions is provided. Remaining open questions and further research requirements are outlined.

1 Summary of discussed topics and key results

1.1 Part II

Following the introductory remarks in part I, part II of the dissertation has given a detailed description of the development and principles of the ACPM approach and provided an overview of the secondary credit market instruments that can currently be applied to actively manage loan portfolios. Moreover, the theoretical background of the ACPM approach has been outlined based on which its value-creation potential has been examined.

The first chapter has introduced banks as intermediaries between supply and demand of capital on financial markets before evidence for legitimization of their existence despite a recent trend towards more complete capital markets has been provided. Subsequently, the different types of banks developed over the course of time have been described. In particular, wholesale banks have been identified as institutions focusing on business with large- and medium-sized corporate and institutional customers.

As the ACPM approach has been driven by the wholesale banking segment, the main focus of the dissertation has been narrowed down to wholesale credit business. Accordingly, an overview of these business activities has been provided: further to describing characteristic loan origination, credit approval and monitoring activities, emphasis has been put on introducing typical credit portfolio risks along with related measurement concepts because they have frequently been referred to in the course of the dissertation. In this context, the probability function of credit asset values has been discussed, with emphasis placed on risk measures by distinguishing symmetric risk measures from their shortfall counterparts. VaR, especially, is a shortfall risk measure commonly used by practitioners. Based on an introduction of the EC concept, risk-adjusted performance measures have been introduced since they allow the evaluation of loan assets according to risk-return aspects. Following the description of credit portfolio risks as well as risk and performance measurement concepts, chapter one has been concluded by outlining typical refinancing and problem loan management/workout activities.

Further to an illustration of the conventional "originate and hold" wholesale lending approach of financial institutions, which is characterized by holding the originated credit assets until maturity or default, chapter two has illustrated in greater detail the most significant forces of change in credit markets that have induced the development of the ACPM approach. In particular, these have been the increasing liquidity of secondary loan markets supporting the exchange of credit risks as well as opportunities to perform regulatory capital arbitrage. Furthermore, advancements in credit risk analytics, especially the development of credit portfolio models, have enabled banks to measure the risks inherent in their credit portfolios in a more refined way than before and to compute the EC required for a credit asset or portfolio. allowing these lending securities to be priced from a risk-adjusted point of view. An overview of the credit portfolio models currently used by leading financial institutions has been provided, illustrating that in practice internally developed models dominate external software solutions. The recent forces of change in credit markets have not only provided opportunities for wholesale asset-focused financial institutions, but they have also confronted them with considerable challenges. In particular, the declining profitability of banking business due to falling new lending margins and growing loan losses have recently challenged the institutions' approaches towards lending business.

After a description of the forces of change in credit markets, the idea to actively manage loan portfolios in order to benefit from the opportunities and master the challenges accompanying these developments has been introduced. The central idea of this ACPM approach is to apply the principles of classical portfolio theory to the management of credit assets by aspiring to create and maintain a risk-return efficient loan portfolio. The generic business models according to which literature on ACPM suggests an implementation of the ACPM approach have been depicted. In particular, the proprietary investor business model has been described in greater detail based on the available information in literature on ACPM. This model foresees the establishment of an ACPM unit that is empowered to take over credit assets from loan originating customer BUs and acts as an independent manager of its institution's credit assets on financial markets.

Further to an illustration of the feasible ACPM business models developed by existing research on this topic, determinants for the design of ACPM units have been identified founded on literature on ACPM. It has been possible to categorize them as internal and external determining factors. The former include the institution's economic performance, the type of initiator and driver for setting up an ACPM unit as well as the institution's governance principles. The latter comprise the credit market environment in which an institution aspiring to set up an ACPM unit operates. Illustrating the generic ACPM business models and identifying the determining factors for their design has particularly been motivated by the objective to test these models and subsequently deduct the optimal approach towards actively managing loan portfolios with the help of the empirical study on ACPM described in part III.

It has been shown that the execution of transactions on secondary credit markets is a central feature of the ACPM approach. A broad range of secondary credit market instruments are at the disposal of an ACPM unit for this purpose. Chapter three has described these instruments and related markets in greater detail. They have also been compared regarding their methods and suitability to transfer credit risks. Furthermore, potential issues such as information asymmetries, additional risks, and regulatory requirements as well as market deficiencies and interdependencies between different subtypes of secondary credit markets that need to be considered when applying these instruments have been illustrated. It has been shown that, given the different characteristics of these instruments, credit portfolio managers need to specifically select the type of instrument best fitting to their strategy to achieve an optimal loan portfolio composition.

Loan sales and syndication are the first group of secondary credit market instruments that have been depicted in greater detail. They enable a direct "true" transfer of credit risks between contract parties. As opposed to loan sales and syndication, credit derivatives, whose importance as instruments for ACPM has risen particularly strongly in recent years, allow credit risks to be transferred in a synthetic way, i.e., without requiring shifting the underlying assets. Markets for these instruments have experienced a considerable growth, with single-name CDS currently having a global market share of about 50% in total outstanding derivatives volumes. However, a caveat related to this enormous growth is that it has by and large been limited to contracts issued on the largest underlying credit names worldwide. Securitization instruments differ from the aforementioned ones in the sense that not all of them enable the transfer of credit risks. This is because ABBs/Pfandbriefe and recourse securitization structures cannot be used to shift credit risks but to obtain collateralized refinancing for loan exposures as well as to manage interest and pre-payment risks instead. By contrast, the other types of securitization instruments described – in particular CDOs, non-agency CMOs, and ABS according to a narrow definition – allow the transfer of credit risks through tranches with identical risk-return characteristics.

Chapter four has described the principles of classical portfolio theory, which serves as the theoretical basis for the ACPM approach. Based on this description, it has been discussed whether the active management of loan portfolios is value creating for an institution.

The first part of this chapter has displayed the results of academic research on portfolio selection of individual investors. The construction of mean-variance efficient portfolios that are located on an efficient frontier plays a central role in this context. If an investor has the opportunity to invest funds in a risk-free asset besides performing risky investments, the market portfolio M remains the only efficient portfolio, and his decision problem is reduced to the choice between which percentage of available funds to invest risk-free and which percentage to invest in M. This is the so-called Tobin separation. Accordingly, the investor's risk preferences are merely relevant for the split of his investments in risk-free funds and in M. The same optimization principle holds if the investor defines risk as deviation below a previously set target return instead of the symmetric standard deviation and consequently includes shortfall risk measures in his preference function.

In the classical setting, the mean-variance principle is based on the assumption that investors have either quadratic utility functions or that asset returns are normally distributed. While the former assumption is frequently critizised as not being realistic, the latter is typically not given in the context of credit assets. Further academic research in the field of portfolio theory has shown, however, that these rather restrictive assumptions do not necessarily need to hold for the validity of the aforementioned portfolio theory. By contrast, with the help of Chebyshev's inequality, e.g., the limitation on normally distributed asset returns can be regarded as a borderline case that can be justified in a broader context with more generalized assumptions on distribution functions.

Based on the results derived from research on the portfolio selection of individual investors, asset pricing models enabling the optimal investor behavior to be determined as well as the return a holder of an individual risky asset can expect in a competitive market equilibrium have been described. These asset pricing models can be displayed in a very general setting. If the more restrictive assumptions underlying the classical Tobin separation hold, the classical CAPM can be derived as a specialized risk-pricing model that has the risk-free rate as an implicit target rate of return.

Common to these asset pricing models is the assumption of complete capital markets, i.e., unlimited market access for all market participants, no market frictions as well as full information efficiency in the market. By using the maximization of market value as an evaluation criterion, it has been shown that the execution of transactions on secondary credit markets does not enhance an institution's market value if the assumption of complete capital markets holds. Consequently, as the ACPM approach is seen to primarily differ from the conventional approach towards bank lending in the sense that it foresees the execution of secondary credit market transactions, it has been concluded that one cannot expect a (market) value creation from actively managing loan portfolios provided markets for debt and equity capital are complete. By contrast, if it is realistically assumed that capital markets are incomplete, it has been shown that such secondary credit market transactions can enhance the market value of a corporation. Thus, it has been concluded that the active management of loan portfolios by means of such transactions is value creating for an institution's credit business compared to the conventional "originate and hold" lending approach under the assumption of incomplete capital markets.

1.2 Part III

The findings of part II have been compared to the results of an empirical study on ACPM. The study was conducted in the beginning of 2005 among 22 leading Western European financial institutions in chosen as participants since they were initially assumed to have established a best-practice ACPM approach. The empirical information has been gathered through personal face-to-face expert interviews accompanied by a questionnaire containing a mixture of closed- and open-ended questions. Besides focusing on the participants' approach towards managing loan portfolios, the questions especially covered the interfaces between these institutions' CPM units, loan origination and, secondary market units.

After having described the goals of the empirical study in chapter one, chapter two has provided a description of the data sample. The methodology to obtain the empirical information, the structure and content of the applied questionnaire, and the approach taken to analyze the empirical information has been discussed in chapter three. In chapter four, evidence on the CPM business models identified in the empirical sample has been illustrated.

A somewhat surprising outcome of the empirical study has been that more than a third of all institutions covered by the survey still pursue the conventional "originate and hold" approach towards bank lending and do not yet actively manage their credit portfolios – despite being leading players in the European wholesale credit business. They perform passive CPM functions within existing risk units instead, thus effectively acting as "risk controllers". Characteristic main tasks of these risk controllers are to influence the definition of target credit portfolios, develop concepts and tools for the measurement of credit risks and perform credit research. They typically do not exert influence on loan origination BUs nor do they engage in secondary credit market transactions to improve the composition of their institutions' loan portfolios.

More than 40% of the institutions covered in the empirical sample have set up an ACPM unit acting as an "active advisor". Active advisors aspire to optimize their institutions' credit portfolio composition by impacting acquisition and renewal decisions of loan contracts on the primary market side and by executing transactions on secondary credit markets if operating in supportive market conditions. While not taking over credit assets from loan origination units, their influence on primary market lending business is typically exerted in the form of non-binding advice towards origination regarding the right price to be charged when granting a loan to customers.

It has been possible to divide these active advisors into two sub-groups depending on their organizational location. These subgroups differ, e.g., regarding their functional competencies: the smaller share of the active advisors in the empirical sample is located in their institutions' central risk or finance units while the larger share is situated in wholesale or SME-/retail asset-focused BUs. The former typically have stronger risk management-related competencies while the latter dispose of stronger competencies and enforcement powers towards the primary market side.

A comparison with the generic business models developed in literature on ACPM has revealed that the "advisors" described in literature differ from the active advisors set up in practice, particularly regarding their mandate to execute transactions on secondary credit markets.

The smallest share of survey participants have set up an ACPM unit operating as "proprietary investor". Most of these units are located in wholesale BUs of their institutions, focusing on managing wholesale credit assets and taking over loans from origination BUs at a self-determined, binding market-based settlement price. In a modified form of this business model, the acquisition of risks related to the underlying credit assets instead of physically taking over the loans is foreseen. The establishment of a shortfall compensation mechanism in case the price origination charges to customers deviates from proprietary investors' settlement price quotation ensures a strong enforcement power of these units towards the primary market side. Being initially set at "zero profitability" through this shortfall compensation, they are required to actively manage the credit assets they have taken over to be profitable. Hence, they are incentivized to engage in various types of secondary credit market transactions to reshuffle and optimize their portfolio composition. As proprietary investors are economically accountable for their loan portfolio, they need to be set up as profit centers instead of as cost centers. As a consequence, the generic "active portfolio manager" business model, which is seen to operate as a cost center by literature despite taking over ownership of credit risks, does not occur in practice in this form.

Most of the CPM units in the empirical sample are located on the private side of their institutions and have access to material non-public information about the banks' credit customers. Fewer units prefer higher flexibility on secondary credit markets and closer contact to other market participants. Therefore, they have chosen a location on the public side of their institution. Some of the most advanced players have split their CPM units into private- and public-sided functions in order to combine the advantages of having a strong impact on the primary market side with maximum flexibility and independence on secondary credit markets.

The CPM business models identified not only pursue different objectives but especially vary concerning perceived implementation degrees related to these goals as well as with respect to barriers on the path to a successful implementation. Irrespective of the current CPM business model pursued, however, the lack of existence and insufficiently liquid secondary credit markets seem to be the most severe barriers on the path to achieving a higher implementation success for several of the CPM units' key objectives and to further enhancing their approach towards managing loan portfolios. This indicates that the development of secondary credit market instruments and recently strong growth of corresponding markets has not been sufficient yet for a smooth and effective functioning of ACPM units. This finding has also confirmed the observation that the credit market environment in which an institution operates is a key external determinant for the set-up of its ACPM unit.

Further to providing an elaborate characterization of the CPM business models distinguished in the empirical sample, it has been tested whether the theoretical finding that the ACPM approach creates additional (market) value for an institution's credit business in incomplete capital markets holds in practice. Astonishingly, none of the survey participants were able to provide an exact quantification of the economic impact actually achieved or at least aspired to from the implementation of an ACPM business model. Mostly, deficient data and (reporting) systems infrastructure or the relatively short time periods since completed implementation of the active advisor and especially the proprietary investor ACPM business models were named as reasons. Consequently, the extent to which an ACPM approach creates value for an institution's credit business – thus justifying its existence – could only be explored in a rather qualitative way.

Four dimensions according to which an ACPM unit is seen to potentially create additional value for an institution's credit business have been distinguished: (I) improvement of primary market credit business, (II) distribution of credit risks on secondary loan markets, (III) subsequent reinvestments of the freed-up capital into higher yielding credit assets, and (IV) repackaging and structuring credit risks and subsequently placing them in the form of standardized securities among secondary market investors.

From this qualitative evaluation, it has become evident that moving from a passive to an active way to manage loan portfolios is accompanied by increased value creation for an institution's credit business. Judging from the business model-characteristic importance ascribed to various objectives and related implementation degrees, however, it is solely the longest and most successfully established wholesale asset-focused proprietary investors which have sufficiently managed to create additional value for their institutions along all four identified dimensions. This may lead to the conclusion that the proprietary investor business model is the optimal approach to actively managing loan portfolios to be implemented in all cases. However, especially since many survey participants voiced hesitation about moving towards such a business model, this conclusion may be premature.

Hence, it has seemed necessary to perform a more refined deduction of the optimal approach towards actively managing loan portfolios. Whether a certain type of ACPM business model can be successfully established is certainly influenced by the existence of specific barriers on the path to an effective implementation of set objectives and depends on if these barriers can be overcome. Further to that, however, the implementation of a certain model is critically influenced by the specific determining factors identified in part II with help of literature on ACPM. The impact which the specification of these determinants has on the choice for a particular CPM business model has been tested founded on the results of the empirical study on ACPM as well as based on additionally performed analyses.

In chapter five it has been illustrated which specific constellations of determinants have triggered the implementation of a certain approach towards managing credit assets among the "best-practice" players in the empirical sample. In this way, the optimal target ACPM model to be chosen has been specified in greater detail.

Generally, the analyses have revealed that "the" optimal ACPM business model to be implemented in all situations does not exist. Quite the contrary, the ideal approach towards managing loan portfolios has proven to be primarily dependent on each institution's specific situation, the individual significance it ascribes to different determinants and also on preferences of decision makers.

An examination of the approaches towards managing loan portfolios taken by the "best-practice" players in the empirical sample has disclosed that certain business models appear to be systematically preferred over others depending on the specific constellations of determining factors an institution faces and the importance it ascribes to specific determinants.

If a player operates in a sufficiently liquid secondary credit market environment with available secondary market prices for the loan assets on which its lending activities are focused, setting up an asset transferring proprietary investor that acquires loans from origination BUs at an NPV-based settlement price has proven to be the optimal ACPM business model to be implemented. In practice, this is the case for wholesale credit asset-focused players. Operating in such a favorable market environment, the proprietary investor has the flexibility to optimally structure its loan portfolio composition through execution of secondary credit market risk distribution and investment transactions as well as by issuing structured products on the basis of its loan portfolio. While it seems particularly recommendable to set up such a business model for an institution that is confronted with a strong profitability pressure, a proprietary investor also appears to be the best business model to protect an institution operating in a rather benign credit market environment against potential downswings.

While it is crucial for an asset transferring proprietary investor to be situated in the customer BU in which the loans to be taken over are originated, implementing its risk transferring counterpart seems to be recommendable if it is decided to set up the ACPM unit at a central location within the organization. Characteristic advantages need to be weighed against disadvantages when considering establishing such a business model instead of an asset-transferring proprietary investor: On the one hand, not physically owning credit assets limits the flexibility of such a unit to act on secondary credit markets. On the other hand, its central location allows it to better discern and capitalize on cross-divisional diversification benefits. The successful implementation for both types of proprietary investor business models can only be guaranteed if the institution has established a well defined and aligned incentive structure for the objectives set for ACPM as well as for units affected by its activities, in particular origination.

If, due to an emphasis on specific preferences, it is aspired to set up an ACPM unit as an active advisor in a sufficiently liquid credit asset segment, it should be ensured that ACPM sets market-based price recommendations towards origination to guarantee the risks of the originated lending assets are properly priced. The advisor should be equipped with a strong mandate and empowerment towards origination as to its recommendations regarding the acquisition and renewal decisions of loan contracts as well as concerning prices to be claimed for the assets. Analogous to the proprietary investor business model, the establishment of a shortfall compensation system may support ACPM's enforcement power towards the primary market side and help to overcome conflicts of interest and cultural differences with origination BUs. Operating as a profit center, the advisor should ideally perform synthetic secondary credit market transactions to distribute credit risks and undertake (re-)investments of the freed-up capital to achieve a risk-return optimal loan portfolio composition. Furthermore, additional income may be earned through generating structured credit products in cooperation with asset-owning origination BUs and subsequently placing the securities among secondary market investors.

An active advisor appears to be the optimal ACPM business model especially if favorable secondary credit market conditions enabling the exchange of risks on these markets are not given. Not being satisfactorily able to optimize its institution's loan portfolio composition on the secondary market side, it should place emphasis on impacting primary market activities to ensure a profitable loan portfolio composition is achieved. The advisor should assume ownership of its institution's loan pricing model to set ideally binding model-based quotes towards origination ensuring credit assets are appropriately priced.

A feasible target ACPM business model combining both types of ACPM units may consist of a proprietary investor in the institution's wholesale banking customer BU and another ACPM unit, set up as an active advisor that is centrally located within the organization.

2 Critical evaluation of approach and further research requirements

In view of the inevitable recent developments in the credit markets they operate in, banks – especially wholesale asset-focused players – have felt strong pressure to restructure their approach to lending business. In this context, the ACPM approach has emerged as a new concept to address the challenges that have arisen with these market developments. Since the promising field of ACPM had been relatively unexplored up to now, the main motivation for writing this dissertation has been to address and close the obvious existing research deficiencies regarding ACPM. After having posed the research questions in part I of the thesis, part II has given an elaborate characterization of the ACPM approach and related activities based on specialized literature and recently observed market developments. The main goal of part II has been to provide the basis for an empirical study on ACPM. The theoretical findings derived in part II have been compared to the results of this study by means of which it has been aspired to comprehensively explore the hitherto relatively unknown field of ACPM in greater depth and detail.

The approach taken to raise the empirical information will be critically evaluated in the following. Besides this, unresolved questions that could not be addressed in sufficient depth and detail within the scope of this dissertation will be addressed based on which further research requirements will be discussed.

2.1 Critical evaluation of approach

It was decided to conduct the empirical study on ACPM among 22 of the largest and most significant Western European financial institutions. Choosing this sample of players was motivated by the following main goals:

As they are among the most advanced European institutions in terms of (wholesale) lending business, the selected participants have as well been assumed to be leaders in the still widely unexplored field of ACPM, which has been initiated by the wholesale credit segment. Through surveying these leading players, it has been expected to get to know what can momentarily be considered as state-of-the-art in terms of managing lending assets. With the help of such "best-practice" results, decision makers in other institutions that have not yet implemented an ACPM business model may obtain guidance regarding which is the optimal approach towards managing lending assets that they should establish.

The scope of the study has been limited to a manageable number of participants. Like this, it has been possible to dedicate sufficient time to the individual questioning held during face-to-face interviews accompanied by a detailed questionnaire. Performing this procedure with a handy sample size has enabled an in-depth exploration and understanding of each participant's approach towards managing its loan portfolio without going beyond an acceptable and feasible scope of this effort. For example, the asset transferal procedure of the proprietary investor business model could be investigated in greater detail by means of this practice. If more participants had been included in the empirical study, such detailed face-to-face questioning would no longer have been feasible.

Ex post, the results of the empirical study seem to confirm that the chosen modus operandi was suitable for the given situation: even among these most advanced European financial institutions in terms of (wholesale) lending business covered by the survey, there is a significant share of players – more than one third in the empirical sample – that do not yet actively manage their predominantly wholesale asset-focused loan portfolios. If even these institutions have not universally implemented an ACPM approach, there is little reason to assume that less significant and advanced players in terms of (wholesale) lending pursue an equally or even more sophisticated lending approach. Thus, including a broader set of European participants in the empirical study would most likely not have enhanced the quality of its results nor would it have brought significantly new insights.

Nevertheless, although the procedure chosen to raise empirical information on ACPM appears to be the right one even in an ex-post evaluation, the focus on a comparably small data sample entails shortcomings of which one should be aware when interpreting and drawing on the results and conclusions of the study.

In view of the relatively recently developed approach towards actively managing loan portfolios and due to its initiation by the wholesale lending segment, there is legitimate reason to assume that by including the largest and most significant Western European institutions, the empirical study has covered the players that have established the most advanced approaches towards actively managing loan portfolios in this region.

Yet, there is the possibility that the focus on such a small, and by far not representative sample size may not have captured the entire information spectrum. This is because the approaches identified towards actively managing loan portfolios may primarily be suitable for large, mostly internationally-oriented wholesale asset-focused institutions. There is reason to assume that they may not necessarily also be suitable for players with a smaller loan book and a predominantly regional, and potentially more SME-retail credit asset-oriented business focus.[873]

A larger sample size would also have enabled the analysis of the empirical information with the help of multi-variate statistical measures rather than with the relatively simple methods applied to analyze the findings obtained from the empirical study in question. In particular, this would have enabled obtaining a more quantitative, hence more accurate deduction of the optimal ACPM business model in chapter five of part III:

---

873 An example of such players not covered by the empirical study are German savings and cooperative banks. Granting loans belongs to their main business activities, albeit in a predominantly regional scope. These institutions supposedly operate in an illiquid credit market environment by focusing on business with private individuals, SMEs, and municipalities. See again chapter 1.3.2 of part II for a description of their typical activities

with the help of suitable statistical methods, the different determinants could have better been ranked concerning their significance for the design criteria of ACPM business models.[874]

The geographic focus of the empirical study has been limited to coverage of Western European institutions. In view of the approach chosen – i.e., raising the information through face-to-face interviews – it would not have been feasible to cover a global sample in the context of this dissertation. However, this implies forgoing knowledge regarding the status and specifics of ACPM in other geographic regions.[875]

2.2 Further research requirements

In the course of conducting the research project at hand and particularly when raising and analyzing the empirical information on ACPM, some issues and open questions have emerged which could not be fully addressed and solved in the context of this dissertation. Besides this, as mentioned above, further research requirements arise from an extension of the approach hereby chosen to gathering the empirical information. Therefore, it will be described in the following sections in which area related to the active management of loan portfolios there appears to remain the most exigent requirement for further research beyond the scope of this thesis.

2.2.1 Tradability of credit risks

Chapter 4.3.2 of part III has described implementation barriers for the objectives of the different CPM units have been described. Among other things, it has been shown that – despite a recent tremendous growth of market volumes for secondary credit market instruments[876] – the insufficient liquidity of the secondary markets in which CPM units operate is regarded as a major barrier for the successful functioning of all types of business models and the successful implementation of their objectives. Besides this, it has been found that the value-maximizing proprietary investor business model can only be regarded as the optimal approach towards managing loan portfolios if the unit has the opportunity to operate in a sufficiently liquid secondary credit market environment.[877]

---

[874] For detailed descriptions of possible suitable statistical methods see, for example, Pflaumer, Heine et al. (2001) chapter 8 concerning statistical tests and chapter 9 regarding regression analyses

[875] It seems, however, as if the empirical information obtained through the empirical study at hand was relatively representative even in an international setting: Comparing the information with the latest publicly available global survey on CPM – as far as comparability of the results is possible – has not revealed obvious differences or contradictions; see again chapter 4.6.2

[876] See again Figure 16, Figure 17, Figure 18 and Figure 25 for the volume growth of secondary credit market instruments

[877] See again chapter 5.3.1 of part III

The most advanced players in terms of ACPM have developed ideas to improve the unsatisfactory status quo regarding secondary credit market liquidity, to help complete the financial markets for credit risk capital.[878] It has been possible to only put these ideas into effect up to now, however. Since many survey participants have voiced a strong interest in new ideas and approaches to tackle the illiquidity issue and because the ability to exchange credit risks has been identified as crucial for the successful set-up and effective functioning of a value-maximizing ACPM unit, it seems essential to perform more elaborate research in this field.

The hitherto developed ideas and concepts collectively aspire to facilitate the exchange of an institution's credit risks, either through capital markets or directly between ACPM units. The main reason why some of them – e.g., the notion of swapping credit exposures directly between ACPM units instead of through credit markets – have not yet been put into effect is often a lack of transparency for a risk acquirer regarding the true risks inherent in the assets to be potentially taken over from a risk distributor. Such possible information asymmetries between asset owners and prospective outside investors become particularly acute if debtor categories for which there is no external credit rating available are to be exchanged. Therefore, it appears advisable to develop concepts on how to overcome information asymmetries propelling the exchange of credit risks.

Since resistance regarding the acquisition of "unknown" risks may complicate the transfer of debt assets in certain – typically unrated – credit segments or make them entirely impossible, a possibility may also be to come up with alternative ideas for how an ACPM unit could potentially transfer or acquire risk exposure to a certain debtor without using secondary credit markets or directly exchanging credit assets.

In this context, a possible alternative approach may be to look for alternative, sufficiently liquid markets on which risks that are highly correlated with a specific debtor's credit risk can be exchanged. For example, one should expect the profitability and consequently the creditworthiness of a corporation engaged in crude oil exploration to be highly correlated with the world market price for crude oil. A falling oil price would most likely be accompanied by pressure on this corporation's profitability, thus increasing its credit default risk. Provided there is a sufficiently high and stable correlation between the oil price and the explorer's credit risk, a financial institution that has a significant credit exposure to this corporation may want to protect this exposure not in a conventional way with the help of the secondary credit markets but acquire protection against falling crude oil prices instead.[879]

---

[878] See also again Figure 46

[879] In practice, protection against a falling oil price could, for example, be acquired through selling a corresponding futures contract; see, e.g., Hull (2006), chapter 2 on the mechanics of futures markets and contracts

The idea of hedging credit risks not through secondary credit markets but with help of other, potentially more liquid markets does not need to be limited to exposure to a single corporation. It may become even more feasible if an institution has loan exposures to a particular sector since there may be a higher and more predictable correlation between market prices of this sector's particular goods and sector-specific credit default risks.[880]

It may be fruitful to devote more detailed research to further developing and potentially implementing this idea to open up new ways for an exchange of an institution's credit risks.

2.2.2 Application of secondary credit market instruments

It has been shown that a key functional competence of ACPM units as opposed to units performing rather passive risk controlling and management activities is the execution of transactions on secondary credit markets. A range of instruments is available for this purpose and have been described in detail in chapter three of part II. Hence, the need for further research requirements regarding availability and application of these instruments seems to be rather small. Nevertheless, in view of the instruments' high innovation rate and volume growth, regular updates in this field seem appropriate. This appears especially important in order for the available knowledge and techniques concerning measurement and management of related risks to keep up with the high innovation pace.[881]

In view of the growing spectrum of suitable instruments enabling a transfer of existing credit risks and given the increasing number of players from different sectors in the secondary credit market acting as buyers and sellers of credit protection,[882] it seems essential to conduct further research with the goal of discerning interdependencies between these sectors related to a transfer of credit risks. In this context, it appears particularly necessary to perform a further examination of the challenges concerning an understanding of the eventual whereabouts of these risks and possible related implications. While the typical buyers and sellers of credit protection are known, the still relatively high opacity of these markets makes it difficult to assess their actually

880 There are several other industries besides the oil sector whose products are exchanged with similar frequency at daily quoted prices. Credit exposures to these sectors could be hedged in a similar way. See, e.g., Hull (2006) p. 32 et seq., Table 2.2 for an overview of futures quotes for different commodity sectors

881 An example for enhanced requirements to measure and manage related credit risks are the recently developed single-name CDOs, see again chapter 3.3.2.2.2. Smithson (2004) gives an introduction in the specifics regarding measuring the risks related to these instruments.. See also again Gibson (2004) regarding characteristic risks of synthetic CDOs

882 For example, hedge funds have recently emerged and rapidly gained importance as buyers and sellers of credit protection on the global credit derivatives market besides banks and insurance companies, see again chapter 3.2.4 and BBA (2003/2004), p. 17

held positions in an accurate way. This is further aggravated by the fact that financial reporting and disclosure requirements for credit derivatives vary between different sectors and countries. Consequently, concerns have been voiced that risks associated with credit risk transfer instruments may be concentrated in a small group of institutions. This may lead to repercussions and possible systemic problems due to contagious effects if a major market participant had severe problems,[883] making it essential to perform further research in this field and develop appropriate measures.

An unresolved question preoccupying virtually all participants in the empirical study is the optimal approach they should pursue to manage their loan portfolio throughout the different stages and conditions of a credit cycle, especially with the help of secondary credit market instruments. Extended methodical research in this field would be particularly beneficial since none of the participants has developed an analytical approach towards active credit cycle management yet. In this context, further investigations should also be made regarding the optimal strategy and tactics to (re)invest capital on secondary credit markets.[884]

2.2.3 Regulatory requirements

The implementation of the "Basle II" guidelines and their conversion into national law is momentarily pending. Following a finalization of this legislation on supranational and national levels, it will be necessary to perform an in-depth examination regarding the impact that the usage of secondary credit market instruments has on an institution's regulatory capital requirements. In this context, more thorough analyses regarding the opportunity to perform regulatory arbitrage following the implementation of the new capital adequacy guidelines may be of particular interest.

When conducting the empirical study on ACPM, an issue racking all surveyed institutions" brains was related to the fact that current accounting rules and regulations are perceived to be an obstacle for the players' activities and transactions performed in the context of actively managing loan portfolios. This particularly applies to the requirements of the new accounting rules "FAS 133" and "IAS 39" regulating the recognition of hedges as eligible for accounting purposes, in particular ruling that credit derivatives are to be valued on a mark-to-market basis. The main issue resulting from this forced mark-to-market valuation of credit derivatives is the often

883 See, e.g., Schich (2003) p. 9 et seqq. on potential issues regarding credit risk transfer between financial institutions and different financial sectors. Further examinations concerning possible systemic problems related to an enhanced credit risk transfer might extend recent research by Allen and Carletti (2005) who discuss possible contagious effects between different industry sectors

884 For example, there seems to be a further research requirement beyond Comer, Boney et al. (2005) regarding the specific question whether market-timing promises to generate better performance than index-investing in fixed-income markets, hence being a recommendable strategy to manage credit investments. See also Footnote 730

significantly increasing volatility of an institution's P&L statement if these instruments are used to hedge default risks of a loan book that is traditionally not held on a mark-to-market but on an accrual basis.[885]

This accounting mismatch may discourage portfolio managers from actively managing their loan portfolios with help of credit derivatives. It may also impede their frequently aspired-to effort to set up an active cycle management strategy. This is especially because the mark-to-market accounting requirement of derivatives could imply that strategic hedging activities induce P&L losses during some phases of a credit cycle that may make it difficult for credit portfolio managers to justify and hence continue holding the hedge positions that were initially opened to protect their loan book against potential downturns in the credit cycle.[886]

If the efforts and ambitions of credit portfolio managers were continually impeded by adverse accounting regulation, this would imply a dramatic step backwards for the only recently emerged field of ACPM. Therefore, it appears to be most advisable to perform further research in this field, identifying the best solution that aligns the interests and motivation of regulators with those of practitioners, thus ensuring a continuation of the current momentum with respect to improving bank lending through ACPM.

2.2.4 ACPM approach

The determination of the optimal ACPM business model to be chosen has been based on a comparison between key determinants faced by the "best-practice" institutions included in the empirical sample and the approach they have taken to actively managing their loan portfolios. Due to the comparably small sample size, a ranking of the determinants' significance for the design criteria could not be provided in a quantitative form but had to be primarily based on qualitative information such as judgments and opinions provided by the interviewees when the empirical information was gathered. As already mentioned before, with help of a broader empirical sample such a more quantitative determination regarding their significance for the design of ACPM units may be performed

In this context, it seems appropriate to expand the spectrum of institutions covered beyond the largest mostly wholesale credit asset-oriented players. It may also be advisable to include a broader set of quantitative determining factors such as one-time

[885] See again Footnote 745 on the accrual accounting logic as well as Footnote 771 on the requirements for hedges to be qualified for accounting purposes under "FAS 133" and "IAS 39"

[886] See Wolcott (2005) giving an overview on the issues practitioners face and the concerns they voice regarding the requirement to obey current accounting regulation when initiating derivative-based hedge transactions to protect their loan exposures. An exemplification of the significant mark-to-market losses on CDS contracts incurred by UBS and Bank of America when hedging loan exposures and the resulting negative publicity underlines the significance of this issue

implementation and running costs of an ACPM unit, for example, which could not be considered in this dissertation due to insufficient availability of information in the empirical sample.

As confirmed by the empirical study on ACPM, the principal asset focus of all types of surveyed CPM business models lies on "plain vanilla" loans, in this context chiefly on large- and mid-corps exposures.[887] Not in the focus of these units is the active management of credits to finance specific large-scale investment projects such as power stations or large equipment such as aircraft, for example. Portfolios containing such specialized finance lending assets may be future addressees and, hence, a possible "next horizon" when expanding the ACPM approach towards other asset classes. Specialized finance lending typically entails large single-name concentration risk exposures for an institution. There are also multiple influencing factors for the riskiness of this asset class. Hence, a refined view on the specific risks inherent in these exposures and especially an exploration of the possible ways towards actively managing these asset classes is essential when thinking about an advanced form to manage them.

Further to investigations regarding an expansion of the ACPM approach to asset classes currently not yet in the focus of ACPM units, research in this field should be extended to other geographic credit markets. Conducting a similar empirical study as the one at hand among players in other comparably highly developed loan markets such as the US or Japan would enable differences between the approaches towards bank lending pursued in these markets and the ones in Europe to be elaborated. This may also help to obtain and exchange ideas and suggestions on how to further improve ACPM activities.

It seems particularly advisable to extend research on the optimal way to manage credit portfolios to institutions located in emerging market economies or that have significant lending exposures to debtors in such countries: owing to comparably underdeveloped markets for equity and debt capital, the banking sector enjoys a considerably higher significance for the financing of economic activities than in industrialized countries[888] – despite a recent growing disintermediation of the credit channel.[889] Hence, researching the optimal approach to bank lending in these nations and potentially transferring knowledge and experience obtained from the "best-practice" loan asset managers in industrialized states seems particularly relevant. It may not only help to improve the economic situation of individual institutions but also contribute to a

[887] See again especially Figure 41

[888] See, e.g., Catao and Rodriguez (2000), p. 3 et seq. as well as Footnote 3 on the higher share of bank deposits in the financial stock of emerging market economies

[889] See, e.g., Hawkins and Mihaljek (2001), p. 5 et seq.

reduction or at least reduced severities of the financial crises in these countries that have occurred time and again in recent years.[890]

Activities regarding the management of problem loans/workout of lending assets have not been covered in great detail by this dissertation. Nonetheless, it has been learned from the empirical study that the management of ailing engagements is typically not a task of the CPM units surveyed but performed either in existing risk functions or in separate, dedicated workout units instead. Clearly defined linkages and interdependencies between these units do not seem to exist yet. Therefore, future research in the field of ACPM should also focus on how to best expand the responsibility of ACPM units to problem loan management/workout functions. This is especially relevant because such an expansion and enhancement of ACPM's competencies appears to be an essential next step on the path to setting up an integrated approach with regard to actively managing lending assets along the entire "credit pipeline" from loan origination to managing down distressed assets. Besides this, it seems particularly beneficial to properly define and clarify functional interdependencies and demarcations between origination, ACPM, and corresponding problem loan management/workout units since a structured feedback mechanism between these units may be an essential step towards a thought-out approach to discern and, hence, inhibit problem loans already at the origination stage. For example, the information advantage that origination units have due to their close customer contacts could be used and leveraged by a problem loan management/workout unit to facilitate the detection of potentially ailing engagements through a system of early warning indicators. Equally, the experience of workout units might be leveraged by ACPM and origination if there is sufficient interaction between these units.

* * * * *

The emergence of the ACPM approach has triggered a fundamental change of the way bank lending business is performed. The hope remains that its advantages are broadly perceived and recognized, leading to its wide-spread implementation as well as inducing a further advancement and sophistication of related business models. Irrespective of its individual realization through tailored business models, however, it should be aspired to make the centralized institution-wide active management of credit risk exposures part of a value-oriented, comprehensive bank management system.

[890] See also again Footnote 5

Appendix

1 Appendix A: Additional figures

Cumulative average corporate default rates by rating classes
In percent

	Rating category	Year 1	Year 5	Year 10	Year 15
Investment grade	AAA	0.00	0.10	0.48	0.65
	AA+	0.00	0.16	0.36	0.36
	AA	0.00	0.13	0.79	1.36
	AA-	0.02	0.56	1.32	1.95
	A+	0.06	0.63	1.75	3.18
	A	0.05	0.51	1.80	2.99
	A-	0.04	0.89	2.42	3.15
	BBB+	0.32	2.81	5.35	8.43
	BBB	0.34	2.38	5.89	8.78
	BBB-	0.46	5.54	10.24	13.77
Speculative grade	BB+	0.64	7.62	13.69	16.50
	BB	1.15	10.95	19.08	21.64
	BB-	1.97	16.27	26.73	31.51
	B+	3.19	21.96	31.59	37.49
	B	8.99	31.53	38.61	44.00
	B-	13.01	39.23	46.48	47.87
	CCC/C	30.85	53.00	58.44	61.58
Average	**Inv. Grade**	0.13	1.31	2.91	4.28
	Spec. grade	5.27	21.58	30.04	34.45

Figure 69: Cumulative average corporate default rates by rating classes[891]

[891] Source: Own illustration based on Standard & Poor's (2004), p. 13. The default rates stem from Standard & Poor's CreditPro™ database, including 10,438 companies, rated by Standard & Poor's as of December 31, 1980 or first rated between December 31, 1980 and Dec. 31, 2003. It needs to be considered that maturities of most obligations are much shorter than 15 years, which results in a smaller sample size for longer time horizons

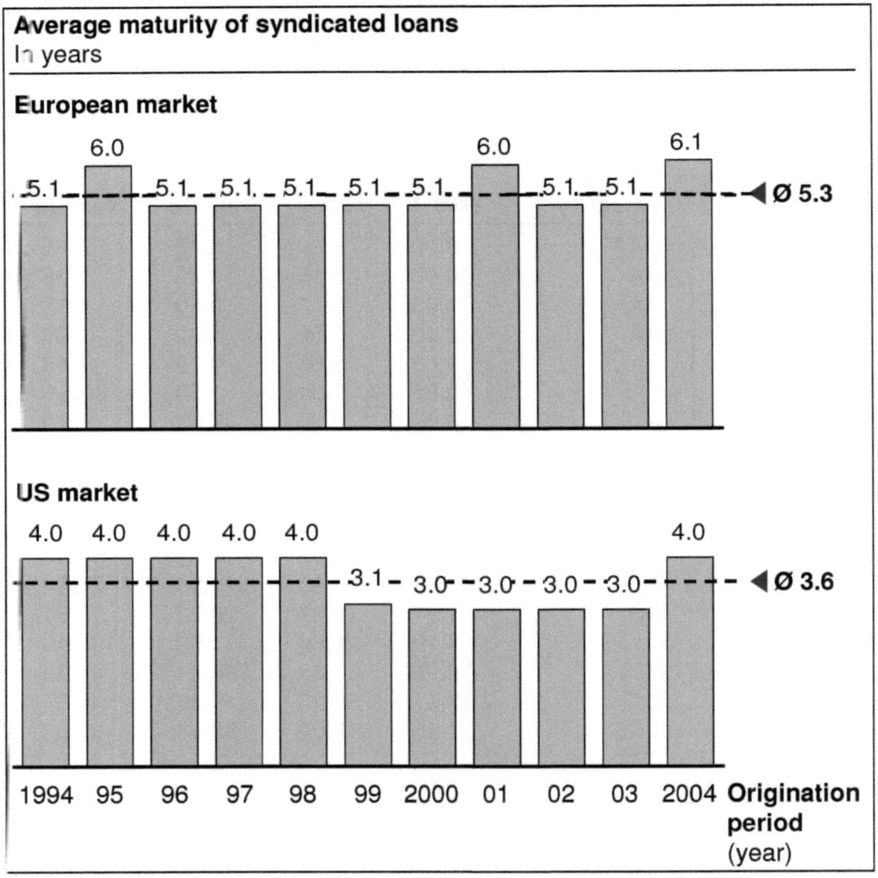

Figure 70: Average maturity of syndicated loans[892]

[892] Source: Own illustration based on Dealogic Loanware database

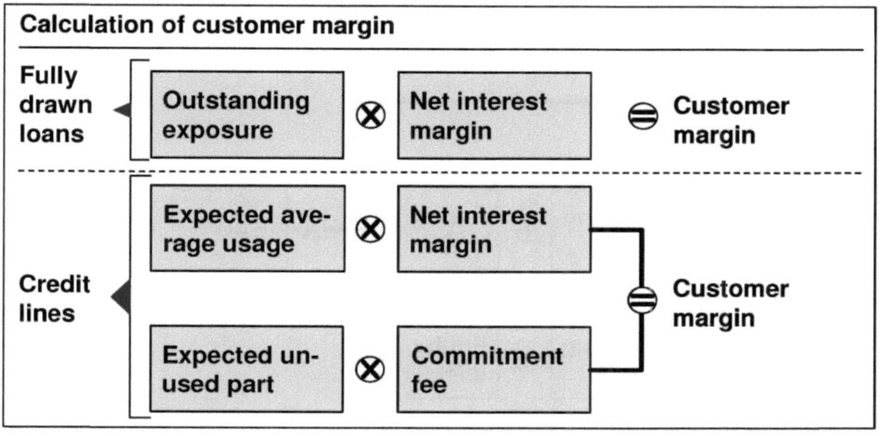

Figure 71: Calculation of customer margin[893]

[893] Source: Own illustration based on results of empirical study on ACPM

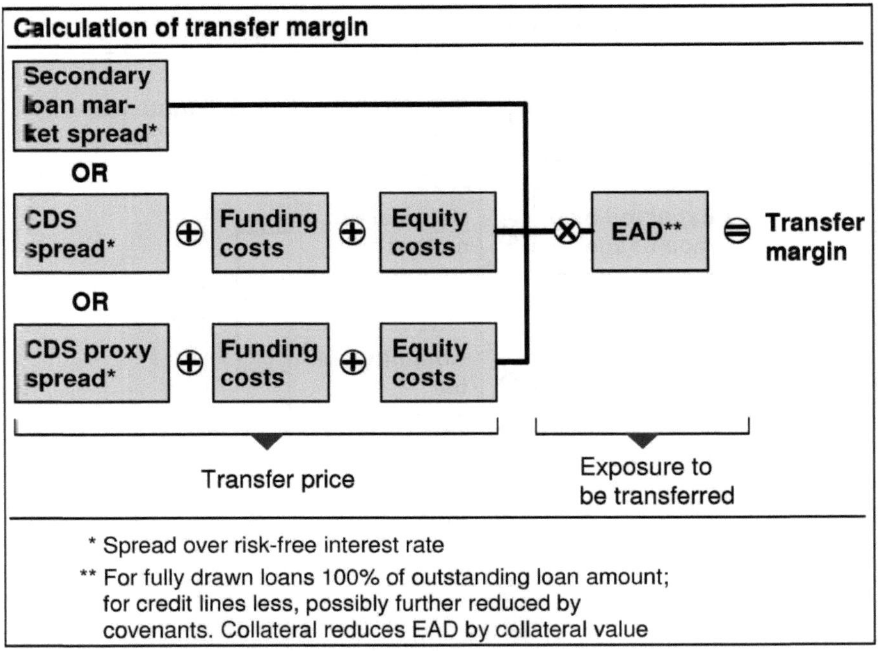

Figure 72: Calculation of transfer margin[894]

894 Source: Own illustration based on results of empirical study on ACPM

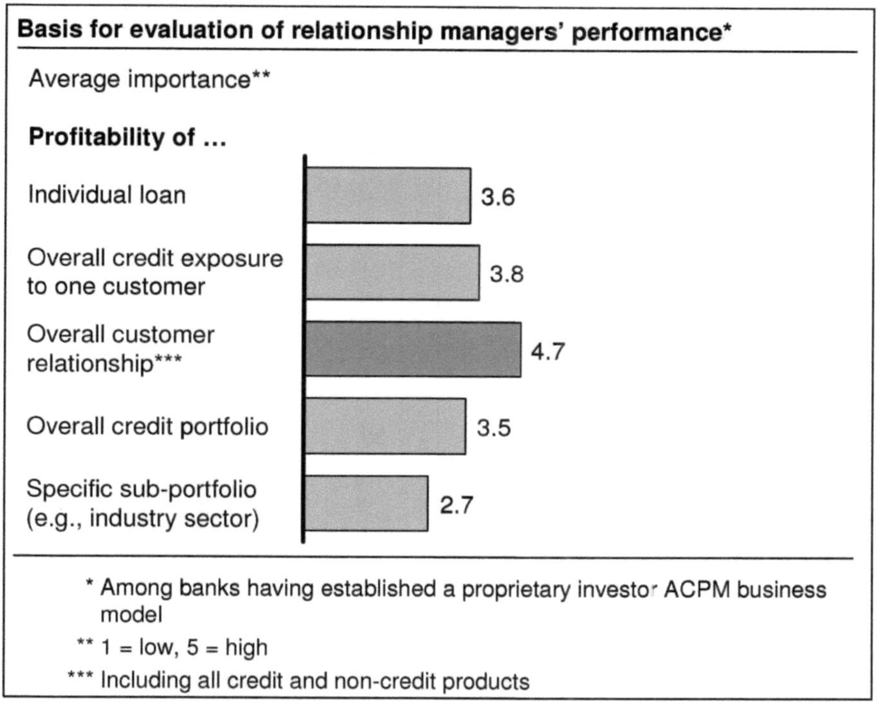

Figure 73: Basis for evaluation of relationship managers' performance[895]

[895] Source: Own illustration based on results of empirical study on ACPM

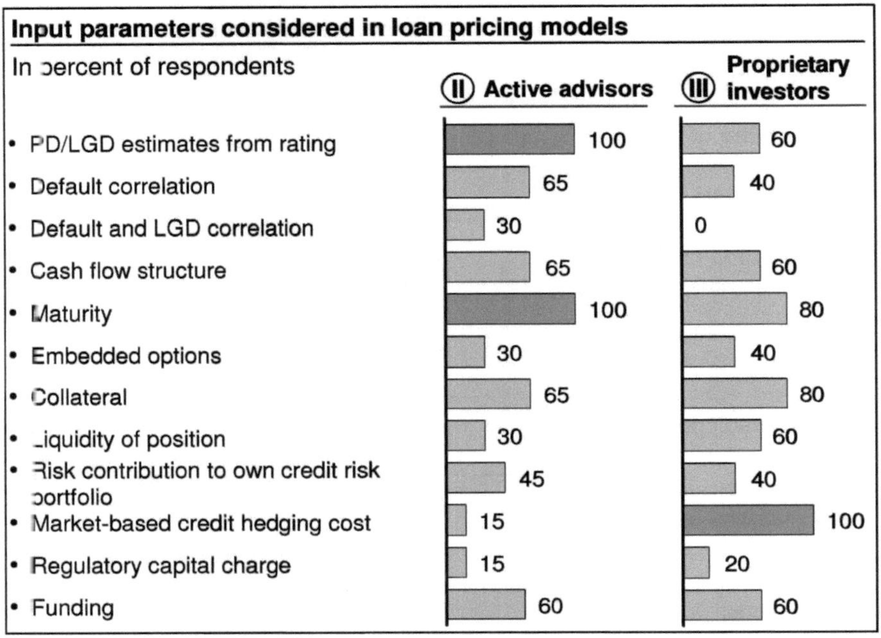

Figure 74: Input parameters considered in loan pricing models[896]

896 Source: Own illustration based on results of empirical study on ACPM

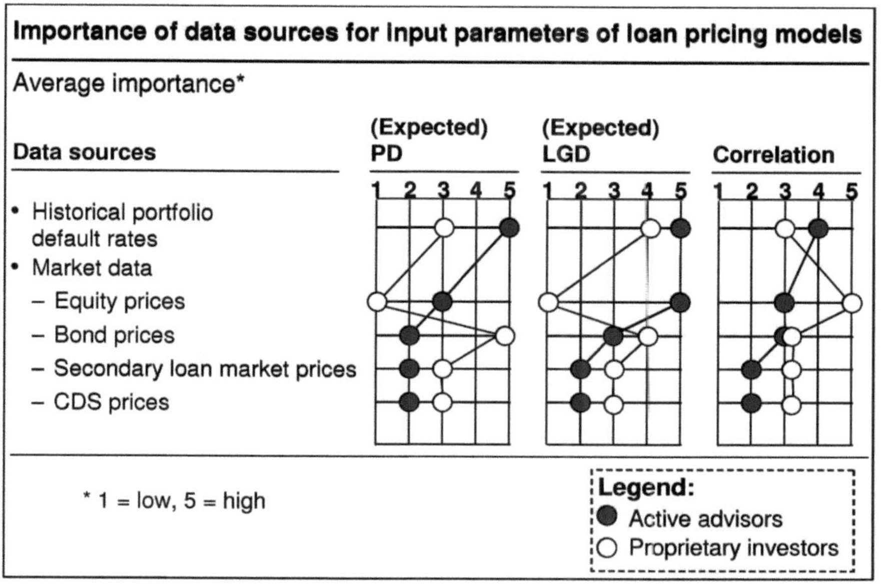

Figure 75: Importance of data sources for input parameters of loan pricing models[897]

[897] Source: Own illustration based on results of empirical study on ACPM

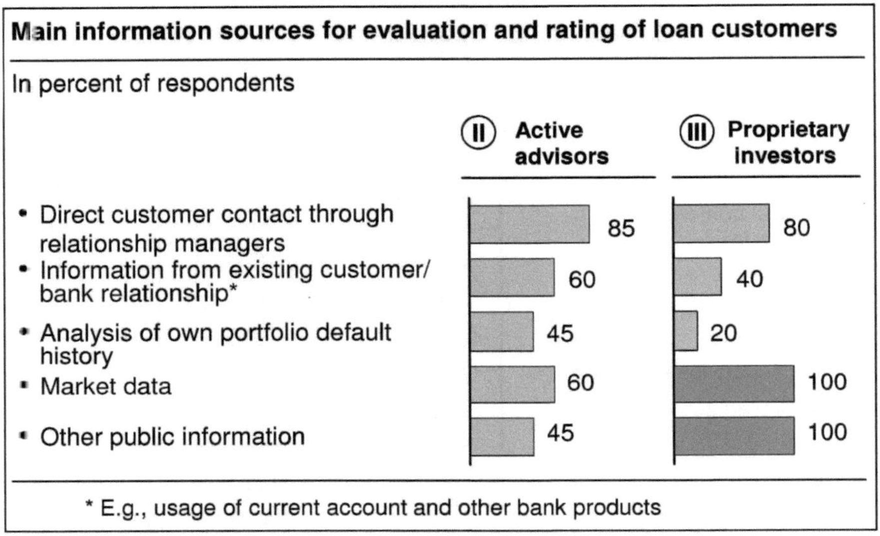

Figure 76: Main information sources for evaluation and rating of loan customers[898]

[898] Source: Own illustration based on results of empirical study on ACPM

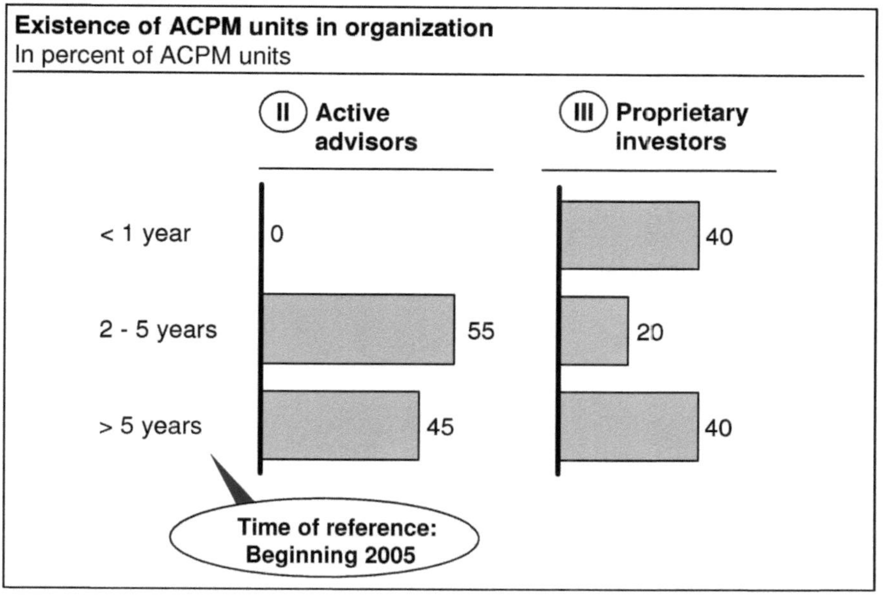

Figure 77: Existence of ACPM units in organization[899]

[899] Source: Own illustration based on results of empirical study on ACPM

Comparison between credit spreads and standard deviations of selected tradable credit products

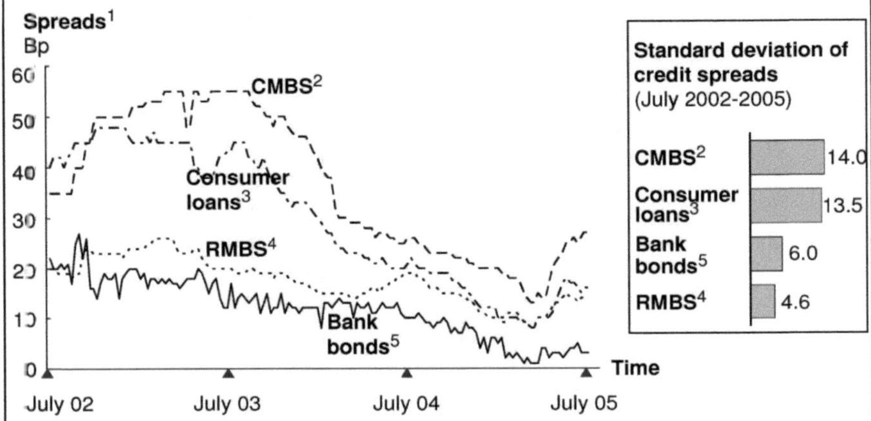

1 Weekly spreads to 3 month GBP Libor (for CMBS and RMBS tranches) and 3 month Euribor (for consumer loan tranches and bank bonds)
2 Maturity 5 years, AAA-rated tranche, UK
3 Maturity 3 years, AAA-rated ABS tranche, Eurozone
4 Maturity 5 years, AAA-rated tranche, UK
5 Average of Eurozone bank bond spreads over Euribor with maturity between 3 - 5 years and AA long-term credit ratings

Figure 78: Comparison between credit spreads and standard deviations of selected tradable credit products[900]

900 Source: Own illustration based on following sources:

Credit spreads of CMBS, RMBS and consumer loans have been retrieved from on J.P. Morgan (2005 a) , Tables 1 and 2, J.P. Morgan (2005 b), Tables 1 and 2, J.P. Morgan (2005 c), Tables 1 and 2, J.P. Morgan (2004 a), Tables 1 and 2, J.P. Morgan (2004 b), Tables 1 and 2, J.P. Morgan (2004 c), Tables 1 and 2, J.P. Morgan (2004 d), Tables 1 and 2, J.P. Morgan (2003 a), Tables 1 and 2, J.P. Morgan (2003 b), Tables 1 and 2, J.P. Morgan (2003 c) Tables 1 and 2, as well as J.P. Morgan (2002 a), Tables 1 and 2

Credit spreads of bank bonds have been taken from Bloomberg database

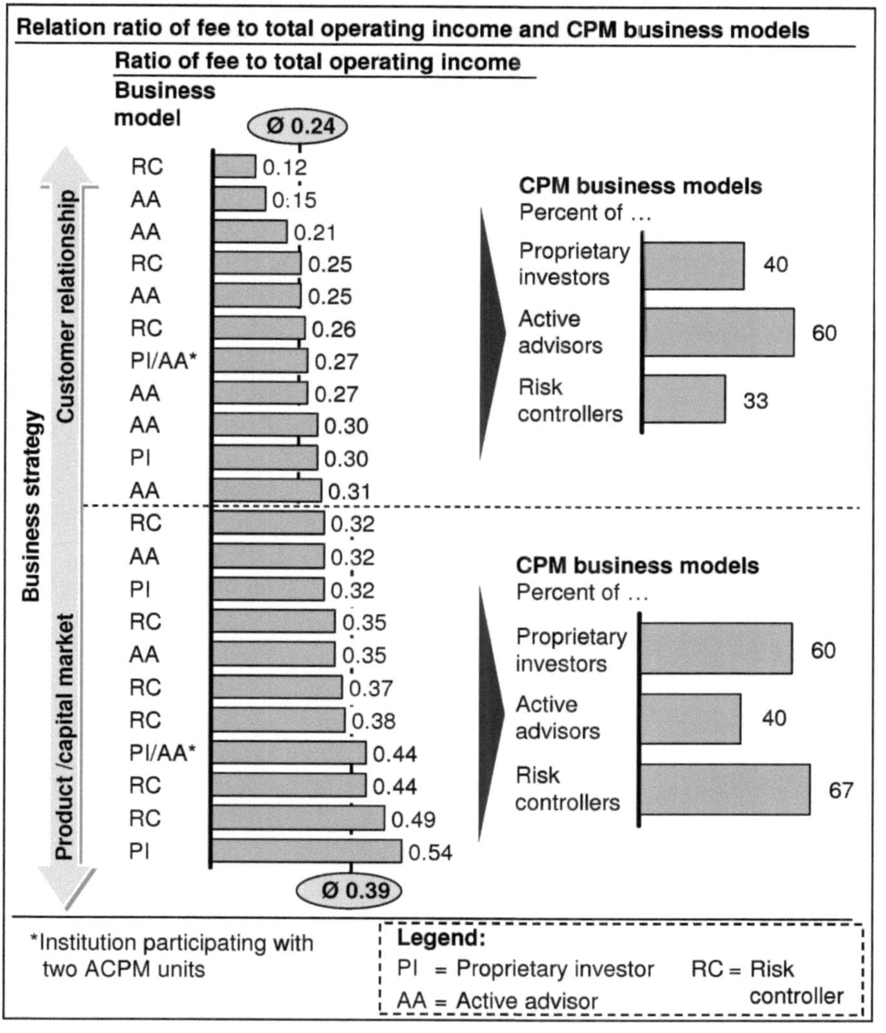

Figure 79: Relation ratio of fee to total operating income and CPM business models[901]

[901] Source: Own illustration. Information on CPM business models based on results of empirical study on

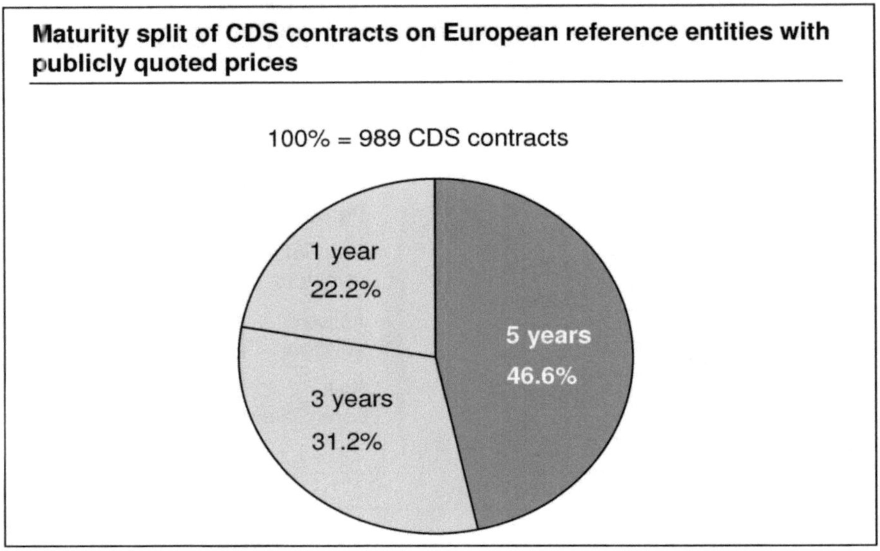

Figure 80: Maturity split of CDS contracts on European reference entities with publicly quoted prices[902]

ACPM. Ratio of fee to total operating income based on research in Datastream and Bloomberg databases and derived from annual reports

902 Source: Own illustration based on research in Bloomberg database; see also Footnote 839 for further annotations

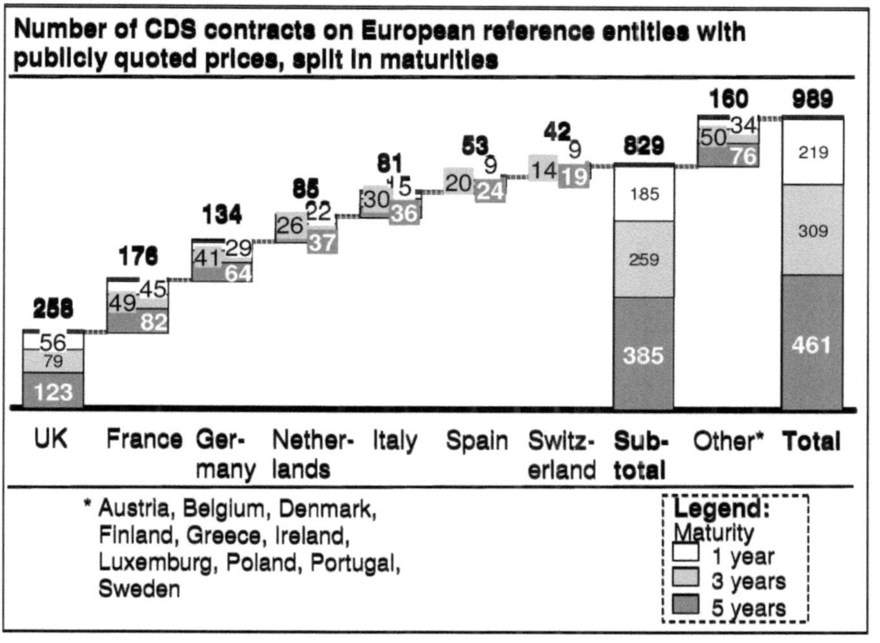

Figure 81: Number of CDS contracts on European reference entities with publicly quoted prices, split in maturities[903]

[903] Source: Own illustration based on research in Bloomberg database; see also Footnote 839 for further annotations

Appendix B: Questionnaire applied in empirical study on ACPM

EMPIRICAL STUDY ON ACPM

I. CREDIT PORTFOLIO MANAGEMENT (CPM) APPROACH

II. RELATION TO/INTERFACES WITH ORIGINATION UNITS

III. RELATION TO/INTERFACES WITH SECONDARY MARKET ACTIVITIES

I. Credit Portfolio Management (CPM) approach

1 Overall goals, strategy, development status and sources of value creation

- For how long do you have (a) CPM unit(s) in your organization?

____

- Which are the overarching goals that you want to achieve with your CPM unit(s)?

____

- How would you describe the development status of your CPM approach?

____

- Which sources of value creation for your CPM unit(s) are most important?

____

2 Design criteria for CPM units

2.1 Reporting structure/organizational setup and governance

How many CPM units (i.e. units responsible for influencing risk/return of credit risk portfolio after primary market origination) do you have in your organization?

- No CPM unit at all
- One central CPM unit
- Two CPM units
- More than two CPM units

According to which criteria do you organize the management of your credit portfolios?

- By business divisions (e.g., retail/wholesale), which? ______________
- By regions (e.g., US, Europe), which? ______________
- By products (e.g., bilateral loans, structured finance), which? ______________
- By customer groups (e.g., retail, corporates, financial institutions), which? ______________
- Other (which?) ______________

Where is/are your CPM unit(s) organizationally located?

- Line of business (e.g., Capital Markets BU), which? ____________________
- Risk Unit
  - Credit approval/Second Vote
  - Risk Management/Risk Controlling
- Finance Function
- Separate BU (e.g., directly reporting to the CEO)
- Other? Please specify ____________________

What are the main reasons for your specific decision? ____________________

On which organizational level is/are the CPM unit(s) located? The head of CPM is...

- Board member
- 2nd level
- 3rd level
- Other: ____________________

What are the main reasons for your specific decision? ____________________

Is/are your CPM unit(s) on the private or public side of your institution, i.e., separated from other BUs (in particular origination unit) through a "Chinese Wall"?

- On private side
- On public side

Please specify the reporting line setup within your CPM unit(s)

- Reporting lines to regional head
- Reporting lines directly to global head
- Other (which?) ____________________

Which main governance issues do you see for CPM within your organization?

1. ____________________

2. ____________________

3. ____________________

2.2 Functional mandate and competencies

2.2.1 Detailed functional mandate

Which of the following credit functions are under the responsibility of your CPM unit/other units? What is the degree of involvement of these units (estimation in percent)

Credit policy setting

Function	Involvement of CPM (%)	FTE	Involvement of other units (which?) (%)
Definition of credit risk appetite of the institution			
Definition of target credit portfolio			
Capital allocation to business units			
Capital allocation to sub-portfolios (e.g., regions, industries, products)			
Setting underwriting guidelines, approval decision criteria, pricing standards			
Definition of decision-making power and decision processes			
Definition of limits: sectors, regions, single concentration limit			
Other (which?)			

Loan origination and underwriting

Function	Involvement of CPM (%)	FTE	Involvement of other units (which?) (%)
Customer/deal information gathering, verification, quality control			
Credit analysis			
Credit rating ("doing")			
Credit rating (final assessment)			
Pricing			
First vote			
Second vote			
Third vote (if applicable)			
Credit control incl. documentation			

Credit portfolio controlling and management

Function	Involvement of CPM (%)	FTE	Involvement of other units (which?) (%)

Credit research			
Ongoing monitoring of single position and credit quality			
Limit and exposure controlling			
Loan loss provision setting			
Performance/risk-return controlling			
Concept and tool development/(re-) calibration, e.g., rating, pricing, structuring			
Tool approval			
Other (which?)			

Secondary credit market transactions

Function	**Involvement of portfolio management** (%)	**FTE**	**Involvement of other units (which?)** (%)
Advising			
Initiating			
Structuring			
Data gathering			
Pricing/negotiating			
Credit decision of PM deals			
Counterparty limit allocation (e.g., on sectors, products, maturities)			
Deciding			
Executing (market access)			
Trading			
Controlling			
Other (which?)			

Problem loan management and workout

Function	Involvement of CPM (%)	FTE	Involvement of other units (which?) (%)
Loan loss provisions			
Other (which?)			

For which decisions of your CPM unit do you have escalation criteria and which criteria are these? ____

2.2.2 Functional competencies

Which competencies does your CPM unit have for the aforementioned credit functions?

Credit policy setting

Function	No competence at all	Informational role/ competence	Advisory power	Veto power	Decision-making right
Definition of credit risk appetite of the institution					
Definition of target credit portfolio					
Capital allocation to business units					
Capital allocation to sub-portfolios (e.g., regions, industries, products)					
Setting underwriting guidelines, approval decision criteria, pricing standards					
Definition of decision-making power and decision processes					
Definition of limits: sectors, regions, single concentration limit					
Other (which?)					

Loan origination and underwriting

Function	**No competence at all**	**Informational role/ competence**	**Advisory power**	**Veto power**	**Decision-making right**
Credit customer/deal information gathering, verification, quality control					
Credit analysis					
Credit rating ("doing")					
Credit rating (final assessment)					
Pricing					
First vote					
Second vote					
Third vote (if applicable)					
Credit control incl. documentation					

Credit portfolio controlling and management

Function	**No competence at all**	**Informational role/ competence**	**Advisory power**	**Veto power**	**Decision-making right**
Credit research					
Ongoing monitoring of single position and credit quality					
Limit and exposure controlling					
Loan loss provision setting					
Performance/risk-return controlling					
Concept and tool development/(re-) calibration, e.g., rating, pricing, structuring					
Tool approval					
Other (which?)					

Secondary credit market transactions

Function	**No competence at all**	**Informational role/ competence**	**Advisory power**	**Veto power**	**Decision-making right**
Advising					
Initiating					
Structuring					
Data gathering					
Pricing/negotiating					
Credit decision of PM deals					
Counterparty limit allocation (e.g., on industry sectors, products, maturities)					
Deciding					
Executing (market access)					
Trading					
Controlling					
Other (which?)					

Problem loan management and workout

Function	**No competence at all**	**Informational role/ competence**	**Advisory power**	**Veto power**	**Decision-making right**
Loan loss provisions					
Other (which?)					

2.3 Asset focus and management principles

2.3.1 Asset focus

Which part of your institution's total credit portfolio (actual exposure, excluding credit lines of banks and sovereigns) is owned/managed by your CPM unit? What was the situation three years ago? Please estimate if necessary.

In percent (100% = EUR ....bn)	**Portfolio composition**	
Products/customer groups	**Cur-rent**	**3 yrs. ago**
Bilateral corporate lending		
Large corps loans		
Mid corps loans		
Small corps loans		
Syndicated loans		
Structured finance		
Project finance		
Other		
Leveraged finance		
Mortgage loans		
Consumer loans		
Other (which?)		

What share of your institution's total outstanding credit exposure in the following regions is integrated in your CPM unit?

In percent (100% = EUR ....bn)	**Share of total business volume** (%)
Domestic (home country)	
Europe	
US	
Emerging markets	
Rest of world	

2.3.2 Asset management principles (approach to asset ownership, management style, pricing, performance measurement/incentivization)

a) Approach to asset ownership

Does your CPM unit have its own book?

- Yes
- No
- Planned for: ___________

Does your CPM unit manage its own P&L?

- Yes
- No
- Planned for: ___________

If yes for which "changes" in your credit assets does the CPM unit bear P&L responsibility?

- Default
- Spread changes
- Changes in absolute return of assets

Which general role towards origination does your CPM unit have?

- Proprietary investor with asset ownership and full responsibility for credit portfolio
- Active portfolio manager with ownership of credit risks and activities on secondary credit markets
- Advisor on strategic direction of loan portfolio
- Risk reporter/controller

Please specify the above-mentioned role

____

Does this role vary across different products/customer groups of your credit portfolio? Does the current role correspond to the targeted role?

	Proprietary investor		**Active portfolio manager**		**Advisor on strategic direction**		**Risk reporter/controller**	
Products/customer groups	**Current role**	**Target role**	**Current role**	**Target role**	**Current role**	**Target role**	**Current role**	**Target role**
Bilateral corporate lending								
Large corps loans								
Mid corps loans								
Small corps loans								
Syndicated loans								
Structured finance								

Project finance								
Other								
Leveraged finance								
Mortgage loans								
Consumer loans								
Other (which?)								

b) Asset management style

How would you consider your management/investment style for individual products/customer groups?

Products/customer groups	Buy and hold approach	Selectively hedge and invest	Originate and trade/asset mgmt. approach	Varying levels of capital, e.g., depending on credit cycle	Other (which)
Bilateral corporate lending					
Large corps loans					
Mid corps loans					
Small corps loans					
Syndicated loans					
Structured finance					
Project finance					
Other					
Leveraged finance					
Mortgage loans					
Consumer loans					
Other (which?)					

Which concept of cycle management do you have?

- No cycle management at all
- Hold economic credit risk constant (e.g., in order to have constant income)
- "Riding the cycle", e.g., higher level of economic risk in peaks, lower level in downturns
- Other (which?)

What are your key cycle management instruments?

- Origination adjustments, which?______________________________
- Secondary market transactions, which?______________________________
- Capital transactions, which?______________________________
- Other, which?______________________________

How do you account for changes in credit qualities in the business originated by the bank?

	Portfolio owned by CPM	Portfolio not owned by CPM
Volume/valuation		
Market valuation		
Model valuation		
Risk		
Capital requirements		
Profitability		
Change of margins due to different standard risk cost		
No accountability		

c) Credit asset pricing (competence, methodology, risk measurement)

Pricing competence

For which products/customer groups does your CPM unit quote prices/hurdle rates to your origination unit? What is the character of the prices quoted by CPM?

	Prices/hurdle rates quoted		Character of prices			
Products/customer groups	**Yes**	**No**	**Binding**	**Recommending**	**Informational**	**Other (which?)**
Bilateral corporate lending						
Large corps loans						
Mid corps loans						
Small corps loans						
Syndicated loans						
Structured finance						
Project finance						
Other						
Leveraged finance						
Mortgage loans						
Consumer loans						
Other (which?)						

How often does the realized asset price deviate from the calculated price?

- % realized price equals calculated price
- % realized price above calculated price
- % realized price below calculated price

What are the main reasons for these deviations in different customer segments? *(please rank by importance on a scale from 1 to 5; 1= lowest, 5= highest importance)*?

	Corporates		**Institutionals**	
	Large Caps (> EUR 100 million)	**Small/ medium caps**	**Large caps**	**Small caps**
Importance of customer relationship				
Overall profitability of customer relationship				
Visibility of credit pricing vs. other products or non-shopped fees				
Other (which?)				

What is your approach to setting prices/values for credit assets?

	Liquid assets			**Illiquid assets**		
Products/customer groups	**Face value**	**Market value, e.g., CDS prices**	**Model value**	**Face value**	**Market value, e.g., CDS prices**	**Model value**
Bilateral corporate lending						
Large corps loans						
Mid corps loans						
Small corps loans						
Syndicated loans						
Structured finance						
Project finance						
Other						
Leveraged finance						
Mortgage loans						
Consumer loans						
Other (which?)						

How often do you mark positions to market/to model?

Products/customer groups	Daily	Weekly	Monthly	Quarterly	Yearly	Other
Bilateral corporate lending						
Large corps loans						
Mid corps loans						
Small corps loans						
Syndicated loans						
Structured finance						
Project finance						
Other						
Leveraged finance						
Mortgage loans						
Consumer loans						
Other (which?)						

If assets are transferred to CPM: Who determines the prices to transfer assets to the CPM unit?

- Originating business units
- Credit management
- CPM
- Credit risk committee
- Other: ______________________________

Is there a rule for selling underperforming assets after a certain period of time?

- Yes: (what is it?) ______________________________
- No

Who bears the cost of underperforming assets?

- Originating unit
- CPM
- Other: ______________________________

Pricing methodology

What is your pricing methodology?

____

How does your internal credit pricing model work for different products/customer groups?

Products/customer groups	Based on historical defaults and losses	Based on observed market prices and derived information (e.g., through no-arbitrage-model)	Other
Bilateral corporate lending			
Large corps loans			
Mid corps loans			
Small corps loans			
Syndicated loans			
Structured finance			
Project finance			
Other			
Leveraged finance			
Mortgage loans			
Consumer loans			
Other (which?)			

Which input factors are considered for your pricing model?

- PD/LGD estimates from rating
- Default correlation
- Default and LGD correlation
- Cash flow structure
- Maturity/duration
- Embedded options
- Collateral
- Liquidity of position/holding period
- Risk contribution to own credit risk portfolio
- Market based credit hedging cost
- Regulatory capital charge
- Funding
- Other (which?):______________________________________

How important are the following key data sources to feed your internal pricing model?

	Importance *(please rank on scale from 1 to 5)*		
Data sources	**(Expected) probability of default**	**(Expected) loss given default**	**Risk contribution to own credit risk portfolio (correlation)**
Analysis of own portfolio default history			
Market data			
Equity prices			
Bond prices			
Secondary loan prices			
CDS prices			
Other (which?)			
Other (which?)			

What are the main information sources for credit evaluation/assessment/rating?

- Originating business units and direct customer contact
- Information from existing customer/bank relationship, e.g., current account and product usage
- Analysis of own portfolio default history
- Other public information
- Market data
- Other (which?) ______________________________

How are the accounting values of your credit assets determined?

- Based on accrual accounting
- Fair value (marked-to-market or marked-to-model)

Other (which?): ______________________________

Which issues do you see with regard to your pricing concept?

- Important factors missing (which?) ______________________________
- Important factors not adequately considered (which?) ______________________________
- Less important factors receive too much attention (which?) ______________________________
- Other conceptual issues (which?)______________________________
- No conceptual issues but other? ______________________________

Where do you think is the most significant improvement potential regarding pricing in your institution?

- Concepts ______________________________
- Tools ______________________________
- Applications______________________________

Risk measuremen

Which credit risks are measured?

- Default risks
- Spread risks
- Collateral value risks
- Liquidity risks
- Other (which?)

Which risk factors are modeled?

- Collateral value
- Rating downgrades/upgrades
- Changes in market evaluation of credit risk
- Changes in liquidity
- Sector/regional risks
- Credit cyclicality
- Credit correlations
- Other (which?)

What are the parameters for your risk measurement model

- Time horizon (in days) ____________________
- Confidence level (in %) ____________________

Do you conduct stress tests on a regular basis?

- Yes
- No

If yes, which factors are stress-tested?

____

How content are you with the degree of sophistication/accuracy of your risk measurement on different levels? What are key issues?

Individual transactions

Fully	**Some-what**	**Hardly**	**Not at all**	**Key issues**
☐	☐	☐	☐	

Counterparties

Fully	**Some-what**	**Hardly**	**Not at all**	**Key issues**
☐	☐	☐	☐	

Entire credit portfolio

Fully	Some-what	Hardly	Not at all	Key issues
☐	☐	☐	☐	

d) Performance measurement/incentivization

Which are the key performance indicators to define your target credit portfolio *(please rank by importance on a scale from 1 to 5; 1= lowest, 5= highest)?* How do you estimate the future importance of these indicators?

	1	2	3	4	5	Future dev.
Performance						
Profit contribution	☐	☐	☐	☐	☐	
ROE improvement	☐	☐	☐	☐	☐	
RAROC/RORAC/economic profit improvement	☐	☐	☐	☐	☐	
Ex-ante RAROC	☐	☐	☐	☐	☐	
Ex-post RAROC	☐	☐	☐	☐	☐	
Returns compared to benchmark	☐	☐	☐	☐	☐	
Other (which?)	☐	☐	☐	☐	☐	
Volume						
Balance sheet impact (e.g., share of customer loan volume)	☐	☐	☐	☐	☐	
Risk assets	☐	☐	☐	☐	☐	
Other (which?)	☐	☐	☐	☐	☐	
Risk						
Country	☐	☐	☐	☐	☐	
Industry	☐	☐	☐	☐	☐	
Product	☐	☐	☐	☐	☐	
Single name	☐	☐	☐	☐	☐	
Credit risk cost	☐	☐	☐	☐	☐	
Ex-ante from pre-calculation	☐	☐	☐	☐	☐	
Actual loan losses	☐	☐	☐	☐	☐	
P&L VaR/economic capital	☐	☐	☐	☐	☐	
Regulatory Capital	☐	☐	☐	☐	☐	
Tier-1 ratio	☐	☐	☐	☐	☐	
Basel I/Basel II capital ratio	☐	☐	☐	☐	☐	
Economic capital	☐	☐	☐	☐	☐	
Other (which?)	☐	☐	☐	☐	☐	

Which are the performance figures used to evaluate CPM
(please rank by importance on a scale from 1 to 5; 1= lowest, 5= highest)?

Net profit contribution

1	2	3	4	5
☐	☐	☐	☐	☐

Returns compared to benchmark

1	2	3	4	5
☐	☐	☐	☐	☐

RAROC

1	2	3	4	5
☐	☐	☐	☐	☐

Economic profit/NPV

1	2	3	4	5
☐	☐	☐	☐	☐

Credit risk cost

1	2	3	4	5
☐	☐	☐	☐	☐

Portfolio VaR

1	2	3	4	5
☐	☐	☐	☐	☐

Reduction of concentration risk

1	2	3	4	5
☐	☐	☐	☐	☐

Approximation of portfolio to target portfolio

1	2	3	4	5
☐	☐	☐	☐	☐

Efficiency (e.g., cost per EUR/USD economic capital reduction)

1	2	3	4	5
☐	☐	☐	☐	☐

Other: ______________________________

1	2	3	4	5
☐	☐	☐	☐	☐

Are there potential conflicts of interest between the goals and management principles of origination and CPM ?

- Yes
- No

If yes, what are they? ______________________________

1. ______________________________
2. ______________________________
3. ______________________________

How do you solve these conflicts of interest?

1. ______________________________
2. ______________________________
3. ______________________________

Where do you allocate diversification benefits?

	Diversification benefits
Add benefits back to BUs	
Keep benefits within PM unit	
Don't measure and allocate at all	
Other (where?)	

Are the objectives for your CPM unit clearly reflected in the incentives for management and staff in CPM and other units?

CPM	Yes	Partially	No
Origination	Yes	Partially	No
Secondary market units	Yes	Partially	No
Risk function	Yes	Partially	No

What do your incentive systems for your CPM look like and how do you align them with the ones in other functions/BUs?

____

3 Objectives, related implementation barriers and approaches to overcome

3.1 Key objectives of CPM unit, degree of implementation and main implementation barriers

What are the key objectives of your CPM unit *(please rank by importance on a scale from 1 to 5)*? To what extent have these objectives been implemented? What are/have been key issues/barriers for success?

Increase transparency of portfolio risk

1	2	3	4	5		Implementation/Achievement (%)	Issues/Barriers
☐	☐	☐	☐	☐			

Increase transparency of portfolio return/performance

1	2	3	4	5		Implementation/Achievement (%)	Issues/Barriers
☐	☐	☐	☐	☐			

Limit unwanted risks, e.g., (unexpected) loss limitation

1	2	3	4	5		Implementation/Achievement (%)	Issues/Barriers
☐	☐	☐	☐	☐			

Discipline origination, especially with regard to risk-adjusted pricing

1	2	3	4	5		Implementation/Achievement (%)	Issues/Barriers
☐	☐	☐	☐	☐			

Capital and exposure management

- Reduce regulatory capital consumption

1	2	3	4	5		Implementation/Achievement (%)	Issues/Barriers
☐	☐	☐	☐	☐			

- Reduce economic capital consumption

1	2	3	4	5		Implementation/Achievement (%)	Issues/Barriers
☐	☐	☐	☐	☐			

- Improve ratios for own credit rating

1	2	3	4	5		Implementation/Achievement (%)	Issues/Barriers
☐	☐	☐	☐	☐			

- Improve qualitative factors/processes for rating

1	2	3	4	5		Implementation/Achievement (%)	Issues/Barriers
☐	☐	☐	☐	☐			

– Free up credit lines to support additional business

1	2	3	4	5		Implementation/Achievement (%)	Issues/Barriers
☐	☐	☐	☐	☐			

– Manage free capital at overall banking level (across divisions)

1	2	3	4	5		Implementation/Achievement (%)	Issues/Barriers
☐	☐	☐	☐	☐			

– Reallocate capital across BU/division

1	2	3	4	5		Implementation/Achievement (%)	Issues/Barriers
☐	☐	☐	☐	☐			

Balance sheet/P&L management

– Reduce balance sheet volume/size

1	2	3	4	5		Implementation/Achievement (%)	Issues/Barriers
☐	☐	☐	☐	☐			

– Increase share of customer business

1	2	3	4	5		Implementation/Achievement (%)	Issues/Barriers
☐	☐	☐	☐	☐			

– Ensure sufficient income, e.g., to cover fixed costs

1	2	3	4	5		Implementation/Achievement (%)	Issues/Barriers
☐	☐	☐	☐	☐			

– Manage revenues (e.g., through reinvestments)

1	2	3	4	5		Implementation/Achievement (%)	Issues/Barriers
☐	☐	☐	☐	☐			

– Other: ____

1	2	3	4	5		Implementation/Achievement (%)	Issues/Barriers
☐	☐	☐	☐	☐			

Improve risk-return structure/diversification/portfolio efficiency of credit portfolio, create shareholder value

– Change risk structure of portfolio

1	2	3	4	5		Implementation/Achievement (%)	Issues/Barriers
☐	☐	☐	☐	☐			

– Change margin structure of portfolio

1	2	3	4	5		Implementation/Achievement (%)	Issues/Barriers
☐	☐	☐	☐	☐			

- Increase liquidity of exposures within your loan portfolio

1	2	3	4	5		Implementation/Achievement (%)	Issues/Barriers
☐	☐	☐	☐	☐			

- Optimize collateral

1	2	3	4	5		Implementation/Achievement (%)	Issues/Barriers
☐	☐	☐	☐	☐			

- Other: ______________________________

1	2	3	4	5		Implementation/Achievement (%)	Issues/Barriers
☐	☐	☐	☐	☐			

Create new secondary markets in credit risk trading

1	2	3	4	5		Implementation/Achievement (%)	Issues/Barriers
☐	☐	☐	☐	☐			

Active spread positioning

1	2	3	4	5		Implementation/Achievement (%)	Issues/Barriers
☐	☐	☐	☐	☐			

Cycle management

1	2	3	4	5		Implementation/Achievement (%)	Issues/Barriers
☐	☐	☐	☐	☐			

- Other: ______________________________

1	2	3	4	5		Implementation/Achievement (%)	Issues/Barriers
☐	☐	☐	☐	☐			

What would need to happen for you to be significantly more effective in achieving your goals?

- Internally in your institution

1. ______________________________
2. ______________________________
3. ______________________________

- Externally in the marketplace

1. ______________________________
2. ______________________________
3. ______________________________

3.2 Basis for implementation decision of CPM unit

What were/are the main implementation steps (phases/milestones) of your CPM unit?

____

How long did it take to achieve these milestones?

____

What were the available/necessary resources?

- Budget: ____
- Personnel: ____
- Tools: ____

What implementation organization has proven successful?
- Implementation through existing line organization
- Implementation through a dedicated project
- Implementation through newly established line unit (CPM)
- Other (which?)

3.3 Issues during implementation and approaches to overcome

What are the lessons learned regarding implementing your CPM ?
1. ____
2. ____
3. ____

What are/were key success factors *(please rank by importance on a scale from 1 to 5; 1= lowest, 5= highest)?*

Clear strategy

1	2	3	4	5		Key success factors
☐	☐	☐	☐	☐		

High ambition level

1	2	3	4	5		Key success factors
☐	☐	☐	☐	☐		

Specific business opportunity

1	2	3	4	5		Key success factors
☐	☐	☐	☐	☐		

Competitive pressure

1	2	3	4	5		**Key success factors**
☐	☐	☐	☐	☐		

Senior executive as driving force

1	2	3	4	5		**Key success factors**
☐	☐	☐	☐	☐		

Right group of motivated, skilled people

1	2	3	4	5		**Key success factors**
☐	☐	☐	☐	☐		

What are/were key issues during implementation and what was your approach to overcome them?

Data availability *(please rank by importance on a scale from 1 to 5; 1= lowest, 5= highest)*

– Availability of portfolio data (LGD, collateral data)

1	2	3	4	5		**Approach to overcome**
☐	☐	☐	☐	☐		

– Data consistency/"cleanness"

1	2	3	4	5		**Approach to overcome**
☐	☐	☐	☐	☐		

– Other: ____

1	2	3	4	5		**Approach to overcome**
☐	☐	☐	☐	☐		

Tools/processes

– Portfolio model (credit VaR)

1	2	3	4	5		**Approach to overcome**
☐	☐	☐	☐	☐		

– Pricing

1	2	3	4	5		**Approach to overcome**
☐	☐	☐	☐	☐		

– Incentives for origination

1	2	3	4	5		**Approach to overcome**
☐	☐	☐	☐	☐		

– Transfer process in/out of portfolio

1	2	3	4	5		Approach to overcome
☐	☐	☐	☐	☐		

People skills

– Credit expertise

1	2	3	4	5		Approach to overcome
☐	☐	☐	☐	☐		

– Secondary market expertise

1	2	3	4	5		Approach to overcome
☐	☐	☐	☐	☐		

– Availability

1	2	3	4	5		Approach to overcome
☐	☐	☐	☐	☐		

Acceptance by BU and other units

1	2	3	4	5		Approach to overcome
☐	☐	☐	☐	☐		

Cultural change

1	2	3	4	5		Approach to overcome
☐	☐	☐	☐	☐		

Top management support

– Board/CRO involvement

1	2	3	4	5		Approach to overcome
☐	☐	☐	☐	☐		

– Divisional support

1	2	3	4	5		Approach to overcome
☐	☐	☐	☐	☐		

– Other: ______________________

1	2	3	4	5		Approach to overcome
☐	☐	☐	☐	☐		

Liquidity of assets

- Liquidity/tradability of assets

1	2	3	4	5		Approach to overcome
☐	☐	☐	☐	☐		

Change of accounting standards (e.g., IAS)

1	2	3	4	5		Approach to overcome
☐	☐	☐	☐	☐		

Other: ______________________________

1	2	3	4	5		Approach to overcome
☐	☐	☐	☐	☐		

4 Economic impact

How would you consider the economic impact of your CPM unit?______________________________

What bottom-line impact (estimation?) did you achieve with implementation of your CPM unit?

	Before implementation	After implementation	Time for recognition in institution	Main drivers
Performance				
Net profit (EUR mn.)				
ROE (%)				
RAROC/RORAC (%)				
Returns vs. benchmark				
Other (which?)				
Volume				
Customer loan volume				
Risk assets				
Other (which?)				
Risk				
Credit risk cost (EUR mn)				
P&L volatility (%)				
Other (which?)				
Capital				
Regulatory capital (EUR mn)				
Economic capital (EUR mn)				
Other (which?)				
Other				
What are running costs p.a. of your CPM unit (EUR mn)?				
What were implementation costs?				

5 Outlook and vision

What is your vision regarding CPM?

___

Which are your key issues regarding achieving this vision?

___

How do you plan to move towards the "next horizon" with your CPM unit?
- In-source functions from other players
- Create new markets
- Other (which?)

What are your future goals/next steps concerning design and development of your CPM unit?

- Scope: ___
- Management style/principles: ___
- Organizational setup: ___

II. Relation to/interfaces with origination units

1 Origination objectives and performance evaluation

Which are the key performance indicators for origination *(please rank by importance on a scale from 1 to 5; 1=lowest, 5= highest)?*

	1	2	3	4	5	N/A
Performance						
– Spread over CPM's transfer price						
▪ NPV-based	☐	☐	☐	☐	☐	
▪ Margin-based	☐	☐	☐	☐	☐	
– Returns compared to benchmark	☐	☐	☐	☐	☐	
– RAROC/RORAC	☐	☐	☐	☐	☐	
– ROE	☐	☐	☐	☐	☐	
– Profit contribution (accrual result)	☐	☐	☐	☐	☐	
Volume						
– Balance sheet impact (e.g., share of customer loan volume)	☐	☐	☐	☐	☐	
– Risk assets	☐	☐	☐	☐	☐	
– Portfolio composition	☐	☐	☐	☐	☐	
– Key target customer penetration	☐	☐	☐	☐	☐	
– New customer acquisition	☐	☐	☐	☐	☐	
Risk (VaR)						
– Country	☐	☐	☐	☐	☐	
– Industry	☐	☐	☐	☐	☐	
– Product	☐	☐	☐	☐	☐	
– Single name	☐	☐	☐	☐	☐	
– Credit risk cost	☐	☐	☐	☐	☐	
– Portfolio VaR	☐	☐	☐	☐	☐	
Capital	☐	☐	☐	☐	☐	
Other (which?)	☐	☐	☐	☐	☐	

What is the basis for origination performance evaluation?

Individual loan

1	2	3	4	5
☐	☐	☐	☐	☐

Overall credit exposure to individual name/counterparty

1	2	3	4	5
☐	☐	☐	☐	☐

Overall relationship including all credit and non-credit products

1	2	3	4	5
☐	☐	☐	☐	☐

Sub-portfolio – region

1	2	3	4	5
☐	☐	☐	☐	☐

Sub-portfolio – industry

1	2	3	4	5
☐	☐	☐	☐	☐

Sub-portfolio – Other

1	2	3	4	5
☐	☐	☐	☐	☐

Overall portfolio

1	2	3	4	5
☐	☐	☐	☐	☐

Are management incentives aligned with these criteria?

- Yes
- Partially
- No

2 Origination competencies and interfaces with CPM

2.1 Pricing

What is your pricing approach towards your customers?

- Return > hurdle rate (transfer price) for each individual transaction/loan
- Return > hurdle rate (transfer price) for credit exposure to each individual name
- Return > hurdle rate (transfer price) for each individual customer relation
- Return > hurdle rate (transfer price) for specific sub-portfolios of names, e.g., industries, regions
- Other:____

How are the costs of hedging for concentration-risk reduction allocated?

	Assets transferred to CPM	**Assets not transferred to CPM**
Origination		
CPM		

2.2 Credit analysis and approval

How is your credit analysis process organized?

- Regional groups
- Industry groups
- Credit qualities/rating
- Other (which?)

What happens if a loan does not meet your hurdle rate criteria?

- Immediate rejection
- Origination/relationship management can approve loan without further requirements
- Origination/relationship management can approve loan only under specific considerations (which?)
- Escalation process, e.g., into credit committee, higher organizational level
- CPM can approve loan without further requirements
- CPM can approve only under specific considerations (which?) ____________________
- Other (which?) ____________________

What are the escalation criteria in case of disagreement between CPM and origination/relationship management?

1. ____________________
2. ____________________
3. ____________________

2.3 Transfer of assets

When are assets transferred to CPM ?

Products/customer groups	**Immediately after origination**	**Upon decision of origination**	**Upon decision of PM**	**Assets are not transferred**
Bilateral corporate lending				
Large corps loans				
Mid corps loans				
Small corps loans				
Syndicated loans				
Structured finance				
Project finance				
Other				
Leveraged finance				
Mortgage loans				
Consumer loans				
Other (which?)				

Which assets does CPM put on its own books/P&L?

- Highly liquid names with secondary market price
- Liquid names without secondary market price
- Small/mid caps/illiquid assets
- No assets at all

For which changes in your credit assets does your origination unit bear (internal) P&L responsibility?

- Loan loss reserves
- Default
- Market value changes
- Model value changes

III. Relation to/interfaces with secondary credit market activities

1 Secondary market business approach

Which is your secondary market business approach regarding CPM *(please rank by importance on a scale from 1 to 5; 1 = lowest, 5 = highest)*? Do you mainly…

Distribute credit risks

1	2	3	4	5
☐	☐	☐	☐	☐

Invest into credit risks

1	2	3	4	5
☐	☐	☐	☐	☐

Trade credit risks

1	2	3	4	5
☐	☐	☐	☐	☐

2 Secondary credit market instruments

Which secondary credit market instruments do you use to invest in and to sell credit risks? How important are these instruments for the management of your credit portfolio *(please rank by importance on a scale from 1 to 5; 1 = lowest, 5 = highest)*?

Invest in credit risks							
	Yes	**No**	**Importance**				
			1	**2**	**3**	**4**	**5**
• Syndication	☐	☐	☐	☐	☐	☐	☐
• Plain vanilla credit derivatives (CDS)	☐	☐	☐	☐	☐	☐	☐
• Synthetic securitizations							
– CDO/baskets	☐	☐	☐	☐	☐	☐	☐
– ABS, MBS	☐	☐	☐	☐	☐	☐	☐
• Cash-based securitizations							
– CDO	☐	☐	☐	☐	☐	☐	☐
– ABS, MBS	☐	☐	☐	☐	☐	☐	☐
• Loan sales	☐	☐	☐	☐	☐	☐	☐
• Bonds/macro-investments	☐	☐	☐	☐	☐	☐	☐

Distribute credit risks							
	Yes	No	Importance				
			1	2	3	4	5
• Syndication	☐	☐	☐	☐	☐	☐	☐
• Plain vanilla credit derivatives (CDS)	☐	☐	☐	☐	☐	☐	☐
• Synthetic securitizations							
– CDO/baskets	☐	☐	☐	☐	☐	☐	☐
– ABS, MBS	☐	☐	☐	☐	☐	☐	☐
• Cash-based securitizations							
– CDO	☐	☐	☐	☐	☐	☐	☐
– ABS, MBS	☐	☐	☐	☐	☐	☐	☐
• Loan sales	☐	☐	☐	☐	☐	☐	☐

3 Reinvestment strategy

Have you defined an explicit reinvestment strategy?

- Yes
- No

If yes, is a detailed reinvestment strategy per segment (e.g., OECD corporates) available?

- Yes
- No

Which tactics do you use when investing into credit risk?

- Buy and hold
- Active Management

If you use active management tactics, which specific approaches do you use?

- Market timing
- Sector plays
- Leveraged plays
- Name picking
- Other, which?___________________

Which is the planning horizon for your reinvestment strategy?

- 1 year
- 1 - 3 years
- > 3 years

How do you measure the performance of your reinvestment portfolio?

- Entirely based on accrual results
- Partly based on accrual results, partly based on marked-to market/model
- Entirely based on marked-to-market/model
- Other, which? ______________________________

Which risk measures do you use for your reinvestment portfolio?

- Unexpected loss
- VaR
- Conditional VaR
- Sharpe ratio
- Other, which ? ______________________________
- No measures at all

4 Issues related to secondary credit market activities

What are the key issues in applying the secondary credit market instruments mentioned above? How can the bank/CPM use the available instruments more effectively?

____

Which key issues do you see regarding the establishment of a broad investor base?

- Lacking direct market access for Credit CPM
- Insufficient contact to market participants
- Other (which?)

How important do you consider an own secondary market access for your credit CPM

- Very important
- Somewhat important
- Not particularly important

Which secondary market functions are essential for your CPM to successfully perform secondary market transactions?

- Syndication desk
- Secondary loan trading desk
- Other (which?)__________

Please specify:

____

Glossary

AEB (2001). "Asociaciòn Espanola de Banca, Cuentas de Perdidas y Ganancias de la Banca en Espana." http://www.aebanca.com (as of 23 November 2005). Diciembre 2001

AEB (2002). "Asociaciòn Espanola de Banca, Cuentas de Perdidas y Ganancias de la Banca en Espana." http://www.aebanca.com (as of 23 November 2005). Diciembre 2002

AEB (2003). "Asociaciòn Espanola de Banca, Cuentas de Perdidas y Ganancias de la Banca en Espana." http://www.aebanca.com (as of 23 November 2005). Diciembre 2003

AEB (2004). "Asociaciòn Espanola de Banca, Cuentas de Perdidas y Ganancias de la Banca en Espana." http://www.aebanca.com (as of 23 November 2005). Diciembre 2004

Akerlof, G. (1970). "Market for Lemons: Quality Uncertainty and the Market Mechanism." Quarterly Journal of Economics 84: 488 - 500

Albanese, C. (1997). "Credit Exposure, Diversification Risk and Coherent VaR." Working Paper, Department of Mathematics, University of Toronto

Albrecht, P. (2001). "Portfolioselektion mit Shortfallrisikomaßen." Mannheimer Manuskripte zu Risikotheorie, Portfolio Management und Versicherungswirtschaft Nr. 133

Allen, F. and Carletti, E. (2005). "Credit Risk Transfer and Contagion." CFS Working Paper No. 25/2, http://ssrn.com/abstract=824226 (as of 20 January 2006)

Allen, F. and Gale, D. (2000). Comparing Financial Systems. Cambridge, MIT-Press

Allen, F. and Santomero, A. M. (1998). "The Theory of Financial Intermediation." Journal of Banking and Finance 21: 1461 - 1485

Allen, S. (2003). Financial Risk Management. Hoboken, Wiley Finance

Altman, E., Caouette, J., et al. (1998). Managing Credit Risk. Hoboken, John Wiley & Sons

Altman, E. I. (1993). Corporate Financial Distress and Bankruptcy - A Complete Guide to Predicting and Avoiding Distress and Profiting from Bankruptcy. New York, Wiley Finance Edition

Altman, E. I. and Saunders, A. (1997). "Credit Risk Measurement: Developments Over the Last 20 years." Journal of Banking and Finance 21: 1721 - 1742

Ambrose, B., LaCour-Little, M., et al. (2003). "Does Regulatory Capital Arbitrage or Asymmetric Information Drive Securitization?" Working Paper, University of Kentucky

American Bankers Association (1999). Banking & Finance Terminology. Washington

Anhamm, C. (2004). "Covered Bonds' Global Expansion." The Banker, February 2004

Anson, M., Chen, M., et al. (2004). Credit Derivatives: Instruments, Applications and Pricing. Hoboken, John Wiley & Sons

Armstrong, J. (2003). "The Syndicated Loan Market: Developments in the North American Context." Working Paper No. 2003 - 15, Bank of Canada

Arrow, K. (1964). "The Role of Securities in the Optimal Allocation of Risk-Bearing." Review of Economic Studies: 91 - 96

Artzner, P., Delbaen, F., et al. (1999). "Coherent Measures of Risk." Mathematical Finance 9(3): 203-228

Asarnov, E. (1996). "Active Loan Portfolio Management: Stages of Implementation." Journal of Lending and Credit Risk Management 79(1): 15 - 22

Atkeson, A. and Cole, H. (2005). "A Dynamic Theory of Optimal Capital Structure and Executive Compensation." NBER Working Paper No. W11083, January 2005

Azarchs, T. (2003). "Demystifying Banks' Use of Credit Derivatives." Working Paper, Standard & Poors

BaFin (1995). Bundesaufsichtsamt für das Kreditwesen: Überblick über die grundsätzlichen Anforderungen an die Offenlegung der wirtschaftlichen Verhältnisse nach § 18 KWG, BAK-Schreiben vom 8. August 1995

BaFin (2002). "Vereinbarung über die Zusammenarbeit der Bundesanstalt für Finanzdienstleistungsaufsicht und der Deutschen Bundesbank bei der Beaufsichtigung der Kredit- und Finanzdienstleistungsinstitute." http://www.bafin.de/sonstiges/mou_021031.htm (as of 19 May 2005)

BaFin (2003). "Bundesanstalt für Finanzdienstleistungsaufsicht. Wir über uns. Aufgaben & Ziele." http://www.bafin.de/bafin/aufgabenundziele.htm (as of 19 May 2005)

Bakalar, N. and Prince, J. (2003). "Synthetic CDOs Come of Age: An Investor's Guide." Research Document, Wachovia Securities, July 2003

Bamberg, G. and Spremann, K. (1989). Agency Theory, Information, and Incentives. Berlin, Heidelberg, Springer

Bankers Trust (1995). RAROC 2020: A Comprehensive Risk Measurement Service

Banks, E. (2004). The Credit Risk of Complex Derivatives. New York, Palgrave MacMillan

Banque de France (2004). "Rapport Annuel de la Banque de France." http://www.banquedefrance.fr/fr/publications/rapport/rapport.htm (as of 23 November 2005)

Barnish, K., Miller, S., et al. (1997). "The New Leveraged Syndication Loan Market." Journal of Applied Corporate Finance 10(1): 79 - 88

Barton, D., Newell, R., et al. (2003). Dangerous Markets: Managing in Financial Crises. Hoboken, John Wiley & Sons

Bavaria, S. (2002). "Syndicated Loans - A Rated Market at Last." Research Paper No. 27, Standard & Poor's

Bawa, V. (1975). "Optimal Rules for Ordering Uncertain Prospects." Journal of Financial Economics 2: 95 - 121

Bawa, V. (1978). "Safety First, Stochastic Dominance and Optimal Portfolio Choice." Journal of Finance and Quantitative Analysis 13: 255 - 271

Bawa, V. and Lindenberg, E. (1977). "Capital Market Equilibrium in a Mean, Lower Partial Moment Framework." Journal of Financial Economics 5: 189 - 200

Baxter, N. (1967). "Leverage, Risk of Ruin and the Cost of Capital." Journal of Finance 22: 395 - 403

BBA (1996). "The British Bankers' Association Credit Derivatives Report."

BBA (2003/2004). "The British Bankers' Association Credit Derivatives Report."

Beck, T. (2000). "Deposit Insurance as Private Club: Is Germany a Model?" Working Paper, World Bank

Beneviste, L. M. and Berger, A. (1987). "Securitization with Recourse, An Instrument that Offers Uninsured Bank Depositors Sequential Claims." Journal of Banking and Finance 11: 403 - 424

Benthien, K. (1993). Risikomanagement im gewerblichen Kreditgeschäft. Handbuch Firmenkundengeschäft. K. Juncker and Priewasser, E. Frankfurt am Main, Fritz Knapp Verlag

Berg, E. (1994). Prozessorientierte Analyse der Abwicklung notleidender Kredite. Kiel, Vauk

Berger, A. and Udell, G. (1993). Securitization, Risk, and the Liquidity Problem in Banking. Structural Change in Banking. M. Klausner and White, L. Irwin, Homewood

Bernoulli, D. (1738). "Specimen Theoriae Novae de Mensura Sortis." Commentarii Academiae Scientiarum Imperialis Petropolitanae 5: 175 - 192

Bhattacharaya, A. (2001). Prepayment Penalty on Mortgage-Backed Securities. The Handbook of Mortgage-Backed Securities. F. Fabozzi. New York, McGraw-Hill

Bhattacharya, S. and Thakor, A. V. (1992). "Contemporary Banking Theory." Journal of Financial Intermediation 3: 2-50

BIS (1988). International Convergence of Capital Measurement and Capital Standards - Basel Committee of Banking Supervision. Basel

BIS (2003a). "BIS Quarterly Review March 2003." http://www.bis.org/publ/qtrpdf/r_qt0303.pdf (as of 13 December 2005)

BIS (2003b). "Credit Risk Transfer." Report submitted by a working group established by the Bank for International Settlements Committee on the Global Financial System. http://www.bis.org/publ/cgfs20.pdf (as of 23 Oct. 2005)

BIS (2003c). "The New Basel Capital Accord - Quantitative Impact Study 3 and Working Paper 2." The Basel Committee of Banking Supervision of the Bank for International Settlements. http://www.bondmarkets.com/europe/esfbaselletter13jan03.pdf (as of 26 Oct. 2005)

BIS (2004a). "BIS 74th Annual Report." http://www.bis.org/publ/ar2004e.htm (as of 23 November 2005)

BIS (2004b). "Credit Risk Transfer." The Basel Committee of Banking Supervision of the Bank for International Settlements

BIS (2004c). International Convergence of Capital Measurement and Capital Standards. A Revised Framework, Bank for International Settlements

BIS (2004d). "OTC derivatives market activity in the second half of 2003." The Monetary and Economic Department of the Bank for International Settlements

Black, F. (1972). "Capital Market Equilibrium with Restricted Borrowing." Journal of Business 45: 444 - 454

Black, F. and Scholes, M. (1973). "The Pricing of Options and Corporate Liabilities." Journal of Political Economy 83(3): 637 - 654

Blanco, R., Brennan, S., et al. (2003). "An Empirical Analysis of the Dynamic Relationship between Investment Grade Bonds and Credit Default Swaps." Working Paper, Banco de Espana

Bleymüller, J., Gehlert, G., et al. (2004). Statistik für Wirtschaftswissenschaftler. München, Vahlen

Bond Market Association (2002). "An Investor's Guide to CMOs." The Bond Market Association

Bond Market Association (2004a). "Asset Backed Securities Outstanding by Major Types of Credit." BondMarkets.com, http://www.bondmarkets.com/story.asp?id=84 (as of 14 December 2004)

Bond Market Association (2004b). "Outstanding Volume of Agency Mortgage-Backed Securities." BondMarkets.com, http://www.bondmarkets.com/story.asp?id=1256 (as of 14 December 2004)

Börner, C. J. (2000). Strategisches Bankmanagement: Ressourcen- und marktorientierte Strategien von Universalbanken. München, Wien, Oldenburg

Börsenzeitung (2005). "HDax-Werte im Überblick - 13.12.2005." Börsenzeitung as of 14 December 2005: 24

Bradley, M., Jarrell, G., et al. (1984). "On the Existence of an Optimal Capital Structure: Theory and Evidence." Journal of Finance 39: 857 - 877

Brav, O. (2004). "How Does Access to the Public Capital Market Affect Firm's Capital Structure?" Working Paper, The Wharton School, University of Pennsylvania

Brealey, R. and Myers, S. (2003). Principles of Corporate Finance. New York, McGraw-Hill

Brealey, R., Myers, S., et al. (2004). Fundamentals of Corporate Finance. New York, McGraw-Hill

Breeden, D. (1979). "An Intertemporal Asset Pricing Model with Stochastic Consumption and Investment Opportunities." Journal of Financial Economics 7: 265 - 296

Brennan, M. and Schwartz, E. (1984). "Optimal Financial Policy and Firm Valuation." Journal of Finance 39: 593 - 607

Breuer, W. (1993). Finanzintermediation im Kapitalmarktgleichgewicht, zugel. Dissertation Universität zu Köln. Wiesbaden

Broome, L., Markell, B., et al. (2004). Securitization, Structured Finance and Capital Markets. Charlottesville, Newark, San Francisco, Lexis

Bundesbank (1992). Die Einlagensicherung in der Bundesrepublik Deutschland

Bundesbank (1994). Monatsbericht September 1994. Frankfurt am Main, Deutsche Bundesbank

Bundesbank (1996). Monatsbericht September 1996. Frankfurt am Main, Deutsche Bundesbank

Bundesbank (1998). Monatsbericht September 1998. Frankfurt am Main, Deutsche Bundesbank

Bundesbank (2000). Monatsbericht September 2000. Frankfurt am Main, Deutsche Bundesbank

Bundesbank (2002a). Monatsbericht Januar 2002. Frankfurt am Main, Deutsche Bundesbank

Bundesbank (2002b). Monatsbericht September 2002. Frankfurt am Main, Deutsche Bundesbank

Bundesbank (2003a). Monatsbericht September 2003. Frankfurt am Main, Deutsche Bundesbank

Bundesbank (2003b). Monatsbericht September 2003. Frankfurt am Main, Deutsche Bundesbank

Bundesbank (2004). Bankenstatistik, Statistisches Beiheft zum Monatsbericht 1, September 2004. Frankfurt am Main, Deutsche Bundesbank

Bundesbank (2005a). Bankenstatistik, Statistisches Beiheft zum Monatsbericht 1, Oktober 2005. Frankfurt am Main, Deutsche Bundesbank

Bundesbank (2005b). Monatsbericht September 2005. Frankfurt am Main, Deutsche Bundesbank

Burghof, H. and Rudolph, B. (1996). Bankenaufsicht: Theorie und Praxis der Regulierung. Wiesbaden, Gabler

Büschgen, H. E. (1998). Bankbetriebslehre: Bankgeschäfte und Bankmanagement. Wiesbaden

Büschgen, H. E. and Börner, C. J. (2003). Bankbetriebslehre. Stuttgart, Lucius & Lucius

Busse, C. (2003). "BayernLB legt die grossen Pläne ad acta." Handelsblatt as of 11 June 2003: 20

Campbell, J., Lo, A., et al. (1997). The Econometrics of Financial Markets. Princeton, Princeton University Press

Caprio, G. and Klingebiel, D. (1999). "Episodes of Systemic and Borderline Financial Crises." World Bank Report

Carlstrom, C. and Samolyk, K. (1995). "Loan Sales as a Response to Market-Based Capital Constraints." Journal of Banking and Finance 19: 627 - 646

Carrington, T. (1984). "U.S. Won't Let 11 Biggest Banks in Nation Fail." Wall Street Journal as of 20 September 1984: 2

Catao, L. and Rodriguez, S. (2000). "Banks and Monetary Shocks in Emerging Markets: How far can we go with the "Credit View"?" IMF Working Paper 00/68, März 2000, http://www.imf.org/external/pubs/ft/wp/2000/wp0068.pdf (as of 21 January 2006)

CECA (2002). "Confederacion Espanola de Cajas de Ahorros: Sector Cajas de Ahorros, Cuenta de Pérdidas y Guanacias Pública, A 31 de Diciembre 2002." http://www.ceca.es/CECA-CORPORATIVO/en/caja_c.html (as of 23 November 2005)

CECA (2003). "Confederacion Espanola de Cajas de Ahorros: Sector Cajas de Ahorros, Cuenta de Pérdidas y Guanacias Pública, A 31 de Diciembre 2003." http://www.ceca.es/CECA-CORPORATIVO/en/caja_c.html (as of 23 November 2005)

CECA (2004). "Confederacion Espanola de Cajas de Ahorros: Sector Cajas de Ahorros, Cuenta de Pérdidas y Guanacias Pública, A 31 de Diciembre 2004." http://www.ceca.es/CECA-CORPORATIVO/en/caja_c.html (as of 23 November 2005)

CECI (2005). "Rapport Annuel du Comité des Établissements de Crédit et des Entreprises d'Investissement." http://www.banque-france.fr/fr/publications/publications.htm (as of 23 November 2005)

Celent Communications (2002). "Commercial Lending Market Overview: The Calm before the Storm". October 2002

Chicago Mercantile Exchange (2003). "Notice Number CMO0405."

Chorafas, D. (2000). Credit Derivatives and the Management of Risk. New York, Prentice Hall

Choudhry, M. (2004a). An Introduction to Credit Derivatives. Oxford, Elsevier

Choudhry, M. (2004b). Structured Credit Products: Credit Derivatives and Synthetic Securitization. Hoboken, John Wiley & Sons

Coleman, E. and Viala, P. (2000). "The Credit Rating." Risk Magazine 47(June 2000): 44 - 46

Comer, G., Boney, V., et al. (2005). "High Quality Bond Funds: Market Timing Ability and Performance." Working Paper, Georgetown University, University of Delaware, April 2005

Credit Suisse (1997). "CreditRisk+: A Credit Risk Management Framework." Credit Suisse Financial Products

Crouhy, M., Galai, D., et al. (2001). "Prototype Risk Rating System." Journal of Banking and Finance 25(1): 47 - 95

Das, S. (2000). Credit Derivatives and Credit Linked Notes. New York, John Wiley & Sons

DeAngelo, H. (1981). "Competition and Unanimity." American Economic Review 71: 18 - 27

DeMarco, P. and Duffie, D. (1999). "A Liquidity-Based Model of Security Design." Econometria(January 1999): 65 - 99

Demirguc-Kunt, A. and Detragiache, E. (2000). "Does Deposit Insurance Increase Banking System Stability? An Empirical Investigation." Working Paper, The World Bank Development Research Group and International Monetary Fund Research Department

Demirguc-Kunt, A. and Sobaci, T. (2000). "Deposit Insurance Around the World: A Data Base." Working Paper, The World Bank

Demsetz, R. (1994). "Evidence on the Relationship Between Regional Economic Condition and Loan Sales Activity." Proceedings of the 30th Annual Conference on Bank Structure and Competition: 370 - 380

Demsetz, R. (2000). "Bank Loan Sales: A New Look at the Motivation for Secondary Market Activity." Journal of Financial Research 23(2): 197 - 222

Dennis, S. and Mullineaux, D. (2000). "Syndicated Loans." University of Kentucky Working Paper

Deutsche Bank (2003). Jahresbericht. Frankfurt am Main, Deutsche Bank AG

Di Clemente, A. and Romano, C. (2003). "Beyond Markowitz: Building Optimal Portfolio Using Non-Elliptical Asset Return Distributions." Working Paper, Department of Economic Theory and Quantitative Methods for the Political Choices, University of Rome

Diamond, D. W. (1984). "Financial Intermediation and Delegated Monitoring." Review of Economic Studies 51: 393 - 414

Diamond, D. W. and Dybvig, P. H. (1983). "Bank Runs, Deposit Insurance, and Liquidity." Journal of Political Economy 91(3): 401 - 419

Diekmann, A. (2002). Empirische Sozialforschung. Reinbek bei Hamburg, Rowohlt Taschenbuch Verlag

DIHK (2005). "Kreditkonditionen unter dem Diktat der Bonität." Ergebnisse einer DIHK Umfrage zur Unternehmensfinanzierung im Mittelstand, Frühjahr 2005

DNB (2000). "De Nederlandsche Bank Statistical Bulletin March 2000." http://www.dnb.nl/dnb/pagina.jsp?lang=en&pid=tcm:13-36068-64 (as of 23 November 2005)

DNB (2001). "De Nederlandsche Bank Statistical Bulletin March 2001." http://www.dnb.nl/dnb/pagina.jsp?lang=en&pid=tcm:13-36068-64 (as of 23 November 2005)

DNB (2002). "De Nederlandsche Bank Statistical Bulletin March 2002." http://www.dnb.nl/dnb/pagina.jsp?lang=en&pid=tcm:13-36068-64 (as of 23 November 2005)

DNB (2003). "De Nederlandsche Bank Statistical Bulletin March 2003." http://www.dnb.nl/dnb/pagina.jsp?lang=en&pid=tcm:13-36068-64 (as of 23 November 2005)

DNB (2004). "De Nederlandsche Bank Statistical Bulletin March 2004." http://www.dnb.nl/dnb/pagina.jsp?lang=en&pid=tcm:13-36068-64 (as of 23 November 2005)

DNB (2005). "De Nederlandsche Bank Statistical Bulletin March 2005." http://www.dnb.nl/dnb/pagina.jsp?lang=en&pid=tcm:13-36068-64 (as of 23 November 2005)

Donaldson, G. (1961). Corporate Debt Capacity: A Study of Corporate Debt Policy and the Determination of Corporate Debt Capacity. Boston, Division of Research, Harvard Graduate School of Business Administration

Duffee, G. and Zhou, C. (2001). "Credit Derivatives in Banking: Useful Tools for Managing Risk." Journal of Monetary Economics 48: 25 - 54

Duffie, D. and Garleanu, N. (2001). "Risk and Valuation of Collateralized Debt Obligations." Working Paper, Stanford University

ECB (2000). "EU Banks' Margins and Credit Standards." European Central Bank Publication December 2000

ECB (2004). "EU Banking Sector Stability." European Central Bank Publication, http://www.ecb.int/pub/pdf/other/eubankingsectorstability2004en.pdf (as of 15 April 2005)

ECB (2005). "EU European Banking Sector Stability." http://www.ecb.int/pub/pdf/other/eubankingsectorstability2005en.pdf (as of 23 November 2005)

Eckbo, B., Giammarino, R., et al. (1990). "Asymmetric Information and the Medium of Exchange in Takeovers: Theory and Tests." Review of Financial Studies 3: 651 - 675

Eckbo, B. and Masulis, R. (1992). "Adverse Selection and the Rights Offer Paradox." Journal of Financial Economics 32: 293 - 332

Eckbo, B. and Norli, O. (2004). "The Choice of Seasoned-Equity Selling Mechanisms: Theory and Evidence." Working Paper, Dartmouth

Ehrbar, A. (1998). Economic Value Added: The Real Key to Creating Wealth. New York, John Wiley & Sons

Eichwald, B. and Pehle, H. (2000). Die Kreditarten. Geld-, Bank- und Börsenwesen, Handbuch des Finanzsystems. G. Obst, Hinten, O., von Hagen, J.et al. Stuttgart, Schäffer-Poeschel: 742 - 814

EinlSG (1998). "Einlagensicherungs- und Anlgerentschädigungsgesetz vom 16. Juli 1998 zuletzt geändert durch Art. 12 des Gesetzes vom 15. Dezember 2003."

Ely, B. and Wallison, P. (2000). Nationalizing Mortgage Risk. The Growth of Fannie Mae and Freddie Mac. Washington, AEI Press

ESF (2005). "ESF Securitisation Data Report." European Securitisation Forum (http:/www.europeansecuritisation.com) (as of 13 Dec 2005)

European Commission (2003). "Empfehlung der Kommission vom 6. Mai 2003 betreffend die Definition der Kleinstunternehmen sowie der kleinen und mittleren Unternehmen (2003/361/EG)."

Fabozzi, F. (2001). The Handbook of Mortgage-Backed Securities. New York, McGraw-Hill

Fabozzi, F., Sanders, A., et al. (2001). Nonagency CMOs. The Handbook of Mortgage-Backed Securities. F. Fabozzi. New York, McGraw-Hill: 267 - 280

Fama, E. (1985). "What's Different about Banks?" Journal of Monetary Economics 15: 29 - 39

Federal Reserve Board (2002). "Risk-Based Capital Guidelines; Capital Adequacy Guidelines; Capital Maintenance: Capital Treatment for Recourse, Direct Credit Substitutes and Residual Interest in Asset Securitizations." Federal Reserve Board, Office of the Comptroller of the Currency, Federal Deposit Insurance Corporation, Office of Thrift Supervision

FinDAG (2002). "Gesetz über die Bundesanstalt für Finanzdienstleistungsaufsicht vom 22. April 2002."

Fishburn, P. (1977). "Mean-Risk Analysis Associated with Below-Target Returns." American Economic Review 67: 116 - 126

Fisher, E., Henkel, R., et al. (1989). "Dynamic Capital Structure Choice: Theory and Tests." Journal of Finance 44: 19 - 40

Flämig, M. (2005). "HVB managt aktiv die Kredite für Firmenkunden." Börsenzeitung as of 7 May 2005

Flesch, H. and Gerdsmeier, S. (1998). "Entwicklungslinien im Bankcontrolling." Die Bank: 294 - 301

Flick, U. (2002). Qualitative Sozialforschung. Reinbek bei Hamburg, Rohwolt Taschenbuch Verlag

Francis, J., Frost, J., et al. (1999). The Handbook of Credit Derivatives, McGraw Hill

Frank, M. and Goyal, V. (2005). "Trade-off and Pecking Order Theories of Debt." Working Paper, Sauder School of Business/Honkong University of Science and Technology; Forthcoming in B. Espen Eckbo (ed.), Handbook of Corporate Finance: Empirical Corporate Finance (Handbooks in Finance Series, Elsevier, North-Holland), Chapt. 7, 2005

Franke, D. (2005). "Börsenhandel mit Krediten - Neuer Marktplatz." Die Bank(Januar 2005): 14 - 15

Freixas, X. and Rochet, J. (1997). Microeconomics of Banking. Cambridge, London, The MIT Press

Froot, K. A. and Stein, J. C. (1998). "Risk Management, Capital Budgeting, and Capital Structure Policy for Financial Institutions: An Integrated Approach." Journal of Financial Economics 47: 55 - 82

Gadanecz, B. (2004). "The Syndicated Loan Market: Structure, Development and Implications." BIS Quarterly Review(December 2004): 75 - 89

Gallati, R. (2003). Risk Management and Capital Adequacy. New York, Mc Graw-Hill

Gehring, B. (1997). Asset-Backed Securities im amerikanischen und im deutschen Recht, Beck

Geiger, H. (1992). Die deutsche Sparkassenorganisation. Frankfurt am Main, Knapp

Gibson, M. (2004). "Understanding the Risk of Synthetic CDOs." Working Paper, Federal Reserve Board, July 2004

Goldstein, R., Ju, N., et al. (2001). "An EBIT-Based Model of Dynamic Capital Structure." Journal of Business 74: 483 - 512

Gonzalez, N., Litzenberger, R., et al. (1977). "On Mean Variance Models of Capital Structure and the Absurdity of Their Predictions." Journal of Financial and Quantitative Analysis 12: 165 - 179

Goodman, L. (2002). "Synthetic CDOs: An Introduction." Journal of Derivatives 9(3): 1074 - 1240

Gorton, G. and Haubrich, J. (1990). The Loan Sales Market. Research in Financial Services: Private and Public Policy. G. Kaufmann. Greenwich. 2: 85 - 135

Gorton, G. and Pennacchi, G. (1995). "Banks and Loan Sales - Marketing Nonmarketable Assets." Journal of Monetary Economics 35: 389 - 411

Graddy, D. B. and Spencer, A. H. (1990). Managing commercial banks. Englewood Cliffs, Prentice Hall

Greenbaum, S. and Thakor, A. V. (1987). "Bank Funding Modes: Securitization vs. Deposits." Journal of Banking and Finance 11: 379 - 401

Greenbaum, S. and Thakor, A. V. (1994). Contemporary Financial Intermediation, Dryden Press

Grill, W. and Perczynski, H. (2003). Wirtschaftslehre des Kreditwesens. Troisdorf, Bildungsverlag EINS

Gropp, R. and Vesala, J. (2001). "Deposit Insurance and Moral Hazard: Does the Counterfactual Matter?" Working Paper No. 47, European Central Bank

Großpietsch, J. (2003). Supply Chain Management in der Konsumgüterindustrie. Köln, Eul Verlag

Gruber, J., Gruber, W., et al., Eds. (2005). Praktiker-Handbuch Asset-Backed-Securities und Kreditderivate. Strukturen, Preisbildungen, Anwendungsmöglichkeiten, Aufsichtsrechtliche Behandlung. Stuttgart, Schäffer-Poeschel

Grundke, P. (2003). Modellierung und Bewertung von Kreditrisiken, zugel. Dissertation Universität zu Köln. Wiesbaden, Deutscher Universitäts-Verlag

Guill, G. and Hennessey, L. (1997). "Organizational Issues and Transactional Capabilities for Credit Portfolio Management." The Journal of Lending & Credit Risk Management(August 1997): 18 - 28

Gupton, G., Finger, C., et al. (1997). CreditMetrics Technical Document. New York, Morgan Guaranty Trust Co.

Hahn, O. (1981). Struktur der Bankwirtschaft. Band I: Banktypologie und Universalbanken. Berlin

Hahn, T. (1993). "Commercial Paper." Federal Reserve Bank of Richmond Econonic Quarterly 79(2)

Haley, C. and Schall, L. (1979). The Theory of Financial Decisions. New York, McGraw-Hill

Halov, N. and Heider, N. (2004). "Capital Structure, Risk and Asymmetric Information." Working Paper, New York University

Hammes, W. and Shapiro, M. (2001). "The Implications of the new Capital Adequacy Rules for Portfolio Managers of Credit Assets." Journal of Banking and Finance 25: 97 - 114

Hannemann, R., Hanenberg, L., et al. (2003). Mindestanforderungen an das Kreditgeschäft (MaK): Eine einführende Kommentierung, Schäffer Poeschel Verlag

Harlow, W. and Rao, K. (1989). "Asset Pricing in a Generalized Mean-Lower Partial Moment Framework: Theory and Evidence." Journal of Financial and Quantitative Analysis 24(3): 285 - 311

Hart, O. D. and Jaffee, D. M. (1974). "On the Application of Portfolio Theory to Depository Financial Intermediaries." Review of Economic Studies 41: 129 - 147

Hartmann-Wendels, T., Pfingsten, A., et al. (2000). Bankbetriebslehre. Berlin, Heidelberg, Springer Verlag

Hartmann-Wendels, T., Pfingsten, A., et al. (2004). Bankbetriebslehre. Berlin, Heidelberg, Springer Verlag

Haubrich, J. and Thomson, J. (1996). "Loan Sales, Implicit Contracts, and Bank Structure." Review for Quantitative and Financial Accounting 7: 137 - 162

Haugen, R. and Senbet, L. (1978). "The Insignificance of Bankruptcy Costs to the Theory of Optimal Capital Structure." Journal of Finance 33(2): 383 - 393

Hawkins, J. and Mihaljek, D. (2001). "The Banking Industry in the Emerging Market Economies: Competition, Consolidation and Systemic Stability: An Overview." Bank for International Settlements Papers No. 4, August 2001, http://www.bis.org/publ/bispap04.pdf (as of 21 January 2006)

Hayre, L., Mohebbi, C., et al. (2001). Stripped Mortgage-Backed Securities. The Handbook of Mortgage-Backed Securities. F. Fabozzi. New York, McGraw-Hill: 151 - 167

Hayre, L. (2001). A Concise Guide to Mortgage-Backed Securities (MBS). Salomon Smith Barney Guide to Mortgage-Backed and Asset-Backed Securities. New York, Wiley Finance

Hayt, G. and Smithson, C. (2000a). "Credit Derivatives The Basics." Journal of Lending and Credit Risk Management(February 2000)

Hayt, G. and Smithson, C. (2000b). "Credit Derivatives: Implications for Bank Portfolio Management." Journal of Lending and Credit Risk Management(April 2000)

Hayt, G. and Smithson, C. (2001). "The State of the Art in Credit Portfolio Modeling." Risk Management Journal(March 2001): 34 - 38

Hayt, G. and Smithson, C. (2001a). "Implementation of New Approaches in Credit Portfolio Management." Risk Management Journal(October 2001): 67 - 71

Hayt, G. and Smithson, C. (2001b). "Managing Credit Portfolios by Maximizing Risk Adjusted Return." Risk Management Journal(December 2000/January 2001): 44 - 47

Hellwig, M. (1994). "Banking and Finance at the End of the Twentieth Century." WWZ Discussion Paper: 26

Hempell, H., S. (2002). "Testing for Competition Among German Banks." Economic Research Centre of the Deutsche Bundesbank

Hennessey, L. and Whited, T. (2004). "Debt Dynamics." Journal of Finance(Forthcoming)

Hill, C. (1996). "Securitization: A low-cost Sweetener for Lemons." Washington University Law Quarterly(Winter 1996): 1061 - 1120

Hirshleifer, J. (1966). "Investment Decisions under Uncertainty: Application of the State-Preference Approach." Quarterly Journal of Economics 80: 262 - 277

Holmstöm, B. and Tirole, J. (1997). "Financial Intermediation, Loanable Funds and the Real Sector." Quarterly Journal of Economics 112: 663 - 691

Howard, L. (1999). "Bancassurance Continues to Evolve in Europe." National Underwriter Property & Casualty-Risk & Benefits Management 103(16): 15

Huang, C. and Litzenberger, R. (1988). Foundations for Financial Economics. Upper Saddler River, Pearson

Hull, J. (2006). Options, Futures and other Derivatives. Upper Saddler River, New Jersey, Prentice Hall

Hull, J., Mirela, P., et al. (2004). "The Relationship between Credit Default Swap Spreads, Bond Yields and Credit Rating Announcements." University of Toronto, Working Paper, http://www.rotman.utoronto.ca/~hull/DownloadablePublications/HPWPaperonCDSSpreads.pdf (as of 22 Dec 2005)

HypBG (2004). "Hypothekenbankgesetz in der Fassung der Bekanntmachung vom 9. September 1998, zuletzt geändert durch Art. 8 des Gesetzes vom 05. April 2004."

Ingersoll, J. (1987). Theory of Financial Decision Making. Savage, Maryland

InsO (1994). Insolvenzordnung, BGBl I 1994, 2866

Institut für Genossenschaftswesen an der Humbold Universität zu Berlin (1993). Genossenschaftsbanken in sich ändernder Umwelt. Berlin, Institut für Genossenschaftswesen

Institut für Mittelstandsforschung (2005). "Mittelstand - Definitionen und Schlüsselzahlen." http://www.ifm-bonn.org/dienste/daten.htm (as of 25 Jan. 2005)

Iscoe, I., Kreinin, A., et al. (1999). "An Integrated Market and Credit Risk Portfolio Model." Algo Research Quarterly(September 1999): 21 - 38

ISDA (2003). "The ISDA Credit Derivatives Definitions 2003."

J.P. Morgan (2002 a). "European Structured Products Weekly." Global Structured Finance Research, J.P. Morgan Securities Inc., London, December 23, 2002, http://www.absreports.com/index.cfm?fuseaction=getResearch (as of 15 November 2005)

J.P. Morgan (2003 a). "European Structured Products Weekly." Global Structured Finance Research, J.P. Morgan Securities Inc., London, October 6, 2003, http://www.absreports.com/index.cfm?fuseaction=getResearch (as of 15 November 2005)

J.P. Morgan (2003 b). "European Structured Products Weekly." Global Structured Finance Research, J.P. Morgan Securities Inc., London, July 7, 2003, http://www.absreports.com/index.cfm?fuseaction=getResearch (as of 15 November 2005)

J.P. Morgan (2003 c). "European Structured Products Weekly." Global Structured Finance Research, J.P. Morgan Securities Inc., London, March 10, 2003, http://www.absreports.com/index.cfm?fuseaction=getResearch (as of 15 November 2005)

J.P. Morgan (2004 a). "European Structured Products Weekly." Global Structured Finance Research, J.P. Morgan Securities Inc., London, October 4, 2004, http://www.absreports.com/index.cfm?fuseaction=getResearch (as of 15 November 2005)

J.P. Morgan (2004 b). "European Structured Products Weekly." Global Structured Finance Research, J.P. Morgan Securities Inc., London, July 5, 2004, http://www.absreports.com/index.cfm?fuseaction=getResearch (as of 15 November 2005)

J.P. Morgan (2004 c). "European Structured Products Weekly." Global Structured Finance Research, J.P. Morgan Securities Inc., London, April 5, 2004, http://www.absreports.com/index.cfm?fuseaction=getResearch (as of 15 November 2005)

J.P. Morgan (2004 d). "European Structured Products Weekly." Global Structured Finance Research, J.P. Morgan Securities Inc., London, January 12, 2004, http://www.absreports.com/index.cfm?fuseaction=getResearch (as of 15 November 2005)

J.P. Morgan (2005 a). "European Structured Products Weekly." Global Structured Finance Research, J.P. Morgan Securities Inc., London, August 8, 2005, http://www.absreports.com/index.cfm?fuseaction=getResearch (as of 15 November 2005)

J.P. Morgan (2005 b). "European Structured Products Weekly." Global Structured Finance Research, J.P. Morgan Securities Inc., London, March 29, 2005, http://www.absreports.com/index.cfm?fuseaction=getResearch (as of 15 November 2005)

J.P. Morgan (2005 c). "European Structured Products Weekly." Global Structured Finance Research, J.P. Morgan Securities Inc., London, January 10, 2005, http://www.absreports.com/index.cfm?fuseaction=getResearch (as of 15 November 2005)

James, C. (1988). "The Use of Loan Sales and Standby Letters of Credit by Commercial Banks." Journal of Monetary Economics 22: 395 - 422

Jensen, M. and Meckling, W. (1976). "Theory of the Firm: Managerial Behavior, Agency Cost and Ownership Structure." http://papers.ssrn.com/sol3/paper.taf?ABSTRACT_ID=94043 (as of 2 February 2005)

Jobst, N. and Zenios, S. (2000). "Extending Credit Risk (Pricing) Models for the Simulation of Portfolios of Interest Rate and Credit Risk Sensitive Securities." Working Paper, The Wharton School, University of Pennsylvania

Jobst, N. and Zenios, S. (2001). "The tail that wags the dog: Integrating Credit Risk in Asset Portfolios." Working Paper, The Wharton School, University of Pennsylvania

Johannsen, K. (2005). "CDS für das DAX Universum handeln." Börsenzeitung as of 25 February 2005(39): 17

Joint Market Practices Forum (2003). "Statement of Principles and Recommendations Regarding the Handling of Material Nonpublic Information by Credit Market Participants." http://www.isda.org/c_and_a/pdf/jmpfStatement.pdf (as of 24 July 2005)

Jones, D. (2000). "Emerging Problems with the Basel Capital Accord: Regulatory Capital Arbitrage and Related Issues." Journal of Banking and Finance 24: 35 - 58

Jones, J., Lang, W., et al. (2000). "Recent Trends in Loan Syndications: Evidence for 1995 - 1999." OCC Economic and Policy Analysis Working Paper No. 2000 - 10

Jorion, P. (2001). Value-at-Risk: The New Benchmark for Managing Financial Risk. New York, McGraw-Hill

Jorion, P. (2003). "Portfolio Optimization with Tracking-Error Constraints." Financial Analysts Journal 59: 70 - 82

Kaduff, J. (1996). Shortfallrisk-basierte Portfoliostrategien. St. Gallen

Kaduff, J. and Spremann, K. (1996). "Sicherheit und Diversifizierung bei Shortfall Risk." Zeitschrift für betriebswirtschaftliche Forschung 48: 779 - 802

Kahane, Y. (1977). "Capital Adequacy and the Regulation of Financial Intermediaries." Journal of Banking and Finance 1: 207 - 218

Kane, M. (2001). An introduction to the Asset-Backed Securities Market. Salomon Smith Barney Guide to Mortgage-Backed and Asset-Backed Securities. L. Hayre. New York, Wiley Finance

Kane, M., Marcus, A., et al. (1984). "How big is the Tax Advantage of Debt?" Journal Of Finance 39: 841 - 853

Kataoka, S. (1963). "A Stochastic Programming Model." Econometria 31: 181 - 196

Katz, D. (1972). Die Andeutung der Ergebnisse: Probleme und Gefahren. Das Interview. Formen-Technik-Auswertung. R. König. Köln, Kiepenhauer & Witsch

Kaufman, G. G. (1992). Banking Structures in Major Countries. Boston

Kaufman, G. G. (2003). "Too Big to Tail in U.S. Banking: Quo Vadis?" Working Paper, Loyola University Chicago and Federal Reserve Bank Chicago

Kealhoffer, S. (1995). Managing Default Risk in Derivative Portfolios. Derivative Credit Risk: Advances in Measurement and Management. London, Renaissance Risk Publications

Keeley, M. C. and Furlong, F. T. (1990). "A Reexamination of Mean-Variance Analysis of Bank Capital Regulation." Journal of Banking and Finance 14: 69 - 84

Kelman, A. (2002). "Mortgage-backed Securities & Collateralized Mortgage Obligations: Prudent CRA Investment Opportunities." Community Investments(March 2002)

Kiff, J., Michaud, F., et al. (2002). "Instruments of Credit Risk Transfer: Effects on Financial Contracting and Financial Stability." NBB Working Paper

Kim, D. (1988). "Risk in Banking and Capital Regulation." Journal of Finance 43: 1219 - 1233

Kimber, A. (2004). Credit Risk From Transaction to Portfolio Management. Oxford, Burlington, Elsevier Butterworth-Heinemann

Kimmel, P., Weygandt, J., et al. (2004). Financial Accounting - Tools for Decision Making. New York, John Wiley & Sons

Kirmße, S. (2001). Kreditrisikosteuerung im Firmenkunden-Portfeuille. Das Firmenkundengeschäft, ein Wertvernichter? K. Dreyer and Rolfes, B. Frankfurt am Main, Fritz Knapp Verlag

Kish, L. (1965). Survey Sampling. New York, John Wiley & Sons

Koehn, M. and Santomero, A. M. (1980). "Regulation of Bank Capital and Portfolio Risk." Journal of Finance 35: 1235 - 1244

Koller, T., Goedhardt, M., et al. (2005). Valuation Measuring and Managing the Value of Companies. Hoboken, John Wiley & Sons

Kraus, A. and Litzenberger, R. (1973). "A State Preference Model of Optimal Financial Leverage." Journal of Finance 33: 911 - 922

Krokhmal, P., Palmquist, J., et al. (2001). "Portfolio Optimization with Conditional Value-at Risk Objective and Constraints." Working Paper, University of Florida

Kruschwitz, L. and Löffler, A. (1997). "Ross' APT ist gescheitert. Was nun?" Zeitschrift für betriebswirtschaftliche Forschung 49(7/8): 644 - 651

Kuritzkes, A. (1998). "Active Credit Portfolio Management." ERisk.com

KWG (1998). Gesetz über das Kreditwesen (Kreditwesengesetz) in der Fassung vom 22. April 2002

Laudi, P. (2003). Fusionen von Genossenschaftsbanken. Bremen, Institut für Finanz- und Dienstleistungsmanagement

Lauer, J. (2004). Das Kreditengagement zwischen Sanierung und Liquidation. Stuttgart, Deutscher Sparkassenverlag

Lehman Brothers (2001). Collateralized Mortgage Obligations. The Handbook of Mortgage-Backed Securities. F. Fabozzi. New York, McGraw-Hill: 169 - 195

Leibowitz, M. and Henriksson, R. (1989). "Portfolio Optimization with Shortfall Constraints." Financial Analysts Journal 45: 34 - 41

Leibowitz, M. and Kogelman, S. (1991). "Asset Allocation Under Shortfall Constraints." Journal of Portfolio Management 17: 18 - 23

Leland, H. E. and Pyle, D. H. (1977). "Informational Asymmetries, Financial Structure and Financial Intermediation." Journal of Finance 23(2): 371-387

Lintner, J. (1965). "The Valuation of Risk Assets and the Selection of Risky Investments in Stock Portfolios and Capital Budgets." Review of Economics and Statistics 47: 13 - 37

Loan Pricing Corporation (2001). Annual Volume 7, Loan Pricing Corporation

Lowell, L. (2001a). Mortgage Pass-Through Securities. The Handbook of Mortgage-Backed Securities. F. Fabozzi. New York, McGraw-Hill: 25 - 50

Lowell, L. (2001b). Z Bonds. The Handbook of Mortgage-Backed Securities. F. Fabozzi. New York, McGraw-Hill: 221 - 238

Maccoby, E. and Maccoby, N. (1972). Das Interview: ein Werkzeug der Sozialforschung. Das Interview. Formen-Technik-Auswertung. R. König. Köln, Kiepenhauer & Witsch

Makowski, L. and Pepall, L. (1985). "Easy Proofs of Unanimity and Optimality without Spanning: A Pedagogical Note." Journal of Finance 11(4): 1245 - 1250

Mao, J. (1970). "Survey of Capital Budgeting Theory and Practice." Journal of Finance 25: 349 - 360

Markowitz, H. (1952). "Portfolio Selection." Journal of Finance 7: 77 - 91

Markowitz, H. (1959). Portfolio Selection. New York, John Wiley & Sons

Markowitz, H. (1991). Portfolio Selection: Efficient Diversification of Investments. Cambridge, London, Blackwell Publishers

Marrison, A. (2001a). "Credit Derivatives, Disintermediation and Investment Decisions." University of Oxford Working Paper

Marrison, C. (2001b). "Risk Measurement for Project Finance Guarantees." The Journal of Project Finance 7(2): 43 - 53

Marrison, C. (2002). The Fundamentals of Risk Measurement. New York, McGraw Hill

Matutes, C. and Vives, X. (1995). "Imperfect Competition, Risk Taking and Regulation in Banking." European Economic Review 44: 1 - 34

Mauer, D. and Triantis, A. (1994). "Interaction of Corporate Financing and Investment Decisions: A Dynamic Framework." Journal Of Finance 49: 1253 - 1277

McDermott, G. (2001). The ABCs of CDO Equity. Salomon Smith Barney Guide to Mortgage-Backed and Asset-Backed Securities. L. Hayre. New York, Wiley Finance

McDonough, W. (1998). "Statement before the Committee on Banking and Financial Services, U.S. House of Representatives, October 1, 1998." Federal Reserve Bulletin, December: 1050 - 1054

McKinsey & Company (2000a). Credit Portfolio View: A Credit Portfolio Risk Measurement & Management Approach, Approach Document. New York

McKinsey & Company (2000b). Credit Portfolio View: A Credit Portfolio Risk Measurement and Management Approach, Technical Document. New York

McKinsey & Company (2005). "$ 118 trillion and counting: Taking Stock of the World's Capital Markets." The McKinsey Global Institute

McKinsey & Company (2006). "Mapping the Global Capital Market 2006 - Second Annual Report." The McKinsey Global Institute

Mello, A. and Parsons, J. (1992). "Measuring the Agency Cost of Debt." Journal of Finance 47: 1887 - 1904

Merton, R. (1972). "An Analytic Derivation of the Efficient Portfolio Frontier." Journal of Financial and Quantitative Analysis 7: 1851 - 1872

Merton, R. (1973). "An Intertemporal Capital Asset Pricing Model." Econometria 41: 867 - 887

Meuser, M. and Nagel, U. (1991). ExpertInneninterviews - vielfach erprobt, wenig bedacht. Ein Beitrag zur qualitativen Methodendiskussion. Qualitativ empirische Sozialforschung. D. Garz and Kraimer, K. Opladen, Westdeutscher Verlag: 441 - 468

Miller, M. (1977). "Debt and Taxes." Journal of Finance 32(2): 261 - 275

Miller, S. (1998). The Development of the Syndicated Loan Asset Class. Bank Loans: Secondary Market and Portfolio Management. F. Fabozzi. New Hope, PA, J. Wiley & Sons: 1 - 23

Modigliani, F. and Miller, M. (1958). "The Cost of Capital, Corporation Finance and the Theory of Investment." The American Economic Review 48(3): 261 - 297

Modigliani, F. and Miller, M. (1963). "Corporate Income Taxes and the Cost of Capital: A Correction." American Economic Review 53: 433 - 443

Morellec, E. (2004). "Can Managerial Discretion Explain Observed Leverage Ratios?" Review of Financial Studies 17: 257 - 294

Mossin, J. (1966). "Equilibrium in a Capital Asset Market." Econometria 34: 261 - 276

Mülhaupt, L. (1980). Einführung in die Betriebswirtschaftslehre der Banken: Struktur und Grundprobleme des Bankbetriebs und des Bankwesens in der Bundesrepublik Deutschland. Wiesbaden, Gabler

Myers, S. (1977). "Determinants of Corporate Borrowing." Journal of Financial Economics 5: 147 - 175

Myers, S. (1984). "The Capital Structure Puzzle." The Journal of Finance 29(3): 575 - 592

Myers, S. and Majluf, N. (1984). "Corporate Financing and Investment Decisions when Firms Have Information that Investors do not have." Journal of Financial Economics 13: 187 - 221

N.N (2002). "The Debt Exchange: Bringing Liquidity to Secondary Loan Trading." URL: http://www.celent.com/PressReleases/20021119/DebtExchange.htm (as of 7 January 2005)

N.N (2003a). "Finanzaufsicht: Engagement bei britischem Fernsehverleiher Boxclever soll möglicherweise komplett abgeschrieben werden. WestLB muss Risikovorsorge drastisch erhöhen." Die Welt 58(179): 13

N.N (2003b). "Kirch hinterlässt tiefe Spuren in Bankbilanzen." Handelsblatt(54): 18

N.N (2005a). "Banken in Wartestellung für Pfandbriefemissionen." Börsenzeitung as of 17 June 2005(114): 5

N.N (2005b). "Covered Bond Council meldet erste Erfolge." Börsenzeitung as of 1 November 2005(210): 3

N.N. (2004a). "Erstes Mindestrating für Sparkassengruppe." Börsenzeitung as of 14 December 2004(242): 5

N.N. (2004b). "Immer mehr Mittelständler nutzen syndizierte Kredite." Frankfurter Allgemeine Zeitung as of 29 October 2004(253): 25

N.N. (2005). "Gutes Rating für die Landesbanken." Frankfurter Allgemeine Zeitung as of 27 April 2005(97): 14

Nöth (2004). eFinance: Portfolioentscheidungen, Handelsstrategien und Sicherheit. Zugelassene Habilitation an der Universität Mannheim

Nourzad, F. (2002). "Financial Development and Productive Efficiency." Journal of Economics and Finance 26(2)

OCC (2004). "Office of the Controller of the Currency Annual Report Fiscal Year 2004."

OGAW (2002). "Richtlinie des EU Rates zu Koordinierung der Rechts- und Verwaltungsvorschriften betreffend bestimmte Organismen für gemeinsame Anlagen in Wertpapieren in der am 4.12.2001 verabschiedeten Fassung der Änderungsrichtlininen 2001/107/EG und 2001/108/EG vom 21. Januar 2002."

Ohl, P. (1994). Asset Backed Securities - ein innovatives Instrument zur Finanzierung deutscher Unternehmen. Wiesbaden, Gabler

Packmohr, T., Mächtlinger, J., et al. (2003). "Jumbo-Angebot 2004. Ausblick auf die Emissionstätigkeit im Jumbo Covered Bond- und Länder Segment." Research Document, Dresdner Kleinwort Wasserstein(October 2003)

Pavel, C. and Phillis, D. (1987). "Why Commercial Banks Sell Loans: An Empirical Analysis." Federal Reserve Bank of Chicago Economic Perspectives 14: 3 - 14

Pennacchi, G. (1988). "Loan Sales and the Cost of Bank Capital." Journal of Finance 43: 375 - 396

PfandBG (2005). "Gesetz zur Neuordnung des Pfandbriefrechts vom 22. Mai 2005 (BGBl. 2005 Teil I, S. 1373 - 1393."

Pflaumer, P., Heine, B., et al. (2001). Statistik für Wirtschafts- und Sozialwissenschaften. München, Oldenbourg Wissenschaftsverlag GmbH

Pflug, G. (2000). Some Remarks on the Value-at-Risk and the Conditional Value-at-Risk. Probabilistic Constrained Optimization: Methodology and Applications. S. Uryasev, Kluwer Academic Publishers

Poppensieker, T. (2002). Kreditportfoliosteuerung mit Sekundärmarktinstrumenten, zugel. Dissertation Universität zu Köln. Wiesbaden, Deutscher Universitäts-Verlag

Pratt, J. (1964). "Risk Aversion in the Small and in the Large." Econometria 32: 122 - 136

Pratt, J. (2000). "Efficient Risk Sharing: The Last Frontier." Management Science 46(12): 1545 - 1553

Pyle, D. H. (1971). "On the Theory of Financial Intermediation." Journal of Finance 26: 737 - 747

Rappaport, A. (1997). Creating Shareholder Value. London, New York, Free Press

Rhoades, T. (2000). Syndicated Lending. London, Euromoney Books

Ritchken, P., Thomson, J., et al. (1993). "On Flexibility, Capital Structure and Investment Decisions for the Insured Bank." Journal of Banking and Finance 17: 1133 - 1146

Rochet, J. (1992). "Capital Requirements and the Behaviour of Commercial Banks." European Economic Review 36: 1137 - 1178

Rockafellar, R. and Uryasev, S. (2000). "Optimization of Conditional Value at Risk." Journal of Risk 2: 21 - 41

Rolfes, B. (1998). Das Konzept des Gesamtbankmanagement. Gesamtbankmanagement - Integrierte Risiko-/Ertragssteuerung in Kreditinstituten. B. Rolfes, Schierenbeck, H. and Schüller, S. Frankfurt am Main, Fritz Knapp Verlag

Roll, R. (1977). "A Critique of the Asset Pricing Theory's Test: Part I: On Past and Potential Testability of the Theory." Journal of Financial Economics 4: 129 - 176

Ross, S. (1976). "The Arbitrage Theory of Capital Asset Pricing." Journal of Economic Theory: 343 - 362

Roth, E., Ed. (1993). Sozialwissenschaftliche Methoden. München, Wien, Oldenburg

Roussakis, E. N. (1997). Commercial Banking in an Era of Deregulation. Westport, London, Praeger

Roy, A. (1952). "Safety First and the Holding of Assets." Econometria 20: 431 - 439

Rubinstein, M. (1973). "A Mean-Variance Synthesis of Corporate Financial Theory." Journal of Finance 28: 167 - 181

Rudolf, M. (1994). "Efficient Frontier and Shortfall Risk." Finanzmarkt und Portfolio Management 8. Jahrgang(Nr. 1): 88 - 101

Rudolph, B. (1979). Kapitalkosten bei unsicheren Erwartungen: das Kapitalmarktmodell und seine Bedeutung für die Theorie der Kapitalkosten. Heidelberg, Springer

Rutter Associates LLC (2004). "Excerpts from 2004 Rutter Associates Survey of Credit Portfolio Management Practices." http://www.rutterassociates.com/pdf/EXCERPT_Survey_of_CPM_Practices_2004.pdf (as of 24 October 2005)

Sanders, A. (2001). Commercial Mortgage-Backed Securities. The Handbook of Mortgage-Backed Securities. F. Fabozzi. New York, McGraw-Hill: 661 - 675

Santomero, A. M. (1984). "Modeling the Banking Firm: A Survey." Journal of Money, Credit and Banking 16: 567-602

Santomero, A. M. (1997). "Deposit Insurance: Do We Need It and Why?" Working Paper no. 97-35, The Wharton School, University of Pennsylvania

Santos, J. (1998). "Commercial Banks in the Securities Business: A Review." Bank for International Settlements Working Paper Nr. 56

Schich, S. (2003). "Tour d'Horizon on Financial Markets: Implications for the Insurance Industry." Discussion Paper, OECD Secretariat

Schierenbeck, H., Ed. (2001). Relationship Management als zentraler Erfolgsfaktor im Firmenkundengeschäft. Das Firmenkundengeschäft - ein Wertvernichter? Frankfurt am Main, Fritz Knapp Verlag

Schierenbeck, H. (2003). Ertragsorientiertes Bankmanagement. Wiesbaden, Gabler

Schierenbeck, H. and Paul, S. (2000). "Die Re-Allokation von Risikokapital als strategische Herausforderung." Beihefte zu Kredit und Kapital 33: 203 - 227

Schiller, B. and Tytko, D. (2001). Risikomanagement im Kreditgeschäft. Stuttgart, Schäffer-Poeschel

Schmidt, T. and Nehls, H. (2004). "Credit Crunch in Germany?" Discussion Paper, Rhine-Westphalia Institute for Economic Research

Schubert, L. (1996). "Lower Partial Moments in Mean-Varianz-Portefeuilles." Finanzmarkt und Portfolio Management 10: 496 - 509

Schüler, M. (2003). "Kreditderivate - die treibende Kraft am Kreditmarkt." Die Bank(April 2003): 251 - 253

Schüller, S. (1984). Organisation von Controllingsystemen in Kreditinstituten. Frankfurt am Main

Schulte, J. (2001). Von der Börse zum Wertpapiermarktorganisator: Wertsteigerung durch Corporate Governance aus ökonomischer Sicht, zugel. Dissertation European Business School, Oestrich-Winkel. Wiesbaden, Deutscher Universitäts-Verlag

Schwazcz, S. (2002). "The Universal Language of International Securitization." Working Paper, Duke University School of Law

Schweizerische Nationalbank (2003). "Die Banken in der Schweiz." http://www.snb.ch/d/aktuelles/index.html?file=publikation/content_pub.html (as of 23 November 2005) 88. Jahrgang

Schweizerische Nationalbank (2004). "Die Banken in der Schweiz." http://www.snb.ch/d/aktuelles/index.html?file=publikation/content_pub.html (as of 23 November 2005) 89. Jahrgang

SEC (2003). "The Securities and Exchange Commission Annual Report 2003."

Sharpe, W. (1964). "Capital Asset Prices: A Theory of Market Equilibrium under Conditions of Risk." Journal of Finance 19: 425 - 442

Sharpe, W. (1973). "A Simplified Model for Portfolio Analysis." Management Science: 277 - 293

Simons, K. (1993). "Why do Banks Syndicate Loans." New England Economic Review(January/February): 45 - 52

Sinn, H. (2003). Der Staat im Bankwesen: zur Rolle der Landesbanken in Deutschland. München, C.H. Beck

Slikker, N. (2004). "Opposites attract?" The Banker(February 2004): 17-18

Smith, K. (1971). Portfolio Management: Theoretical and Empirical Studies of Portfolio Decision Making. New York

Smithson, C. (2000). "The State of Play in Loan Portfolio Management." http://www.rutterassociates.com/surveys_a.htm (as of 9 June 2005)

Smithson, C. (2003). Credit Portfolio Management. Hoboken, New Jersey, John Wiley & Sons

Smithson, C. (2004). "Hedging a portfolio of structured credit assets." Risk Magazine(October 2004): 88 - 90

Smithson, C., Brannan, S., et al. (2002). "Results from the 2002 Survey of Credit Portfolio Management Practices." http://www.rutterassociates.com/surveys_a.htm (as of 9 June 2005)

Spremann, K. (1996). Wirtschaft, Investition und Finanzierung. München, Wien, Oldenbourg

Spremann, K. (2003). Portfoliomanagement. München, Oldenbourg

Standard & Poor's (2004). "Special Report Ratings Performance 2003." Standard & Poor's Research(February 2004)

Steiner, M. and Wallmeier, M. (1997). "Totgesagte leben länger." Zeitschrift für betriebswirtschaftliche Forschung 49(12): 1084 - 1088

Stiglitz, J. (1973). "Taxation, Corporate Financial Policy and the Cost of Capital." Journal of Public Economics 2: 1 - 34

Stöcker, O. (2001). "Die Renaissance des Pfandbriefes in Europa." Der langfristige Kredit 52: 113 - 118

Strebulaev, I. (2004). "Do Tests of Capital Structure Theory Mean What They Say?" Working Paper, University of Stanford

Stulz, R. and Johnson, H. (1985). "An Analysis of Secured Debt." Journal of Financial Economics 14: 501 - 521

Suchman, E. and McCandless, B. (1940). "Who Answers Questionnaires?" Journal of Applied Psychology 24(December 1940): 758 - 769

Süchting, J. and Paul, S. (1998). Bankmanagement. Stuttgart, Schäffer-Poeschel

Swalm, R. (1966). "Utility Theory - Insights into Risk Taking." Harvard Business Review 47: 123 - 136

Tavakoli, J. (2001). Credit Derivatives & Synthetic Structures: A Guide to Instruments and Applications. New York, John Wiley & Sons

Teller, N. (2004). "Corporate Customers and Institutions - Crucial for Commerzbank's success." German Corporate Conference, Frankfurt

Titman, S. and Tsyplakov, S. (2004). "A Dynamic Model of Optimal Capital Structure." Working Paper, University of Texas at Austin and University of South Carolina

Tobin, J. (1958). "Liquidity Preference as Behaviour Towards Risk." Review of Economic Studies 25: 65 - 86

VDH (2001). "Der Pfandbrief - Europas grösster Bondmarkt." Verband Deutscher Hypothekenbanken

VDH (2002). "European Mortgage Securitisation: A Valuer's Guide." Verband Deutscher Hypothekenbanken(November 2002)

VDH (2004). "Der Pfandbrief. Europas grösster Bondmarkt." Verband Deutscher Hypothekenbanken

Viswanath, P. (1993). "Strategy Considerations, the Pecking Order Hypothesis, and Market Reactions to Equity Financing." Journal of Financial and Quantitative Analysis 28: 213 - 234

Von Neumann, J. and Morgenstern, O. (1973). Spieltheorie und wirtschaftliches Verhalten. Würzburg

Wagenaar, W. (1972). Sequential Response Bias: A Study on Choice and Chance, The Institute for Perception

Wheeler, D. (2001). A Guide to Commercial Mortgage-Backed Securities. Salomon Smith Barney Guide to Mortgage-Backed and Asset-Backed Securities. L. Hayre. New York, Wiley Finance

Whetten, M. and Adelson, M. (2004). "The Bespoke - A guide to Single Tranche Synthetic CDOs." Research Document, Nomura Securities International(November 2004)

Wicki, L.-P. (1996). Bankweites Wertschöpfungspotential einer Informatik-Plattform. Eine Modellbetrachtung am praktischen Beispiel unter Berücksichtigung des integrierten Kundenbetreuer-Arbeitsplatzes im Retail Banking und Verrechnungsaspekten, zugel. Dissertation Universität St. Gallen. St. Gallen

Wilson, T. (1997). "Measuring and Managing Credit Portfolio Risk: Part I and II." Journal of Lending and Credit Risk Management(July 1997): 61 - 72, 76 - 78

Wolcott, R. (2005). "Credit managers hope for new accounting blueprint." Risk 18(2): 38-41

Wolter, H.-J. (1993). "Shortfall-Risiko und Zeithorizonteffekte." Finanzmarkt und Portfolio Management 7: 330 - 338

Zagst, R. (2002). Interest Rate Management. Berlin, Heidelberg, New York, Springer

Zenger, C. (1992). "Zeithorizont, Ausfallwahrscheinlichkeit und Risiko: Einige Bemerkungen aus der Sicht des Praktikers." Finanzmarkt und Portfolio Management 6: 104 - 113

Robert Schmidt

The Behavioral Economics of Foreign Exchange Markets

A Psychological View on Human Expectation Formation in Foreign Exchange Markets

Frankfurt am Main, Berlin, Bern, Bruxelles, New York, Oxford, Wien, 2006.
XX, 334 pp., num. fig., tab. and graf.
European University Studies: Series 5, Economics and Management. Vol. 3178
ISBN 978-3-631-54814-1 · pb. € 56.50*

This book deals with psychological factors, which may be important for understanding the observable exchange rate movements. Thus, the study belongs to the new research field of behavioral economics, which considers the relevance of psychological factors in economic contexts. The main objective of behavioral economists is to develop a more realistic view of the actual human behavior in the context of economics. Central to the concept of behavioral economics is the assumption that humans' actual behavior deviates from the ideal of economic rationality due to at least two reasons: first, decisions are usually based on an incomplete information basis and, second, the information processing of human beings is limited by their computational capacities. Due to these limitations people are forced to apply simple heuristics in information processing. Our aim is to analyze the relevance of simple heuristics in the context of foreign exchange markets. In our view, the decision situation in foreign exchange markets can serve as a prime example for decision situations in which simple heuristics are especially relevant as the complexity of the decision situation is very high.

Contents: The exchange rate disconnect puzzle · Patterns of exchange rate dynamics and the role of speculation · Behavioral economics as an alternative approach · Experimental and empirical evidence